Amsterdam's Atlantic

THE EARLY MODERN AMERICAS

Peter C. Mancall, Series Editor

Volumes in the series explore neglected aspects of
early modern history in the western hemisphere.
Interdisciplinary in character, and with a special
emphasis on the Atlantic World from 1450 to 1850,
the series is published in partnership with the
USC-Huntington Early Modern Studies Institute.

Amsterdam's Atlantic

Print Culture and the Making of Dutch Brazil

Michiel van Groesen

PENN

UNIVERSITY OF PENNSYLVANIA PRESS

PHILADELPHIA

Copyright © 2017 University of Pennsylvania Press

All rights reserved. Except for brief quotations used for purposes of review or scholarly citation, none of this book may be reproduced in any form by any means without written permission from the publisher.

Published by
University of Pennsylvania Press
Philadelphia, Pennsylvania 19104–4112
www.upenn.edu/pennpress

Printed in the United States of America on acid-free paper
1 3 5 7 9 10 8 6 4 2

Library of Congress Cataloging-in-Publication Data
ISBN 978-0-8122-4866-1

CONTENTS

INTRODUCTION Amsterdam, Dutch Brazil, and the Atlantic World
1

CHAPTER 1 Anticipation
14

CHAPTER 2 Jubilation
44

CHAPTER 3 Appropriation
72

CHAPTER 4 Friction
102

CHAPTER 5 "Amsterdamnified"
127

CHAPTER 6 Recollection
157

CONCLUSION Toward a Public Atlantic
187

NOTES
199

BIBLIOGRAPHY
231

INDEX
255

ACKNOWLEDGMENTS
263

INTRODUCTION

Amsterdam, Dutch Brazil, and the Atlantic World

In his popular guidebook *The Present State of the United Provinces* (1669), the English physician and diplomat William Aglionby made two important observations about the people of Holland. First, "they all love their Liberties, even those that have made but a few years stay in that *Province*, as if the genius of it had a secret power of mens inclinations." And, second, "the *Hollanders* are very constant in their resolutions, and seldome desist till they have obtain'd their end."[1] Many seventeenth-century English travelers echoed these cultural characteristics and emphasized how privileges and resolve converged in public life. "The people say and print what they please, and call it liberty" observed John Ray, the naturalist who visited Holland in 1663.[2] Most Englishmen viewed the relative freedom of expression with a mixture of envy and contempt. As early as 1617, the trader James Howell with thinly veiled admiration described "this City of Amsterdam" as "a great Staple of News."[3] Others, however, were quick to point out that the relatively unimpeded circulation of rumors and opinions was not always a blessing. When analyzing the growing popular discontent on the eve of the Civil War in 1641, the pamphleteer John Taylor complained that "too many places of England [are] too much Amsterdamnified by severall opinions," a choice of words that showed little appreciation for the endless political exchanges that at times disrupted the young republic's stability.[4]

If there was one political issue in the United Provinces that divided opinions at the time when Taylor coined his term, it was Dutch Brazil. Despite being nearly five thousand miles away, the rise and fall of Dutch Brazil was one of the most heavily covered news stories of the Dutch Golden Age. The stakes in Brazil were high. The attack on America signified the desire of the

States General, the main political body of the United Provinces, to relieve the country of Spanish military pressure after the first phase of the Eighty Years' War, from 1568 to 1609, had been fought mainly on Dutch soil. The foundation of the West India Company in 1621, immediately after the expiration of the Twelve Years' Truce, represented the perfect opportunity to turn the tables on the Habsburgs and transfer part of the war to America, where the threat to the religious freedom and economic interests of the Dutch was minimal and the vulnerable Spanish treasury could be dealt a potentially crippling blow. Initially the plan worked. From 1624 onward, the West India Company ruled in northeast Brazil, first in Bahia, and later in Pernambuco and six adjacent captaincies (Figure 1). Targeting Brazil was a collective effort. The West India Company represented the interests of thousands of shareholders, urban dwellers from the middle classes who had invested small sums in the Company in the hope of making a profit. The active participation of ordinary citizens and the intimate connection between military progress in the Atlantic world and the fortunes of the war in the Low Countries are the main reasons that news from Brazil was avidly followed at home until 1654, when Dutch imperial ambitions finally collapsed.

The city of Amsterdam played a pivotal role in gathering, constructing, and disseminating Atlantic news. During the rise and fall of Dutch Brazil, it was both the leading financial center and the main information hub of early modern Europe. Its relatively tolerant religious and ideological climate attracted authors, free thinkers, and opinion makers, while its extensive trade network ensured that newspapers, pamphlets, prints, maps, and scientific treatises published here were certain to make an impact across the Continent.[5] As a result, Amsterdam's political power was much greater than the theory of republican government in the United Provinces permitted. The city council's opinion carried great weight in the provincial States of Holland, which in turn dominated the process of decision making in the States General.[6] A similar tension between federal theory and political disparity shaped the dynamics in the boardroom of the West India Company. Although the organizational setup ensured that Amsterdam did not have a majority vote, the city had raised nearly half of the starting capital, was home to the largest and most powerful chamber, and often provided the venue for the meetings of the Company's CEOs, the Heeren XIX (Gentlemen Nineteen). The decentralized system generally worked well, but it also "promoted an exceptional amount of controversy, power struggles, and non-official commentaries."[7] The domination of Amsterdam's cultural

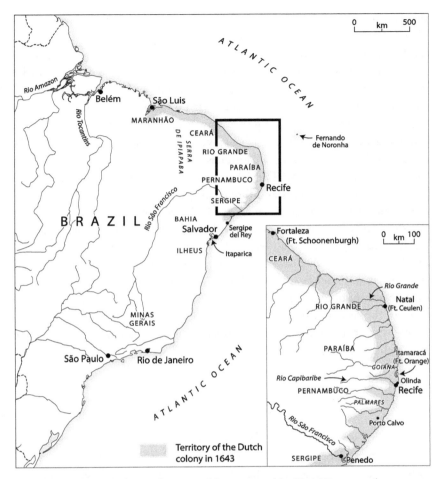

FIGURE 1. Dutch Brazil, c. 1643. Map prepared by UvA-Kaartenmakers. Reprinted with permission.

sector, and its preeminence in public debate, further undermined the formal checks and balances devised in the charter of the West India Company.

Like most cities in the Northern Netherlands, Amsterdam was a semi-autonomous entity, its power founded on privileges, exemptions, and unwritten yet long-practiced customs. In the absence of a strong central government, many political decisions were taken by the urban authorities, from the burgomasters in the town hall and the clergymen and elders in the consistories to the Company directors in the West India House. The urban population lived physically closer to those in power than was the case anywhere else in early modern Europe. This proximity may have raised the level of popular participation in politics and the effectiveness of public opinion.[8] The regents who dominated urban politics collectively strove to pursue their own interests and were quick to legitimate and cement their power by suggesting a common identity when things were going their way. "To maintain their authority with less popular envy or discontent, [they] give much to the general opinion of the people in the choice of their Magistrates," another Englishman, Sir William Temple, observed in 1673.[9] The urban policies the regents represented, however, often led to divisions and discussions, occasionally within Amsterdam but more often with other local or provincial governments. As different factions mobilized the urban community through extensive patronage networks, political disagreements pervaded the lower strata of society. The literate middle classes—the burghers—voiced their opinions through pamphlets that caused the patricians to take notice and either change their tone or increase their efforts to win public support.[10] Dutch Brazil became such a defining political topic in the seventeenth-century discussion culture because it provided both moments of collective patriotism and sharp divisions among sections of the ruling elite and their respective supporters.

Amsterdam's Atlantic

Amsterdam's views of Dutch Brazil are situated at the intersection of Atlantic history, urban history, and the history of communication. They can be brought back to life by investigating what the homefront knew, thought, said, and wrote about the evolving political situation in Brazil and why all this mattered for the (Dutch) Atlantic world. Rumors, news, spin-doctoring, and propaganda determined the opinions of armchair travelers not just in government circles but also at public meetings, inside private homes, and on the streets. The making of news and opinion on Dutch Brazil was an exclusively European affair. An ambitious early attempt to establish a printing press in Recife failed in 1643 because the master printer died prematurely, meaning that Amsterdammers—as for any other political topic—relied on local print media.[11] I will take all Dutch perspectives on Brazil into account, but the view from Amsterdam as the epicenter of news and public opinion will prevail.

To this arguably most opinionated of early information societies, I introduce the unique dynamics of the seventeenth-century Atlantic world.[12] I trace the genres of information and their itineraries and argue that transoceanic news formed the indispensable foundation for every form of European agency in the Atlantic world. In a logistically well-developed city like Amsterdam, this was especially obvious. By the time ships from Brazil had unloaded their cargo at the warehouses of the West India Company, word of mouth on events in the colony had long infiltrated the city and inspired discussions—in taverns and brothels as well as in the loggias of the stock exchange. Well before soldiers had signed off and received their final payment at the West India House, newspapers sold from the bookshops near Dam Square had already published the first bulletins on naval triumphs or military setbacks in Pernambuco. And while exotic commodities were expensive, even the most valuable information often cost very little: eyewitness reports from across the Atlantic Ocean were available much more widely in the city than sugar or brazilwood.

The stunning nine-leaf map of Amsterdam by Balthasar Florisz. van Berckenrode, meticulously depicting every house within the city walls, reveals the nearly unlimited urban pride and self-confidence on the eve of Dutch Brazil.[13] The central sheet shows the heart of Amsterdam's communication circuit (Figure 2). Every time a ship from Pernambuco arrived at the waterfront, orally transmitted information immediately entered the city, on smaller boats along the Damrak or on foot. Either way it was only a five-minute journey to the city's political and commercial heart. To get there one had to pass along Amsterdam's book alley called *Op 't Water* (On the Waterfront). Well before anyone had even considered the possibility of a "Dutch" Brazil, the printed travel accounts from the bookshop of Cornelis Claesz, international best-sellers at the turn of the seventeenth century, familiarized literate Amsterdammers with Spanish domination in the Americas.[14] After Claesz's death in 1609, other booksellers Op 't Water continued to cater to readers with an interest in Brazil. The Blaeu family, arguably the most important publishing dynasty in the United Provinces during the Golden Age, occupied a prime location, right next to the Corn Exchange and the Old Bridge, the walkway connecting the city's old and new parts. Here, from 1646 onward, Johan Blaeu sold to affluent customers his lavish wall map of Dutch Brazil. By offering detailed cartographic representations of the northeastern captaincies, decorated with stunning scenes from daily life in the colony, Blaeu's maps were perhaps the most tangible expression anywhere in Amsterdam of the country's newly established Atlantic authority.[15]

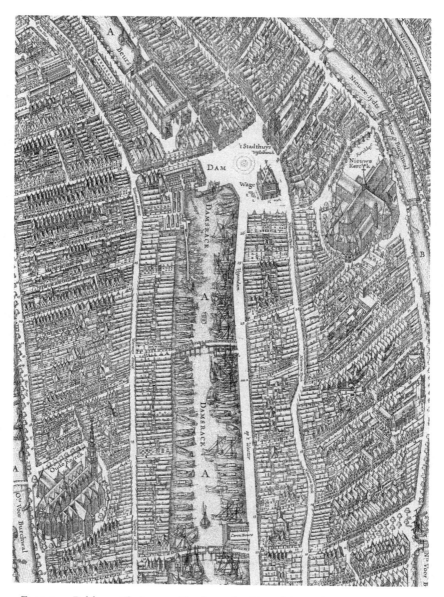

Figure 2. Balthasar Florisz. van Berckenrode, *Map of Amsterdam*, 1625 (detail). At the bottom of this image, close to the waterfront, the Coren beurs (Corn Exchange) and the Oude Brugh (Old Bridge) can be seen. Amsterdam's book alley Op 't Water runs parallel to the Damrack artery that separates the medieval center with the Old Church (left) from the city's fifteenth-century extensions. At the top, the Dam is bordered by the Stadthuys (City Hall) with the Wisselbanck (Bank of Exchange), the Nieuwe Kerck (New Church), and the Beurs (Stock Exchange). Courtesy of Rijksmuseum, Amsterdam, inv. nr. RP-P-1892-A-17491D.

The major civic institutions were centered around "the Dam," the meeting place par excellence for all the different immigrant groups that had accounted for the city's explosive population growth after 1585, when Amsterdam replaced Antwerp as the leading urban center in the Low Countries. Here was the old city hall, a comparatively small building where the *vroedschap* (city council) congregated, with a notice board for official placards and ordinances.[16] The same building also housed the Bank of Exchange, the first institution of its kind administered by the urban authorities. Just off the west side of Dam Square was the Nieuwe Kerk, one of the two grand parish churches dating from the late medieval period. Reformed preachers played an important role in informing their flock from the pulpit about the progress of the war against Spain. And finally, across the Dam, at the square's southeastern entrance was the Beurs, the world's main stock exchange. In addition to being the natural habitat of large traders and shareholders in the East and West India Companies, the Beurs also attracted people looking for news.[17] Jan van Hilten, the city's leading newspaperman who distributed weekly bulletins from the Atlantic world, held shop in the Beursstraat, right next to the exchange. Another leading manufacturer of news, the printmaker Claes Jansz Visscher, also lived and worked in the immediate vicinity of the financial center. Because of their proximity to both the economic bustle of the port and the city's major political, financial, and religious institutions, publishers like Van Hilten and Visscher formed a crucial chain in the process of making Atlantic news, transforming rumors into credible reports that in turn nurtured both carefully constructed propaganda and bitter dissent.[18]

By sharing information and facilitating public opinion, Claesz, Blaeu, Van Hilten, and Visscher were some of the key Amsterdam figures in the making of Dutch Brazil, and they will be discussed in detail in what follows. The urban media landscape, however, also attracted many smaller printers and publishers to the developing Atlantic storyline. The competitive international market for news and opinion ensured that the minority views that were inherent to a federal body politic received disproportionate attention in Amsterdam. The relative scope and impact of the various early modern media are of course hard to establish, but individual emotions and experiences were more prevalent than they are in society today, and notions of "media" and "mediation" should be historicized only with caution. The case of Dutch Brazil, in fact, also shows the limitations of the technology of print at a time when, as Clifford Siskin and William Warner have recently reminded us, "the eye, the hand, and the interiority of the individual . . . still sustained the vital middle position in the transmission of information."[19] Print may have initiated and stimulated popular interest in Brazil, but public opinion and its reflections in print ultimately determined how and why Dutch Brazil came to be "Amsterdamnified." To take a single city's view of a single Atlantic province as this book's unit of analysis, then, is an attempt to do methodological justice to the intrinsically different configurations of the media before modernity.

Atlanticizing Dutch Brazil

The choice to focus on Amsterdam is also a deliberate attempt to use Dutch Brazil to tell a bigger story, one that examines what we could consider to be a "public Atlantic." Why did Brazil matter so much to people in Amsterdam? Timing, as always, was essential. The emergence of Dutch Brazil occurred at the moment the federation of seven provinces had reached the lowest point in its short history. During the Twelve Years' Truce, a theological and ultimately political conflict between Calvinists and libertines in the Reformed Church had brought the country to the brink of civil war and ended in controversy when Stadtholder Maurits of Orange ordered the public execution of Holland's most respected politician, Pensionary Johan van Oldenbarnevelt. The Synod of Dordrecht that followed effectively turned the Remonstrants, a formerly influential group within the Reformed Church that had helped build the new state since the start of the Revolt, into dissenters. It seemed as if society would never be the same again. After the turmoil of the Truce years, the resumption of the war with Spain brought the welcome return of a common enemy but also a period of unexpected hardship. Internal divisions, financial constraints, and military defeats meant that the Dutch were under siege from the moment the war recommenced.[20] Under this cloud, the West India Company, more than any other institution, embodied the new spirit of the war. The mere promise of an attack on Brazil galvanized Dutch society, and public anticipation was extraordinarily high when the first major fleet set sail in December 1623.

The opening of a second front in the Atlantic world coincided with the rise of the printed newspaper as a major new forum for news, providing a weekly impetus to check or revise existing geopolitical perceptions.[21] This popular new carrier of information created an overwhelming appetite for reports from Brazil because initially, amid the political and military sorrow at home, those reports were almost too good to be true. Other (new) media followed suit. Dutch military progress helped reinvent the genre of visual news in the form of printed broadsheets, used by the authorities to manipulate the flow of Atlantic information in their favor. Reports from Brazil pervaded many other genres too, creating a culture of relentless interaction with the authorities and with other opinions that appeared in print to create a vibrant public debate. By the 1630s and early 1640s, coverage of Dutch Brazil had evolved into the early modern equivalent of a multimedia experience. By the later 1640s, however, when bad news began to filter through, the same media that, by applauding events in Brazil, had shaped a public Atlantic had now acquired enough authority to shatter popular support for the West India Company, nourished by a motley crew of political detractors. Impulsiveness, partisanship, and dissent found an outlet in printed pamphlets, a checkered and volatile genre that had truly come of age by the time Dutch Brazil began to divide opinions. All this media interest in Brazil turned Amsterdam into what Filippo De Vivo has termed a "resonating box" in which rumors and oral, handwritten, and printed opinions echoed within the city walls until the entire urban space was filled with political information.[22]

The particular blend of public opinion and popular participation that defined the political culture of the United Provinces could also spiral out of control, potentially leading to great disorder. This is what had happened during the Twelve Years' Truce, and it is also what eventually happened again in spectacular fashion in the case of Dutch Brazil in the late 1640s and 1650s. Scholars have not placed enough value on the capacity of Atlantic issues to derail (or lift) European society. By emphasizing public opinion, I therefore aspire to achieve two broader goals. First, I will demonstrate the relevance of Atlantic history for the Dutch Republic, in that information from across the ocean transformed opinion making at home in a way other colonial ventures had never done. And, second, I will demonstrate the relevance of the Dutch Republic for Atlantic history, urging scholars to look beyond the discourse of empire that has traditionally favored Spain and Britain (and to a lesser extent Portugal and France) and appreciate the crucial role of news, information, and public opinion in the making of the Atlantic world. Scholars who are investigating the reactions to transoceanic developments in locations where political debate was more subdued are encouraged to use my observations as a frame of reference.

For this reason, the urban perspective is crucial. Amsterdam merchants had felt restricted by the monopolistic charter of the West India Company from the day it was founded, campaigned aggressively for free trade in the

1630s, and, by the end—in the words of Charles Boxer—"did not care whether they traded to Brazil under the Dutch or under the Portuguese flag."[23] The Amsterdam city council's increasing detachment of the West India Company paralyzed the States General and initiated the fall of the colony. But "Amsterdamnification" was not only politically charged, it also had a public dimension. By virtue of its position at the center of a global trading network, Amsterdam had become the most important European arena for maritime news and thus for a public examination of the Atlantic world that could not materialize in more autocratic societies. By arguing that developments in Dutch Brazil made an impact well beyond traditional economic narratives, I take the Dutch Atlantic out of the customs houses and into the coffee houses, as it is here that the real scholarly value of the imperial moment in Dutch history lies.[24]

Dutch Brazil *is* that imperial moment. The triangle of a protracted colonial rivalry in the Atlantic world with broad geopolitical implications, local and provincial particularism in the mother country that generated perpetual debate, and a home front that was easily mobilized by a thriving printing industry and high literacy rates is unique. Other Dutch ventures in the Atlantic, in New Netherland, Elmina, Suriname, or the Caribbean, did not have the same political substance or popular appeal, while news from the East Indies did not make the headlines as frequently because it did not carry the implicit promise of imminent Spanish ruination. Both the volume and the sheer quality of publicity inspired by Dutch Brazil, and hence the impact of its capricious storyline on the formation of opinions at home, are unrivalled in the early modern period.[25] If an early modern public Atlantic can in fact be located, Dutch Brazil provides the sharpest lens.

Dutch Brazil featured in prints and paintings, in poems and ballads, in sermons and plays, in art and architecture, in private correspondence, diaries, *alba amicorum*, cabinets of curiosities, and many other forms of communication that reflected and facilitated popular participation in urban politics. Thinking about a public Atlantic raises several questions that remain to be answered before such a concept can take shape. To understand the production and circulation of Atlantic news, it is important to explore how printing houses handled the tension between a permanent demand for news and the infrequent and irregular arrival of ships. Did the public believe what they heard and read given that the ocean obstructed them from gaining credible information from other sources or from checking the facts for themselves?[26] The authorities recognized the need for reliable reporting, but they also desired to manage the news flow and construct their own political narrative that presented Brazil as a success story. Could they bend public opinion in their favor without jeopardizing their credibility? Which information did they protect from public view, as an implicit admission that too much communication might lead to too much popular interest? How did citizens participate in Atlantic affairs? What happened when they found out that colonial realities were radically different from colonial representations, for example, when stylized modes of representing Brazil were exposed by the oral information of thousands of sailors and soldiers who returned after having crossed the ocean? Was the relationship between the authorities, the media, and the public reconfigured when bad news washed ashore? And why, as the imperial moment faded, did the collective memory of progress and decline diverge from the way events in the Atlantic world had unfolded?

These questions would have been recognized by contemporaries as key issues of the Atlantic communication system, in Amsterdam and beyond.[27] Evidently the interest in news and information was not confined to one city. Dutch Brazil also captured the hearts and minds in towns like Middelburg, the capital of the maritime province of Zeeland, and The Hague, the seat of federal government. Public opinion from Amsterdam cannot be regarded as representative of all the different ideas about Dutch Brazil that circulated in the United Provinces, and it is not my objective to argue otherwise. The city was simply too idiosyncratic—ethnically, culturally, politically, economically, and demographically—to justify its use as an archetype. Moreover, some of the views on Brazil emanating from Amsterdam could not have been voiced so sharply had it not been for the radically opposing stances on how the colony should be governed that also carried great political weight. This is particularly true for the Atlantic opinions of two groups: the more orthodox members of the Reformed Church, whose influence in Amsterdam (and Holland in general) was professionally curbed by the powerful regent dynasties who formed a more liberal bloc, albeit strictly within the confines of the public Church; and the towns and province of Zeeland, Amsterdam's increasingly bitter rival in West Indian affairs. Their opinions, of course, will also be given the attention they deserve.

Across the borders of the United Provinces, Amsterdam's Atlantic left a mark too. The struggle for geopolitical dominance in Brazil meandered across different European conflicts and alliances. The war between the Dutch and the Habsburgs, one of the longest upheavals in early modern Europe, partially overlapped with the Union of the Crowns between Spain and Portugal (1580) that effectively turned Portuguese Brazil into a satellite of Madrid—and therefore a legitimate military target for the West India Company. Yet when the Union fell apart in 1640, and Portugal under the Braganças proclaimed its independence from Spain, the war in Brazil was far from finished. Although the Dutch supported the Portuguese Restoration and signed a provisional Ten Years' Truce with the new king João IV in 1641, they only grudgingly accepted its implications in Brazil, where the West India Company was now no longer spearheading the war against Spain (although Philip IV would not give up his claims on Brazil for another twenty-five years). In 1648, the geopolitical complexion changed definitively when the Dutch concluded peace with Spain in Münster while in Pernambuco they faced a Luso-Brazilian revolt—the so-called "War of Divine Liberation"—that was tacitly supported in Bahia and Lisbon. To make matters worse for the West India Company, the Portuguese also recaptured Angola and São Tomé. By the time the Dutch had scaled up the war against Portugal, João IV had regained support from England, sealed by the marriage between his daughter Catherine and Charles II.

In France and the Holy Roman Empire, the struggle in the Atlantic world was followed with more than average interest as well, judging from the column inches Brazil commanded in French and German news media of the time. German Protestants hoped that the imperial overstretch of Habsburg Spain would ease the pressure from the Catholic enemy in the devastating Thirty Years' War, if only ever so slightly. France under Richelieu supported any undertaking that undermined Madrid's military supremacy. Further south, in Venice, Paolo Sarpi had claimed that there would be no better way to break the strength of the Spaniards than for the Dutch to invade America.[28] But there were more mundane reasons to explain foreign interest in Brazil as well. High Germans, as well as Scandinavians, Englishmen, Scots, and French Huguenots, made up such a sizeable contingent of the West India Company's regiments that it is practically impossible to consider the Dutch Atlantic truly "Dutch."[29] Their oral and written testimonies, presented to their families and friends across Europe, will be regarded here as part of Amsterdam's Atlantic because their experiences in Brazil were generally similar to those of their Dutch colleagues. Johan Maurits of Nassau-Siegen, the outstanding governor of Dutch Brazil, was himself a German nobleman, who before his departure for Pernambuco had spent most of his life at the princely courts of Siegen, Herborn, and Kassel. Much of the cultural capital he construed in Recife he subsequently injected into the aristocratic milieu inside *and* outside the United Provinces.[30] Politically, then, Dutch Brazil may have been Dutch, but socially, ethnically, and culturally, it was much more diverse. This diversity, in combination with the colony's myriad of geopolitical implications, guaranteed that public discussions fuelled in Amsterdam commanded great attention across Europe.

※

In the preface to his masterful study *Tempo dos Flamengos* (1947), José Antonio Gonsalves de Mello, the great twentieth-century Pernambucan scholar of Dutch Brazil, wrote with awe about the numerous manuscript reports from Recife available in the archives in the Netherlands. For him, these documents lifted the "time of the Flemings" above the canonical list of political milestones that prior generations of Brazilian scholars had recited. "The Dutch regime never tired of ordering paper, ink and pencils from Holland," he wrote approvingly. The handwritten testimonies enabled the social historian to meticulously reconstruct the building of a tropical version of Amsterdam in Recife—complete with tall and slender houses made of bricks, a synagogue, and a network of canals.[31] With this wealth of unedited material now available to him, Gonsalves de Mello continued, "the collections of pamphlets and other printed matter produced in the Netherlands before and during the occupation of Brazil, which because of their rarity are so difficult to study here, are only of secondary importance."[32] This book argues otherwise. As the mirror image of *Tempo dos Flamengos*, it focuses instead on the paper, ink, and pencils that remained in Amsterdam first to build and ultimately to deconstruct Recife at home. The fact that so much information was publicly available to contemporaries—mainly in print—is what makes Dutch Brazil both unique and immediately relevant to scholars of the early modern Atlantic world. Only by understanding how a much-anticipated colony came to be Amsterdamnified can we appreciate the lasting relevance of Dutch Brazil for Atlantic history.

CHAPTER 1

Anticipation

In the summer of 1601, anyone in Amsterdam with an interest in the Atlantic world could get a glimpse of two Brazilians for as little as two-and-a-half *stuivers*. All he or she needed to do was go to the Warmoesstraat, the city's main shopping street, enter the bookstore of Zacharias Heyns, "In The Three Cardinal Virtues," and buy a copy of *Dracht-thoneel*. This pocket-sized costume book contained images of familiar and unfamiliar populations organized by applying European categories of civility and gender to cultures from different parts of the world. Each of the 139 woodcuts was accompanied by a quatrain in Dutch, explaining to the reader some of the ethnographic qualities of the men and women on display. Featuring in Heyns's catalog of people were "The Brazilian" and "The Brazilian woman," posing as a pair according to costume book protocol (Figure 3). The man is holding typical weaponry of bow and arrows. His muscular body is clearly visible as he is almost entirely naked, with the exception of several plumes on his head and a perfectly arranged cluster of feathers covering his lower back. The long-haired woman, naked like her counterpart, turns away from the viewer for reasons of chastity. Readers are able to see only the head of the young child she carries on her arm. The two quatrains add little information to the illustrations, apart from the emphasis the second poem places on the role of the woman as a mother and the practice of washing her baby immediately after birth. The gloomy background filled with disorderly vegetation completes the two images.[1]

By putting native Brazilians on display in an attractively priced costume book, Heyns catered to the demands of the cosmopolitan population of Amsterdam at the turn of the seventeenth century. Interest in overseas travel soared, and printed books on exotic destinations became instant best-sellers. Zacharias Heyns was one of the city's most productive publishers and was perfectly positioned to understand the commercial potential of this kind of

FIGURE 3. Zacharias Heyns, *Dracht-Thoneel*, Amsterdam, 1601, [H4ʳ]–[H5ʳ]. Courtesy of Koninklijke Bibliotheek, The Hague, KW 3110 G 15.

information. Born and raised in Antwerp and trained in the workshop of the great Christopher Plantin, Heyns left when Catholic troops conquered his hometown in 1585. Like so many immigrants from the Southern Netherlands, he eventually settled in Amsterdam, where he experienced the enormous expansion of commerce and shipping literally on the doorstep of his house near the Old Bridge. Political and mercantile information on Asia had already converged here to become a marketable commodity. When powerful local magistrates like Pieter Hasselaer and Reynier Pauw decided to start investing in the Brazil trade in the late 1590s, depicting native Brazilians was an obvious commercial choice.[2]

Brazil would not be making any headlines for another twenty years. Since the perception of (and interest in) hard news arrived only with geopolitical commitment, topical genres like handwritten corantos did not pay any attention to the Atlantic world. In the meantime, Amsterdam burghers patiently awaited their city's future as a hub of Atlantic information without being supplied with political instructions of how to get there. For now, maps and literary genres such as costume books and travel accounts dominated the information flow. So what exactly did Amsterdammers know about Brazil before the period of geopolitical engagement? When and how did the circulation of exotic representations begin to fuel popular anticipation of a "Dutch" Brazil? And who were the main mediators in this gradual transition? Zacharias Heyns's *Dracht-thoneel* offers an emblematic view of the early urban imagination of Brazil in three related respects. First, knowledge in Amsterdam was based on information from abroad, mostly but not exclusively from France. Second, it was outdated. And third, and most importantly in the context of this book, it carried no immediate political connotation as yet.

A Second-Hand Discovery

The Dutch encounter with Brazil in the final decade of the sixteenth century was an imaginative and indirect one that took place in Amsterdam, not in the Atlantic world. Local booksellers interested in transatlantic information reached out to a broad urban and international audience and relied on proven vehicles of mediation. Costume books and (illustrated) travel accounts had been popular genres in the sixteenth-century European book market. In Antwerp, since 1570, atlases had emerged as a third successful means of communicating information from overseas. All three genres were visually attractive and written in the vernacular, and the information they contained was unpretentious and accessible. Because they were mostly small and woodcuts were relatively cheap, they were affordable for the middle classes. Judging from his publication strategy, Zacharias Heyns was one of a handful of Amsterdam booksellers in the late 1590s to recognize their commercial potential for the domestic market. More than other publishers, he explored the possibilities of different genres to distribute information on the Atlantic world.

In 1598, Heyns set out to capitalize on local interest in overseas expansion by producing a pocket atlas, *Le Miroir du Monde*, based on maps from Abraham Ortelius's *Theatrum Orbis Terrarum*. Since its publication, Ortelius's atlas had rapidly developed into an indispensable item on private and public bookshelves across Europe and had gone through many revised editions. Peeter

Heyns, Zacharias's father, had written short poems for the first pocket-sized version of Ortelius's masterpiece, foreshadowing his son's decision to issue a similar work in his newly adopted hometown. In the copy of *Le Miroir du Monde* now in the Amsterdam University Library, Brazil features on the world map that opens the volume as a distinctive geographical entity, given a different color from the rest of South America to indicate its place in the Portuguese orbit (Figure 4). Heyns's pocket atlas became so fashionable that local competitors quickly replaced his crude woodcuts with copper engravings to push him out of this segment of the market.[3]

Two years later, Heyns tried his hand at arguably the most popular of all late sixteenth-century genres, the travel account. His *Wijdtloopigh Verhael* (Wide-Ranging Story), based on the journal of the physician Barent Jansz Potgieter and rewritten and expanded by Heyns to include literary references and nautical information, was the first Dutch eyewitness report of the Atlantic world

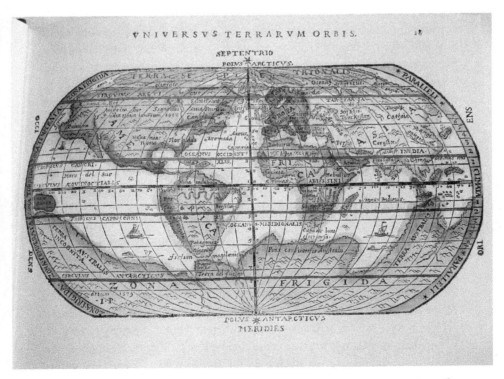

FIGURE 4. Zacharias Heyns, *Miroir du Monde*, Amsterdam, 1598, 18. Courtesy of Special Collections, University of Amsterdam, OTM: O 60-1004.

printed in Amsterdam.[4] It related the misfortunes of the first Dutch attempt at circumnavigation that failed to traverse the Strait of Magellan. Brazil did not feature beyond the occasional reference, but perceptive readers could still make out the contours of the Portuguese Atlantic, riddled with marvelous indigenous peoples and tropical diseases. The volume contained eight woodcuts, including spectacular depictions of the mythical Patagonian giants the crew had supposedly encountered. Once again, the book's instant popularity meant that Heyns's images were upgraded by more technologically advanced publishers, in this case, the internationally oriented firm of the De Brys in Frankfurt. They, by drastically changing the woodcuts, emphasized at an early stage the manipulative potential of information that could not be checked by European readers.[5]

Then, the following year, Heyns provided a first ethnographical round-up of the Atlantic world by publishing *Dracht-thoneel*. Costume books materialized Europeans' efforts to classify human diversity in the rest of the world according to local systems of dominance to impose an interpretative grid on a bewildering range of new data. Clothes, or the lack of them, signified social rank and habits of behavior.[6] *Dracht-thoneel* too can be read through this prism. Heyns portrayed the Brazilians in the book's penultimate section together with other Amerindians, following the images of Old World peoples but preceding an eclectic closing parade of Plinian archetypes like a cyclops and a monkey-headed monster from Peru, and several Catholic fathers including a Jesuit and a Capuchin. The position of the Brazilians at the back end of *Dracht-thoneel*, and the way Heyns represented them, reveals that Amsterdammers were meant to rank them comparatively low in the hierarchy of civilization. Only the Patagonian pair, practically antipodes who were living at the southernmost tip of the American landmass, were portrayed entirely naked like the Brazilians.[7]

Although Zacharias Heyns denounced its inhabitants in no uncertain terms, knowledge of Brazil as a political entity remained scant. How Portugal had struggled to develop the colony and how it had managed to revive its fortunes after 1549 with the establishment of Salvador as the seat of royal and ecclesiastical government were not publicized. For now, Brazil was a silhouette colony in the Amsterdam print media, a differently colored patch on the map, rather than an Atlantic province with a clear-cut public image. Against this backdrop, it did not matter much that, for *Dracht-thoneel*, Heyns had copied the Brazilians, like the majority of his ethnographic illustrations, from what is regarded as the first European costume book, *Receuil de la diversité des habits*

(1564), published by the Huguenot printer Richard Breton.[8] That the Amsterdam images of Brazilians originated in Paris is no coincidence. Effective censorship laws in Portugal and Habsburg Spain meant that French representations of Brazil dominated the European imagination for a considerable time, originating in the years between 1555 and 1560 when a troubled settlement dubbed "Antarctic France" experienced its brief prime in the area around Rio de Janeiro.[9] This period, when Brazil became a contested possession, generated political interest in the colony, a key catalyst for the production of information. For Amsterdam booksellers, French Brazil—the first Reformed settlement society in America—proved an inspirational reference point to create a wider awareness of what the future might bring. Its main mediator was one of Zacharias Heyns's fiercest rivals in the local book market, Cornelis Claesz.

Cornelis Claesz was arguably the leading publisher in the United Provinces around 1600 and played a crucial role in making Amsterdam the European center for Atlantic information.[10] Like Heyns, Claesz was of Southern Netherlandish origin. He had already moved to Holland during the early stages of the Dutch Revolt, and, when the city of Amsterdam finally joined the war against King Philip II of Spain in May 1578, Claesz immediately settled on Amsterdam's book alley *Op 't Water* (On the Waterfront).[11] Located halfway between the maritime rumors of the harbor district and the official announcements from Dam Square, he built a major publishing firm with an international reputation. In the 1590s, as the overseas ambitions of Dutch merchants rapidly materialized, Claesz began to specialize in travel accounts, maps, and navigational literature. Brazil, as the most established trading destination in the Atlantic world, was high on his list of priorities.

When looking for suitable texts to be published, any Dutch bookseller with a half-decent international network would have known of three authors who brought Brazil's incipient role in geopolitics to the attention of a European readership.[12] All three can be linked to the period of French Brazil. The first, André Thevet, departed for Guanabara Bay in 1555 as chaplain to Nicolas Durand de Villegagnon, the projected leader of "Antarctic France." Although an illness forced Thevet to return within three months, his account, *Les Singularitez de la France Antarctique* (1557), earned him the position of royal cosmographer to Henri II. In *Singularitez*, Thevet discussed the rise and fall of French Brazil from a Catholic viewpoint. When Huguenot ministers arrived in the settlement, the author claimed, theological disputes accelerated the downfall of the colony, the remains of which were eventually wiped out by the Portuguese. The dispute in Guanabara Bay between Catholics and Huguenots formed an Atlantic prelude to the religious wars that were to ravage France in the following decades, ensuring that French Brazil acquired public notoriety across Europe.[13] In an age of confessional strife, an overtly Catholic work was an unlikely candidate for translation in an emerging Protestant metropolis like Amsterdam. Claesz, then, did not re-issue or translate Thevet's book. But information transcended all borders. Thevet's woodcuts of Tupinamba Indians, indiscriminately labeled "Brazilians" by Richard Breton for his costume book, were later brought to Amsterdam by Zacharias Heyns.[14]

Thanks to Cornelis Claesz, the other two eyewitnesses of Brazil became household names in Amsterdam bookshops. The German soldier Hans Staden, a native of Homburg in Hesse, had been enlisted by the Portuguese to counter the looming French threat around Rio de Janeiro. Before the actual arrival of the French, however, he had been taken prisoner by the Tupis. His spectacular captivity tale, first published in German in Marburg in 1557, became one of the cornerstones of Brazilian Americana. It lacked the political urgency of Thevet's narrative, but it appealed to more universal sentiments of disbelief at the ethnographic marvels on offer across the Atlantic. Staden, in true Protestant fashion, recounted how he had experienced the threat of being eaten as a test of his Christian faith. After the book's publication, Europeans increasingly began to view cannibalism as something quintessentially Brazilian (Figure 5). In 1595, as Dutch expansion was about to commence, Cornelis Claesz published a translation of Staden's account in a cheap octavo edition. In the introduction, he pointed to the potential of Brazil as a land for evangelization, settlement, and profit. The book remained popular throughout the seventeenth century, when more editions were published in the Low Countries than anywhere else in Europe.[15] In the 1630s, when the Dutch in Brazil entered into an at times awkward military alliance with cannibalistic Tapuya Indians, the Amsterdam news publisher Broer Jansz would issue three reprints in quick succession.

Twenty years after the demise of French Brazil, at the nadir of the French wars of religion, Andre Thevet's Catholic explanation for its loss produced a belated reply from the Protestant side. Written by Jean de Léry, one of the Huguenot ministers who had travelled to the colony in the late 1550s, *Histoire d'un voyage fait en la Terre du Brésil* (1578) was even better positioned than Staden's tale to make an impression in Amsterdam. Its anti-Catholic rhetoric tied in smoothly with Bartolomé de las Casas's story of the gruesome behavior of Spanish conquistadors in America—a powerful trope that Dutch opinion makers utilized as the mirror image of their own experiences with Philip II's

FIGURE 5. "Hans Staden Witnesses a Tupi Cannibalistic Ritual." In Theodore de Bry, *Americae tertia pars*. Frankfurt 1592, 127. Courtesy of Special Collections, University of Amsterdam, OTM: OF 63-731 (3).

tyranny in the Netherlands.[16] The Iberian Union of the Crowns of 1580, in the eyes of the Dutch, effectively legitimated the expansion of the "Black Legend" to Brazil (but not, interestingly, to the Portuguese).[17] Cornelis Claesz, who had coproduced an illustrated Dutch translation of Las Casas's *Brevisima Relacion* in 1596 and would go on to publish two further editions, recognized the political appeal of De Léry's work. In 1597, he printed its first Dutch edition.

De Léry's *Histoire* was a scathing attack on the rule of Nicolas Durand de Villegagnon, a Protestant sympathizer who reverted to Catholicism in Brazil and thus wrecked the dream of a Huguenot refuge in America. De Léry also slated the work of Thevet, who, for his *Singularitez*, had relied on hearsay rather than personal experience. Its polemical tone made De Léry's work both popular and controversial in Reformation Europe. Yet for all his confessional antagonism, De Léry was also one of the most gifted observers of indigenous

Brazilian culture. He devised an elaborate ethnological comparison of Tupi cannibalism with the Christian Eucharist, constructing an analogy of spiritual nourishment. And he even went so far as to confess, after returning to a divided France, that he regretted not being among the savages any longer. De Léry thus placed the man-eating customs in an existing European framework of interpretation that allowed for an understanding of cannibalism—a type of cultural relativism that would later influence Michel de Montaigne in his essay on the subject.[18]

In his *Histoire*, De Léry inadvertently—and with a delay of almost two decades—sent out a strong political message to readers in Amsterdam. He expressed great regret that French Brazil had not succeeded. The colony, he insisted, was unusually rich:

> And certainly, since the country of our Tupinamba is capable of nourishing ten times more people than it has—I myself when I was there could boast of having at my disposal more than a thousand acres of land, better than any in all of Beauce—who can doubt that if the French had remained there (which they would have done, and there would now be more than ten thousand of them, if Villegagnon had not rebelled against the Reformed Religion) they would have drawn the same profit from it as the Portuguese, who have adapted themselves so well to that land?[19]

The Tupis, moreover, welcomed strangers with applause and flattery.[20] If the Dutch would come to develop any ambitions in Brazil, in other words, they might even count on support from within the Habsburg empire. In reissuing a text containing such political implications, Claesz turned French Brazil, a frustrated Reformed attempt to create a colonial settlement in the tropical part of the Atlantic world, into a mental prototype for subsequent Dutch efforts.

The printed books by Zacharias Heyns and Cornelis Claesz form the vantage point of political representations of Brazil in the Dutch Golden Age. These publications were readily available in Amsterdam around 1600, more readily and more widely perhaps than elsewhere in Europe, although the images of Brazil they disclosed were not typical for the Netherlands. If anything, these books were indicative of the second-hand nature of the Dutch "discovery" of Brazil. Yet the moment of their publication is not without significance. This was the time when many merchants in the city were prepared to invest in the long-distance trade. Representations of Brazil as the vulnerable hindquarters of Habsburg America were regarded as an invitation to take action. In late 1590s Amsterdam, the first reports of success in Asia meant that Dutch confidence in overseas expansion surged, and several leading merchants began to shift their focus to the Atlantic world, where similar achievements would directly impair Spanish interests.

Reading Habits

Of course, in order to gauge the popular impact of Brazil in late sixteenth- and early seventeenth-century Amsterdam, analyzing the production of books is only half the story. Who read these books? Did readers understand the objectives authors and publishers had with the various literary genres? And how did all parties collectively shape Amsterdam as a forum for different political opinions where Brazil would be discussed with such vigor in the second quarter of the seventeenth century? The single most important condition for the rise of a public Atlantic was the exceptionally high literacy rate in the urban centers of Holland. Amsterdam's educational practice distinguished itself from that in other European commercial hubs in two important ways. Schooling was available for both boys *and* girls—a meaningful aspect of public life as Dutch Brazil began to mature in the 1630s and 1640s and women needed to take care of family interests while their husbands sailed to the colony. In addition, the city was willing to provide funds to teach the most basic elements of reading and writing to the poor.[21] As a result, about 60 percent of bridegrooms in early seventeenth-century Amsterdam could write their names in the local marriage register. Brides were generally about 35 percent literate around 1600. Both numbers continued to rise until the end of the seventeenth century, when immigrants also gradually reached the higher percentages of native Amsterdammers. Moreover, indications are that the literacy rates of dissenters such as Lutherans and Jews were relatively high, another important prerequisite for the discussion culture of the Dutch Golden Age.[22]

But that many could read does not mean that they did, let alone that they read about Brazil. Here the evidence becomes more circumstantial. The sales figures of the firms of Zacharias Heyns and Cornelis Claesz at least suggest that their titles reached a relatively broad urban audience. In 1605 Heyns left Amsterdam, but it was not until four years later, in April 1609, that his remaining books were auctioned by the Weeskamer (Orphan Chamber), a municipal institution. His back catalog still contained 198 copies of *Dracht-*

thoneel. If we estimate an original print run of around 1,250 to 1,500 copies—not unusual for these kinds of small books—then Heyns must have managed to sell the large majority of copies he had printed within four years. What is more, the remaining copies were purchased by four different Amsterdam booksellers, including Cornelis Claesz, in lots of fifty. Clearly they all estimated that the costume book still had commercial appeal.[23] Claesz could not have sold many copies of *Dracht-thoneel*, because he died in August of the same year. When his stock catalog of books and copper plates was auctioned in 1610, a new generation of publishers jumped at the chance to acquire the material to reprint his successful maps and travel accounts. In the years following Claesz's death, his most important works on non-European topics were reissued with the imprints of other Amsterdam booksellers.[24]

Both Heyns and Claesz had been immigrants. The explosive growth of the city through migration—between 1578 and 1622, Amsterdam's population tripled from 30,000 to 100,000 inhabitants—connected the city to the Protestant diaspora in Europe, and increased its scope as a center for news and political information. Demand for knowledge continued to increase in absolute terms, then, but it remains difficult to establish what people knew exactly about Brazil and how knowledge varied from one person to the next. Individual merchants had been trading in the Atlantic world for several decades, transporting sugar and brazilwood to the Low Countries in close cooperation with New Christians in Portugal and Brazil.[25] This means that a select group of affluent Amsterdammers had been to Pernambuco and Bahia, and knew much more than what could be found in print. But for merchants there was no incentive to share the information they had gathered with their fellow citizens. Keeping things secret was long considered standard business practice.[26] Other potential sources of eyewitness information might have included sailors from the Low Countries, who occasionally were interrogated by the Inquisition in Brazil and Lisbon for suspected Protestant beliefs.[27] But their stories of orthodoxy and repression do not appear to have resonated in the Amsterdam media landscape, and were never printed.

Inventories of private libraries give a rudimentary understanding of the circulation of knowledge among armchair travelers, but, again, this information comes with a caveat. Books were luxury items, and, although many Amsterdammers could read, few in the Golden Age could afford to collect more than a dozen printed volumes. A typical collection of books consisted of a Bible, a handful of devotional texts, some educational works, and an occasional literary treatise of axioms or emblems. There were, of course, exceptions. Ministers, for example, possessed many books, sometimes so many that their collections were publicly auctioned after their death. Their private libraries can be used as a yardstick for the circulation of printed matter on Brazil among the upper middle classes. Johannes Halsberch for example, a clergyman born in Kortrijk in Flanders, migrated to Amsterdam in 1590. On the request of the Vereenigde Oost-Indische Compagnie (VOC, the Dutch East India Company), he translated a book on the wisdom of the Christian religion against heathens, Muslims, and Jews—so he had a semiprofessional interest in Dutch expansion. Yet judging from the books on his own shelves he attached very little importance to Brazil. Among the books he owned when he died in 1607 were works by Ptolemy and Strabo, copies of Sebastian Münster's obsolete *Cosmographia*, José de Acosta's natural history of the New World, and a series of travel accounts to America printed in Basel in 1555. Halsberch even possessed printed Jesuit relations, but he did not own a single book that specifically concerned Brazil.[28]

The famous Jacobus Arminius was a close friend of Halsberch and was very moved by his death. Like Halsberch, Arminius had studied in Geneva with a stipend from the city of Amsterdam, and in 1588 he was called on to become the main preacher in the Old Church. The bulk of his library must have already been in his possession before he moved to Leiden in 1603 to become professor of theology. So did Arminius have an interest in Brazil? He too owned authoritative classical works by Ptolemy and Strabo (and Pliny), as well as Münster's *Cosmographia* and, again, the outdated collection of voyages by Simon Grynaeus and Johan Hüttich issued in Basel. Yet, unlike Halsberch, Arminius also possessed a pocket edition of Jean de Léry's *Historia Navigationis in Brasil*. He even owned a copy of Montaigne's *Essais*.[29] If and how Arminius read those books, however, remains an open question. The relative dearth of printed information on Brazil in two comparatively well-stocked private libraries suggests that very few Amsterdammers before 1620 possessed reliable knowledge of Brazil. A substantial analysis of contemporary Dutch auction catalogs corroborates these Amsterdam findings: interest in America was still driven by classical literature and not yet specifically oriented toward assessing single colonies. For information on Brazil, readers relied on De Léry.[30]

In the public domain, it was no different. The city council in 1578 had founded a library, housed in the New Church on Dam Square, with the explicit brief to give open access to everyone, even to those "who differed from our understanding of religion." Most of the visitors, according to the libertine burgomaster Cornelis Pietersz Hooft, were "of a very young age."[31] The printed catalog of 1612 reveals that Münster's *Cosmographia* and Ortelius's *Theatrum Orbis Terrarum* were joined on the shelf they were chained to by André Thevet's *Cosmographie Universelle*, a two-volume work that included information on Brazil but that, according to the catalog, had been "mutilated by a rascal."[32] Ten years later, at the eve of Dutch Atlantic expansion, the library had broadened its geographical section with the *America* series issued by the De Bry family, which included the accounts of Staden and De Léry—in Latin.[33] Yet here, too, traditional scholarship dominated. Modern local publications like Zacharias Heyns's costume book or Cornelis Claesz's travel accounts did not feature in any of the inventories—private or public—but then, because of their size, they did not represent any monetary value and were therefore unlikely to be named in auction catalogs at all. Despite the apparent circulation of these mundane books in Amsterdam, library catalogs both public and private suggest that readers could be forgiven for being immersed in a culture of stereotypes and, at best, rumors of Brazil's commercial potential.

Orality

So how to explain the apparent discrepancy between the production and reception of information on Brazil in Amsterdam? Despite the explosive rise of print culture around 1600 and the relatively high literacy rates, the production of books and maps can tell only part of the story. Calvinist contempt for public display meant that the representational culture of encounters like in Rouen, where fifty Tupinamba Indians adorned Henri II's 1550 joyous entry, or in Antwerp, where a local sugar merchant headed a procession accompanied by a "well-mannered" African slave from his Brazilian plantation, was inconceivable in Amsterdam.[34] Logistically, however, the city had all it took to become a hotbed of Atlantic information. Ever since the eruption of the Dutch Revolt in the 1570s, Amsterdam had attracted news from all corners of the Netherlands and beyond. Written information—let alone printed information—played only a limited role in the everyday circulation of news. Oral communication remained the most important source of news, especially for developments that had taken place in the proximity of Amsterdam or that otherwise relied on eyewitness reporting. The taverns in the harbor district were the venues of tall stories of maritime adventure, and anecdotal information on Brazil must have circulated here long before the period of political engagement. Rumors, however, were unreliable. The best way to verify what was being said, contemporaries agreed, was to check it against a trustworthy written piece of evidence.[35]

Many handwritten letters during times of war, however, were composed for propaganda purposes and were just as unreliable as word of mouth.[36] Only business correspondence was less susceptible to partisanship. Information from Brazil occasionally featured in the letters of firms involved in the Atlantic trade.[37] In the final quarter of the sixteenth century, as the collective sharing of information gradually became a more attractive business model for merchants than secrecy, these letters developed into a new genre, the handwritten newspaper, which quickly acquired authority in the urban information market.[38] These so-called corantos, written by professional hacks, contained factual descriptions of international developments. In the 1590s, Amsterdam emerged as the genre's center in the Low Countries, an advantageous position it would exploit even further when handwritten newspapers were replaced by printed ones around 1620.[39] Their readership, crucially, consisted not only of private individuals but also of the urban authorities. The directors of the VOC in Amsterdam, for example, had a standing order for handwritten tidings and expressly forbade their members to take the corantos outside the East India House, a clear indication that demand for the news they contained was high.[40]

Although Brazil was not a regular feature in the early news media, information from the Atlantic world was easily incorporated in the urban infrastructure of communication. Every time a ship arrived in the port of Amsterdam after a transatlantic voyage, its first obligatory stop was at the Nieuwe Brugh. Physically this "New Bridge," a stone structure built to replace an old wooden bridge in the early 1560s, marked the boundary between the open sea and the city's orderly network of canals; metaphorically, it separated the Atlantic world from Amsterdam's highly sophisticated communication circuit. All incoming ships called here to pay their tolls at the Paalhuys, the small building on the bridge (Figure 6). Those "coming overseas from East and West" were obliged by decree immediately to drop off messages and private letters for the city's inhabitants. The letters were numbered by a clerk and put on a list on a notice board outside. "Throughout the day and especially in the evening," one contemporary observer wrote, "the bridge is teeming with people who come here just to discuss maritime affairs."[41] In 1624, the very year the Dutch first got a foothold in Brazil, the city council accommodated public discussion on the New Bridge by constructing a gallery where burghers could sit down and gaze across the open water to witness the ocean-going vessels while sharing the latest information from overseas.[42] In the 1640s, even directors of the West India Company supposedly went to the bridge for Atlantic news.[43]

A lively culture of conversation widened the participation in political discourse, and oral communication about Brazil explains why the name Pernambuco had attained a familiar ring early on. "In our time," one contemporary observer wrote, "there are two means of leading the common folk by the ear—namely, the pulpit and the stage."[44] In 1596, the poet Jan van Hout wrote a farce for a festival of one of the chambers of rhetoric in Leiden, Holland's university town twenty miles south of Amsterdam. The play was titled *Loterijspel* (Lottery Play), a generic name related to its function rather than to its content. Rhetoricians, in close cooperation with the urban authorities, organized lotteries for the benefit of the common good. To succeed in attracting more buyers, the farce would need to appeal to a wide audience.[45] Here we can deduce that knowledge of the commercial potential of Brazil had started to reach the middle classes. In a dialogue between two of the farcical characters, the worldly wise Steven and the provincial Bouwen, the former boasted of his voyage to "Ver en de Boc," a vulgar pronunciation of Pernambuco. Since Bouwen had never heard of this place, Steven explained that, in order to reach the province, one had to cross the equator. Usually only Spanish vessels sailing from Seville called at the port, according to Steven, but nowadays it was being visited by Dutchmen too.[46] The urban audience was meant to chuckle at the peasant's ignorance,[47] but this presupposed prior knowledge of the Brazilian province and its place in the Atlantic trading network.

That local navigators sailed to Brazil, then, was evidently public knowledge beyond the harbor district where traders recruited their personnel. The spread of maritime information also acquired an institutional dimension in the 1590s. Pilots obviously learnt the art of traversing the Atlantic on board, but, before 1600, Amsterdam already had two masters teaching ocean-going navigation.[48] These navigational schools were a key link between the city's maritime and nonmaritime sectors. Not only did they disseminate specific Atlantic knowledge to a small number of urban inhabitants and provide a venue to discuss and develop geopolitical strategies of expansion, but they also opened up the maritime sector to trends in the book trade. Long before their courses were included in the curriculum of the prestigious Athenaeum Illustre, the city's institute of higher education founded in 1632, the two programs in ocean-going navigation had mathematical and cartographical components that could be learned from books and maps, a development that required basic

FIGURE 6. Jan Abrahamsz Beerstraten, *The Paalhuis and the New Bridge*, c. 1660, oil on canvas, 84 × 100 cm. Courtesy of Rijksmuseum, Amsterdam, inv. nr. SK-A-20.

reading, writing, and counting skills among the lower-middle-class pupils. Here—in the context of Brazil—the worlds of orality and print first came together.[49]

In the final decade of the sixteenth century, publications on Brazil moved from the shop windows of Amsterdam bookstores into the cabins of transoceanic navigators—a transition in which Cornelis Claesz again played a crucial role. Many of his regular customers earned their money in the maritime sector, and authors wishing to promote overseas expansion recognized his reputation as a skillful mediator. Jan Huygen van Linschoten's *Reys-gheschrift* of 1595 included six chapters with practical information on Brazil, from the ideal Atlantic crossing between Cape Verde and Fernando de Noronha to the prevailing winds on sea routes to profitable regions like Bahia and São Vicente.[50]

Van Linschoten had lived in Goa and written an important guide to open up the Asian trade to Dutch merchants, the famous *Itinerario*. His authority as a pathfinder was undisputed, and his publications resonated also with a wider urban audience. That he now turned his attention to Brazil was highly significant.[51] The following year, Van Linschoten wrote another eighteen pages about the customs of Brazilian Indians, largely based on the Dutch translation of De Léry that Claesz was preparing for the presses at the same time. Brazil, author and publisher explained, was a place where many East Indiamen made landfall and deserved a detailed description.[52]

Lucas Jansz Waghenaer, the compiler of a series of important pilot guides, reported the latitudes of several locations in Brazil in his *Enchuyser Zee-caertboeck* of 1598—the only overseas destination he considered worth mentioning (Figure 7). He also added brief transoceanic itineraries to Brazil from the Canary Islands and from Guinea.[53] Four years later, for the fourth edition of his landmark *Thresoor der Zeevaert* issued in Amsterdam by Claesz, Waghenaer provided even more details. In a newly written addendum, he made profiles of the coastline of Pernambuco from a navigator's perspective in order to help ships' captains to establish their position in the Atlantic.[54] In this vibrant environment of navigational know-how it is conceivable that the Amsterdam globe maker Jacob Floris van Langren was correct when he claimed that sev-

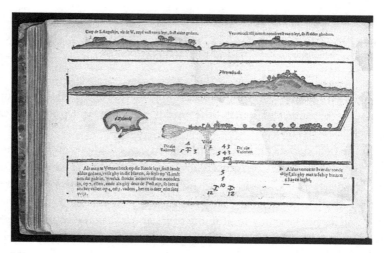

FIGURE 7. "Coastline of Pernambuco." In Lucas Jansz Waghenaer, *Thresoor der Zee-vaert*, 4th ed. Amsterdam 1592, unpaginated leaf. Courtesy of Special Collections, University of Amsterdam, OTM: OF 63-792.

eral of his countrymen had travelled to Pernambuco with the aid of his globe.[55] Globes, like nautical charts and rutters, were intended to facilitate travel and trade that ultimately would lead to profit and, albeit unintentionally, to a broader understanding of the world. The new knowledge navigators gathered in Brazil in turn penetrated other sectors of Amsterdam's maritime economy. In 1608, many exotic curiosities from America were on sale in Amsterdam when a party of collectors from Venice visited the city, and, two years later, a German diplomat too recorded that lots of rarities from the West Indies were available here.[56]

Two-Speed Atlantic

The political implications of presenting Brazil as an integral part of the Habsburg Empire, like the poet Jan van Hout had done, soon generated a more channeled interest for the colony. With its long coastline, its disjointed defensive apparatus, and its highly profitable commodities, Brazil formed an obvious commercial and military target. Based on years of anti-Spanish propaganda and encouraged by Jean de Léry's first-hand observations, the Dutch anticipated that the native population might well be eager to join forces with their Protestant "allies," since both had been suffering under the same "tyranny."[57] In 1599, this assumption could be tested for the first time when a squadron of a massive Dutch fleet that had attacked the Canary Islands drifted south of the equator and raided the Bay of All Saints. At almost the same time, the Amsterdammers Laurens Bicker and Cornelis van Heemskerck commanded an expedition to Río de la Plata, which, on the way back, called in Bahia and Pernambuco. Hendrik Ottsen, one of the expedition's captains, documented the crew's apprehension when navigating along the Brazilian coast. He recorded his encounter with Governor Francisco de Sousa in Salvador, who held the ships for several weeks and interrogated the officers about their objectives before eventually releasing them. Ottsen's account, published by Cornelis Claesz in 1603, included an engraving of the Dutch fleet in the Bay of All Saints.[58]

In the same year, the States General dispatched a fleet of seven vessels under Paulus van Caerden and Jochem Swartenhondt to harass the Brazilian coast. The 1603 privateering expedition formed a watershed moment in Dutch Atlantic policy, as now, for the first time, the political authorities targeted Brazil. Inspired by the instant success of the VOC in overwhelming Portu-

FIGURE 8. Hendrik Vroom, *Return of the Hollandtsche Tuyn*, after 1605, oil on canvas, 144 × 279 cm. Courtesy of Rijksmuseum, Amsterdam, inv. nr. SK-A-1361.

guese trading posts in Asia, the States General supplied Admiral Van Caerden with enough mortar and stones to build a stronghold on the coast—if one contemporary historian is to be believed.[59] When the expedition returned to Amsterdam in 1605, Hendrik Cornelisz Vroom painted a "ship portrait" of the admiral's ship *De Hollandse Tuyn* shortly before entering the city harbor (Figure 8). Vroom, the leading marine painter in the Netherlands, had made a name for himself by recording the return of the second naval expedition to the East Indies in 1599, which epitomized immediate Dutch success in Asia.[60] His design for the return of Van Caerden's fleet was practically identical. Enthusiastic inhabitants of Amsterdam—some well-to-do judging from their clothes, some more rough-edged—celebrated the return of the ships after eighteen months, both on the shore and in small boats approaching the sailors. The vessels answered the people's patriotism by flying the flags of the United Provinces. The painting's message to its select group of viewers was clear: another fleet had braved the oceans and had safely returned, and more exotic riches could soon be expected to fuel the city's status as a maritime and economic entrepot. The West could become the new East.

First-hand stories of the Atlantic world started to infiltrate the city. Jochem Swartenhondt in particular was ideally positioned to impress the Amsterdam authorities. After spending many years in the service of the Amsterdam Admiralty, he bought an inn on the Nes, a street in the city's medieval quarter. He changed its name from Prince van Orangien to Den Swarten Hondt (The Black Dog), and turned it into a first-class establishment, entertaining many notable guests.[61] But no matter how much "spin" was put on events, Swartenhondt's sudden career change also reflects that the expedition to Brazil was not the breakthrough his distinguished clientele had hoped for. A lack of victuals on the inbound voyage had led to a mutiny that Admiral Van Caerden had only barely managed to control, and the States General paid the admiral only a modest sum after his return to *patria*.[62] One sailor who took part in the expedition kept a log, but it is telling that neither Cornelis Claesz nor one of his rivals in the Amsterdam book market considered it a good investment. When it ultimately appeared in print, it was issued only in German. Its observations of encounters with "savage" Brazilians with painted bodies and tattooed hands—the sort of information that might have dampened belief in an anticipated alliance—were lost on many Amsterdam readers.[63]

The urban media landscape was now sufficiently mature to take the Atlantic storyline to the next level. Literary genres, despite their fondness for outdated information and susceptibility for stereotypes, had familiarized readers with Brazil. Maps and navigational literature had demonstrated that the colony was within reach of local ships. Merchants oozed optimism after the instant success of the VOC since its establishment in 1602 and were ready to invest in a Dutch Atlantic empire. But, in order for opinion makers to turn their knowledge of Brazil into popular anticipation of a "Dutch Brazil," merchants needed the support of the government. It was here that the inevitability that characterized the years between 1595 and 1605 suddenly ebbed away and a two-speed Atlantic emerged: a still burgeoning economic one and a stagnating political one. Discussions over the charter of a projected West India Company between the States of Holland and Zeeland were put on hold because of geopolitical developments closer to home. Madrid and The Hague had opened peace negotiations that eventually would lead to the Twelve Years' Truce on the condition that the States General would not establish an Atlantic sister company of the VOC. By 1606, the diplomatic overtures provided an impediment for any sort of new political initiative in the Atlantic world.[64]

Urban interests, not for the last time, were at odds with federal policy. The Amsterdam city council vehemently opposed attempts to conclude a truce, precisely because little progress could now be expected in the Western Hemisphere for another twelve years. Within the city, political developments were a bitter blow to the ambitions of one man in particular, the staunchly

Calvinist merchant Willem Usselincx. Usselincx had traveled to Spain, Portugal, and the Azores where he gradually developed his ideology of large-scale Protestant migration to the New World and the subsequent conversion of Native Americans, following in the footsteps of Jean de Léry and theorists of settlement such as the Englishman Richard Hakluyt.[65] Peace with Spain—if only temporarily—would obstruct these plans, yet, despite the intense lobbying of Usselincx and other hardliners like Petrus Plancius, the Truce faction led by the libertine Holland pensionary Johan van Oldenbarnevelt maintained the upper hand. Usselincx's subsequent barrage of pamphlets, keenly read, one suspects, by Oldenbarnevelt's many opponents across the city, did little to endear him to the political elite. All his proposals were shelved until the resumption of hostilities in 1621; by then, to Usselincx's chagrin, commerce would trump evangelization as the main incentive for Atlantic expansion.

The armistice with Spain, then, required restraint from the Amsterdam authorities. Individual investors carried on their fluid cooperation with New Christian intermediaries and Portuguese sugar planters. Between one-half and two-thirds of the carrying trade between Brazil and Europe in the 1610s was in the hands of the Dutch, generally in the service of Amsterdam's Portuguese community. In the dockyards of the United Provinces, up to fifteen ships a year were built exclusively for the Brazil trade.[66] Shipbuilding was one of the main industries in the Dutch Golden Age, and, although Amsterdam was not its main center, most of the repair work on ocean-going vessels took place on the artificial Rapenburg island on the city's eastern edge, where the wharves of the VOC were located.[67] The sector provided work for thousands of blue-collar workers, many of whom will have experienced at first hand the increasing economic importance of Brazil and the Atlantic world for the urban economy. The sugar industry, too, flourished. Forty to fifty thousand chests of sugar were imported annually during the Truce, with the number of sugar refineries in Amsterdam alone rising to twenty-five before 1622.[68]

Knowledge of the Brazil trade flowed through the city—among traders, shipmasters, insurers, and notaries, for example—but made little public headway.[69] With little new information forthcoming, the literary genres continued to dominate perceptions of Brazil. It was not until the armistice drew to a close that the colony returned as a regular feature on the political agenda. By the late 1610s Amsterdammers began to submit increasingly bold requests to the States General for military support in the Western Hemisphere. In May 1617, the VOC pleaded with the regents to order the Amsterdam Admiralty to prepare a war ship, which could be sent to Brazil or the West Indies to take

Iberian captives. This, according to the directors of the Company, would be the only way to make the Habsburgs agree to a long-awaited exchange of hostages.[70] Four weeks later, the Amsterdam burgher Leonart de Beer who had lived in Brazil for twenty-five years, according to the minutes of the regents' meeting, claimed that indigenous inhabitants had informed him of a natural inlet on the coast "where previously no person from the Republic had been." In the context of the Truce, this was a politically charged way of telling the authorities to stake a legitimate claim on as yet "undiscovered" overseas land.[71] De Beer intended to set sail to this location and vied for recognition of his voyage. The regents, however, decided that before they would allow him to take command of the region, De Beer needed to hand in a substantial dossier with more information on his intended destination.[72] What happened next is unknown, but clearly the idea of establishing a Dutch outpost in Brazil began to regain momentum in Amsterdam.

Among the supplications to the States General in the final Truce years, in hindsight, one stands out. It was submitted by a woman from Middelburg, Catharina Willems, in June 1618. She informed the regents of the predicament of her husband, who had sailed to Brazil but had ended up a long way south of the equator due to contrary winds. When he had gone ashore to find fresh water for his crew, he had been captured by the Portuguese and taken first to Rio de Janeiro and later to Salvador de Bahia. Here the man had since been imprisoned "in miserable circumstances." Initially he had been sentenced to death, but fortunately the Portuguese had mistaken her husband, the ship's captain, for a mere sailor. Now she pleaded with the States General to send a letter to Governor Luis de Sousa in Salvador asking for the release of her husband.[73] Catharina's request was unsuccessful, either because the States were reluctant to interfere or because the Brazilian authorities refused to let the man go in spite of Dutch appeals. But Catharina was eventually reunited with her husband because he managed to escape after thirty months of imprisonment. By early 1620 he had returned safely to Middelburg.[74] Four years later he would go back to Brazil to avenge his "miserable" detention.

The man who suffered in his prison cell in Salvador for two-and-a-half years was Dierick Ruiters. Before he had been taken captive, he had acquired a lot of expertise on Brazil, where in 1617 he had witnessed the arrival of the Inquisition in Sergipe. After his return to Middelburg, he decided to put his knowledge to the service of the common good by writing a book, which appeared in print in 1623 under the title *Toortse der Zee-vaert* (Torch of Sea Travel). Ruiters's *Toortse* was by no means a traditional captivity narrative in the mold of Hans Staden's *Warhaftig Historia*. Instead, it was to the Atlantic what Van Linschoten's *Itinerario* had been to Asia: a practical guide to the networks of trade, the position of European competitors, and the opportunities for the Dutch should they at last decide to enter the field of play. "It will be highly useful to you," Ruiters claimed in his introduction, "to take this with you on your voyage: after all, it is better to tread a path already found, than to find a new one." There was good reason to listen to his advice. Ruiters recounted the number of times that Dutch sailors had been killed on the shores of Brazil immediately after having landed there. Others had been imprisoned for long periods of time, sometimes for as much as six or seven years, and it had only been due to good fortune, the author concluded, that he had been able to escape.[75]

Ruiters's personal motives to compose such a detailed travel companion were predictable: under the cloak of economic potential, he intended *Toortse* to be read as a call for battle. He meticulously described the best routes to

FIGURE 9. Dierick Ruiters, *The Bay of All Saints*, c. 1620, ink on paper, 29 × 42 cm. Courtesy of Nationaal Archief, The Hague, Verzameling Buitenlandse Kaarten Leupe, inv. nr. 4 VEL 717.

Brazil, before explaining the more practical do's and don'ts for Dutch ships arriving on the shores that were still unknown to many. He advised captains, for instance, to fire a few shots before landfall to scare off enemy troops who were patrolling the coastline, unless they wanted to establish friendly relations with the American Indians, who would be frightened off by cannon fire—a finely nuanced approach to the possibility of an indigenous alliance in Brazil. The real strategic value of *Toortse der Zee-vaert* was to be found in the description of the region around Salvador. Ruiters, fully aware that the directors of the new West India Company that had been founded in June 1621 were plotting their first move in the Atlantic, argued for an attack on the Bay of All Saints. Salvador was perched on top of a steep cliff, but, according to Ruiters, this should not deter the Company from attacking the colonial capital. With the urban population amounting to around three thousand, he estimated that only half of the inhabitants were able-bodied men. More important, Salvador "was unprotected, without any gated wall which could be an impediment to enter from outside."[76] The city, in other words, was vulnerable, and the directors—as well as the general reader—should prepare for a sustained attack. While the printed version of *Toortse* circulated in public, preparing the hearts and minds for a transoceanic naval campaign, the most confidential details of Bahia's defenses remained behind closed doors. The accuracy of Ruiters's intelligence was unsurpassed: hand-made drawings of Rio de Janeiro, Pernambuco, and the Bay of All Saints, including the main fortifications and the locations of the major administrative buildings, still survive in the archives of the West India Company (Figure 9).[77]

Anticipation

Finally, two years after the truce had expired, one person embodied the long-standing Dutch inclination to invade Brazil. Amsterdam merchants eagerly joined the aggressive initiatives from Zeeland in planning for war in the Atlantic world. The setup of the West India Company reflected the federal structure of the United Provinces (Figure 10). Its board of nineteen directors, the Heeren XIX (Gentlemen Nineteen), was made up of representatives of five different regional "chambers": eight from Amsterdam, four from Zeeland, and two each from Holland's Northern Quarter (Hoorn and Enkhuizen), the Maas (Rotterdam and Dordrecht), and the city and countryside of Groningen. The nineteenth and final director was a representative of the States General, evidence

38   Chapter 1

FIGURE 10. *The United Provinces*, c. 1648. Map prepared by UvA-Kaartenmakers. Reprinted with permission.

of the "national" importance of the Company that was designed to enter into military conflict abroad. The Company's federal structure meant that every piece of policy was subject to discussion almost by default. The preeminence of Amsterdam was further reflected in its place as the regular seat of the meetings of the nineteen executives. Each chamber had its own capital and its own regional board of directors, usually formed by the main investors.[78]

In Amsterdam, the urban authorities ordered that a building on the Haarlemmerstraat, originally designed to be a Meat Hall, be renovated to serve as the local West India House (Figure 11).[79] Now that commercial appeal and a strong political incentive to attack Brazil converged, albeit belatedly in the eyes of some, the urban population started to prepare for the upcoming maneuvers. Anticipation was high, judging from the diary of Arnoldus Buchelius, a VOC director and West India Company supporter from the first hour. Buchelius described the nervous rumoring about Jesuits from Spain who had come to Holland in disguise, trying to prevent the establishment of the new company. He also recorded the Company's efforts to market its shares in order to raise capital. In July 1621, less than two months after the Company charter had been signed, he noted how placards were printed and attached to the walls of public buildings in the various towns in Holland.[80] In Amsterdam, five eminent merchants led by the former burgomaster Jacob Gerritsz Hoing, would be present at the Admiralty office on the Oudezijds Voorburgwal every Monday and Thursday from nine to eleven in the morning to register the names of would-be participants in the joint-stock company.[81] Suddenly, the prospect of an attack on Brazil attained its own kiosk in Dutch urban centers.

FIGURE 11. "Het West-Indische Huys." From Claes Jansz Visscher, *Map of Amsterdam*, c. 1625 (cartouche, bottom-right corner). Courtesy of Rijksmuseum, Amsterdam, inv. nr. RP-P-1880-A-3846.

Despite the public awareness these placards generated, the Company found it difficult to assemble sufficient funds. The VOC had acquired a reputation for not paying shareholders dividends as promised, a policy that did not do the West India Company any favors. Meanwhile, the towns in the Northern Quarter, Hoorn and Enkhuizen, protested against the inclusion of the salt trade in the Company's monopoly. Prospective shareholders, moreover, were all too aware of the military (and hence financial) risks of attacking Spain in the Atlantic world. As a result, the new company depended more on small investors who were perhaps less informed about overseas trade and geopolitical affairs than on the wealthy merchants who had financed the VOC. The *Groot-Kapitaalboek* of the Amsterdam Chamber, the register of the main shareholders who participated in the newly established West India Company, contained the names (and occupations) of local carpenters, bakers, butchers, brewers, blacksmiths, sailmakers, booksellers, apothecaries, and notaries—many of whom advanced several hundreds or even thousands of guilders.[82] All these burghers of Amsterdam worked for their living in ways that were not directly connected to the business of politics. For the professionals of the West India Company, the responsibility to inform the middle classes about their investment, no matter how small, meant they would need to use popular media far more aggressively than the VOC to advertise their objectives and achievements.[83]

Only in 1623 had the Company finally collected enough capital to launch its "Grand Design," a wave of attacks in Brazil, West Africa, and the Caribbean. It anticipated that, as the marine painter Hendrik Vroom had envisioned more than twenty years before, the West could in fact come to mirror the East. This message was reinforced by Willem Usselincx in yet another Amsterdam pamphlet of which the title, *Voortganck vande West-Indische Compaignie* (Continuation of the West India Company), hinted at the sudden abortion of his own plans in the advent of the Truce. Usselincx listed no fewer than eight reasons why the West India Company deserved to receive more support from investors than the VOC. The West was much closer than the East, meaning lower wages for sailors and the possibility of completing two campaigns per year. Atlantic trade did not require new ships, and existing vessels would not need as many repairs. Most important, much of the trade network was already in place, and the Company could count on the unconditional support of the States General, who nominated one of the nineteen directors. On the pamphlet's title page, an illustration of three Dutch ships before a mountainous (and thus exotic) backdrop was accompanied by a battle-cry in verse:

> The West Indies can be of great profit to the States,
> It reduces the enemy's power, and renders silver plates.[84]

In December 1623, the first Atlantic fleet of the West India Company left from the island of Texel, no longer with the intention to discover the potential of a Dutch Atlantic empire but simply to make it happen. The expedition was commanded by Admiral Jacob Willekens, a cousin of the powerful Amsterdam magistrate Reynier Pauw who controlled the local Company chamber.[85] On the day of departure, the authorities enabled the general public to pledge its loyalty to the patriotic cause one more time by orchestrating a day of public prayer, an important civic ritual in the United Provinces intended "to ask the Lord for his support for the solace of our common fatherland."[86] That Willekens' fleet was destined for the Bay of All Saints, a vital piece of intelligence, was the subject of speculation on the city streets, according to Arnoldus Buchelius. "One notices how confidential our deliberations are," he cynically remarked, "and how some people are undercutting the common interest"—an observation with prophetic qualities on the eve of Dutch Brazil.[87]

And then the waiting began. The months between the fleet's departure in December and the arrival of good news in August are characterized by an intense collective anticipation. Several publishers cashed in on these sentiments, and a brief look at their commercial strategies explains why 1624 became such a crucial year in the history of Dutch Americana. References to the riches awaiting the nation in the Atlantic world popped up everywhere in print. During the early months of the year, the publisher Nicolaes van Geelkercken issued *Wonderlicke avontuer van twee goelieven* (Marvelous Adventure of Two Lovers), a romantic story in prose. This literary genre had been tried and tested for decades, but this time, in the margins of a predictable tale of two lovers, it had a political pretext. Tapping into the collective sense of anticipation, the author decided to send the male protagonist to Brazil, after a succession of adventures on European battlefields. This was a fair reflection of how the West India Company had attracted its personnel for Willekens's fleet. The fictional character, however, "received good financial terms, and could send [his lover] two months of pay," a somewhat rosier picture than could realistically be expected. Upon arrival in the West Indies, he described Brazil "as a true Earthly Paradise, whose nature and features exceed those of all European countries." The title page of the edition displayed the gold and pearls of the Atlantic world he subsequently described in great detail.[88]

Before the summer, while still awaiting confirmation of military success, Van Geelkercken also contributed to a pamphlet titled *Reys-boeck van het rijcke Brasilien, Rio de la Plata ende Magellanes* (Travel Book of the Abundant Brazil, Río de la Plata, and the Strait of Magellan),[89] a work that brought together various pieces of existing textual and cartographic information. After the printed text was finished, the publisher put the book on the shelf, waiting for the opportunity to maximize its commercial potential as soon as good news would arrive. When this happened, Van Geelkercken hastily added images of the invasion and included a rather bland textual account of the campaign that had resulted in the Dutch takeover. A similar strategy of controlled delay was applied to a political proposal that may have been circulating for even longer. In April 1623, a certain Jan Andries Moerbeeck appeared before the States General in The Hague to argue for the vulnerability of Brazil, as "many of the Portuguese nation are from the Jewish Religion, and many others are born and sworn enemies of the Spanish nation"—testifying to the broadly shared assumption nurtured by Jean de Léry that the Dutch were likely to receive support from within the colony.[90] The Amsterdam publisher Cornelis van de Plasse waited until the news of victory had broken before putting the rallying call in print. In retrospect, talk of New Christian support for a Dutch invasion must have appeared ill-informed, but, for a publisher who had anticipated news of the triumph for so long, commercial momentum outweighed the desire for accuracy.

Like his colleagues, the Amsterdam publisher and newspaperman Broer Jansz had shown little previous interest in books on the Atlantic world, but, in 1624, he suddenly published three works on America and Brazil. In January, he issued *Gheluck-wenschinghe aen de West-Indische vlote* (Blessing to the West India Fleet), the most explicit printed expression of support for the West India Company's "Grand Design," reminiscent of the day of public prayer organized by the States General. In July, a month before news from Brazil reached Holland, Jansz cooperated with an Amsterdam colleague to produce *West-Indische Spieghel* (West Indian Mirror), a historical and geographical account of the various American colonies, supposedly written by the well-informed (but fictitious) Peruvian author Athanasius Inga. The booksellers appealed directly to the anticipated audience by dedicating the work to the directors and "supporters of the West India Company." And several months later, Jansz joined up with two other Amsterdam colleagues to produce a new edition of Jose de Acosta's *Natural and Moral History of the West Indies*, the first Dutch edition of this standard work to appear since 1598. Evidently the bookshops On the Waterfront were well stocked with Americana in anticipation of good news from across the ocean. Everybody in Amsterdam, it appears, was waiting merely for the celebrations to begin.

Amsterdam's "discovery" of Brazil was a slow process. From the 1590s onward, literary texts were widely available—they were cheap and attractive, and urban literacy rates were high—but the information they contained was outdated, without any concern for topicality. Genres like costume books, maps, and travel accounts on Brazil, nevertheless, resulted in sufficient name recognition for the colony to feature on the stage, an emerging platform for public debate during the Golden Age. Specialized navigational knowledge of the Atlantic world also rapidly increased, but public exposure was limited. The early news media, in the shape of handwritten corantos, mentioned Brazil only on rare occasions. The missed opportunity of French Protestants in Rio de Janeiro, as reported by the Huguenot Jean de Léry, carried political implications that the Amsterdam publisher Cornelis Claesz presented to urban readers exactly at the time when local merchants began to invest in the Atlantic world. Literary genres receded only when the political urgency increased. Already before the period of real geopolitical engagement, however, the mechanisms of public communication dictated that disappointing news made little headway. The only eyewitness account of the much anticipated Van Caerden expedition was never printed in Dutch, in spite of the obvious appeal of the genre in the Amsterdam book market. During the Twelve Years' Truce, the Brazil trade prospered, and the city's shipbuilding and sugar industries flourished. Yet it was only when the political momentum began to build, and the West India Company was finally founded in 1621, that opinion makers expressed a strong interest in Brazil once more. As the first fleet set sail for the Atlantic world, Amsterdam booksellers upped the ante and began to prepare the urban audience for a major triumph.

CHAPTER 2

Jubilation

In spite of the collective anticipation, few people in Amsterdam could have envisaged that the conquest of Habsburg America would be so easy. On 10 May 1624, soldiers in the service of the West India Company overwhelmed Salvador de Bahia, capital of colonial Brazil. Only forty-eight hours earlier, they had arrived in the Bay of All Saints, daunted perhaps by the town's strategic location but eager to attack after departing from the United Provinces some five months earlier. When Vice-Admiral Piet Heyn launched the campaign by capturing the newly constructed battery at the heart of the bay, the outcome was never in doubt. By the evening of the first day Dutch troops reached the Benedictine convent just outside the recently erected city walls, where many of them spent the night. As soon as it was dark, demoralized colonists, Indians, and African slaves began to stream out of the town, ignoring the pleas of Governor Diogo de Mendonça Furtado and a handful of loyalists to stay. Led by Bishop Marcos Teixeira, the population regrouped in the Reconçavo to prepare for a sustained period of guerrilla warfare. Dutch soldiers entered the town unopposed on the morning of the second day, arrested the governor, and immediately began to make themselves feel at home by stripping the cathedral of its images to prepare it for Calvinist worship.[1]

The conquest of Salvador constituted the political arrival of the Dutch in Brazil, and the attack on Bahia—an operation aimed at the jugular of the Portuguese colony—developed into the most lavishly celebrated military victory in the war against Spain until that point. Predictably, given the anticipation surrounding the campaign they had created themselves, the Amsterdam print media seized the moment. "Bahia" would remain the foundational moment of the widespread public interest in Brazil for an entire generation. A new genre, the printed newspaper, assisted in the rapid establishment of the city's clear supremacy as the center of Atlantic news.[2] Dutch Brazil, as the main ongoing political storyline of the second quarter of the seventeenth century, would become its staple diet. The newspapers' weekly periodicity turned them into the sources for other print media and explains their key role in constituting public opinion.[3] A detailed analysis of the production, circulation, and reception of printed newspapers and rival genres in the urban news market serves to explain why the Amsterdam mediation of events in Brazil generated such euphoria, why embedded journalism would ultimately trump the more independent press in successfully framing the triumph, and why Dutch Brazil would remain such an attractive news topic in subsequent decades.

Newspapers

News of Dutch success in Brazil arrived in Amsterdam with a delay of three months and two weeks on 24 August 1624. Inevitably, as tensions had increased during the summer, rumors of success had started to do the rounds. Some of these speculative stories were persistent enough to be mentioned by one of the two weekly newspapers that appeared in Amsterdam every Saturday. At times when a victory on foreign shores could reasonably be expected, the rival newspapers of Broer Jansz—the partisan publisher who had so publicly supported the West India Company earlier in the year—and his more level-headed colleague Jan van Hilten included weekly bulletins on developments in the Atlantic world. The printed corantos were the main carriers of news in the city since their emergence in 1618. Within a few years, they had pushed the handwritten media out of the market, and, in the summer of 1624, they were avidly purchased every Saturday by readers who anticipated news of victory in Brazil.[4] To keep hold of the public's attention until the moment that hard news arrived, the Amsterdam coranteers created a weekly rhythm of snippets of Atlantic information even when they had little or no copy.[5]

Jan van Hilten was a reliable journalist who generally tried to check his facts before he considered news stories from abroad fit to print. Born in Hamburg, he was one of the city's many second-generation immigrants. His father had been accepted as a member of the Amsterdam booksellers' guild, and, by the time Jan took over the coranto and moved to a new location near the stock exchange, he strongly identified with the local cause. In July 1624, when there was a sense in the city that good news from the Atlantic could arrive at any moment, his *Courante uyt Italien, Duytslandt &c.* (Coranto from Italy, Germany, etc.) jumped the gun by reporting that "word has it that Colonel Van Dorth has captured the Bay of All Saints."[6] Since Van Hilten could not get confirmation of the story, he did not provide any follow-ups to the claim in subsequent issues, and the urban audience had to wait for another month. The newspaper of Broer Jansz, *Tijdingen uyt verscheyde Quartieren* (Tidings from Various Quarters), was emphatically Calvinist and Orangist. Jansz was more openly patriotic than his rival, which led to accusations that he reported only good news. In the late 1630s, satirical commentators from the Southern Netherlands even advised him "to lie some more about Brazil, since it is far enough away from here."[7] But both papers enjoyed a healthy readership in Amsterdam because, as one news addict put it, "one can always find something in one newspaper that is not available in the other."[8] The number of competing local corantos gradually increased to five in the mid-1640s.

The English diplomat Henry Wotton once called Amsterdam "a magazen of rumours," and one of the key functions of the newspapers was to verify and refute the unconfirmed tales that circulated.[9] The schoolmaster David Beck, who lived in The Hague, reported in his diary on Sunday 25 August that after a service in the local church, he had heard "whispers of good news from the West Indies, brought here by some richly laden ships—or so they said."[10] Beck was a close personal friend of Jacob Willekens, the fleet's admiral, and had more than a passing interest in Brazil. He regularly acquired a copy of Van Hilten's *Courante* in The Hague and visited the coranteer's shop whenever he took a barge to Amsterdam. A second entry in his diary, two days later, reveals not only how rumors could come into being but also how difficult it was for the Amsterdam newspapers to compete in this environment. Beck professed to have heard that Stadtholder Maurits had been talking to two Jesuits from Pernambuco in the garden of his residence. The Brazilian fathers had intended to go to Spain to tell King Philip IV how the West India Company had taken control of Salvador and the Bay of All Saints, but then had been captured by a Dutch pirate. After having been brought to The Hague, they had a personal one-and-a-half-hour audience with Maurits to tell him their version of the conquest.[11] Such stories quickly spread in the dense urban network of the maritime provinces, as daily contact between people stimulated and structured the flow of information. That same evening, Beck discussed "the West Indian trade" at home, with his mother-in-law, his wife's uncle, and his illiterate niece.[12]

On the same day, Tuesday 27 August, the rumors were confirmed at the West India House in Amsterdam, and almost immediately the news became public knowledge. It was Jan van Hilten who secured the scoop. He had decided not to wait until his regular Saturday issue but produced a *Courante extraordinarij*—a plano sheet of which both sides were filled with information on the conquest of Salvador (Figure 12). Eight months after the fleet had left from Texel, the news of Dutch success in America was important enough to warrant such a special issue, the first of its kind from the Van Hilten firm.[13] The *Courante extraordinarij* informed readers accurately of the main developments, but the structure of the news bulletin indicates that reliable information had been at a premium. The coranto included what was by all accounts a protracted passage on the individual experiences of the projected governor, Colonel Johan van Dorth, whose ship had been separated from the rest of the fleet on its way to Brazil. Van Hilten explained how Van Dorth had sighted the mainland before the others and had immediately fired shots at the fortifications along the coast. When the colonel realized that the other ships had not yet arrived, he returned to sea and came back to the bay only two days after Dutch troops had secured the city. According to Van Hilten, Van Dorth "wished he could have been there" to witness the triumph. But the *Courante extraordinarij* also criticized the colonel for announcing the arrival of the fleet prematurely, "so that [the Portuguese] were alerted to the impending attack."[14] In the only setback in the early phase of the occupation, Van Dorth became one of the first victims of Portuguese guerrilla tactics. After having been ambushed by a group of colonial and indigenous forces, a Brazilian Indian decapitated the colonel when he was lying pinned down under his horse. His head, retrieved by one of the surviving Dutch soldiers, was ceremoniously buried in the cathedral that for so long had been the main building of the clergy in Brazil.[15]

The regular *Courante* of the following Saturday contained more information that the authorities would have liked to cover up. Van Hilten recounted in great detail how Company soldiers had plundered the city. Captains had supposedly each gathered up to forty thousand guilders worth of gold, while a one-legged soldier had unearthed diamonds and others had stumbled upon a chest with silverware. Inevitably, fueled by abundant wine, infighting had broken out.[16] Alongside such unlikely stories, the newspaper report also contained factual inaccuracies. Van Hilten systematically referred to Salvador as a city situated on an island, an error that can be attributed only to the need to publish the available information in a hurry, as maps of the Bay of All Saints had

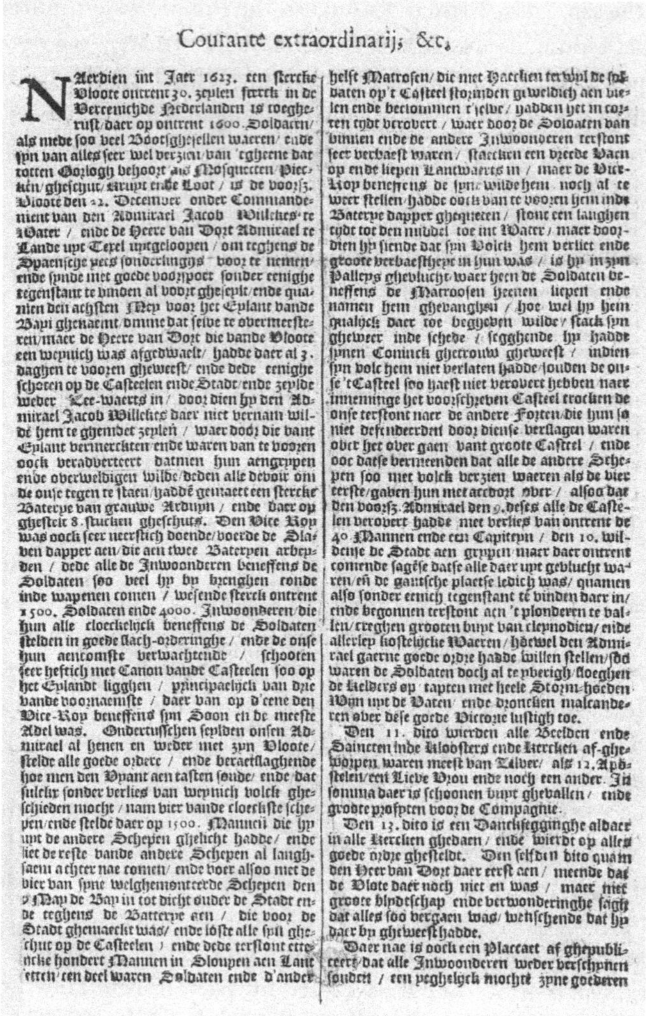

Courante extraordinarij; &c.

Naerdien int Jaer 1623. een stercke Vloote ontrent 30. zeylen sterck in de Vereenichde Nederlanden is toegherust/ daer op ontrent 1600. Soldaten/ als mede soo veel Bootsghesellen waeren/ ende syn van alles seer wel verzien/ van 'tgheene dat totten Oorlogh behoort als Mosquetten/ Piecken/ gheschut/ cruyt ende Loot/ is de voorsz. Vloote den 22. December onder Commandement van den Admirael Jacob Willekes te Water/ ende de Heere van Dort Admirael te Lande uyt Texel uytgeloopen/ om teghens de Spaensche vers sonderlinghs voor te nemen/ ende synde met goede voorspoet sonder eenighe tegenstant te vinden al voort gheseylt/ ende quamen den achsten Mey voor het Eylant vande Bayi ghenaemt/ omme dat selve te overmeesteren/ maer de Heere van Dort die vande Vloote een weynich was afgedwaelt/ hadde daer al 3. daghen te vooren gheweest/ ende dede eenighe schoten op de Casteelen ende Stadt/ ende zeylde weder Zee-waerts in/ door dien hy den Admirael Jacob Willekes daer niet vernam wilde hem te ghemoet zeylen/ waer door die vant Eylant vermerckten ende waren van te vooren ooch verasseert datmen hun aengrypen ende overweldigen wilde/ deden alle devoir om de onse tegen te staen/ hadden gemaect een stercke Baterye van grauwe Arduyn/ ende daer op ghestelt 8. stucken gheschuts. Den Vice Roy was oock seer neerstich doende/ voerde de Slaven dapper aen/ die aen twee Bateryen arbeyden/ dede alle de Inwoonderen beneffens de Soldaten soo veel hy by brenghen conde inde wapenen comen/ wesende sterck ontrent 1500. Soldaten ende 4000. Inwoonderen/ die hun alle cloeckelyck beneffens de Soldaten stelden in goede slach-orderinghe/ ende de onse hun aencomste verwachtende/ schooten seer heftich met Canon vande Casteelen soo op het Eylandt ligghen/ principaelijck van drie vande voornaemste/ daer van op d'eene den Vice-Roy beneffens sijn Soon en de meeste Adel was. Ondertusschen seylden onsen Admirael al henen en weder met zyn Vloote/ stelde alle goede ordere/ ende beraetslaghende hoe men den Vyant aen tasten soude/ ende dat sulckx sonder verlies van weynich volck gheschieden mocht/ nam vier vande cloeckste schepen/ ende stelde daer op 1500. Mannen die hy uyt de andere Schepen ghelicht hadde/ ende liet de reste vande andere Schepen al langhsaem achter nae comen/ ende voer alsoo met de vier van syne welghemonteerde Schepen den 9 May de Bay in tot dicht onder de Stadt ende teghens de Batterye aen/ die voor de Stadt ghemaeckt was/ ende loste alle sijn gheschut op de Casteelen/ ende dede terstont etteliicke hondert Mannen in Sloupen aen Lant setten/ een deel waren Soldaten ende d'ander helft Matrosen/ die met Haecken terwyl de soldaten op 't Casteel stormden geweldich aen vielen ende becommen t'selve/ hadden het in corten tydt verovert/ waer door de Soldaten van binnen ende de andere Inwoonderen terstont seer verbaest waren/ staecken een witte Vaen op ende liepen Lantwaerts in/ maer de Vice-Roy beneffens de syne wilde hem noch al te weer stellen/ hadde ooc van te vooren hem inde Baterye dapper ghequeeten/ stont een langhen tydt tot den middel toe int Water/ maer door dien hy siende dat syn Volck hem verliet ende groote verbaestheyt in hun was/ is hy in zyn Palleys ghevlucht/ waer heen de Soldaten beneffens de Matroosen heenen liepen ende namen hem ghevanghen/ hoe wel hy hem qualijck daer toe begheven wilde/ stack syn ghewe er inde schede/ segghende hy hadde synen Coninck ghetrouw gheweest/ indien syn volc hem niet verlaten hadde/ souden de onse 't Casteel soo haest niet verovert hebben naer inneminge het voorschreven Casteel trocken de onse terstont naer de andere Forten/ die hun so niet defendeerden door dien se verslagen waren over het over gaen vant groote Casteel/ ende ooc datse vermeenden dat alle de andere Schepen soo met volck verzien waeren als de vier eerste/ gaven hun met accoort over/ alsoo dat den voorsz. Admirael den 9. deses alle de Castelen verovert hadde met verlies van ontrent de 40 Mannen ende een Capiteyn/ den 10. wildense de Stadt aen gryppen maer daer ontrent comende sagense datse alle daer uyt gevlucht waren/ en de gantsche plaetse ledich was/ quamen also sonder eenich tegenstant te vinden daer in/ ende begonnen terstont aen 't plonderen te vallen/ creghen grooten buyt van cleynodien/ ende allerley kostelijcke Waeren/ hoewel den Admirael gaerne goede ordre hadde willen stellen/ so waren de Soldaten doch al te yverigh/ sloeghen de kelders op tapten met heele Storm-hoeden Wyn uyt de Vaten ende droncken malcanderen over dese goede Victorie lustigh toe.

Den 11. dito wierden alle Beelden ende Saincten inde Kloosters ende Kercken af-ghewopen waren meest van Silver/ als 12. Apostelen/ een Lieve Vrou ende noch een ander. In somma daer is schoonen buyt ghevallen/ ende groote profyten voor de Compagnie.

Den 13. dito is een Dancksegginghe aldaer in alle Kercken ghedaen/ ende wierdt op alles goede ordre ghestelt. Den selfden dito quam den Heer van Dort daer eerst aen/ meende dat de Vlote daer noch niet en was/ maer met groote blydschap ende verwonderinghe saghe dat alles soo vergaen was/ wenschende dat hy daer by gheweest hadde.

Daer nae is oock een Placcaet af ghepubliceert/ dat alle Inwoonderen weder verschynen souden/ een yeghelijck mochte zyne goederen

FIGURE 12. Jan van Hilten, *Courante Extraordinarij*, Amsterdam, 27 August 1624, recto. Courtesy of Koninklijke Bibliotheek, The Hague.

circulated in Amsterdam for years and the location of Salvador had never been the subject of discussion.[17] Some of the other information Van Hilten included was vague—a deliberate ploy not to jeopardize his credibility by making more needless mistakes. There were no names of towns and fortifications in Brazil, and the newspaper even avoided mentioning the number of ships that had sailed under the flag of the West India Company. Once again this information had been public knowledge since the turn of the year, but being the first to bring the news in print was all that mattered for now.

Relatively little is known about the process of making a printed coranto, but it is clear that, for the Amsterdam newspaper journalists, speed of publication was their most important asset. Jan van Hilten reduced the time of printing by about half by having the text set up in duplicate, so that the same issue could be printed on two presses simultaneously. Although he did not own a press himself—he relied on the labor of a local printer—this probably meant that he could wait for news for a few hours longer than Broer Jansz, who did possess a press but just a single one. The structure of every coranto was identical. The oldest news, arriving from places far away from Amsterdam, was listed first. Atlantic news was always included on the back of the sheet, among the domestic bulletins, since it was gathered by newspaper "reporters" in the harbor district, within easy walking distance of the printing shop. When fresh news arrived, Van Hilten wanted to communicate it to readers as quickly as possible and deleted older news to make room. If necessary, the latest information from Brazil, the West Indies, and Africa was printed in a smaller type to fit the newspaper's idiosyncratic format.[18] The corantos were then sold at the bookshop and at various busy locations across the city by street vendors and itinerant booksellers.[19]

In the first hours and days after news of a major Atlantic event had arrived, when demand for news was high and many local publishers were looking for easy gain, the newspapermen struggled to print stories without losing their precious credibility. Within a few days of a story breaking, however, the Amsterdam corantos usually dominated the news cycle—inside the city, but also elsewhere in Holland and throughout the United Provinces.[20] Hardly anything is known of the newspapers' weekly print run, but if eighteenth-century figures are extrapolated, an estimate of two thousand copies each is not unlikely. The number of weekly readers was certainly much higher, because reading newspapers was a social affair. People shared their copies, and sometimes they also read them out loud.[21] Newspapers were read by the authorities too, since the stories of ordinary sailors on the Amsterdam waterfront were complementary to official bulletins circulating in the corridors of power. And both Van Hilten and Jansz also issued French and English editions. They helped cement the position of Amsterdam as a center for political information, and the efficiency of the publishing industry in the Dutch Golden Age also explains the increasing interest from abroad. Diplomats and political agents in the United Provinces sent the weekly newspapers to their contacts across Europe, giving unprecedented scope and authority to the opinions of the Amsterdam media.[22]

Middle-class readers too devoured the information the newspapers provided. David Beck often received Van Hilten's newspaper from his uncle in Amsterdam and typically sat down with friends "until [they] had read the printed *Courant* in its entirety."[23] The poet and historian Pieter Corneliszoon Hooft, who spent the summers in Muiden Castle ten miles east of Amsterdam, routinely complained that the newspapers reported lies and were always one step behind the news. For readers of Hooft's social pedigree—he was the son of a respected Amsterdam burgomaster—the essence of credibility was trust, which depended on social authority.[24] He perceived anonymous reports in printed corantos issued by publishers with an eye for commerce as distinctly inferior to traditional letters written by people whose status guaranteed their credibility. Yet at the same time there could have been few readers who were as addicted to reading printed newspapers as Hooft. He would get restless if his cousin in Amsterdam was late in sending him the weekly bulletins: "The tidings of the day before yesterday have made me so ardent for what follows, that I sent a messenger with my letter asking for more information when the ferry returned because of bad weather."[25] His critical attitude toward the two Amsterdam corantos did not stop him from reading both, and he read foreign newspapers too, "because no matter if they contain good or bad news, they tell me something about the world." No wonder that he occasionally confessed that the papers had occupied him until late at night.[26]

Public Relations I

The media frenzy of the first few days required a solid response from the authorities. The West India Company was a joint-stock enterprise, and favorable information was crucial to its share price and long-term financial welfare. In an atmosphere of fierce competition for news from Brazil, the Company directors were unable to control the print media. Van Hilten's reports of looting and lack of leadership from Van Dorth, however, emphasized the need to manage the flow of information and mobilize support for the objectives and achievements of the Company. Since suppressing the forums for news was virtually impossible in Amsterdam, the directors opted to manipulate them to their advantage. Two local *bewindhebbers*, Rombout Jacobsz and the influential Albert Coenraedtsz Burgh visited the States General in the first week after news from Brazil had arrived to ask for an official ban on undesirable media coverage that could lead to public concern.[27] The regents too saw the benefit of a positive story. On Friday 30 August, six days after the news had broken, they granted the directors' wish.[28]

By then the governing bodies had launched an ambitious campaign to impose the "official" version of events on the general public. First, they penciled in two feast days for the upcoming Sundays, the first one in the towns and villages of the United Provinces, the second a week later on the frontiers in an effort to demoralize the enemy. In Breda, where Habsburg forces under General Ambrogio Spínola had just started to lay siege to the city, defending troops were ordered to fire their cannons to "let them know that God had honored the Provinces with such a magnificent success."[29] The urban governments and church consistories orchestrated their own celebrations in a further push to win public support.[30] The schoolmaster David Beck recorded that the jubilations had taken place in a wonderful atmosphere, at least until the evening when most of the bonfires had died down and "the masses had gradually become unruly."[31] One seasoned reporter, chronicler Willem Baudartius, claimed that Amsterdam's "Portuguese" inhabitants—thus referring to the small contingent of Sephardic Jews living in the Vlooienburg neighborhood—had actively participated in local celebrations, while, in contrast, "the *Spaniards* in Lisbon and in all of the monarchy" had been sad and sorrowful.[32] In any event, the authorities could be certain that by the evening of Sunday, 1 September—a week after the first rumors had reached the city—everyone in Amsterdam knew about the emphatic Atlantic triumph of the West India Company.

The next step for the political operatives was to dictate the way the victory would be stored in the collective consciousness. Early modern Europeans often distrusted written texts, particularly those issued by authorities keen on public approval, but they placed faith in images of extraordinary events. If it was not so recorded, moreover, an event lost some of its actuality, as well as its power to move later generations.[33] The West India Company decided to distribute news of the Dutch victory in Brazil by means of a so-called news map, a visually attractive broadsheet that could be understood by everyone at first glance thanks to its combination of an illustration of the geographical setting and the unfolding of the battle with an extensive printed caption.[34] As their mouthpiece the directors chose the leading producer of topical prints in Holland, the print publisher Claes Jansz Visscher. Visscher, a native Amsterdammer, was a member of the local consistory and a deacon of the Nieuwe Kerk, the urban center of Calvinist orthodoxy since the Synod of Dordrecht of 1618–19 had witnessed the triumph of hardliners over libertines. As an artist, he had distinguished himself with anti-Arminian imagery including a famous engraving of the execution of Johan van Oldenbarnevelt, which may explain his employment by the West India Company.[35]

In the developing story that was Dutch Brazil, the news map would become the genre that epitomized "embedded journalism." Visscher, in constructing his news map of military success in Salvador, was assisted by the cartographer Hessel Gerritsz, an employee of the Company who had access to business intelligence and occasionally joined the fleet. Together Visscher and Gerritsz would be responsible for making around a dozen news maps of Atlantic victories in the 1620s and 1630s.[36] If possible, their designs were checked by an eyewitness before they were published: admirals and ship's captains navigating the Atlantic were to ensure that "everything could be cut into the plate and put into print truthfully, with a brief account underneath."[37] Subsequently, the news maps, often promoted through an advertisement in one of the two newspapers, were sold in Visscher's bookshop just off Amsterdam's Dam Square and marketed by street vendors. They were also made public on official notice boards at the West India House and the town hall.[38]

Visscher and Gerritsz published their first news map less than a week after the news of victory in Salvador had been confirmed (Figure 13). Visscher could have already drawn the outlines of the Bay of All Saints based on Dierick Ruiters's sketch of the area, meaning that the effect of the sudden rush in the production process on the artistic quality of the news map was negligible. On the extreme left and right of the illustration, Visscher depicted the two main defensive bulwarks of the Portuguese, one on the mainland and the other on the island Itaparica. In the heart of the image, the engraver added to Ruiters's drawing the Forte do Mar, newly constructed in order to defend the warehouses of the lower city. Perched on top of the cliff were the most important buildings of Salvador, their functions explained by the illustration's legend in the bottom-right corner. The remaining space in the composition was reserved for the impressive Dutch fleet and for an inserted map of Salvador and the Reconçavo in the bottom-left corner of the image. Typically for the news map genre, the illustration portrayed both the sinking of the Dutch ship *Groningen*, to the left of the middle, and the soldiers' disembarkation and their subsequent march toward the city gates on the right—developments that represented different stages of the two-day siege. The caption, a prose text in Dutch, related the story

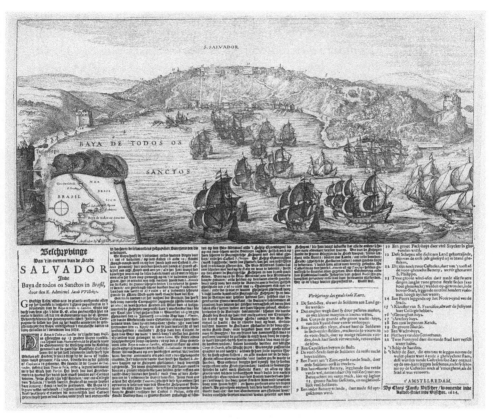

FIGURE 13. Claes Jansz Visscher, *Beschryvinge van 't in-nemen van de Stadt Salvador*, Amsterdam, 1624, ink on paper, 33.6 × 39.5 cm. Courtesy of Rijksmuseum, Amsterdam, inv. nr. RP-P-OB-79.371.

of the expedition, while the legend, corresponding to the numbers 1 to 22, reiterated the most important features of the invasion.[39]

Visscher, as would any professional spin doctor, dramatized the Company's attack. The news map distorted the geographical proportions of the bay to the extent that the fleet appeared to be under crossfire from the two main fortifications, whereas, in reality, the structures were too far apart to hurt incoming vessels simultaneously.[40] To make the victory look as unblemished as possible, Visscher made no mention of Colonel Van Dorth's erratic conduct or of looting Company forces inside the city walls. The media strategy worked. In a phase of sudden political and military success, the cooperation between the

West India Company and a highly skillful print publisher like Visscher ensured the visual dominance of a carefully constructed representation of Dutch success.[41] The Company directors must have been extremely pleased with the design, for, when another opportunity presented itself to bend the public imagination in their favor, two months later, they once again turned to Visscher. The joy that had been triggered by the initial news had now faded, and the time had come to put the achievement of defeating the Portuguese into the broader context of the war against the Habsburgs. Visscher's brief was clear when, in October, the perfect opportunity for another bout of roaring rhetoric presented itself.

On the second day of the siege and in the days that followed, Dutch troops had managed to capture almost the entire administrative and religious elite of Salvador. Fourteen of the highest-ranking men were taken as hostages to the United Provinces, including Governor Diogo de Mendonça Furtado and Domingo Coelho, the provincial of the Society of Jesus in Bahia and *qualitate qua* the leading Jesuit in Portuguese America. Their capture provided a propaganda boost for the Company directors, who ordered Visscher to depict the group of fourteen in October 1624, one day after they arrived in Amsterdam (Figure 14).[42] After this exclusive "photo opportunity," which saw the artist portray the men against the backdrop of Salvador to remind his audience of their Brazilian origins, the Company imprisoned the Portuguese officials in two separate locations in Amsterdam. The governor and his son were held in the West India House at the Haarlemmerstraat, where the local directors convened. The Jesuits were sent to the Rasphuis, a former Catholic convent in the Kalverstraat where the city's petty thieves and other lowlife were put to the service of the common good, ironically enough, by grating imported brazilwood to extract dyes for the textile industry.[43]

The Company directors (and, one assumes, a shrewd print publisher like Visscher) knew full well that the presence of the Jesuit fathers in the heart of the officially anti-Catholic province of Holland would create a buzz. Only three years before, when another Jesuit had been imprisoned in Amsterdam, sympathizing burghers had liberated the man and smuggled him out of the city, to the embarrassment of the local authorities.[44] The arrest of the leading Jesuits from Brazil was, therefore, certain to make a great impact on public opinion in the United Provinces. Visscher made the most of the commercial opportunity. He added an explanation to the illustration to identify the prisoners and rounded off with a fictional dialogue, titled *Steyger-praetjen* (Chat

FIGURE 14. Claes Jansz Visscher, *Steyger-Praetjen*, Amsterdam 1624, ink on paper, 36.6 × 22.8 cm. Courtesy of Het Scheepvaartmuseum, Amsterdam, inv. nr. A.0145 (250) 2.

on the Wharf). This theatrical dialogue between a sailor who had taken part in the expedition to Brazil and a patriotic "Batavian" who had remained at home eager for good news pushed all the right anti-Spanish and anti-Catholic buttons for an audience that was intimately familiar with the rhetoric of war.

The anonymous author of *Steyger-praetjen* opened with the capture and imprisonment of the fourteen colonial officials, establishing the connection with Visscher's illustration. The sailor and the "Batavian" gleefully recounted that the Jesuits were now locked in a building that, until Amsterdam's "Alteration" of 1578, had belonged to the nuns of the Order of St. Clare. They joked about the Jesuits' supposed desire for material goods and how these "Papists" would deny access to Heaven to believers who did not give financial support to the Society. Then the men turned to discussing the main reason for the Spanish presence in the Americas: greed. The dialogue proceeded in predictable fashion by placing Habsburg rule in Brazil in the context of Spanish tyranny abroad. Both men pledged their support to the States General and the House of Orange before promising to serve the cause of the United Provinces by

> taking from [the Spaniard] that which has supported
> his dominance for so long, that is his great tyranny,
> and the annihilation of thousands through murder, hanging, burning,
> just what our parents used to suffer in [the Netherlands].⁴⁵

The analogy between the fate of the American Indians and the ordeals of the Dutch population in the early years of the Revolt helped assign legitimacy to the conquest. After decades of rhetorical preparation, the first triumph in the Atlantic world merely confirmed what the Dutch had been saying all along. The operation to rescue the indigenous population and threaten the very source of Madrid's avarice had finally begun. As the "Batavian" recited Bartolomé de Las Casas's list of Spanish cruelties—cutting off hands, noses, and ears, hanging the innocent, quartering children—the sailor concluded that the conquistadors must have profoundly enjoyed these brutalities, for he could not explain them otherwise. He reveled at the thought of divinely inspired revenge, while, at the same time, victories in America would relieve the position of the "naked, innocent Indians," who had done nothing wrong apart from handing their riches to the invaders.⁴⁶ To make the rhetoric of *Steyger-praetjen* more recognizable and more powerful still for a Dutch audience, the sailor and the "Batavian" systematically labeled the enemy as Spanish, conveniently ignoring that, in reality, Salvador had been administered by the Portuguese.

"Social" Media: Poetry and the Pulpit

Corporate propaganda served as a catalyst for an undertow of spontaneous, nationwide joy. In the United Provinces, the medium of choice to express individual views in the immediate aftermath of a significant news event was occasional poetry. These poems, often overtly patriotic, were rooted in the tradition of the *geuzenliederen* (beggars' songs), which had been written and composed since the early phase of the Revolt. Already in the 1570s and 1580s, publishers had assembled these political songs, of which the "Wilhelmus" devoted to William of Orange—still the Dutch national anthem today—is the most illustrious. By the 1620s, the material had been augmented and reissued so often that the inhabitants of the United Provinces practically shared a national songbook. Rhetoricians, poets, and especially Reformed ministers now extended the familiar language of military victory to the Atlantic world where the enemy, and therefore the tune, was the same.[47]

In the wake of victory, amateur poets too relied on the trusted combination of anti-Catholic and anti-Spanish rhetoric. Some of their verses were printed, while others circulated in manuscript—yet all were intended to contribute to an increasingly broad and interactive debate. The influential poems written by Reformed ministers may be considered a reflection of opinions distributed from the pulpit—a respected urban venue of communication to summarize and give meaning to news bulletins. Official days of public prayer were purposely designed to structure the flow of information and generate a biblical interpretation of events, but ministers also used important political turning points such as "Bahia" as *exempla* in regular sermons to promote the practice of godliness among the faithful.[48] Their sermons were rarely printed, but their song collections were generally cheaply produced, without unnecessary musical notations that affected the price. On the songbooks' title pages, poets and publishers asserted that their works were aimed specifically at "the common people," and ministers, therefore, used biblical language, rhetorical strategies, and melodies that were easily accessible.[49]

The authorities' public relations strategy had carefully placed the triumph in Brazil in the right context, and many of the descriptive details in individual poems referenced the phrasing in the official news map. A good example of the interweaving of Scripture and militant rhetoric is provided by Johannes Haselbeeck in his 314 verses on the victory in Bahia. Haselbeeck, who would later serve as a minister in Brazil for three years, opted to thematize fear in the Spanish ranks, inspired by Exodus 23:27.[50] By using the straightforward symbolism of a foul-eyed cat who, in apparent safety up in a tree, watched a "hostile" dog below, he alluded to the strategic location of Salvador, towering above the Bay of All Saints. The colonial population, giants as it were in this uneven setting, had looked at the Beggars—the Dutch if necessary continued to identify with their grandfathers—as if they were dwarves. When suddenly the giants felt less secure, they saw no option other than to abandon the city.[51] Haselbeeck then followed the news map's embedded report almost word for word by mentioning how the city's inhabitants had left their houses in a hurry, the tables still made for breakfast. He also referred to the imprisonment of the colonial dignitaries in Amsterdam, the subject of the second Visscher news map, but mentioned only the Jesuits explicitly. Now that they had been shipped to Holland, the minister remarked tongue in cheek, it could finally be established whether they liked Dutch cuisine.[52] Haselbeeck's poems circulated in manuscript and were ultimately printed in 1629.

Relations between the church and the secular authorities were often tense in Amsterdam, but essentially they were mutually supportive institutions, especially at times of prosperity. Urban ministers, usually well educated, were in the perfect position to mediate political information and mobilize public support.[53] The most eloquent among them attracted large crowds to their sermons every Sunday, and even pamphleteers acknowledged that, in controversial issues, "one minister could do more harm from the pulpit than one-hundred printed pamphlets." The Amsterdam city council attempted to soothe local clerics by extending social liberties and occasionally tax privileges, but, as with the print media, they could not exert full control. In the 1620s, when the popular Amsterdam minister Adriaan Smout scolded the Dutch East India Company (the VOC) for not taking care of their employees' next of kin, the local directors were ultimately forced to apologize for their spiritual indifference. In the first two decades of its existence, however, the West India Company could generally rely on the support of the Reformed Church. Some ministers and elders had purchased shares, and many others supported the Company's aggressive Atlantic policy in the belief it would hurt Catholic interests.[54]

Jacob Revius, a reputable lyricist from Deventer, was one of these ministers for whom the secular and the spiritual worlds overlapped. He had spent part of his youth in exile in Amsterdam, where he attended the Latin School and mingled with some of the founding participants of the VOC. Perhaps more familiar than Haselbeeck with boardroom rhetoric, he directed his militant verses straight at the defeated Spanish monarch. In the first of two poems, simply titled *Opt veroveren van Todos os Santos* (On the Conquest of All Saints), he used what would become a trusted metaphor in an Atlantic context, jeering at Philip IV for losing to the Dutch not only his mistress, meaning the Portuguese possessions in the East Indies, but now also his legitimate wife, America:

> She complains that you [Philip] have made her dig the earth,
> and have loaded her shoulders with mud and rubble,
> she complains that you have made her look for the deepest
> in herself, only to satisfy your money-greed.[55]

He proceeded by accusing the monarch of torturing the Americans and predictably noted that they were not the only ones to have been tortured by him.

In recognition of Revius's status as an emerging voice in public opinion, his poems were published in Willem Baudartius's Amsterdam news chronicle before they appeared as part of a stand-alone publication several years later.[56] Revius also did not stray too far from the reliable anti-Spanish rhetoric of earlier generations, showing the persistence of preconquest stereotypes. In a second poem, he stressed the significance of the victory in unraveling Spain's seemingly unlimited economic and military power. Using the trope of Spanish dishonesty, Revius accused Madrid and its allies in the Low Countries of pretending not to care about the loss in Brazil, a jibe at Portuguese discomfort with the Habsburgs' neglect of its colonial empire. But behind this façade the Spaniards realized quite well what God and Stadtholder Maurits had taken away from them. In a pun on the name Salvador, the minister reminded the enemy that it now lacked its best guardian. Moreover, by snatching away the bay, the king was now also without the support of "all his Saints." And, since the "Holy Spirit" and "Hope," two names of defeated Habsburg vessels, had sunk in an effort to defend the city, Revius concluded, Philip IV must have lost his belief all together.[57] Such puns must have gone down well with patriotic readers, but Revius's verses had a more serious dimension. The conquest of 1624 was seen by some as the first step in bringing down Habsburg America as a whole, another echo of the months of anticipation that had preceded the weeks of unbridled joy.

Occasional poetry was also the medium par excellence to give rise to a personality cult. Apart from the obligatory adulations of the stadtholder, three men acquired celebrity status in Bahia: Jacob Willekens, Piet Heyn—whose heroics would outlive Dutch Brazil by more than two centuries[58]—and the unfortunate governor-to-be Johan van Dorth. Three poems devoted to Van Dorth were composed by Petrus Gakelius, vice-principal (*conrector*) of the Latin School in Zutphen, who had acquired a reputation for writing funerary verses. Once again, Baudartius, in Amsterdam, was the first to put the poems into print. In 1626, they were also collected to form an entire book of Gakelius's devout epitaphs, *Lacrymae Ecclesiae*. The Zutphen schoolteacher devoted two poems in Latin to the unfortunate colonel and one in Dutch.[59] One of the two Latin poems opened by praising Van Dorth for defeating the Portuguese (rather than the Spanish), a brief peek at geopolitical reality amid the stereotypical rhetoric of the year's vernacular poetry.[60] But it was the opening line of the Dutch poem that best captured the patriotic spirit of the three epitaphs. "Jan van Dort has remained dead in the service of the Fatherland," it read. Further on, Gakelius called the colonel a "brave hero" and, for the second time, "a servant of the Fatherland." The poem, as was customary in the funerary genre, concluded with a moralistic line warning readers that their number could soon be up.[61]

The glorification of supposedly exemplary servants of the federation like Willekens and Van Dorth indicates the sense of belonging that the government had intended to nurture by distributing the news through "official" channels in Amsterdam and proclaiming moments of nationwide celebration. The unisono voices of amateur poets testify to the success of the West India Company's public relations campaign among the middle classes. Dutch pamphleteers, who usually thrived on discord and who had torn apart the discussion culture in the 1610s during the religious conflict between Remonstrants and Counter-Remonstrants, suddenly displayed perfect harmony. Willem Teellinck, for example, an aggressive advocate of strict Calvinism and early proponent of the Further Reformation, issued a text based on Psalm 116:12–14 that—so the title page claimed—had been the first sermon to be preached in Salvador after the conquest.[62] Teellinck's emphasis on Dutch gratitude for the successful military campaign, based on Scripture, was intended to harmonize the homefront in the mid-1620s. In Amsterdam, hardline Calvinists like Visscher and Baudartius were more vocal than the more numerous local libertines in celebrating the defeat of the Spanish arch-enemy. But they were also better positioned to make their voices heard after the Synod of Dordrecht had established orthodoxy and effectively relegated the libertines to the fringes of society.[63]

The Historical Record

Arguably the most talented opinion maker in Amsterdam in these years, Nicolaes van Wassenaer, had sympathized with the Remonstrant cause. Twice annually, he wrote a chronicle titled *Historisch Verhael*, which summarized political, religious, and military developments both at home and abroad for Dutch readers who wanted to be informed about world affairs. The quarto volumes, densely printed and full of juicy details, formed an authoritative historical record of events in the years between 1621 and 1635 (Figure 15).[64] Unlike Baudartius, Van Wassenaer did not give pride of place to institutional documents, and, also in marked contrast to Baudartius, he assembled and reprinted vari-

FIGURE 15. Nicolaes van Wassenaer, *Historisch Verhael*, vol. 7, Amsterdam 1625, title page. Courtesy of Special Collections, University of Amsterdam, OTM: O 63-965.

ous dissident opinions. The popularity and influence of his chronicle were such that the States General kept a close eye on the information it contained, and Van Wassenaer occasionally walked a tightrope.[65] In everyday life, he worked as a physician in the service of the Amsterdam Admiralty, the largest of the five federal colleges of the Dutch navy, and he claimed to have intimate knowledge of what had happened in Salvador from conversations with injured veterans. By the time volume eight appeared in the fall of 1625, the physician had managed to obtain reports about the interrogations of the Jesuit provincial Domingo Coelho during his Amsterdam imprisonment. These alleged transcripts are among the most intriguing representations of the conquest of Bahia and its aftermath, drawing as they do on the widespread tendency to deride the enemy that was already present in some of the occasional poetry.[66]

Van Wassenaer implied that he had spoken to Coelho himself, so readers would have no doubts about the credibility of the information he presented. The provincial, according to the author, was a man of humble disposition. He was soft spoken, blessed with good judgment, and well versed in Latin. Some Jesuits even regarded him as "divine" and honored him as an extraordinary man.[67] The chronicler did his best to give a meticulous and agreeable representation of Coelho's character in the knowledge that this would place even more emphasis on the sinister details that were to follow. Jesuits, Dutch pamphleteers had after all insisted for decades, were notoriously unreliable.[68] True to form Coelho, according to Van Wassenaer, adopted a haughty tone when he was being interrogated. He claimed that some considered him to be of higher rank than the governor or even the king himself. How, then, could it be possible that such a holy man was now being held in such terrible surroundings? The response he received was taken straight from the Dutch rhetorical handbook: here in Amsterdam, free burghers were not subjected to the dictates of the Spanish monarch, and the provincial would be treated in the same way as Dutch prisoners were being treated in Spain.[69]

Several episodes in the alleged transcripts were subject to similar rhetoric. Coelho, for example, spoke highly of the governor of Brazil during the interrogations. He was prepared, if necessary, to defend him against Spanish accusations of having failed to take his responsibilities. Mendonça de Furtado, unlike what some of his detractors in Bahia had stated, had dutifully assembled money to build a ring of defensive walls and a new fortification at sea level in time for the Dutch attack. He had managed to maintain order among the armed forces in the city, just as the Crown had desired.[70] Through his Jesuit puppet, Van Wassenaer must have enjoyed laying the blame for the loss of

Salvador indirectly at the court in Madrid. The Dutch accounts of 1624, after all, had emphasized how easily Piet Heyn had conquered the newly financed "royal" fortress. Elsewhere in his description of the interrogations, Van Wassenaer displayed an even stronger bias. Following Visscher and Baudartius, he attempted to capitalize on the awkward relationship between the Spanish monarch and his Portuguese subjects:

> [Coelho] confessed that the Portuguese suffered from the King of Spain, who was a nuisance to everyone, and who possessed so many empires that he could not possibly rule them all. That there were also many of his officials, who acted so rudely that they had brought despair to the subjects, which had resulted in wars. That [the Portuguese] had lost the better part of the East Indies by the hatred unleashed, and that one now intended to attack the West Indies, citing the example of Bahia.[71]

Did the provincial really use such strong terms to criticize the Habsburg monarchy? The Jesuits in Bahia, although not always trusted allies of the king, had generally supported metropolitan policies.[72] Was Coelho forced to concur with the line of rhetoric his Dutch interrogators presented him with, or did Van Wassenaer willfully construct these comments to reinforce the existing anti-Spanish sentiments of his readership? The readers of *Historisch Verhael* presumably did not care. This was entertainment, not journalism, which should be read in the same way as Visscher's *Steyger-Praetjen*, where no one would ever consider the "Batavian" to be a flesh-and-blood character. Van Wassenaer continued to describe the provincial's sorrows in predictable fashion by making him cry out for his beloved King Sebastian, the Portuguese monarch whose ill-timed death in 1578 had brought about the Union of the Crowns, and bemoan the fatal battle of Alcácer El-Quibir in Morocco, where the king had perished. Since Sebastian's death, Portugal had found itself loathed by its former friends. Had the country not been under Spanish rule, it would still have enjoyed the adoration of the whole world and would have been able to continue its mercantile activities without peril.[73]

When the interrogators first mentioned the Society of Jesus, the readers of *Historisch Verhael* must have been on the edge of their seats. After the expiration of the Truce, anti-Jesuit sentiments in the United Provinces had soared. The canonizations of Ignatius of Loyola and Francis Xavier had been celebrated just south of the border, in Antwerp, in ostentatious fashion. The subsequent uncovering of a Jesuit conspiracy to burn down large parts of Amsterdam, as one Reformed minister insisted, had caused panic among the people.[74] Coelho allegedly acknowledged that the Society of Jesus was disliked more than any other order and that he was familiar with the rationale behind this aversion. The Society, the interrogators suggested to him, stirred up the Old World royalty and nobility and, by doing so, had caused many wars. The Jesuits did not hesitate to kill monarchs if necessary, either in public or by secretly placing explosives that, so Van Wassenaer claimed, "we have seen all too often during our time."[75] Of course Coelho denied the accusations and insisted that no Jesuit was allowed to interfere in government. He explained that sometimes they were called upon to advise rulers but that they would never recommend waging war, as this was prohibited by the Society's constitutions.[76] In Salvador, Coelho continued, the governor once had consulted the entire administrative elite before an attack on a group of rebellious Indians. The provincial's stance at this time had been a very principled one. The superior-general of the Society in Rome would not permit him to get involved in such matters, and he had, therefore, left the meeting.[77]

Whereas, for Coelho, this episode might have illustrated the noninterventionist attitude of the Society under his supervision, Van Wassenaer's readers surely reached a different verdict. Having been brought up with stories of Spanish tyranny, they must have interpreted Coelho's departure from the meeting as a refusal to protect the lives of the innocent Brazilians the Society was supposed to convert to Christianity. That the Jesuits in Bahia had been actively advocating a more humane attitude toward Indians was of no consequence at all.[78] Van Wassenaer conveniently overlooked reality in favor of recognizable rhetoric. Arguably more important still for the Dutch image of the Society was the conclusion to Coelho's enforced introspection. The provincial admitted that it was allowed for Jesuit fathers to advise monarchs in maintaining their religion and to propagate the faith among their subjects. How this was done was left unexplained, Van Wassenaer added in one of his rare explicit comments. If it were up to him, the chronicler stated, he would certainly have an opinion on these matters, as such controversies pleased him a great deal. But, instead, he would allow every reader "to judge for himself."[79] Regardless of Coelho's (manipulated) efforts to explain and justify the influence of the Jesuits, the conclusion to the paragraph did more for the prolongation of the existing stereotype than for the rebuttal of Jesuit intrusion in political affairs. Not everyone appreciated Van Wassenaer's contribution to public debate. The following year, despite the mediation of the Amsterdam pensionary Adriaen Pauw, the States General wrote to the city council that the chronicler was no longer allowed to put anything in print without prior approval.[80]

Information Warfare

The West India Company's ambitions of information management did not stop at the city gates. Almost all international representations of the invasion issued in 1624 and 1625, both texts and images, were copied or derived from the Visscher news map, and the Company was instrumental in widening the circle of readers to whom it presented the "official" version of the conquest in an attempt to give credence to the notion of a "Dutch" Brazil. At home, Visscher and Gerritsz issued another edition with a caption in Latin verses, while abroad the seismic shock of the conquest led to a dozen copies of the news map. In France, Melchior Tavernier, the king's print publisher and a producer of news maps in his own right, printed the illustration and translated text. In the Holy Roman Empire, during the Thirty Years' War, news maps of military triumphs were very common, and here the impact of the first major Protestant victory in the Americas was most significant. At least eleven different copies of Visscher's news map appeared, many of them with a 1624 imprint, with various German translations.[81] The copies produced in centers of the German book trade such as Frankfurt am Main and Strasbourg lost little in quality compared to Visscher's original.[82] Most others, however, clearly carry the marks of being produced in a hurry by booksellers firmly fixed on commercial profit. Victory in Brazil, after all, could not have been achieved without the help of many German soldiers in the service of the West India Company, and the news map was certain to appeal to this second homefront across the border.

Visscher's design also made inroads in Europe's broader iconography of Brazil, altered and modified only to meet the stylistic conventions of the different genres it infiltrated.[83] Within Amsterdam, a stone mason was ordered to make a gable stone, based on Visscher's design, perhaps for Jacob Willekens's house in the vicinity of the Zuiderkerk (Figure 16). Beyond the walls of the city, the marine painter Andries van Eertvelt, trained in Holland by Hendrick Vroom but active in Antwerp, used the news map as inspiration for a painting of the invasion (Figure 17).[84] His panel is a remarkably truthful copy of Visscher's composition, testifying to the high artistic quality of the Amsterdam engraving. To

FIGURE 16. Amsterdam gable stone, *Baya d[e] Todos os Sanctos*, date unknown, 38 × 82 cm. Current location: Rozenstraat 144, Amsterdam. Photograph by Frank Lucas, Vereniging Vrienden van Amsterdamse Gevelstenen. Reprinted with permission.

FIGURE 17. Andries van Eertvelt, *The Conquest of Salvador, May 1624*, c. 1624, oil on panel, 67.3 × 106.7 cm. Courtesy of National Maritime Museum, Greenwich, London, inv. nr. BHC0268.

convince viewers of the exotic settings of the bay, Van Eertvelt added four red parrots to the composition, one of only a few small adjustments he made. The bright red or orange flags tied to the masts of the largest Dutch ships point either to the custom of raising the red "blood flag" to announce the start of a naval battle, or to the painter's sympathy—or that of his benefactor—for the House of Orange. In 1632, Stadtholder Frederik Hendrik's personal art collection included a similar painting possibly made by François van Knibbergen.[85]

The image reached another segment of the German book market when it was incorporated into an emblem book with hundreds of European, mainly German, cityscapes. The final volume of *Thesaurus Philo-Politicus*, published in 1625 by Daniel Meisner and the engraver Eberhard Kieser in Frankfurt, included Salvador as the only overseas panorama, a testimony to the impression the Dutch conquest of the previous year had made in the Holy Roman Empire (Figure 18). The city was depicted under the adage *Haec maxima dona vigescunt* and thus made to stand for the greatest gifts one could receive from God. In the *subscriptio* to the emblem in Latin and German verses, these gifts were extended to good health, intelligence, and good fortune. Although the

FIGURE 18. Eberhard Kieser, "Haec maxima dona vigescunt." In Daniel Meisner, *Thesauri philo-politici pars sexta*. Frankfurt, 1625, [B3ᵛ]. Courtesy of Koninklijke Bibliotheek, The Hague, KW 959 E 35 (3).

hand coming from the clouds signaled the emblematic character of the *pictura*, the representations of city and bay were copied after Visscher's news map. The engraver modified the image slightly to underline Salvador's new status as a city under Dutch control. The six ships sailing peacefully in the Bay of All Saints, as well as the *Forte do Mar* and other fortifications, sported the banners of the United Provinces, while the bell tower of the erstwhile Catholic cathedral now seemed to have distinctly northern European features.[86]

By the time Meisner's emblems appeared, however, the geopolitical situation had already been reversed. The "Voyage of the Vassals," a majestic Iberian armada under Don Fadrique de Toledo, reached the Bay of All Saints in April 1625.[87] Although Willekens had returned to Amsterdam and Heyn had left for Angola, the besieged would have been able to withstand an attack had it not been for the mutiny and disorder among the soldiers, which reflected a lack of leadership. After four weeks, well before a Dutch relief fleet reached Brazil, demoralized officers surrendered the city.[88] Throughout the summer, rumors from Antwerp so consistently suggested that the Habsburgs had recaptured Bahia that the English ambassador in The Hague, Sir Dudley Carleton, attested in August that "howsoever wee have here no certayne newes, and are willing to flatter ourselves with a beliefe to the contrary, none of our marchants of Amsterdam will venture any wagers; which is here an argument of much despayre."[89] The practice of betting on the outcome of battles against Spain was widespread in Holland and, for some, added personal interest to the culture of anticipation that surrounded news from the Atlantic world.[90] One week later, the Heeren XIX too admitted that they heard many stories that Bahia had indeed fallen. Because nothing definitive had been reported for four and a half months, Van Hilten added in his coranto, "many still doubt its veracity."[91] In early September, Carleton wrote that "they here lay even wagers the Spanish printed relation of the losse of the place is false: which I can not but wish, for very much depends upon that place."[92] Two weeks later, however, the loss of Bahia was finally confirmed.

Arguably the best indication of the power of Claes Jansz Visscher's corporate representation of victory, paradoxically, came with the loss of Salvador. The court-inspired exaltations in Madrid of the recapture of Bahia are well known: Maíno's painting for the Hall of Realms at the Buen Retiro and Lope de Vega's play *El Brasil restituido* are the most prominent.[93] Yet the reaction in the Habsburg Netherlands, just south of the border, to the international media strategy of the West India Company is equally intriguing. In a political culture where news maps played little or no role in public affairs, a "counter" news map appeared in 1625 (Figure 19). It was clearly made in a hurry, as it combined a

Jubilation 69

survey of the formal terms of surrender as agreed between Don Fadrique and Company officer Willem Stoop in Bahia with an old woodcut depicting the Dutch siege of Sluis of 1604![94] The publisher had done little to transform the image other than to scratch out the names of Flemish towns and add a few

FIGURE 19. *La rivee de l'arme navalle de Spaigne devant la Baye au Bresil*, ink on paper, 40.1 × 30.7 cm [1625]. Courtesy of University Library, Leiden, Coll. BN 054-16-001.

opaque references to Brazil. The textual section, however, was more astute because it was printed in two languages, French and Dutch—an innovation that soon would be picked up in Amsterdam. Although primarily aimed at a Southern Netherlandish readership, news bulletins like these crossed the permeable border between South and North.[95] Intentionally or not, they must have partly compensated for the silence in the Dutch media.

Printed farther away from Amsterdam but hurtful on a different level was a second spiteful news map, made by Wilhelm Peter Zimmerman, an Augsburg print publisher (Figure 20). Zimmerman had copied Visscher's design of the Dutch conquest in 1624, as one of many printers in the Holy Roman Empire, and it is clear at first glance that his news map of 1625 was derived from the Dutch news map of the previous year as well.[96] The perspective is identical, only the vessels—in this case, Spanish galleys—indicate that this broadsheet was meant to celebrate the recapture rather than the capture of

FIGURE 20. Wilhelm Peter Zimmerman, *S. Salvador die Sadt von Spanier eingnumen*, ink on paper, 33 × 41.5 cm. Augsburg [1625]. Courtesy of Collection Atlas van Stolk, Rotterdam, inv. nr. 1610.

Salvador. Zimmerman left his readers in no doubt that this news map was as topical as his first copy of Visscher's design. The explanatory note at the bottom tried to persuade customers that for a good understanding of the present situation in Brazil they needed to buy the second news map now that the colony had changed hands once again. Artistically as well as politically, both the bilingual news map from the Southern Netherlands and Zimmerman's image of the Habsburg restoration constituted a rather bitter conclusion to the efforts of the West India Company to control the flow of information. Both in terms of geopolitics and of news management, what should have been a breakthrough in America in the end provided only embarrassment.

The successful invasion of Salvador was a major news event in Amsterdam. The media attention that followed the arrival of good news in the final week of August 1624 was typical for the news cycle of Atlantic events. An extended period of anticipation culminated in a climactic form of reporting. What started as a rumor was first verified by the Amsterdam corantos, which quickly developed into the gatekeepers of public opinion. The sounding of bells, orchestrated bonfires, and expressions of gratitude in the local churches represented the first attempts of the authorities to channel and mediate the victory. The officially approved (and distorted) version of transoceanic events appeared in the form of a printed news map, the combined effort of Company intelligence and artistic expertise. This news map was visually so attractive and powerful that it would dominate the way the victory was framed after the initial enthusiasm had died down. A plethora of stylized individual opinions, often mimicking the official spin, reflected the widespread joy in urban society. Amsterdam chronicle writers digested the different genres and created a popular and authoritative record where news and opinions could be retrieved by future generations. The variety of genres, the unanimity and ubiquity of jubilation, and quite simply the huge number of column inches and pamphlets meant that the conquest of Salvador in 1624—as the first major Dutch victory since the resumption of the war with Spain—acquired canonical value. The Atlantic dimension of the war had arrived to considerable excitement, and the resonance of the opening triumph meant Brazil would not retreat from public scrutiny until the conflict would be resolved, one way or the other.

CHAPTER 3

Appropriation

The fall of Salvador reverberated in Amsterdam for several years. Demoralized troops returned in the summer of 1625 to a series of inquests and legal wranglings that continued until the end of the year. As an Atlantic media hub, the city imploded spectacularly. Ordinary readers received very little news about the defeat, and even Johannes de Laet, director in the Chamber of Amsterdam as well as the West India Company's official chronicler, confessed to having relied on Spanish sources for most of his information. The investigation into the surrender had produced inconsistent stories and allegations, according to De Laet, and it was difficult to know what to believe—a bleak contrast with the exhaustive analysis of victory the year before.[1] The detention of the Portuguese governor and the Jesuits in Amsterdam, a source of ongoing rhetorical joy in the aftermath of the conquest, now turned into a painful diplomatic affair that involved the French ambassador, the Jesuit provincial in Brussels, Archduchess Isabella and even Philip IV himself.[2] When the Company eventually released the prisoners in November 1626, a leading Catholic merchant in Amsterdam organized a lavish celebration dinner at his house on the Oudezijds Voorburgwal that was a cause of great public humiliation for the urban authorities. When Domingo Coelho and the other Jesuits left the city several days later, their departure attracted a crowd of curious onlookers.[3]

The unmistakable reality check of Dutch Atlantic ambitions extended to the Amsterdam print media, where the memory of Bahia would echo caution for a decade, if not longer. When in 1630 the West India Company captured Olinda and Recife, the media frenzy surrounding the first invasion was missing, and jubilation quickly gave way to concerns for consolidation. As the Dutch slowly expanded their influence in Brazil, further limitations of the print media as carriers of information became apparent. There are two explanations for this shifting balance in Atlantic mediation. First, patriotic psychology determined that, although newspapers continued to publish weekly bulletins, spin-doctors customized their strategies to dominate the news flow, and chronicle writers still summarized events to shape opinion making, they all did so more reservedly than six years before. Second, as thousands of eyewitnesses of Dutch Brazil returned to Amsterdam in the early 1630s, the ubiquity and sheer variety of Atlantic information undermined the preeminence of the print media. Communication and discussion were increasingly being personalized and thus decentralized. Returning soldiers and sailors told of military stagnation, hunger, and disease. Faced with this new public order, the media could no longer cartelize the flow of information, and the West India Company could no longer manage it to bring exclusively good news. This chapter will analyze how the narratives of the boardroom and the urban population gradually diverged and how the limited geographical scope of early modern Amsterdam—and hence the physical closeness between regents, widows, shareholders, and innkeepers—fueled the explosive potential of public opinion in an urban context.

Lessons Learned

The memory of Bahia dominated representations of Brazil until the launch of the next major campaign in 1630 and in some ways even beyond that point.[4] Initially humiliation and pessimism reigned. The regular channels of communication were practically silent. The only eyewitness account of the unorderly defense of Bahia that was printed, written by the German soldier Johann Gregor Aldenburgk, appeared in Coburg—far away from Amsterdam—and has still never been translated into Dutch.[5] With another major setback to absorb in Breda, which fell to Spinola's troops, and the death of Stadtholder Maurits, the common explanation was that the quick succession of reverses was a form of divine punishment. These sentiments were articulated most forcefully by Ewout Teellinck, a Calvinist minister with millenarian tendencies, in three pamphlets based almost entirely on Scripture, in which three fictional *Wachters* (Watchmen) brought "tales of gloom" to the United Provinces. Teellinck's "Second Watchman" reported on the fall of Bahia and concluded, quoting Jeremiah 25:29, that the Lord had said, "Look for I begin to bring evil upon the city which is called by my name [Salvador], and should ye be utterly unpunished? Ye shall not be unpunished."[6]

Amid feelings of despair, however, two sentiments also prolonged the memory of conquest and helped the public deal with defeat. The first was a

74 Chapter 3

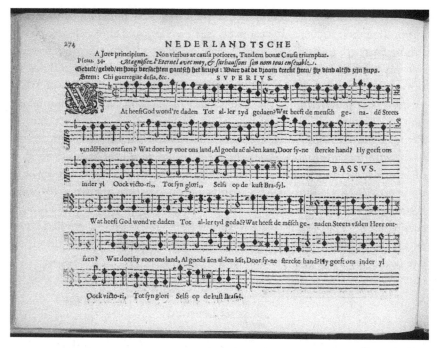

FIGURE 21. Adriaen Valerius, *Neder-landtsche Gedenck-clanck*. Haarlem, 1626, 274. Courtesy of Special Collections, University of Amsterdam, OTM: OL 1.

subdued sense of pride that, despite the mission's eventual collapse, a key stronghold of Habsburg America had briefly been seized. At the very least, the Portuguese *donatários* needed to shore up their defenses along the Brazilian coastline, a costly process that further widened the cracks in the Luso-Spanish relationship.[7] Adriaen Valerius's prestigious national songbook of 1626, explicitly printed for educational purposes, included a hymn on victory in Salvador that was not withdrawn after the city's return to Habsburg control (Figure 21).[8] Second, the ease of the initial triumph, as well as its timing amid military adversity in Europe, instilled hope for a better future. Informed readers of news bulletins recognized that, with a more professional hierarchy and a bit of good fortune, the West India Company could achieve more lasting success. In subsequent years, relatively inconspicuous expeditions in the Atlantic were given disproportional coverage in both independent and embedded media. In modern terms, Brazil became a trending topic in Amsterdam.[9]

The invasion also resulted in the emergence of a nationwide celebrity in Piet Heyn. His daring contribution to the conquest of Bahia meant that his next campaigns in the Atlantic were followed very closely by the print media, and his reputation would reach dizzying heights in 1628 after he captured the New Spain treasure fleet in Matanzas Bay, Cuba. Yet the foundation of his star status lay in his Brazilian ventures, as Heyn himself insisted, and he further encouraged the nation's pride and hope with actual military results. Unlike in 1625 when his auxiliary fleet, returning from an expedition to São Paulo de Luanda, had been too weak to relieve the besieged troops in Salvador,[10] the admiral launched another attack on Bahia in March 1627 when he was better provisioned. His force was too small to conquer the city for a second time, but he did capture or sink twenty-six enemy vessels and dispatched four richly laden ships to the United Provinces. After seizing yet more prizes in another raid on the bay later that same year, the Heeren XIX awarded him a gold chain and a medal and capitalized on his success in public by ordering another news map, produced in Amsterdam by Claes Jansz Visscher and Hessel Gerritsz.[11]

This news map, printed on a plano sheet, was twice the size of the news maps of 1624 and confirmed the status of the genre as the prime medium for good tidings from the West India House (Figure 22).[12] Several colored copies have survived, but not all copies include the comprehensive textual explanation, showing both the increasing versatility of the genre in the Amsterdam book market and the news map's use as a colorful souvenir that could be framed and displayed as a token of identity. The engraving enabled armchair travelers to observe Salvador from so close up that they could almost look through the windows of the cathedral. Heyn's ship was depicted at the heart of the composition, fighting the two vessels of the Portuguese admiral and vice-admiral at the same time, while being within firing distance of the batteries in the Forte do Mar. More than any other Atlantic news map, the broadsheet glorified the power of the fleet and its admiral, whose portrait was included in the bottom-right corner. The news map's elaborate textual segment alluded to the collective desire for retribution. One of the more regrettable episodes of the occupation of Salvador, the death of Governor Van Dorth, had now "finally" been avenged. Van Dorth's supposed murderer, the indigenous captain Francisco Padilha, was mortally wounded by a bullet that went through his armor. "His death," the author wrote, "was a great discouragement to the defensive forces."[13] Heyn's display of naval prowess carried the implicit promise that the West India Company would return to Brazil, and the disappointing conclusion to the

FIGURE 22. Hessel Gerritsz, *Vertoon van de exploicten door den manhaften Pieter Pietersz Heyn*, Amsterdam, 1628, ink on paper, 77.5 × 57 cm. Courtesy of Het Scheepvaartmuseum, Amsterdam, inv. nr. A.0145 (131).

first conquest gradually gave way to more substantiated feelings of hope and potential vindication.

The late 1620s brought a change of fortune to the Netherlands, as the new stadtholder Frederik Hendrik besieged and captured Grol, Wesel, and finally 's-Hertogenbosch in quick succession.[14] In June 1628, the painter Peter Paul Rubens anxiously reported from Antwerp that another attack on Salvador was in the cards, and such rumors must have also circulated north of the border.[15] Heyn's capture of the New Spain treasure fleet supplied the Company with enough funds to launch its second invasion. A Dutch trader in Pernambuco provided the Heeren XIX with crucial military intelligence. He used streets in Amsterdam as a reference point, explaining the length of one of Olinda's streets as one-third of the Breestraat and the valley adjacent to the western walls as as wide as the Nieuwmarkt.[16] The directors kept the location of the attack secret, but the newspapers estimated that Brazil was the most likely destination and passed this information off as a fact in the months of renewed anticipation that followed. Given the overwhelming success of the first invasion, the outcome of the second campaign was confidently awaited at home— and with good reason. Sixty-seven vessels with over seven thousand men under Admiral Hendrick Lonck and Colonel Diederick van Waerdenburgh arrived before the coast in February 1630, where the conquest of Olinda—like that of Salvador—was a matter of hours rather than days. The Portuguese put up strong resistance in Recife for two more weeks, but, other than burning the sugar warehouses, there was little they could do to frustrate the invaders. By early March, the West India Company was in control of the province's main settlements.[17]

Two months later, once again, the authorities made sure that the good news reached Amsterdammers from every class and age. Church bells were sounding, grace was being said in every parish, and printed sheets with images of Pernambuco that could be cut out and used as a card game introduced young children to the restoration of Dutch Brazil (Figure 23).[18] But the urban population was now used to hearing reports from the Atlantic, and, even though the news was just as good, the sheer surprise and excitement of 1624 were missing. Given also that they were in the ascendancy at home, the victory in Pernambuco was often presented as one in a series of military successes.[19] A few songs—cheaply produced and aimed at the lower classes—mocked Spain (and the pope) for losing control of Brazil again, but the reaction to victory in the mainstream media indicates that the West India Company had learned from its publicity mistakes.[20] The corantos again competed to bring the good news first, but this time they followed the "official" reports almost verbatim—a reward for the Company's efforts of information management.[21] The most significant eyewitness report shored up and intensified the official story: Johannes Baers, yet another Reformed minister, recounted that, as Company soldiers entered Olinda, the population had left their houses in a hurry. The doors had been left open, and the tables were still set—an almost word-for-word reminder of reports from Salvador. He also testified that the churches were "cleansed" within a few days, enabling him to conduct services on Easter Sunday, and he noted with approval that many African slaves had come to church, "who, in their own way, were quiet, pious, and listening diligently."[22] When Van Waerdenburgh set up his quarters in Olinda's Jesuit convent, Baers reported it without any sense of *Schadenfreude*. Instead, he emphasized the commitment and piety of the authorities, vouching that he had been woken up at night by the sound of the colonel getting up to pray. According to Baers, Van Waerdenburgh then lay awake for several hours to continue his worship of the Lord.[23]

The collective memory of failure also had a bearing on policy. Casting their eye over the misfortune of Johan van Dorth and subsequent excesses, the Heeren XIX this time took the precaution of sending a triumvirate to Brazil, the Politieke Raad (Political Council). They were later joined by two of the Company's nineteen directors, Matthias van Ceulen from Amsterdam and Johan Gijsselingh from Zeeland—a setup that generally operated efficiently and received little public scrutiny.[24] The one story that *was* eagerly covered by all the Amsterdam media told how Admiral Lonck, having taken possession of Olinda, went on a reconnaissance mission on the narrow, sandy road to Recife where he was ambushed by nearly three hundred African slaves. All but five of the party of forty Dutchmen were killed, but Lonck survived because he was on horseback at the time of the surprise attack. According to the German soldier Ambrosius Richshoffer, the admiral's horse was wounded by two arrows, but he nevertheless returned to Olinda safely.[25] The parallel with Johan van Dorth's survey mission outside the walls of Salvador was glaringly obvious,[26] and, for those who believed in divine intervention—and that included most if not all seventeenth-century Amsterdammers—Lonck's narrow escape had great symbolic value. It demonstrated that, faced with opposition identical to that encountered in Salvador, the outcome six years on was much better.

More instrumental for the prolongation of success than the symbolism treasured by the media were military developments in Europe and Brazil. Olivares found the Portuguese nobility reluctant to participate in another armada

Appropriation 79

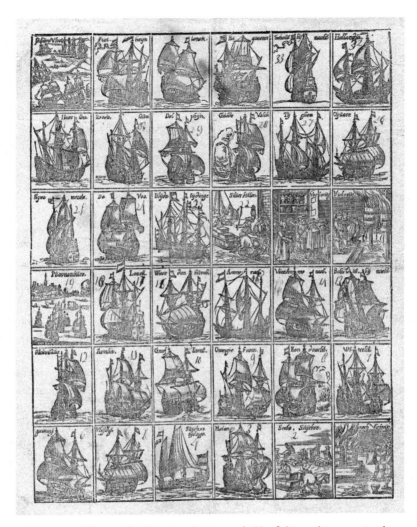

FIGURE 23. Sheet with thirty-six playing cards (?) of ships taking part in the campaigns at Matanzas ("Silver vloot," 1628) and Olinda ("Pharnambuco," 1630) [1630], ink on paper, 39.5 × 30.5 cm. Courtesy of Collection Atlas van Stolk, Rotterdam, inv. nr. 1713.

to relieve Brazil, a foreboding of growing recalcitrance against Madrid.[27] At the same time, the Dutch constructed fortifications in and around Recife with astonishing speed. Half a dozen bastions were started and, for the most part, finished in 1630, only two of which were former Portuguese structures.[28] In

January 1631, returning ships brought reassurances that the settlement was now secured and that an estimated garrison of five hundred soldiers would be capable of defending Recife and the adjacent island of Antonio Vaz. With the bridgehead properly protected, Van Waerdenburgh shifted his attention to breaking the resistance of Matias de Albuquerque and the remaining loyalists.[29] In February, Dutch troops were confident enough to celebrate that, with the help of God, they had succeeded not only in conquering Pernambuco but in consolidating their victory for a full year.[30] Van Waerdenburgh ordered the demolition of Olinda, the most likely place of rebellion, and sent its church bells to the West India House in Amsterdam as a tangible symbol of lasting Dutch hegemony.[31]

Consolidation

The mediation of victory developed along predictable lines. The West India Company once again employed Claes Jansz Visscher to develop a news map that must be considered the culmination of the genre (Figure 24). The spin-doctor had worked tirelessly to make his product yet more attractive. Anticipating the translations of his reportage that were inevitably to follow, Visscher in 1630 decided to optimize his commercial formula.[32] The textual report of the invasion was printed in two languages, Dutch and French. The first of four illustrations was placed along the top of the composition, across the width of the two printed plano sheets. Visscher visualized the dominance of the Company by the array of Dutch flags, proudly flying within Olinda's fortifications. The second illustration, depicting a typical sugar mill, indicates that Visscher was misinformed about the ins and outs of the sugar industry. Viewers with more intimate knowledge, Amsterdam's Sephardic merchants, for example, would have noticed that the small illustration portrayed an obsolete and long-abandoned method of extracting liquid sugar from cane.[33] Hessel Gerritsz, the Company cartographer, contributed a map of Brazil from Rio Grande in the north to Salvador in the south and a bird's-eye view of the battlefield that testified to the soldiers' courage in making their approach to Olinda from the most difficult angle where the city rose highest above the surrounding countryside.[34]

The Company directors were pursuing an aggressive strategy of market saturation through (apparent) differentiation. The collage-like news map could be separated into several parts, depending on the customer's wishes and spending power. The chosen segments, for example, could be combined to

FIGURE 24. Claes Jansz Visscher, *De stat Olinda de Pharnambuco, verovert by den E. Generael Hendrick C. Lonck, Anno 1630*, Amsterdam, 1630, ink on paper, 97 × 118 cm. Courtesy of Het Scheepvaartmuseum, Amsterdam, inv. nr. A.0145 (130).

create a news map aimed at an exclusively national readership, omitting the French translation. At least one copy survives where Visscher left out the two main maps and the illustration of the sugar mill and combined the remaining parts for an elongated yet still attractive version. The map alone could be sold separately too, and an abridged version of the text—without any of the images—was for sale as a news pamphlet in Hessel Gerritsz's shop.[35] Print publishers abroad saw little point in copying this skillfully crafted media strategy, which required significant artistic and financial investments. After his association with the West India Company had ensured his primacy in the media landscape at home, Visscher now successfully cornered the international market as well. The separate illustrations that made up the news map remained in the mainstream of Europe's Brazilian iconography, inspiring illustrious artists such as Matthias Merian and Wenceslaus Hollar.[36]

The Dutch, the leading mapmakers of early modern Europe, were particularly keen on using cartography to support their claims. Having arrived relatively late on the Atlantic scene, their maps, globes, and atlases were meant to convince an international audience of the legitimacy, enforceability, and durability of Dutch claims.[37] By the early 1630s, according to one employee, the West India Company had a better knowledge of Atlantic geography than did the Spanish or the Portuguese. The Habsburgs by now were having Dutch books on the art of navigation translated into Spanish, instead of the other way around.[38] The cartographic elements of Visscher's news map, moreover, represented a new geographical reality rather than a specific military event—appropriation rather than triumph. The strategy of visual distortion was adapted accordingly: in contrast to the actual situation, the maps suggested that the Dutch had knowledge (and had assumed control) of the interior. The depiction of several riverbeds, up to a dozen miles inland judging from the map's scale, featured tree-lined waterways and upstream islands, which implied a certain familiarity with Olinda's hinterland. Visscher made the landscape more recognizable to European viewers by filling the empty spaces at the top with hills, vegetation, and a village—the latter so close to the shore that it could well have been spotted by the soldiers. The absence of Portuguese toponymy other than Olinda and Recife can be regarded as an implicit invitation for the West India Company to take control. As the Dutch in subsequent years began to realize the territorial opportunities suggested, Visscher's news map transformed from a somewhat premature representation of expansion in Brazil into the earliest acknowledgment of the Company's achievements.[39]

The West India Company was of course prudent enough not to share strategic information with third parties—as the case of Dierick Ruiter's sketches of the early 1620s has shown.[40] Once Pernambuco had been secured, however, the benefits of appropriating the province in public, both at home and abroad, outweighed the risk of communicating details to third parties. This U-turn in cartographic representation after more than a century of Iberian censorship was a balancing act between withholding what had to remain secret and disclosing what could be used to advance Dutch claims. Moreover, the *bewindhebbers* had to take into account that to keep things secret caused suspicion among ordinary shareholders in Amsterdam that things were not going well, as one contemporary observer suggested.[41] By doing it sensibly, as Visscher did on the Company's behalf, the suggestion of openness had far-reaching implications in early modern Europe. It gave the impression that, in contrast to the Habsburgs, the Dutch did not need secrecy because their dominance over Pernambuco, and later also the adjacent captaincies, was secure and manifest.

For this mode of rhetoric to work, reports of success in Pernambuco were considered incomplete without stressing the need to make permanent the victory. Although the storyline of consolidation was not particularly mediagenic, the Amsterdam print media ardently developed it. Throughout 1630, Jan van Hilten's *Courante* made regular mention of the feverish construction works.[42] Barent Lampe, Nicolaes van Wassenaer's (less gifted) successor, literally copied Colonel Van Waerdenburgh's claims that Recife especially could be impregnable.[43] Social media also settled for a more judicious tone: one patriotic amateur poet explicitly called on the directors of the Company to send auxiliary troops to Pernambuco.[44] This was a line of thought that proved functional and tenacious. The verses calling for reinforcements were reprinted in songbooks of 1645, 1656, and 1661, when the geopolitical impact of the campaign in Pernambuco had already been reversed. Even high-brow poetry focused on consolidating Dutch Brazil: Elias Herckmans, an admired Amsterdam lyricist and merchant, reserved praise in his masterpiece *Der Zee-vaert Lof* (In Praise of Seafaring, 1634) for such unpoetic actions as the use of shovels to strengthen Recife's fortifications.[45] Herckmans's eye for a pragmatic approach to Atlantic expansion was something special. He would later serve in Brazil, first as a member of the Political Council in Recife, then as governor of Paraíba, Itamaracá, and Rio Grande, and ultimately as vice-admiral of an unfortunate expedition to Chile.[46]

The Amsterdam directors, too, refused to get overexcited. They extended their media strategy by commissioning the local notary Daniel Bredan to write a pamphlet in Spanish, calling upon the people of Brazil to abandon their suspicions and embrace the new regime.[47] Although the text was primarily aimed at colonists and planters in Pernambuco, it was probably also useful on the European market or perhaps even to make an impact among the Sephardim in the Low Countries. In any event, it fitted nicely alongside newspaper reports of colonists who decided to switch sides. Some of these deserters like the Brabander Adriaen Verdonck or the mulatto Domingos Fernandes Calabar provided further intelligence to the Company—and encouragement to the public. By October 1630, Pieter Corneliszoon Hooft wrote optimistically to the Amsterdam magistrate Albert Coenraedtsz Burgh that "if we could get the Atlantic for ourselves, I can see the time of Solomon dawn for us, and silver will lie like mud in the streets of Amsterdam."[48] In general, however, consolidation was not nearly as spectacular and beloved a topic for newswriters at home as conquest. During the calendar year 1631, reports from Brazil in the Amsterdam corantos demanded fewer and fewer column inches. Adriaen Pater's important yet (for him) fatal battle against a numerically superior enemy, a commendable piece of maritime skill and daring, never acquired the heroic appeal of privateering expeditions in the buildup to Lonck's invasion.[49]

Obtaining credible information from across the Atlantic was difficult, probably more so than at times when the authorities wanted good news to be distributed. Every homecoming ship from Pernambuco rendered substantial coverage in each of the two Amsterdam corantos, as only eyewitness reports enabled Van Hilten and Jansz to verify prior bulletins. For the first five to six years, however, the newspapers did not consider everything they learned suitable for circulation. The situation in Recife ranged from the unenviable to the outright grueling, as hunger and disease defined a settlement where the only way in and out was by ship. This part of colonial reality rarely featured in the media. The Amsterdam newspapers reported fairly systematically how provisions sent from Lisbon did not reach the Portuguese troops in the *Arraial*, but seldom pointed out that the population of Recife suffered from similar shortages.[50] Unsuccessful Habsburg attempts to recapture Recife or Olinda did figure in the news reports, whereas equally unsuccessful Dutch efforts to expand their influence beyond these settlements did not.

In June 1633, the German commander Sigismund von Schoppe occupied the island of Itamaracá and in December, he captured the strategically important Fort Reis Magos, but it was not until Christmas 1634 that victory in

Paraíba decidedly tipped the balance in Dutch favor.[51] In Amsterdam, Visscher this time reserved four-fifths of his composition for the Brazilian landmass, a clear indication of the tendency to present Dutch expansion as a natural and irreversible process (Figure 25). The iconographic appropriation of Brazil was supported by the texts. Visscher described the piety of the indigenous inhabitants, two thousand of whom had switched sides since 1630 after having first chased away the two Jesuit fathers they had obeyed for (too) long. Now that the governing Albuquerque family was losing even local support, the text concluded confidently, they were better off leaving Brazil altogether. The indigenous appreciation for Dutch success was a particularly strong signal of legitimacy since opinion makers in the United Provinces had insisted for decades on the likelihood of an alliance with the Amerindians.[52] Portuguese families who had left to escape the impending attack returned to their houses. According to Visscher's news map, they too had grown estranged from the authorities in Bahia, as pamphleteers in Holland and Zeeland had already predicted prior to the invasion of Salvador. In the summer of 1635, the Polish colonel Christoph Arciszewsky managed to break Albuquerque's resistance, expand Dutch power to the interior, and allow the Company to finally begin the exploitation of Pernambuco's sugar industry.[53]

Dutch domination in northeastern Brazil was ultimately confirmed in 1637, when West India Company forces conquered the key defensive stronghold at Porto Calvo. Visscher did not produce a news map of this decisive victory, probably because his clients had found an even more gifted Amsterdam artist to convey their message. Yet it is testimony to Visscher's success as a spindoctor that his two main rivals for making news from Brazil in mid-seventeenth-century Amsterdam, the journalist Jan van Hilten and the cartographer Johan Blaeu, each produced a news map of the triumph at Porto Calvo that prolonged the iconographic program set in motion in the late 1620s.[54] Van Hilten's broadsheet in particular mimicked Visscher and provided the natural and artistic conclusion to the gradual visual appropriation of the colony (Figure 26). Those who had followed the Company's progress through successive Amsterdam news maps had, literally, witnessed the Dutch move away from the coast to take possession of the interior. As the offensive of the mid-1630s faded, and the focus shifted from military affairs to reviving the export of sugar, the news maps lost their key role in informing and influencing the public at home.

By now, Company officials in Recife had finished their cartographic survey of the coastline, effectively confirming that the public appropriation of the province had been completed.[55] As military expansion in Brazil gave way to

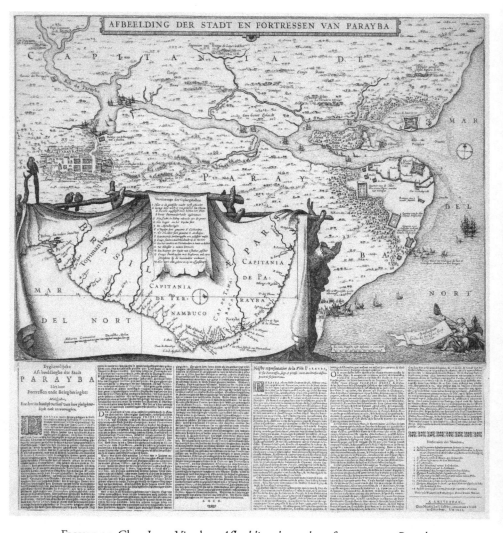

FIGURE 25. Claes Jansz Visscher, *Afbeelding der stadt en fortressen van Parayba*, Amsterdam, 1635, ink on paper, 63.3 × 67.6 cm. Courtesy of Collection Atlas van Stolk, Rotterdam, inv. nr. 1762.

(Facing page)
FIGURE 26. Jan van Hilten, *Auctentijck verhael van de belegheringhe ende veroveringhe van Porto Calvo*, Amsterdam, 1637, ink on paper, 61.4 × 39.7 cm. Courtesy of Het Scheepvaartmuseum, Amsterdam, inv. nr. A.0145 (134).

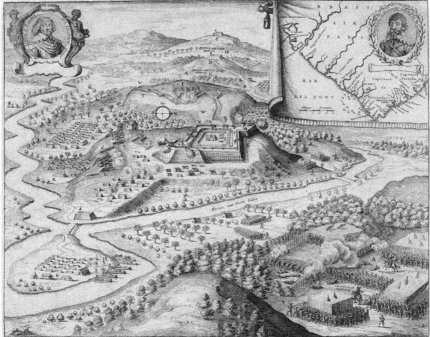

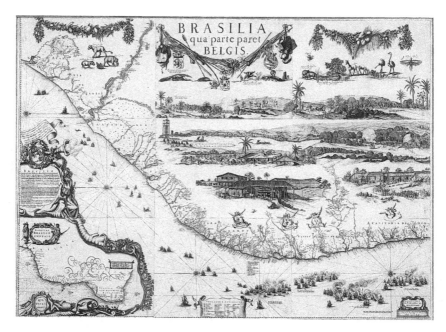

Figure 27. Clement de Jonghe, *Brasilia qua parte paret Belgis*, Amsterdam [1664], 101 × 163 cm. Courtesy of Maritiem Museum Rotterdam, inv. nr. WAE 598.

the settlement of the colony to focus on sugar production, the West India Company adjusted its public relations strategy. Johan Blaeu was ideally positioned to emulate Visscher in shaping the image of Dutch Brazil. He had close professional (and occasionally kinship) relations with influential directors and major shareholders of the West India Company such as Samuel Blommaert, Laurens Reael, and Albert Coenraedtsz Burgh. Another Amsterdam director, Hans Bontemantel, even protected Blaeu against persecution when the provincial authorities tried to ban Socinian and Remonstrant books he had printed.[56] From the mid-1630s onward, Blaeu became the Company's favored cartographer, a shift in preference reflected in the fact that the directors chose him rather than Visscher to produce the official news map of victory in Porto Calvo. By combining the cartographic pioneering of Hessel Gerritsz with a highly advanced navigation chart by the brothers Johannes and Philips Vingboons, Blaeu subsequently devised a map of the colony for his atlas in 1642.[57] Four years later, he crafted his monumental nine-leaf wall map of Dutch Brazil, improved with information Georg Marcgraf had assembled in the colony's interior.[58] Blaeu sold this map, the ultimate glorification of the West India Company's ambitions in the Atlantic world, to affluent customers in his shop at the Old Bridge. In subsequent decades, it would be improved and reprinted by leading Amsterdam map publishers like Huych Allart (1659) and Clement de Jonghe (1664) (Figure 27).[59]

More conventional maps also facilitated more conventional forms of appropriation. An obvious strategy was to replace Portuguese and Spanish names with Dutch nomenclature. Well-known settlements like Olinda, despite having been destroyed in 1631, retained their names. So did the captaincies whose names had been familiar to the public at home since the beginning of the century. Life on the sugar plantations continued to be dominated by the Portuguese, and their terminology was introduced into Dutch writings, rather than being replaced with neologisms that had no chance of entering the day-to-day jargon of the *engenhos* anyway. Military prizes, however, whether strategically located towns or, more often, fortresses, were appropriated by a systematic process of renaming. Thus, Fort Reis Magos at the entrance to the Rio Grande was rebaptized Fort Ceulen in honor of Matthias van Ceulen, the Amsterdam representative of the Heeren XIX who had assisted in the attack on the stronghold. By then several fortresses in Recife had already been named after high-ranking Dutch officers. The town of Nossa Senhora das Neves in Paraíba had seen its name changed into Filipeia after the Habsburgs took control of the Portuguese colony in honor of Philip II. The Dutch in 1635 renamed it Frederikstad, cancelling the homage to the Spanish monarch and replacing it with the name of their own stadtholder—a particularly rewarding adjustment from their point of view. Johan Maurits's construction of a major urban extension to Recife on the island Antonio Vaz by the name of Mauritsstad (or Mauritia) constituted the climax of terminological appropriation.[60]

A Multimedia Experience

To measure the success of the concerted campaign of appropriation, it is important to establish that the public identified with the West India Company's cause. Private inventories reveal how copies of news maps were not only purchased and read but framed and put on display inside urban homes, communicating to visitors the owner's patriotism, worldliness, and support for the effort in Brazil. Janneke Hendrix, for example, the widow of a former Amsterdam *bewindhebber*, owned an oak-framed copy of Visscher's news map of Salvador, which she kept in the attic of her house on the Nieuwezijds Voorburgwal. The cloth bleacher Cornelis Nason possessed the same image as an oil painting, which was on display in the best room of his house near the bleacheries, just outside the city walls. If the Utrecht painter Jacob Duck's *Bordello Scene* (c. 1635) is to be believed, Visscher's wall map of Olinda and Recife even adorned the walls of taverns where soldiers and prostitutes had a merry time together (Figure 28).[61] The audience for the more luxurious maps made by Blaeu was to be found in the upper middle classes. Frederik van Alewijn, an urban magistrate, had a framed map of northeast Brazil in the reception room of his canal house on the Herengracht, displaying his loyalty for all of his guests to see. So did Matthias van Ceulen, the Company director who twice served in the colony and who may have used the map to enrich stories of his own experiences in the colony.[62]

It was outside, however, on the streets of Amsterdam, where Dutch Brazil made an everyday impression—regardless of individual spending power or economic allegiance. These "spatial media" created a different narrative that was more difficult for the Company to control. The city's built environment, the mundane rituals and occasional excesses of oceangoing life, and non-European additions to the urban population provided everyday reminders of the Atlantic world that mitigated and at times contradicted corporate communication. For the average urban citizen, for example, the sugar industry transformed Amsterdam in a very noticeable (and much more egalitarian) way than print. The number of refineries in the city, which had started to appear during the Twelve Years' Truce, increased from twenty-five in 1620 to forty in 1650, a development directly related to the expansion of Dutch power in Brazil. These buildings were of an extraordinary size for the time, sometimes reaching six stories. Their chimneys emitted soot and stench over the city, a problem the authorities sought to reduce by forbidding the use of coal as heating fuel. Residents continued to complain of "great sorrow, vexation, and discomfort." Ultimately the regents restricted the refineries to the more remote areas west of the Keizersgracht and east of the Nieuwmarkt "in order to banish the smells and other inconveniences that tarnish the city."[63] Meanwhile, the price of sugar as a consumption good remained high even when peace in Brazil allowed the trade to flourish, and, in Amsterdam, the product was known first and foremost for its preciousness, something that would be thematized in contemporary art.[64]

Equally evident, and equally problematic for some ordinary citizens, was the presence of new ethnic groups from Brazil. Already in the mid-1620s there were "three negroes and five negresses" who were captured in Atlantic waters by Dutch privateers and brought to Amsterdam, where together with their

FIGURE 28. Jacob Duck, *Bordello Scene*, c. 1635, oil on panel, 41.3 × 54 cm. Courtesy of RKD Netherlands Institute for Art History, The Hague, no. 196998.

Sephardic masters they remained for three months and were "free to go where [they] pleased." When another Portuguese merchant came from Brazil and settled in Amsterdam, he brought his slave Juliana, who refused to join him when he wanted to depart for Barbados many years later. Like Juliana, most of the Africans in Amsterdam were servants. Several of them were buried in the Sephardic cemetery in Ouderkerk aan de Amstel, a small town well outside the city gates—inside or outside the cemetery fence depending on their conversion to Judaism. Other black men and women appear to have been (or become) free, living together in a basement in Amsterdam in 1632. According to various witnesses, they were "a wild and bad little people" who "made noise and violence everyday, against the Dutch as well as the Portuguese," and were "not being employed, nor in anyone's service." One black woman had been confined to (and later escaped from) the local prison for female criminals;

others were accused of obtaining charity from the Reformed Church under false pretenses.[65] For many Amsterdammers, these experiences must have overshadowed claims in the print media that slaves in Recife were listening diligently to Reformed preaching.[66]

Twenty-four years after Zacharias Heyns's woodcuts, there were now also genuine Brazilians in Amsterdam. The West India Company had transported thirteen young Potiguar Indians from Paraíba to the United Provinces as early as 1625, in anticipation of the conquest of Olinda and Recife. Eight of them were taught how to read and write by the Chamber of Amsterdam. "Ships, money, and everything is in abundance there like the stars in the sky," one of them would later report.[67] The training was to the Company's initial satisfaction: in early 1630, three Potiguars returned with Lonck to Brazil, and the following year the Company reported that the Indians had indeed become sufficiently acquainted with "our laws, government, and our nation." After the conquest of Recife, the directors tried to expand the program by sending twenty-five Indian boys to study in Holland, but in the end the costs must have outweighed the benefits.[68] Nonetheless, in 1636, the Irish adventurer Bernard O'Brien, who had escaped from indigenous captivity on the Amazon, reached Holland where, to his astonishment, he found "many Indians from Brazil who are seeking employment in the service of the States." On the streets of Amsterdam, O'Brien, accompanied by his Indian "boy," could even speak Tupi when he encountered the former Jesuit and *procurador de los Indios* Manuel de Moraes, a mestizo from São Paulo who had sided with the Dutch.[69]

In the harbor district, too, any impact the print media may have had was reduced by the harsh realities of everyday life. Recife now featured alongside destinations in the East Indies on the rolls of recruiters, and anyone who entered one of the taverns, whether Dutch or foreign, sober or drunk, could find himself enlisted by the next morning.[70] Potential soldiers, usually poor men who had traveled to Holland looking for work—perhaps even instigated to do so by optimistic media coverage—sometimes spent several weeks on the streets and were bound to fall into the hands of professional recruiters. Women played an important role in this scheme. Peter Hansen Hajstrup, a brash young man from Schleswig, encountered a prostitute in one of the Amsterdam inns who was "so well dressed that anyone must think she came from nobility."[71] Hansen, wisely, claimed to be very young and inexperienced. He escaped from the tavern but ended up on a Recife-bound vessel all the same and would serve in Pernambuco for nearly ten years. Stephen Carl Behaim, from Nuremberg, was threatened and harassed to repay lodging debts in Amsterdam until he had no choice but to enlist with the West India Company.[72] Thousands must have suffered a similar fate. When these sailors or soldiers-to-be then gathered at the West India House, the people living in the immediate vicinity were certain to notice their presence. In Amsterdam, in the final days before departure, soldiers swore an oath to the Company and graced the streets they had long infested one more time. They marched toward the docks in orderly fashion, carrying colored flags with a gold-embroidered GWC logo of the Geoctroyeerde West-Indische Compagnie and the coat of arms of the city of Amsterdam, suggesting to onlookers that the time for unruliness was over and a more disciplined tour in Brazil was ready to begin.[73]

Life on board was hard, explaining why returning ships could be a source of both excitement and disappointment, and occasionally disturbance.[74] When minister Johannes Baers arrived from Brazil in Texel with Lonck's fleet, countless boats practically covered the water's surface to welcome them, and, in Amsterdam, the streets were so crowded that the returning soldiers could barely disembark.[75] This scene was no exception. Ambrosius Richshoffer recalled how, after safely crossing the Atlantic in 1632, he was grateful to see that many people awaited on the docks, "especially a lot of womenfolk" looking for their husbands, sons, and brothers. Some in the crowd were happy to be reunited with their loved ones; others were distraught at not finding theirs on board, but they all treated the men who did return to brandy, wine, and food. Heartened by this reception, Richshoffer and his comrades paraded through the streets of Amsterdam toward the West India House, firing their last rounds of ammunition to celebrate their safe return, "so that hardly anyone dared to look out of their windows."[76] After having been discharged, the troops usually had to stay in town for several weeks in order to receive their pay. For many, this period led directly to another conscription and a swift return to Brazil, as the salary they eventually received went straight to the innkeepers who had provided lodging—a profitable arrangement that both recruiters and the West India Company were eager to preserve.

Micromanagement

With the grand narrative of embedded journalism pushed to the background by the implications of Atlantic expansion in Amsterdam, different agendas began to come to the fore. The West India House on the Haarlemmerstraat was the urban gateway to Brazil: literally for sailors and soldiers like Ambrosius

Richshoffer and metaphorically for the burghers of Amsterdam who had no intention of crossing the ocean themselves but nevertheless developed a personal interest in Brazilian affairs. Here the first encounters of corporate communication and more intimate economic experiences took place.[77] If anything, these encounters revealed to those who had mediated Dutch Brazil that there were many different ways of appropriating the colony, even within the city walls.

Two or even three times a week, the *bewindhebbers* of the Amsterdam Chamber assembled in the West India House to discuss Atlantic affairs. In the mid-1630s, their number included experienced directors such as Matthias van Ceulen, who had returned from Brazil, and the highly respected Remonstrant and would-be burgomaster Albert Coenraedtsz Burgh, who, in the aftermath of the Bahia campaign, had visited the Brazilian Jesuit fathers in their Amsterdam prison cells. They were joined by prominent merchants such as Jacob Reepmaecker, Daniel van Liebergen, and the German-born Nicolaes van Setterich, and by younger ones like Eduard Man, a deacon of the English Reformed Church originally from Plymouth, and Jan Raey, both of whom would still be on the board in the late 1640s when the situation in Brazil had dramatically changed.[78] Together they formed a representative blend of Amsterdam's elite with an interest in West Indian trade. Typically, during their meetings, the directors discussed a wide array of Atlantic issues like motivating potential settlers to move to the colonies; hiring shipbuilders to work at the docks, loading and unloading ships from Africa, the Caribbean, or New Netherland and (publicly) selling their cargoes; and responding to letters they had received from their colleagues in other chambers or from the States General in The Hague.

The minutes of the directors' meetings have survived only for the years 1635 and 1636,[79] but they provide a vivid impression of the impact the rise of Dutch Brazil had on the everyday lives of people in Amsterdam and of the way ordinary inhabitants, by now well informed of military progress, seized the opportunity to participate in the politics of the Atlantic world.[80] A permanent fixture on the directors' agenda were the requests of citizens who usually felt they were entitled to some form of payment by the West India Company. Women in particular appealed to the directors for money their husbands or sons had earned during their tours in Brazil. Wives, widows, and mothers of seamen in Holland were used to managing the household on their own. In their view, by the mid-1630s already, the public appropriation of Pernambuco and the adjacent captaincies was no longer an issue: Dutch Brazil was a political reality that had a significant impact on their private lives. The Company tried to assist the needy with various forms of poor relief.[81] It was the task of the directors to distinguish between those who had a legitimate claim and should, therefore, be paid and those who did not. A closer look at one of their meetings can offer an impression of how Dutch Brazil invaded the "intimate economic networks" of Amsterdam, created by marriage and kinship.[82] It also demonstrates how well informed some of the supplicants who came to the West India House were, through printed media, handwritten letters from soldiers or sailors in Brazil, or both.

On Thursday 22 February 1635—in the week news of the victory in Paraíba broke in Amsterdam—sixteen directors attended that day's meeting.[83] Only Jan Raey and Pieter Blaeuwenhaen were absent because they were representing the interests of the chamber in The Hague as members of the Heeren XIX. Marcus de Vogelaer, an eminent merchant with Southern Netherlandish roots who also traded in Russia and previously a *bewindhebber* of the VOC, presided over the meeting.[84] The socioeconomic difference between the directors behind the table and the individuals appearing in front of them is remarkable. The first supplicant of the day was one Susanna Bussen, mother of the drummer Godefroy Ruiter. She came to the meeting well prepared, presenting the directors with a printed salary slip to support her request for two months of her son's wages to pay for her daily expenses. The directors decided to postpone making a decision. They wanted the Heeren XIX to establish a ruling that could apply to all such requests uniformly across the five regional chambers, focusing on the bureaucratic issue of which Company officials were entitled to sign these documents. Susanna left the West India House empty-handed for now, but her request had succeeded in persuading the directors to review their administrative procedures. Two weeks later, the matter was settled, meaning that Susanna (and others like her) probably received the money.[85] After Susanna, Jannetje Jans entered the room. She was the wife of a local carpenter who had left for Pernambuco on a ship named *de Brack* ten months before, and she also requested two months of her husband's salary. Perhaps because she did not present any paperwork, her request was turned down. Yet she came back to the West India House a number of times in the weeks that followed, and in May, the directors awarded her the payment she was entitled to after all.[86]

The women who came to the Haarlemmerstraat on this particular Thursday are more than just faces in the crowd. Their relatively simple background, and the candid nature of their requests, demonstrates the accessibility of the directors and the public function of the local chamber of the West India Company in an urban setting. Susanna's plea in particular shows that, before taking action, individual callers could obtain information on what was required for a favorable decision. There is no reason to believe that supplicants came to the boardroom with more confidence on this particular day than on any other because of the good news from Paraíba. The Company was simply one of Amsterdam's most important employers in the second quarter of the seventeenth century, indirectly providing work for many segments of society—from shipbuilders to rope makers and from warehouse personnel to local bookkeepers, clerks, and other white-collar workers.[87] For women who had seen their husbands or sons depart for Brazil, the West India House constituted a place of potential relief from the miserable financial circumstances in which they lived. Some may have had good reason to request advance payment of an employee's salary; others perhaps just gave it a try in the hope that the directors would be compassionate.

The individual requests are testimonies of an individual form of appropriation of Brazil that was more powerful than anything the Company spin-doctors could achieve in the world of print. They suggest a broad familiarity with the many opportunities that the emergence of Dutch Brazil represented. Supplicants who came to the Haarlemmerstraat for an audience with the directors, one assumes, meticulously followed Atlantic developments in the printed media and by word of mouth, and one cannot help but wonder if Susanna Bussen and Jannetje Jans said grace in church that same week for the triumph in Paraíba with as little reservation as in 1624 or 1630. The regents, of course, still held an information advantage. They were primarily responsible for the Company's commercial welfare (and their own), but they were conscientious enough to give every supplicant due attention and to make reasonable decisions in the interest of the urban population on which the chamber and the Company ultimately depended. A sailmaker who applied for an annual salary rather than a daily wage, for example, could therefore be successful in his appeal to the directors. A soldier who had been captured by the Portuguese and returned to Amsterdam penniless had a good chance to receive his overdue salary.[88] In general, the *bewindhebbers* were receptive to many kinds of private initiative, especially if these also enhanced the public image of the Company.

After the individual appeals for the day had been settled, the directors moved on to discussing the incoming correspondence. On 22 February 1635, the first letter, written by a certain Pieter Croon three days earlier, was the most important one. The directors decided to award him a large sum to pay for the safeguarding of the cargo of two Company vessels that had just returned from the Atlantic, *de Windhond* and *de Buijsman*, and to check on the ships two or three times a day.[89] Six more letters followed: the first one from Cornelis van Wijckersloot, one of the major investors in the Amsterdam Chamber who lived in Utrecht; the second from the *bewindhebbers* of the Groningen Chamber; the third from Raey and Blaeuwenhaen who reported from The Hague; and, finally, three letters from Brazil, dating from late December and early January. The first two of those were written from Paraíba, in all likelihood to provide the directors with news of the takeover of the captaincy's main fortifications. The third one was written by Servatius Carpentier, one of the members of the Political Council in Recife, and probably contained the same official information about the expedition to Paraíba as was sent to the stadtholder and the States of Holland.[90] Typically, in the days and weeks that followed, an "Extract from the Letter of the Political Council in Brazil" appeared in print.[91] After the six letters had been dealt with, the next issue concerned a request from Recife to send fishnets of good quality. The directors ordered the *equipagemeesters* who were responsible for outfitting the chamber's ships to report to the directors in eight days' time. From their midst, they selected Van Ceulen to monitor the process on their behalf, "because he had the necessary expertise." Then, as the meeting reached its conclusion, director Jacques de La Mine suggested the ordering of more peas, beans, and rye because there had been "grave reports" on the supply of food in Brazil. The other directors agreed and decided to write to their colleagues in Zeeland, the Maas, and the Northern Quarter to send their remaining victuals to Pernambuco too as soon as possible.

Geopolitics

While the Amsterdam directors managed the demands of individual citizens and other participants in the microcosm of their local chamber, thereby communicating details of the situation in Brazil to men and women in various professions, important decisions with macrocosmic implications were being made in The Hague. Here, away from the prying eyes of the urban population, the burgomasters of Amsterdam played an intricate political game that compromised the efforts of their fellow regents at the West India House, foreshadowed the city's diminishing support for Brazil, and was deliberately not made public. The imbalance of the conflicting agendas in the urban elite would continue to rot for decades.

In 1629, the geopolitical situation in Europe and the Atlantic world had forced Philip IV to authorize Isabella, in Brussels, to seek an armistice with the Dutch. The States General managed to delay the start of formal negotiations until the Heeren XIX had finished preparing for the attack on Pernambuco. This time Amsterdam was pressing for an early truce, but Calvinist fears of a resurgence of Arminianism and Catholicism ensured that the States of Holland remained divided. Zeeland and the West India Company, meanwhile, campaigned vigorously—and at times publicly—against any accord, and by the time the news of victory in Pernambuco arrived in Europe, negotiations had broken down.[92] Two years later delegates secretly reconvened in The Hague, but, by now, the ongoing Dutch appropriation of Brazil had completely changed the complexion of the talks. Philip IV and Olivares insisted unwaveringly on the surrender of Pernambuco, for which they proposed various compensation packages. In 1633, as the Heeren XIX continued to ask for more financial support from the States of Holland, the Amsterdam authorities were even prepared to agree to a complete withdrawal from Recife—a stern warning of things to come—but there was no chance of persuading enough other towns to accept this deal. The deadlock over Brazil was the main reason the peace talks collapsed.[93]

On such an overtly political topic, there was a great discrepancy between classified and public information. Of course, opinion makers mentioned the possible repercussions of a future truce. Willem Usselincx, again, had been quick to point out how well war had served the interests of the West India Company, even before he knew of the capture of Olinda. Those in the United Provinces arguing for a truce now, he claimed, had to be either Papists, "free spirits," Remonstrants, or other apostates of the Reformed religion[94]—a line of thought that was probably supported inside the West India House, albeit in more diplomatic terms. In most of the pamphlets arguing for and against the truce, however, Brazil did not play a particularly prominent role. Newspapers did not cover the negotiations at all, and avid newspaper readers may therefore not have assigned sufficient importance to the ongoing diplomatic proceedings. Pieter Corneliszoon Hooft, for all his political nous, did not mention the negotiations in letters to his cousin Joost Baek, with whom he corresponded on a regular basis about local and global affairs. Instead he attributed great value to the military progress in Paraíba and at Cape Santo Agostinho that was being reported in newspaper bulletins and other publications.[95]

As the biased, patriotic coverage continued in the media, only those who were privy to the mechanisms of high politics were able to see that the very foundation of Dutch Brazil was under threat. Two Remonstrants exiled for their libertine views—Hugo Grotius and Willem van Oldenbarnevelt—did correspond about the truce talks, not distracted as much perhaps by the public relations efforts of the West India Company. Both men were hoping for a settlement to allow them to return to Holland. In the wake of Lonck's "wonderful" conquest, Grotius had already noted from Paris how Pernambuco would bring further differences of opinion over the negotiations.[96] And when news arrived in Brussels, three years later, of a supposed Dutch breakthrough in Brazil, Van Oldenbarnevelt immediately saw the bigger picture: "This will lead to even greater dispute over the truce," he wrote to Grotius in June 1633.[97] Two weeks later, Van Oldenbarnevelt expressed the hope that Diederick van Waerdenburgh, the colonel who had just returned home from Pernambuco, "would be able to decipher the truth about the importance of the West Indies" for the negotiators.[98] Another seven days later, however, he reckoned that "there was little movement, unless the West India Company would be compensated, which is unlikely."[99]

Only in 1636 did Brazil's crucial role in the negotiations become the main subject of a printed text, not so much in an attempt at historical accuracy but rather as a prelude to another conflict that was going to be fought out in public and would have an even greater effect on the colony's future. Published anonymously, *Reden van dat die West-Indische Compagnie oft Handelinge, niet alleen profijtelijck, maer oock noodtsaeckelijck is, tot behoudenisse van onsen Staet* (Reason why the West India Company or its trade is not only profitable, but also necessary for the endurance of our State) criticized "persons of standing and quality in our Lands" who belittled the colony's importance. "What would the writers of Histories say to later generations," the pamphleteer asked, "if we were to surrender a conquest that must be highly estimated for a treacherous and uncertain peace?"[100] The author explained that "he had not a penny of personal interest in the West India Company, but was merely a patriotic advocate of the True Faith." Still, he insisted that Brazil could be a steady and reliable foundation of the state only if it were properly defended. "Should we not be employing all our prudence and our power" he wondered, "to make sure that this foundation will be conserved, improved, and embellished in order for other Nations to seek their commerce more and more in our quarters?"[101]

This rhetorical question was a clear attack on the truce party—and once again all eyes were on Amsterdam. The city council, led by the powerful Bicker family, had been prepared to sacrifice Brazil to enable private merchants—

among them many Sephardic Jews and New Christians—to participate for their individual benefit in a trade that was circumscribed by the monopoly of the West India Company. In October 1630, the Heeren XIX and the States General had provisionally opened the Brazil trade to independent merchants to attract immigration and boost the colonial economy, on the condition that they paid taxes to the Company and used only Company ships. Four years later, in the wake of the disagreements over the truce, the edict was renewed with much lower freight rates—to the satisfaction of the Amsterdam elite. Disgruntled shareholders of the Company, in turn, became increasingly disturbed about the profits individual merchants made and wanted to see the Company's monopoly reinforced in its entirety.[102] Gradually, the contrasting positions over a truce with Spain in the early 1630s evolved into a new confrontation over the issue of free trade. In this debate, the anonymously published pamphlet of 1636 proved to be merely the opening salvo, but, for those who lacked intimate knowledge of the internal differences in preceding years, the bitter tone of the clash would be a profoundly alienating experience.

In political and military terms, the early 1630s represented the beginning of the success story of Dutch Brazil. The Company expanded its influence in the northeast, albeit rather slowly, and orchestrated a campaign of public appropriation in the Amsterdam media that built on its earlier public relations strategy. Its attempts at information management were initially successful because even "independent" media like newspapers followed the corporate storyline of consolidation and appropriation. As thousands of eyewitnesses returned from the Atlantic world, however, Dutch Brazil became a multimedia event that was difficult for any one party to control. Individual concerns of Amsterdam citizens gradually drifted away from the political narrative of the print media. The conquest of Paraíba is a case in point. While Claes Jansz Visscher was busy designing yet another news map, women whose husbands and sons had signed up for a tour in the Atlantic world communicated their everyday problems to the directors at the West India House. The preeminence of the press was further checked by developments in the highest political circles that did not yet make any headlines but that augured more vehement disagreements that would eventually spill over and drench the local discussion culture.

In the public realm, for now, the future looked bright. Newspapers continued to report how the Dutch were succeeding in making their military advantage in Brazil count, and, in 1636—effectively affirming that all was going well—the Heeren XIX decided to move on to the next phase by sending to Recife a governor-general capable of ruling over such an important province. They chose Count Johan Maurits of Nassau-Siegen, the cousin of stadtholder Frederik Hendrik, who had distinguished himself in military operations in the Netherlands, most notably in the successful recent siege of Schenkenschans. He was a zealous Calvinist who had received an exemplary humanist education at various German courts, but his pedigree as a commander was probably his most important asset in the eyes of the Company directors. The war in Brazil was far from over, and Johan Maurits was the ideal candidate for securing and expanding the Dutch sphere of influence. The Count accepted the position, arrived in Recife in January 1637, and immediately got to work.[103]

CHAPTER 4

Friction

Johan Maurits of Nassau-Siegen quickly proved that, in appointing him governor-general, the directors had made the right choice. Within a month of his arrival in Brazil, West India Company troops conquered the strategic fortress at Porto Calvo, effectively putting an end to Portuguese guerrilla resistance in the northeast. Johan Maurits's May 1638 campaign to recapture Salvador de Bahia, surrendered so meekly thirteen years earlier, constituted the climax of the news cycle and the pinnacle of optimism in Amsterdam. "In Brazil, there is good hope, that they will soon take the city of Salvador," the *Athenaeum Illustre* professor Caspar Barlaeus wrote in a private letter to Pieter Corneliszoon Hooft. "But these and other things I have understood from the weekly newspapers, who print tenacious inventions alongside truthful reports."[1] Rumors in the city's Sephardic community even suggested that Bahia had already been taken.[2] The West India Company, however, would not make a triumphant return to Salvador—the first major military disappointment since the takeover of Olinda and a first, small blemish on the reputation of the new governor-general.

During Johan Maurits's tenure, Sergipe in the south and Ceará in the north fell to the Dutch. Across the Atlantic, naval forces established a trading post in Elmina, near the chief slave-supplying areas in West Africa. Off the coast of Recife, a major Dutch fleet defeated what would turn out to be the last unified Habsburg armada intent on recapturing northeastern Brazil, under the Count of Torre, in January 1640. The subsequent Portuguese overthrow of the Spanish regime was welcomed in both Brazil and the United Provinces, but Johan Maurits was anxious to ensure that it did not bring change overnight to Luso-Dutch relations. After Dutch and Portuguese diplomats signed a ten-year truce in June 1641, delays in its ratification—in both Lisbon and The Hague—allowed the West India Company to make its military strength count on two more occasions. Dutch troops occupied Maranhão in November, while a fleet under Admiral Cornelis Jol conquered some of Portugal's most important strongholds in West Africa, such as Benguela, São Tomé, and, most significantly, the great slave depot of São Paulo de Luanda. Under Johan Maurits's rule, the Dutch Atlantic empire flourished as never before.[3]

The string of successes enabled the Amsterdam print media to continue their patriotic narrative, but by now embedded journalism had lost its primacy. Just as Johan Maurits made Dutch Brazil reach its zenith in political terms, the public face of the colony turned sour. In the world of print, tensions that had been rumbling for years came to the surface. The discussion culture that had catapulted Dutch Brazil into the public eye as a news story would now begin to reveal its darker side. Soldiers told of hunger, disease, and tropical warfare. Ministers recognized that the colony was not all that the media had promised it would be. Pamphleteers detected and exploited the discrepancy between the authorized versions of events and the stories that arose in oral accounts and private correspondence. It was impossible to reverse this trend because, by the 1640s, practically everyone in Holland's urban network had access to eyewitness information. As the audience broadened, the encouragement for publishers and printers with commercial motives to discuss the colony increased, but the tone of the narrative changed. The broadening of the information flow coincided with vocal discord over the future of Brazil at the highest political level, and occasionally pamphleteers and ministers chose to thematize the political gridlock in public for their own purposes. The very open confrontation between monopolists and free traders heralded the destructive potential of the discussion culture that would come to full maturity in the late 1640s.

Broadening the Audience

Johann Philipp Mulheiser from Bad Bergzabern in southwestern Germany was one of thousands of soldiers who traveled to Brazil during Johan Maurits's tenure. He had studied theology in Leiden but returned home to the war-ravaged Palatinate to fight under Bernard of Saxe-Weimar in the battle of Breisach. In 1639, he enlisted as an ensign with the West India Company and departed for Brazil as part of the auxiliary force of 2,500 men under Cornelis Jol and Jan Lichthart that the Heeren XIX sent to Recife in the wake of the defeat of Torre's armada. Mulheiser's tour of duty in the colony lasted four years, most of which he spent in the immediate vicinity of Recife and on Itamaracá. In October 1640, he participated in a naval expedition that captured a Spanish ship with seventy-seven African slaves on board, but generally he stayed ashore, commanding a small company that patrolled the sugar plantations in Pernambuco. When the population of Maranhão revolted against Johan Maurits's regime in late 1642, Mulheiser was one of many infantry troops sent to Fort Ceulen on the Rio Grande estuary, where he remained for fourteen months. In August 1644, he returned to the United Provinces as part of the governor-general's homebound fleet.[4]

Mulheiser was an educated, highly articulate man. He would go on to translate political pamphlets from German into Dutch in the 1650s and was even considered a minor poet in the vibrant literary milieu in Dordrecht, where he settled down after returning from the Atlantic world. Yet he never wrote an account of his time in Brazil, and he would have been forgotten like so many of his comrades had it not been for his *album amicorum*, which he took to Brazil and which he continued to use after his return to Europe.[5] The album contains just over one hundred names of friends collected in the colony, including those of high-ranking officers like Elias Herckmans, Jan Lichthart, Pieter Mortamer, and Adriaen van Bullestrate, the physician Willem Piso, minister Vicente Joachim Soler, and even Johan Maurits himself, who signed his name below his motto "Qua Patet Orbis" in late August 1640.[6] The remaining names Mulheiser collected indicate the many different ways in which personal relations could be forged in Brazil. A certain William Scot, garrisoned at Fort Ernestus in Mauritsstad, hailed "my dear Mulheiser" as "a poet among the Barbarians." Some inscriptions included mottos in Latin, Greek, or Hebrew, like those of Nicolaus Vogellius, *predikant* in Porto Calvo, and Samuel Bachiler, an Anglican clergyman in Recife. The album as a whole provides ample evidence of the multinational, multiconfessional, and ethnically diverse make-up of Brazil's colonial population under Dutch rule.[7]

The album's greatest value, however, lies in the more than four hundred names it contains from the period *after* Mulheiser's return to the United Provinces. The sheer number of names is a clear indication of how many people in towns like Amsterdam had direct access to eyewitness information from Brazil. Within twelve months of his return in August 1644, Mulheiser obtained 112 inscriptions for his album—an average of more than two per week—in every major town in Holland and Zeeland. As a former theology student, he arranged meetings with *predikanten* everywhere he went, and he may well have informed them of the difficulties of the Reformed missionaries he had encountered in Brazil.[8] In October 1644, in Amsterdam, Mulheiser met Gerardus and

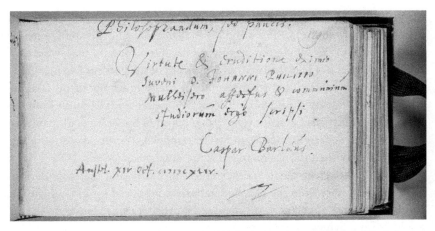

FIGURE 29. Caspar Barlaeus, inscription "Philosophandum, sed paucis." In Johann Philip Mulheiser, *Album Amicorum*, fol. 129ʳ. Courtesy of Koninklijke Bibliotheek, The Hague, KW 129 F 6.

Isaac Vossius, orientalist Jacob Golius, and Caspar Barlaeus, who around the same time started working on his hagiographic account of Johan Maurits's reign in Recife, *Rerum per Octennium in Brasilia* (Figure 29).[9] A few months later, in Leiden, Mulheiser also met Antonius Thysius the Younger, who at the time was preparing a book on glorious naval battles, *Historia Navalis*, which devoted many chapters to admirals with whom the German ensign had served.[10] Through such meetings—and there must have been many more that were left unrecorded—oral accounts of Brazil slowly infiltrated the printed realm.

What exactly Mulheiser and his contacts discussed informally is of course unknown, and the ensign must have told different stories of his time in the Atlantic world to different people, but that they all talked about Brazil is certain: alongside predictable expressions of friendship, many of Mulheiser's contacts acknowledge in writing having heard from him about his adventures. Their inscriptions with references to the ensign's experiences in Brazil give a tantalizing impression of the wide scope of an "oral Atlantic" in the United Provinces. In The Hague, in 1645, Mulheiser encountered Holland pensionary Jacob Cats and several members of the exiled Heidelberg court, including Elizabeth Stuart, the daughter of James I. The following year, again in The Hague, he spoke with the English diplomat William Boswell, and a few years later he also met the Swedish envoy Harald Appelboom, right at the time, in 1653, when the latter was officially mediating between the United Provinces and Portugal.[11]

Mulheiser also must have discussed Brazil with authors who had written poems about the colony in the late 1620s and 1630s, like Jacobus Revius and Dionysius Spranckhuysen.[12] Yet, alongside celebrities, the album contains many names of ordinary people, like fellow citizens of Dordrecht or the party of five men from Bad Bergzabern who visited Mulheiser at his house or several of his relatives who came to Holland.[13] Also in Dordrecht, Mulheiser received a visit from the cartographer Cornelis Golijath, who thanked him in Spanish for his companionship before departing once again for Pernambuco; as time passed more former comrades visited the ensign to reminisce about a shared past.[14]

Just how different the men's experiences in Brazil (and therefore the stories they told) were from the polished narratives produced in print by the authorities becomes apparent in the unedited journal of Peter Hansen Hajstrup, a soldier from Schleswig, who spent nearly ten years in Brazil in the service of the Chamber of Amsterdam.[15] Hansen arrived in Recife a few months after Mulheiser had gone home and a few months before the Portuguese revolt would erupt in June 1645.[16] The themes he confided to his private diary are universal: hunger, fear, the threat of treason, and injuries sustained in battles with the Portuguese were some of the conscripts' most pressing concerns. Danger was everywhere. Hansen almost died on one of his first expeditions into the interior when his survival was ensured only by a Brazilian ally who helped him swim to safety across a river. Once, after being overwhelmed by a force of more than eight hundred Luso-Brazilians, only a handful soldiers returned to Recife alive—an example of the hyperbolic lining of some of the personal memories, but a tall story to be told at home all the same. Several years later, when Portuguese soldiers attacked an *engenho* that Hansen and several others were assigned to defend, the Company forces survived by setting fire to the remaining gunpowder. One bullet went through Hansen's hat, and he escaped with minor injuries above his eye. The following year, he was wounded more seriously at the first Battle of Guararapes (1648) and had to be bandaged and nursed by a comrade from Schleswig. The injuries ruled him out of the fateful second Battle of Guararapes in February 1649, but he subsequently managed to resume his duties.[17]

Hansen also reported regular bust-ups between the troops, often as a result of an evening of heavy drinking, and frankly admitted his own active involvement in these brawls. On one of his first days in Brazil, while standing guard at the entrance gate to the new bridge that connected Recife to Antonio Vaz, Hansen struck a lieutenant with his rifle and had to appear before a military court the following day. Because of his inexperience, he was released with a reprimand. The Company could not afford to be too strict with its men, as the future of the colony depended on them and it was difficult to recruit more orderly troops. Yet Hansen showed few signs of improving his conduct: on seven occasions, according to his notes, he got involved in fights with fellow soldiers. Four times he was arrested and locked up, one time he killed an ensign with a blow to his head, once he pulled a sword on a colleague and challenged him to a duel, and once he shot an innocent bystander in the leg when quarrelling with another soldier from Schleswig.[18] Multiple stories of similar misconduct must have reached Amsterdam and other towns to the dismay of shareholders and pious Calvinists hoping for a prosperous Protestant settlement in the South Atlantic.

Hansen, moreover, was unapologetic and unashamed of his actions. He censored his diary on two occasions—the only sections he did not consider appropriate for his likely readership of relatives. For both episodes, Hansen switched from German to Portuguese, a language of which he must have picked up the basics in Brazil, and on both occasions the tales had a sexual connotation. In the first instance, Hansen reminisced about a girlfriend who had passed away; four years later he aimed to conceal the story about a fellow soldier whose African mistress had had a stillborn child.[19] Whereas for Hansen there was a clear distinction between such personal affairs and more public brawls, both types of mischief were conspicuously absent from more stylized travel accounts that were edited before publication in Amsterdam. Even worse, perhaps, Hansen's misbehavior does not appear to have been out of the ordinary. It certainly did not form an obstacle to his rise through the ranks of the West India Company. Having arrived in Brazil as a soldier in December 1644, he was promoted to the rank of corporal two years later and eventually became *monsterschrijver* in November 1647. A *monsterschrijver* was responsible for the administration of a company—and had to keep records of payment.[20] Being able to write and perform simple calculations must have been two of Peter Hansen Hajstrup's more useful traits, and he remained in the colony until the surrender of Recife.

Slavery

Around half of Dutch Brazil's colonial population in the mid-1640s consisted of soldiers like Mulheiser and Hansen, but the flourishing colony attracted others too. Amsterdam notarial documents of the late 1630s and early 1640s indicate that dozens of local carpenters, masons, glassblowers, coppersmiths, and bakers left the city on short-term contracts to build a prosperous future in Pernambuco, creating ever more personal connections between colonists and family members who remained at home waiting for money and news.[21] By the time Johan Maurits's governance in Mauritsstad had come to an end, an official census of Dutch Brazil showed that, alongside thousands of soldiers, roughly three thousand freemen and citizens of Recife, Itamaracá, Paraíba, and Rio Grande had Dutch or northern European roots. The total estimated population was around fifteen thousand, a figure that also included Sephardic Jews, loyal Indians and a rapidly increasing number of African slaves.[22]

Although slaves were an everyday feature in Brazil, the soldiers' accounts—published or unpublished—generally make little mention of them. On one occasion, in Rio Grande, Hansen commanded a small force of Brazilians and loyal Africans that spent a week tracking down four runaway "Negroß," eventually arresting them with his typical abrasiveness and then selling them on for his own profit.[23] Despite prior public condemnations of the slave trade as typically "Iberian" and "Catholic"—for example by Willem Usselincx and Dierick Ruiters—slaves could count on very little sympathy in the Dutch Atlantic world. Once the Heeren XIX realized that there would be no Brazilian sugar without an African labor force, any lingering moral objections were abandoned. Slaves captured at sea by Company ships had already been sold for a profit since the early 1620s, and, from 1636 onward, seemingly unimpeded by criticism or dissent at home, the Company began transporting slaves from Guinea and later Angola to Pernambuco where they were put to work by the *moradores* on the sugar plantations. Upon arrival in the colony, Johan Maurits called for an increase in the trade, explaining once again to the directors that "it is not possible to accomplish anything in Brazil without slaves." In the ten-year period from 1636 to 1645, before the Portuguese revolt brought the trade to a halt, the Dutch imported more than twenty-five thousand slaves into Brazil.[24]

It is difficult to gauge whether, and if so to what extent, the Company's participation in the transatlantic slave trade was denounced at home. In the regular print media, the activities of the West India Company in West Africa commanded little attention. In Amsterdam, the urban population may have occasionally seen Africans on the streets but not *as* slaves, nor did they witness the gruesome practices of the middle passage or the sale of black men and women on the market in Recife.[25] Yet some in the city certainly felt that the trade in humans was morally wrong, and it is conceivable that echoes of the disapproval voiced a little more loudly in earlier decades could still be heard. The popular Amsterdam poet Gerbrand Adriaensz Bredero had included a clear condemnation of the slave trade in his burlesque play *Moortje* (Little Moor), an adaptation of Terence's comedy *Eunuchus* first performed in 1615 and printed two years later:

> Inhumane custom! Godless rascality!
> That men sell human beings, into horselike slavery!
> In this city too there are those, who engage in such trade
> in Farnabock: but it cannot be concealed from God.[26]

At the time of writing, the passage referred to Sephardic Jews in Amsterdam who traded with their compatriots in Olinda, but by the time the Dutch were in command of "Farnabock" the biting reference to local involvement in the transport of slaves to Recife must have made for some uneasiness among the more principled theatergoers. *Moortje*, a much-loved play ever since its conception, appears to have grown in popularity at precisely the moment the West India Company entered the trade. In September and October 1637, the "Old" Chamber of Rhetoric in Amsterdam brought Bredero's play back to the stage—not in the Schouwburg, the city's grand theater on the Keizersgracht that was not finished until January of the next year, but in the fencing school that served as a makeshift theater during the building works. In 1638, a new edition of the play even appeared in print, referring to the recent performances on its title page, and further editions followed in 1644 and 1646. In January 1646, *Moortje* premiered in the Amsterdam Schouwburg, filling the theater for three consecutive nights. Until the end of the decade, the play was performed at least once a year, presumably in front of a sizeable urban audience since it yielded high ticket revenues.[27]

When the West India Company was founded, the directors had agreed, after consulting compliant Calvinist theologians, that the trade in human beings was morally not justified. At the time, there were also compelling economic reasons not to enter the trade. Hugo Grotius, however, argued in *De Jure Belli ac Pacis* that classical authors had defended slavery as an obvious consequence of a just war, considering that the only alternative was the murder of captured enemies. Most theologians too accepted that slavery was a legitimate human condition, justifying it by quoting Genesis 9:20–27, which recounted how Ham had dishonored his father Noah, who subsequently condemned Ham's son Canaan and his entire lineage to perpetual servitude.[28] By the time the Company entered the trade in West Africa, ministers rallied to validate the change in policy.[29] No one did so more forcefully than Godfried

FIGURE 30. Godfried Udemans, *'t Geestelyck Roer van 't Coopmans schip*, 2nd ed. Zierikzee 1640, title page. Courtesy of Koninklijke Bibliotheek, The Hague, KW 516 E 17.

Udemans, a Reformed minster from Zierikzee who in 1638 published his influential treatise *'t Geestelyck roer van 't coopmans schip* (The Spiritual Helm of the Merchant's Vessel) in which he directly addressed the Heeren XIX and discussed the matter of slavery at length (Figure 30).[30]

Udemans started by acknowledging that slavery was a "grave issue," pointing out that any form of servitude was contrary to God having created human beings in His own image. But then he cited Genesis 9 and several passages from the New Testament that insisted that "whosoever committed sin shall be the servant of sin." He who was sinful and refused to obey the "sweet yoke of his creator," Udemans explained, deserved nothing more than "to fall into the dirtiest and most profound slavery."[31] This provided him with the stepping-stone to argue that Christians could not enslave fellow Christians but *could* enslave heathens justly brought into slavery, for example during a just war as Grotius had argued or if they had been purchased from their parents or other honest masters for a fair price. He used the example of Angola, where, according to what he had been told, this was common practice. He also perhaps foresaw that slaves procured in Guinea would not satisfy the demand in Dutch Brazil for African labor. This practice, Udemans claimed, was affirmed in Leviticus 25:44–46, which stated that "both thy bondmen, and thy bondmaids, which thou shalt have, [shall be] of the heathen that are round about you; of them ye shall buy bondmen and bondmaids . . . and they shall be your possession." But, and this was crucial to Udemans's legitimation of slavery, these laborers had to be treated with respect and had to be introduced to the True Faith. If they were "tyrannized," as they were under their Habsburg masters, the slaves were entitled to run away, and Udemans warned the Company not to sell slaves to "Spaniards, Portuguese, or other crude people." Moreover, converted slaves should be freed after several years of service.[32]

This section of Udemans's ethical compass would soon be at odds with corporate policy: the West India Company sold the majority of African slaves to Catholic *moradores* and made little effort to convert slaves to Protestantism.[33] Yet, as a whole, *'t Geestelijk roer* served as a useful justification for the volte-face in the Dutch attitude toward slavery. The treatise was revised and reprinted in 1640 and again in 1655, which can be interpreted either as a testimony to Udemans's success in explaining the rationale behind the slave trade or as an indication of the need to reiterate his message to a readership that was not immediately or collectively convinced. From the scattered evidence, it seems that the Dutch conscience was not entirely soothed overnight. Even after the appearance of *'t Geestelyck roer*, when Cornelis Jol set out to conquer

São Paulo de Luanda and the Dutch slave trade reached an early peak in quantitative terms, there were traces of embarrassment or at least appeals to public discomfort over the trade. One Amsterdam pamphleteer in 1640 rather awkwardly explained that the "trade in blacks from Angola, Guinea &c. is the seed that the Company must sow in order to reap dividends from Pernambuco, and . . . it cannot be put into question"—apparently some still did—"that the revenues will increase with the import of more slaves."[34]

Three years later, a self-proclaimed loyal supporter of the West India Company, countering the pleas of private investors to open up the lucrative slave trade in Angola, wondered whether individual merchants "could be trusted to sell slaves to planters instructing them in the Reformed religion; or, instead, would they be more intent on maximizing profits on their bodies, without caring for their souls?" The Company ensured that the Africans were sold to [Reformed] Christians, the pamphleteer reckoned, and the trade "was not appropriate for private persons."[35] Although by now the Dutch trade in slaves was booming, both on the Gold Coast and in Angola, the anonymous author apparently believed that there were still readers in Holland who would sympathize with this kind of argument, and he was right. Willem Usselincx, now well into his seventies, accused the States General in October 1644 of "stealing" rather than buying African slaves and of treating them badly on the sugar plantations. Another five years later the armchair chronicler Jacques Joosten compared the slave trade in Dutch Brazil to the Ottoman trade in Christian slaves, "although the Turks in general treat the Christians better."[36] The Heeren XIX, however, had moved on from any moral issues over the transport and sale of human beings. In the late 1640s, when circumstances forced them to allow private investors a share of the Angola trade, they issued a decree that contained no further allusions to the spiritual well-being of the slaves and that unequivocally regarded them as commodities.[37]

To Go Public or Not to Go Public: Religious Dilemmas

Disgruntlement over the ethics of the transatlantic slave trade remained on the fringes of public debate and never matured into a heated discussion, but the issue touched on the more widely shared concern of Reformed orthodoxy. Opinionated ministers, in their sermons and writings, criticized the perceived lack of Calvinist zeal in the colony and the unprecedented religious tolerance that the Company and Johan Maurits extended to Roman Catholics and Jews.

Toleration, in the Dutch Atlantic world, was deeply ambivalent.[38] In 1622, in a document intended to attract capital for the newly established company, an anonymous supporter of the Heeren XIX had plainly stated that the Company would introduce the gentiles and savages to the Holy Scripture.[39] Although the Company charter of the year before had not mentioned the projected conversions to Calvinism—to the disappointment and anger of Reformed ideologists of Atlantic ventures—many would-be shareholders nevertheless expected the directors to be committed to the Reformed cause. Nearly half the directors in the Amsterdam Chamber served as elders in the local *kerkenraad* (consistory), where they would have taken part in weekly or monthly debates about missionary work and confessional orthodoxy in Brazil—at least until 1636 when the church founded a local "Indies Committee" for this purpose.[40] Even then, there were always local directors among the deputies *ad res Indicas*. The Company and the consistory and *classis* (presbytery) of Amsterdam interacted regularly, and together they nominated suitable ministers for the various congregations in Brazil. Yet, despite their concerted efforts, their influence on religious uniformity across the ocean was limited. Again, as with the issue of slavery, the reality of Dutch Brazil was not as straightforward as the media-fueled expectation of the 1620s had suggested, leading to domestic antagonism on yet another topic.[41]

Godfried Udemans's vision of the Dutch mission in Brazil echoed the views of Willem Teellinck as expressed fourteen years earlier. "To build the House of the Lord well in both Indies," Udemans wrote in *'t Geestelyck Roer*, "there must be good order and discipline."[42] This, in theory, was what everyone wanted, including some of the more "libertine" directors of the Amsterdam Chamber. Both the East and West India Companies had the obligation to bring everyone in their service into the public Church. Christians, of course, were among these, to be convinced "with friendly admonitions and good examples, and if that is insufficient, with fines and other penalties," referring to the command in Luke 14:23 to "goe out into the high wayes and hedges, and compell them to come in, that my house may be filled." Eventually non-Christians too had to be forced to go to church, by all means necessary. "As disinclined children," Udemans explained, and "out of fear of political might, they have to be pulled towards the Church, expecting that over time, the Lord shall make their hearts willing, and draw them to hearing his Word." The conversion of Brazilians and Africans, then, was a matter of the highest importance. "If the authorities fail to do so," Udemans warned, "the blindness of the pagans and the unruliness and wickedness of the Company servants will impede the construction of the Lord's Church."[43]

A second, closely related source of anxiety was the survival of Catholicism in Brazil. Udemans acknowledged that, like slavery, this was a *casus conscientiae* for the Heeren XIX and for the Political Council in Recife. But here the minister was not prepared to sacrifice any existing moral standards for the well-being of the Company. "Concerning the issue whether one should allow the Portuguese living under our jurisdiction in the East and West Indies, for political reasons, to openly worship according to the rules of the Papist Religion? To that we answer unequivocally: No."[44] Such a refutation was doubtlessly appreciated by suspicious Calvinist readers at home, but at the same time it was clearly at odds with Johan Maurits's policies in Brazil. Just one year before *'t Geestelyck Roer* appeared, the governor-general had permitted the return of the mendicant orders, with the single exception of the Jesuits (and even this was not strictly adhered to). Only in 1639, when the rumored arrival of the Count of Torre's fleet led to increased nervousness in the colony, did Johan Maurits round up the remaining Benedictines, Carmelites, and Franciscans on grounds of the threat to security and have them confined to Itamaracá and then deported to the Caribbean. To Udemans's chagrin, the *moradores* and other Portuguese inhabitants of Dutch Brazil were left untouched.[45]

The practice of toleration was publicized sufficiently widely in Amsterdam for the Sephardic Jews to take notice. They left in substantial numbers for Brazil, welcomed by the accountants of the West India Company because of their crucial role as investors and intermediaries in the Atlantic sugar network. In 1636, to underline their importance to the colony, the Company gave them permission to build a synagogue, an unprecedented form of religious liberty not extended to Jews anywhere else in the Americas.[46] Once again, the Reformed establishment complained. At a meeting of the Classis of Recife in October 1638, ministers agreed that "the great freedom of Jews and Papists, the unruliness of the 'Negros', the desanctification of the Sabbath, and cursing and swearing" should be prohibited once and for all.[47] Nearly six years later, however, the same body complained that slaves still ignored the Sabbath, that the placards against swearing and against open Jewish worship needed to be renewed, and that priests continued to preach in public churches, organized processions under the pretext of funerals, constructed crucifixes, and built chapels and churches without the approval of the authorities.[48] The ministers sent letters of protest to the Heeren XIX and the Classis of Amsterdam, who shared their concerns. But since the colony needed Reformed settlers to change its religious complexion more lastingly, few mentions were made of these ongoing problems in print. Once again, public representations in the print media and private tales of Brazil, by now abundantly available in Holland, diverged. Ironically, new immigrants to Dutch Brazil in these years were mostly yet more Sephardic Jews from Amsterdam who continued to identify strongly with the colony, inspired by their *haham* Menasseh ben Israel who as "a Portuguese with a Batavian spirit" even dedicated two books to the West India Company.[49]

The writings of Vicente Joachim Soler are a good example of how, amid the religious disarray, the clergy tried to keep up appearances. Soler, an instrumental figure in the Brazilian church, was an orthodox Calvinist and a staunch supporter of Johan Maurits. He was born in Valencia, became an Augustinian friar, but then converted to Calvinism in France before applying for service in the West India Company.[50] In early 1636, he arrived in Pernambuco. Three years later, the Huguenot bookseller Boudewijn du Preys in Amsterdam—himself an early investor in the West India Company—published an elaborate letter Soler had written to a group of fellow Protestants in Normandy. The letter, translated into Dutch, was intended to attract more Reformed souls to Brazil, as Soler too regarded immigration as the ideal medicine for the colony's sorry moral state. In the pamphlet, *Cort ende sonderlingh verhael* (Short and Remarkable Story), Soler gave an optimistic account of the conversions of Brazilian Indians in the *aldeias*.[51] "It is true that the kingdom of God grows among the Indians," he wrote. "At our last meeting, they spontaneously sent representatives of their people to ask for some of our ministers." And there was more good news:

> When the inhabitants of the villages wish to marry or baptize their children, they go to the nearest church, or the minister goes to their village if this is a long way. Each time the army returns, I marry and baptize many people. They now adopt Christian names instead of using the names of birds and fishes, as they used to."

The more notorious segments of the colonial population also profited from Calvinist attempts at civilization. Usually, Soler continued, "the blacks mix like dogs. Now they are made to marry, albeit at the cost of great effort. I often marry them, and as a result they bring me their children to baptize." And there was even a glimmer of hope for the remaining Catholics:

> On the [Portuguese Papists], I have already written saying that they are now beginning to be more submissive, for at the start of my time here they were so stubborn that they would not speak to us. They are now friendly, and no longer refuse to hear preaching.[52]

The rest of the pamphlet was devoted to a buoyant description of Dutch Brazil as a tropical version of the Garden of Eden—at a time when in reality the population of Recife, Soler's place of residence, experienced constant sorrow and frequent bouts of hunger and dearth.

Private letters by Soler, however, provide a unique insight into the discrepancy between the public image of Dutch Brazil he attempted to fashion and his true worries. Written between 1636 and 1643 to the *bewindhebbers* of the Company's Zeeland chamber and to his friend André Rivet, professor of theology in Leiden, they are much more negative in tone and sometimes downright depressing regarding the prospects of Protestantism in the colony. They are also extremely critical of the toleration extended to other religious groups. Shortly after his arrival, in June 1636, Soler wrote to the directors in Zeeland:

> There is no sign of fear of God, no justice, and vices thrive. In one word, I seem to be in Sodom or still worse. Most ministers remain silent about all this; some, instead of tilling the soil of the Lord full of weeds, cultivate the lands and fields which are acquired at the expense of your Company.[53]

At home, the Amsterdam classis shared Soler's views. Even though there were only ten to twelve ministers in Brazil at any given time, the Classis was forced to recall at least two preachers whose conduct was unacceptable.[54] There was a brief upturn in fortunes in early 1638, a few months before Soler wrote the letter that was eventually published in Amsterdam, but, by the time that letter appeared in print, Soler was again complaining about the lack of discipline:

> The Indians . . . receive no education. Due to the shortage of ministers, the Dutch call on the Catholic priests to baptize their children and bless their marriages. The papists enjoy the same freedom as they do in Rome and practice their superstition in five temples in the village of Olinda.[55]

The situation progressively deteriorated. "The Jews multiply," Soler wrote to Rivet in ominous fashion in May 1640. They "enjoy great freedom and take on airs more than ever. It is as clear as the Sun that they ruin the traffic, suck the blood of the people, frustrate and violate the Company." Even Johan Maurits himself, Soler claimed, "declares to nurture a great hatred" for the Jews but found it politically impossible to check them.[56]

At times of friction, the Company efforts at information management backfired. While political and economic reasons prevented the directors from eliminating heterodoxy, the campaign to evangelize and catechize the Tupi in Brazil was also frustrated by the Classis of Amsterdam. The church superiors prohibited the printing and distribution of a trilingual catechism Soler and his colleague David van Dooreslaer had written (in Dutch, Portuguese, and Tupi), "as much for its theses as for the material used; and also because it was very dangerous to deviate even the slightest from the old and established formulas." The theological inaccuracies in the Brazilian catechism caused a public row in Holland in 1641 when the West India Company ordered an Enkhuizen printer to produce the compendium anyway, regardless of the Church's objections. When the catechisms were finally shipped, however, they were not being put to use.[57] A 1645 inventory of books in Recife reveals that 2,951 copies (of an estimated print run of 3,000) still collected dust in a local warehouse four years after the controversy had ended. For these and other reasons, Udemans and Soler criticized the assembled authorities for having failed to bring order, discipline, and Protestant ideology to Brazil. In the fall of 1645, when news of the rebellion by Portuguese sugar planters reached Amsterdam, Reformed ministers were among the first to express their bitterness about recent developments in Brazil.[58]

"The Explosion of the Public Sphere"

Disputes over the (im)morality of the slave trade, the (dis)honorable conduct of the colonists, the excessive religious freedom given to Jews and Catholics, and the lack of zeal in converting Indians and African slaves were all overshadowed by the public thunderstorm over the issue of free trade in Brazil, a political conflict so full of resentment that it had a detrimental effect on relations between the different chambers of the West India Company. Advocates for the monopoly, often from Zeeland, were pitted against the free trade faction around the Amsterdam magistrates, as the conflict laid bare the internal divisions already apparent during the Truce negotiations of the early 1630s. When the States General allowed the Company to reimpose the monopoly in December 1636, merchants in Amsterdam were convinced that envy of their riches in the other chambers had prompted this move.[59] Local pamphleteers in favor of free trade sharpened their pens. For the next eighteen months, readers would be treated to one of the most bitter pamphlet wars of the Dutch Golden Age. In the maelstrom of mutual antipathy, potentially unifying reports of the Company's military endeavors and prudent leadership—so dominant at home when Portuguese resistance had threatened Dutch expansion in Brazil—disappeared from view.

Two pamphlets written and printed anonymously in 1637 capture the acrimonious atmosphere of the debate. The first, *Vertoogh by een Lief-hebber des Vaderlants vertoont* (Disputation by a Supporter of the Fatherland) championed the cause of free trade (Figure 31). The author immediately set the tone in the salutation, announcing how he would demonstrate that the "unfounded assertions of the *Zeeuwen* and other peripheral chambers to close the free trade" would ruin the entire Company. The directors, so far, had sent only soldiers to Brazil—something that must have struck a chord in Dutch society—but no traders. "Will these soldiers alone, with their weekly pay of fifteen *stuivers*, consume enough to empty the Company's warehouses, and bring about the promised riches," the pamphleteer asked his readers. "Or was the Company driven by the honor of possessing such a vast land"? Perhaps, the author thought, this was fitting for a prince, but, for those who administered the resources of widows and orphans, it was a form of godless arrogance.[60] He proceeded by categorizing those in charge of the Company as *conquesteurs*, a spiteful allusion to the way in which a previous generation of Dutch pamphleteers had traditionally portrayed Spain under Philip II. The Company had naively expected Portuguese colonists to hand over more than half their revenues, but in response the planters had brought their sugar mills to a standstill, planting grains and cotton instead. This reaction was perfectly understandable, the author argued. The Duke of Alva's levy of a much lower tax had seen the king of Spain lose the entire Netherlands. Free trade would solve all these problems at once, as it would bring not only investments but also peace, more settlers, and eventually Dutch ownership of the Pernambucan *engenhos*.[61]

The identification of defenders of the monopoly with the Duke of Alva, the epitome of evil in Dutch patriotic thought, was vile enough to warrant a strong response. The second pamphlet, written by a self-styled "investigator of the truth," was published under the title *Examen over 't Vertoogh teghen het ongefondeerde ende schadelijck sluyten der Vryen Handel in Brasil* (Assessment of the Disputation Against the Unsubstantiated and Harmful Closure of Free Trade in Brazil), which indicated that this was a direct reply to the scornful attack of the

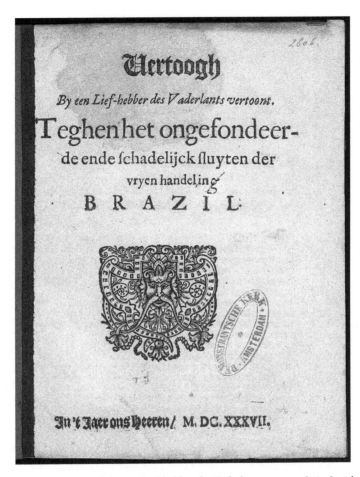

FIGURE 31. *Vertoogh by een Lief-hebber des Vaderlants vertoont* [1637], title page. Courtesy of Koninklijke Bibliotheek, The Hague, Kn. 4514.

Amsterdam-led free-trade brigade (Figure 32). The author took offense at the patronizing reference to the non-Amsterdam chambers of the Company as "peripheral," an epithet that would thus only acquire more appeal among urban pamphleteers. For this and other reasons, the author realized, intelligent readers would not believe the arguments put forward in the *Vertoogh*, but he wanted to make sure that "simple" people would not get the impression that the *Vertoogh* was correct for want of a reply. Its readers, after all, had been treated to little more than "passions without any style, order, substance, and common sense,

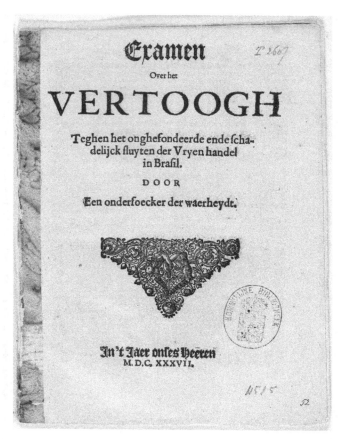

FIGURE 32. *Examen over 't Vertoogh teghen het ongefondeerde ende schadelijck sluyten der Vryen Handel in Brasil* [1637], title page. Courtesy of Koninklijke Bibliotheek, The Hague, Kn. 4515.

that was full of exclamations, vanity, extreme utterances, and threats."[62] The decision to reimpose the monopoly, the author insisted, may have been subjected to factional politics within the Company, but it had been made by the States General in the interest of the fatherland, and it merely confirmed the charter of 1621. Those who now proposed to break the Company's control of the Brazil trade could be driven only by "insatiable greed."[63] Finally, nobody in his right mind would have brought up the Duke of Alva, which led the author to suspect that the *Vertoogh* had been written by a "Portuguese stranger" to Dutch affairs, a reckless fomenter of hostile sentiments.[64]

Whereas federal unity had characterized the phase of warfare against Habsburg Brazil, the Dutch now accused each other of sympathizing with the enemy from Portugal or being more greedy than Alva had ever been. In the *Examen*'s final paragraph, the author professed to assume that his reply had settled the issue and that harmony between the opposing factions would now return, but he certainly realized that the truth was altogether different.[65] The embittered cycle of accusations and increasing resentment that now accompanied the political disagreements jeopardized the future of both the Company and its colony in Brazil. Readers of the arguments for and against free trade realized this as well. A political animal like Hugo Grotius sensed the danger of the issue very early on. Nine days before the States General was to unleash the anger of private investors in Amsterdam by reinstating the monopoly in December 1636, Grotius asked Nicolaas van Reigersberch to keep him informed about the resolution. He indicated that what was being said in Amsterdam, in his perception, was nothing but harmful.[66] The polarization over the issue of free trade in the United Provinces even reached the Dutch expat community in Paris, some of whom "are in passionate disagreement with everything from Holland," Grotius wrote to Van Reigersberch. "I myself would like to hear the arguments from both sides before giving a balanced judgment."[67]

Grotius did not depend on printed matter for information since Van Reigersberch was a High Court judge in The Hague who had good connections. In May 1637, he informed Grotius that there was "a bit too much animosity from both sides," but, four weeks later, he reported that a settlement had been reached, that the monopoly would be preserved as the States General had ordered, and that Bahia was about to fall into Dutch hands—thus reverting to the more standard form of reporting in an attempt to close the book on internal strife.[68] Yet it was probably in the wake of this provisional settlement that *Vertoogh* and *Examen* were published, and things truly got out of hand. Arnoldus Buchelius, who also had inside knowledge, implied in his diary that these "little books, both in manuscript and in print" were being studied by the authorities before a decision would be made—an unusual piece of evidence that the Dutch were on occasion truly "governed by opinion."[69] In early 1638, Van Reigersberch wrote to Grotius that the conflict rumbled on and that the ongoing disagreement "caused very great damage" to the Company.[70] Grotius, pragmatic and involved as ever, proposed opening up the trade in some commodities, while other goods should remain within the confines of the monopoly. If the Company would agree, he suggested a trial period to find out if such a solution would be viable.[71] In April, Van Reigersberch announced to Grotius that the Heeren XIX, urged on from Brazil by Johan Maurits, had reached the same conclusion: slaves, ammunition, and brazilwood remained exclusively in the hands of the Company, while private investors were allowed to participate in the sugar trade. The directors had reached this solution without any further mediation from the federal government, and this, Van Reigersberch wrote, "pleases not only the States General but also the shareholders."[72] Yet the public row had brutally exposed the frailties of Dutch Brazil and its governing body. Rumors of further disputes were difficult to suppress, and, in December 1638, Van Reigersberch intimated to Grotius that "the English think it may well go wrong in Brazil, and others too tell me that the policy of the West India Company is turning sloppy as a result of discord."[73] In 1639, for the first time in many years, the Amsterdam burgomasters explicitly prohibited the writing and publishing of slanderous booklets and tidings.[74]

Elizabeth Eisenstein, in a recent study, talks about "the media explosion of the 1640s" where she discusses the printed testimonies of antagonism during the English Civil War.[75] The situation in the United Provinces concerning the public disagreements about Brazil at the same time was remarkably similar. The combination of a free press, a topic that had generated shared moments of delight and disappointment for close to two decades, and a very public spat that was, on the one hand, familiar—because it involved the politics of particularism at the heart of so many issues in the Dutch Golden Age—but at the same time new because of the level of resentment created great distress throughout the country.[76] Small wonder, then, that pamphleteers in England, when lamenting the alarming increase of friction at home, complained that public opinion in London was being "too much Amsterdamnified by severall opinions."[77] Once the debate over free trade had been settled to the satisfaction of all parties, the astonishment that a storyline that had united the country for so long had now become a divisive issue was so strong that the apprehension just would not go away. Throughout the later 1640s, as the West India Company's position in Brazil gradually deteriorated, the differences of opinion between the regents in Amsterdam, arguing for peace with Spain, and their colleagues in Zeeland, who wanted the war to go on, continued to center on the topic of Brazil. Other divisive issues were instinctively absorbed in this battle between the two leading maritime provinces. The half-hearted efforts of the Heeren XIX to set up a merger with the VOC in the mid-1640s further added to the impression—held by Buchelius, Van Reigersberch, and others—that the directors lacked the competence to deal with the complicated issues at hand.[78]

Paying the Price

Hesitant policies and bad publicity affected the value of West India Company shares on the Amsterdam exchange. The share price, nominally set at one hundred at the Company's foundation in 1621, peaked in the late 1620s and early 1630s after Piet Heyn's capture of the New Spain treasure fleet and the conquest of Olinda. It fluctuated as the Dutch troops were first confined to Recife and then defeated Albuquerque's guerrilla forces, dropped during the heated debate over free trade, and soared to 134 percent of its starting value in May 1640, when news arrived that Johan Maurits had successfully defended Pernambuco against Torre's armada. At the end of the same month, however, Nicolaas van Reigersberch noted that "West Indian shares tend to fall rather than to rise" because of the profits made by private merchants.[79] The following year, just when Portugal regained its independence, peace at last dawned, and the Company's outlook brightened with healthy performance figures in the sugar and slave trades, the shares indeed began to nosedive and were already lurching as low as 68 percent by the time Johan Maurits left Brazil in May 1644. Part of this fluctuation can be explained by taking into account outside factors, like the fallout of the irrational optimism during the "tulipmania" of the late 1630s, but part of it can be understood only by recognizing the lack of trust among shareholders in decisions made by the Heeren XIX and the waning of public confidence in the Company's long-term prospects after the opening up of the sugar trade.[80]

Information about the Company's economic forecasts was, of course, crucial for shareholders in order to reflect on their own participation. The merchant Cornelis Lampsins resigned as director of the Zeeland chamber in 1630 when it appeared that private merchants would be allowed a share of the Company trade, and he estimated that he too would be able to make a bigger profit as an independent trader. Later he returned as *bewindhebber* after it was decided that holding an official position in the Company no longer impeded one's private affairs. These were calculated yet earnest decisions, but there were more unsavory consequences of the fluctuating stocks as well. Speculators and "double dealers" with well-placed friends, occasionally even within the Company boardroom, could minimize their risk by trading with inside knowledge. Although there was no open trade in shares of the East and West India Companies, as buyers first had to register in the record books of one of the chambers, the streets around the Amsterdam exchange were teeming with stockbrokers looking to assist those wishing to buy and sell, if one contemporary observer is to be believed.[81] Cornelis Bicker, initially a major shareholder in the Amsterdam chamber, sold all his shares in the West India Company in the mid-1630s, just before the urban authorities, led by his brother Andries, began to argue in favor of free trade in the knowledge that sooner or later this decision would damage the Company's value on the stock exchange. Other investors loyal to the powerful Bicker clan had the same inside information, and they too used it to sell their stocks before their value was likely to decline.[82]

Private and public interests began to diverge among the regent elite. The average shareholder without access to privileged knowledge suffered from the Company's deteriorating reputation. The irreversible slump in the share prices from the early 1640s onward led to bankruptcies, something that not even the famous tulip craze had managed to inflict.[83] The iron salesman Nicolaes Pathuys, for instance, was forced in 1642 to sell his house in the Amsterdam harbor district because he had invested in the Brazilian enterprise.[84] Among the subscribers of shares in the Amsterdam Chamber of the West India Company were also corporate urban bodies. The local bakers' guild had invested 1,800 guilders in the mid-1620s, the carpenters' guild 1,000 guilders, and the surgeons and shearers 600 guilders each—thus spreading the impact of the economic slide throughout the middle classes. Elsewhere ordinary people suffered too. Below the urban elite who made up the chamber's *hoofdparticipanten*, the major shareholders who participated in the process of decision-making, the local population invested smaller but still substantial amounts. They included Reformed ministers, physicians, apothecaries, and university professors.[85] Artisans and shopkeepers participated as well, sometimes for amounts as small as twenty-five guilders.[86] Parishes and charity institutions also invested in the Company, thus giving credence to the rhetorical reference to "the money of widows and orphans" from pamphleteers. The parish of Zuidwolde, in thinly populated Drenthe, collectively had invested 2,000 daalders in Groningen and another 1,500 in the Amsterdam chamber, thus spreading the risk. The regents of the hospital of St. Anthony, an old men's home in Groningen, even purchased shares for 400 guilders with the specific intention of financing the care of one of its patients and raised this amount by 50 percent in 1639 when the Company issued a new prospectus in order to raise yet more capital.[87]

As the share price slumped, one-time investors like Nicolaes Pathuys may have been forced to knock on the doors of the very same charity institutions that had invested public money in the Company. Donations to charity in Amsterdam were collected in churches or through collection boxes outside private houses or in public places like the orphanage and the Bank of Exchange.

The West India Company too played a noble role in raising money for the poor. In the 1630s and 1640s, twenty-four directors of the Amsterdam chamber had a collection box hanging outside their houses. The urban population could also donate to charity at the Company warehouse on the waterfront. At the West India House, there were two boxes, one outside, the other inside the accounting office where Company employees or their family members picked up their pay. Deacons emptied the boxes once a month, collecting sizeable sums when the Company prospered, as in 1629, shortly after Piet Heyn had captured the New Spain treasure fleet, or in 1634 when the Dutch were about to break the resistance of the Portuguese in the Arraial. This money would be used for the benefit of Company personnel. Deacons, for example, managed the wages of Reformed employees to assist their family members at home. Yet, as Atlantic prospects began to stutter, "poor monies" dropped. Amsterdam directors who had gifted or legated thousands of guilders to charity in the 1630s were no longer as generous. Regular donations diminished too, like the statutory one penny per thousand from all goods imported by the Chambers of Amsterdam and Zeeland. As the particularism and friction increased and share prices continued to fall, Company supporters and employees gradually came to depend on charity, rather than the other way around.[88]

All individual and collective participants who had a financial interest in the West India Company followed the news of developments in Brazil, read pamphlets printed in Amsterdam and Zeeland, and monitored decisions being made in The Hague with growing concern. They agonized as friction increased within the ranks of the West India Company. A minister and ardent supporter of Dutch Brazil like Vicente Joachim Soler made very conscious decisions about which information to make public and which information not to share. Orthodoxy and toleration continued to collide, however, and, as the number of eyewitnesses of Dutch Brazil continued to increase, such contentious notions must have reached the Amsterdam waterfront. Given the city's well-developed media landscape, it was only a matter of time before they would also reach the printing houses.

And there were more serious problems to come. In May 1643, after years of lobbying, the Heeren XIX finally managed to convince the States General to agree to the recall of Johan Maurits.[89] His patronage of the arts and sciences; his building activities in Mauritsstad; his repeated requests for more funds, more settlers, and more troops; and his inability to provide the large and ever-increasing shipments of sugar needed to reduce the financial problems of the Company meant that the relationship between the count and the directors had become distinctly icy as early as 1641. The decision of the Heeren XIX to reduce the garrisons in Brazil, vehemently opposed by Johan Maurits, was pushed through after his departure, despite the preliminary warning of a revolt in Maranhão. In his "political testament" of May 1644, Johan Maurits advised his three colleagues (and successors) in the High and Secret Council to maintain loyalty and discipline among the troops by means of prompt payment and adequate rations, to display courtesy and respect for the *moradores* and their Catholic religion, and to persist in the tactful and tolerant dealings with the native population. Very soon, however, the realities of colonial Brazil were to catch up with the aspirations of the Company directors. Even the welfare system could not protect them from what was to come.[90]

CHAPTER 5

"Amsterdamnified"

In the spring of 1649, in a tavern on Amsterdam's Dam Square, vehement discussion was taking place on the future of Dutch Brazil. Four men sitting around a table tried to establish what had gone wrong in Recife and what should be done about it. The colony had seemed destined for economic and geopolitical success when the West India Company had first assumed control. Since June 1645, however, the Dutch had experienced a revolt from Portuguese planters that would become known in Luso-Brazilian historiography as the "War of Divine Liberation." Supported by the authorities in Bahia and quietly approved by the court in Lisbon, Portuguese and allied forces made quick advancements, and, by the end of the year, the Dutch were being besieged in Recife, with most of the colony in the hands of their enemies. Only Itamaracá and several coastal forts in Paraíba and the Rio Grande estuary remained in Dutch possession. Across the ocean, Angola and São Tomé were also lost to the Portuguese. With ever more soldiers departing for the South Atlantic—delayed only by the "blind obstruction" from Amsterdam—the Company suffered two unexpected military defeats in Pernambuco in 1648 and early 1649 that effectively sealed the fate of the colony. As far as many inhabitants of Amsterdam were concerned, Dutch Brazil by now no longer had a future worth fighting for.[1]

This was also the opinion of the innkeeper who overheard the conversation while pouring drinks and complained to her guests that the misery and imminent disaster in Brazil were a form of divine punishment for not concluding a peace agreement with Portugal. "If there had been no sins," she insisted, "there would have been no plague," something she had learned "from various passages in the Bible." Soon her husband joined the conversation too. Before settling down as a publican in Amsterdam, he had been a sea captain for many years, which gave him some authority on the matter. He explained to his four customers that his wife "always cited Scripture," especially, he said, when he had had one drink too many. Already before dawn on any given Sunday, she would have said prayers in at least four different churches across town—something that clouded her political views. His own opinion on the situation in the Atlantic world was more straightforward: it had been the stubborn and selfish privateers from the province of Zeeland who had obstructed the signing of a peace treaty with Portugal in order to maximize their chances of seizing prizes and who had thereby squandered the future of Dutch Brazil. Inspired by these views, the four customers continued their discussion with renewed vigor.[2]

This chapter sees the bitter triumph of "Amsterdamnification" in the face of the approaching defeat in the Atlantic world. After more than two decades of incessant reporting on Brazil, the news cycle in Amsterdam had come full circle. The corantos of Jan van Hilten and Broer Jansz, by now competing for the readers' attention with three other local newspapers, informed the audience of another major transoceanic news event, only this time their bulletins fueled discontent rather than euphoria.[3] Ordinary Amsterdammers who had lost their investments, their loved ones, or both, vented their anger at the West India Company's mismanagement. Their grievances were often shaped by pamphleteers who thrived on discussion. Reflecting on how for many, Dutch Brazil had become an increasingly personal affair, these professional authors connected individual sentiments that had been brewing for a decade, if not longer, to the regents' political battle against the corruption of the Company directors and the stubborn belief in Brazil in Zeeland.[4] The myriad individual opinions culminated in the rhetorical *praatjes*-genre that reached its apogee in 1649 and gave ordinary Amsterdammers a clear voice as part of fictional dialogues like the one in the tavern on Dam Square. By the time the West India Company surrendered Recife in January 1654, everything that could be said had already been said. As the conformation of defeat arrived, the print media suddenly fell silent.

The Blame Game

The periodical press's first reaction when news of the revolt reached Holland was one of disbelief and denial. On Saturday 2 September 1645, both leading Amsterdam newspapers reported the setback in Recife but immediately played down its significance. Broer Jansz, in his *Tijdingen*, mentioned how the planters of Brazil during a wedding at one of the *engenhos* had plotted to murder the entire Dutch hierarchy present there in order to don the victims' clothes and gain entrance to the bastions of Recife. But the Dutch had discovered the conspiracy in time, and ten or twelve of the planters had died as opposed to "only two or three on our side." "Apparently," Broer Jansz concluded casually, "they had targeted Recife" (Figure 33).[5] Jan van Hilten assured his readers that God had prohibited the plot from happening and reported that the Company had announced a day of public prayer to express gratitude for His support. In the same bulletin, however, he also mentioned how "many Dutchmen" from outside the city were streaming into Recife for protection.

The Heeren XIX, in session at the moment the news arrived, made a more sensible assessment of what had happened. Given the warnings they had received from Johan Maurits, they instantly comprehended the seriousness of the *moradores*' insubordination and sent a delegation to The Hague to confer with the States General, a meeting that took place on the day the public first

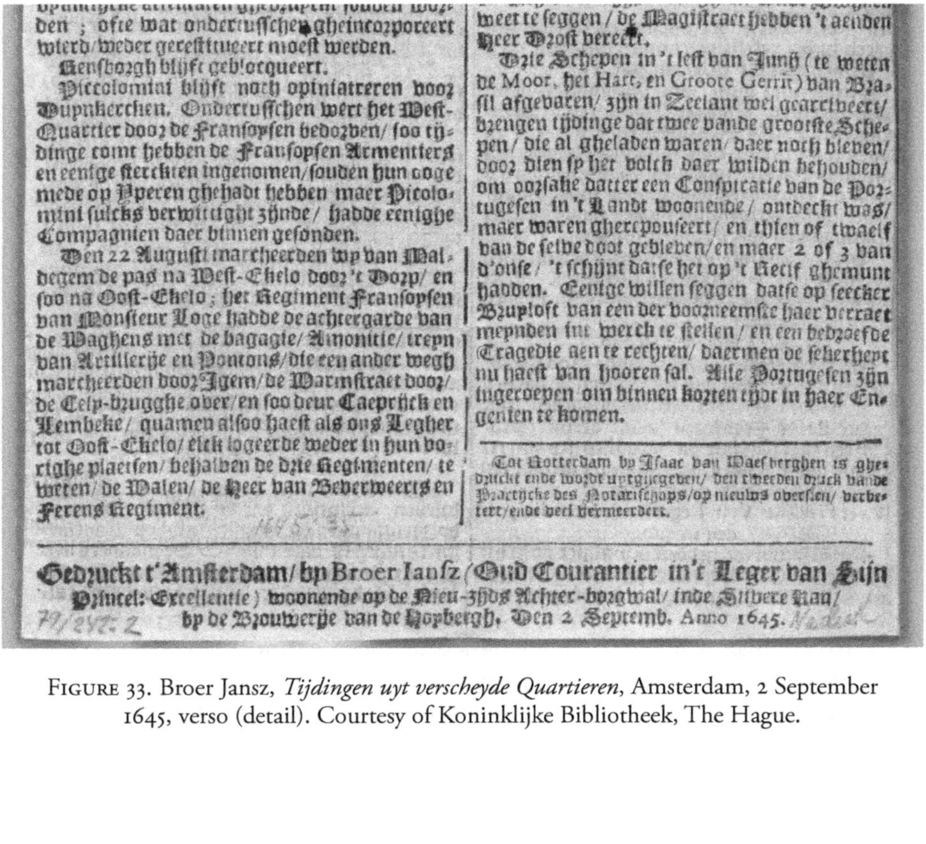

den ; ofte wat ondertusschen gheincorporeert wierd/ weder gerestitueert moest werden.

Rensborgh blijft geblocqueert.

Piccolomini blijft noch opiniatreren voor Duynkercken. Ondertusschen wert het West-Quartier door de Fransoysen bedorven/ soo tijdinge comt hebben de Fransoysen Armentiers en eenige stercksken ingenomen/ souden hun ooge mede op Yperen ghehadt hebben maer Picolomini sulcks verwittight zijnde/ hadde eenighe Compagnien daer binnen gesonden.

Den 22 Augusti marcheerden wy van Maldegem de pas na West-Ekelo door 't Dorp/ en soo na Oost-Ekelo; het Regiment Fransoysen van Monsieur Loge hadde de achtergarde van de Waghens met de bagagie/ Amonitie/ treyn van Artillerye en Pontons/ die een ander wegh marcheerden door Igem/ de Warmstraet door/ de Celp-brugghe over/ en soo veur Caeprijck en Lembeke/ quamen alsoo haest als ons Legher tot Oost-Ekelo/ elck logeerde weder in hun vorighe plaetsen/ behalven de drie Regimenten/ te weten/ de Walen/ de Heer van Beverweerts en Ferens Regiment.

weet te seggen/ de Magistraet hebben 't aenden Heer Drost vereert.

Drie Schepen in 't lest van Junij (te weten de Moor, het Hart, en Groote Gerrit) van Brasil afgevaren/ zijn in Zeelant wel gearriveert/ brengen tijdinge dat twee vande grootste Schepen/ die al ghéladen waren/ daer noch bleven/ door dien sy het volck daer wilden behouden/ om oorsake datter een Conspiratie van de Portugesen in 't Landt woonende/ ontdeckt was/ maer waren gheexpouseert/ en thien of twaelf van de selve doot gebleven/ en maer 2 of 3 van d'onse/ 't schijnt datse het op 't Recif ghemunt hadden. Eenige willen seggen datse op seecker Bruyloft van een der voornaemste haer verraet meynden int werck te stellen/ en een bedroefde Tragedie aen te rechten/ daermen de seekerheyt nu haest van hooren sal. Alle Portugesen zijn ingeroepen om binnen korten tijdt in haer Engenien te komen.

Tot Rotterdam by Isaac van Waesberghen is ghedruckt ende wordt uytgegeven/ den tweeden druck vande Practijcke des Notarischaps/ op nieuws oversien/ verbetert/ ende veel vermeerdert.

Gedruckt t'Amsterdam/ by Broer Iansz/ (Oud Courantier in 't Leger van Sijn Princel: Excellentie) woonende op de Nieu-zijds Achter-borghwal/ inde Silvere Kan/ by de Brouwerije van de Hopbergh. Den 2 Septemb. Anno 1645.

FIGURE 33. Broer Jansz, *Tijdingen uyt verscheyde Quartieren*, Amsterdam, 2 September 1645, verso (detail). Courtesy of Koninklijke Bibliotheek, The Hague.

read about events in the newspapers.[6] Quickly it became clear to everyone that there was no point in denying the gravity of Luso-Brazilian disobedience. The overriding feeling on the homefront as events gradually unfolded was one of betrayal. So, who was to blame? The media singled out two parties for betraying the colony: a small group of Company officers in Recife who were accused of having conspired with the authorities in Bahia and the planters in Pernambuco who had pledged their loyalty to the High and Secret Council but who could no longer bear the burden of debt to the Company, accumulated for the purchase of African slaves for a total sum of around four million guilders. The duplicity of each of these two groups was personified by a single individual who bore the brunt of public anger.

The first was Major Diederick van Hoogstraten, who led the group of officers that voluntarily surrendered the strategic Fort van der Dussen at Cape Santo Agostinho. Treason and rumors of treason had been permanently at the forefront of officers' and soldiers' minds in Brazil. In the early 1630s, the West India Company had benefited greatly from intelligence from the mulatto Domingos Fernandes Calabar. In the years that followed, judging from the diary of Peter Hansen Hajstrup, Company soldiers regularly discussed the presence of double agents within their own ranks, but none of this had prepared the Dutch—both in Pernambuco and at home—for the perfidious conduct of Van Hoogstraten and a handful of his officers. In July 1645, two weeks after the fighting had commenced, the High Council had appointed Van Hoogstraten as head of a mission to Bahia to complain to the governor about his encouragement of the rebels. Upon his return to Recife, the major disclosed how he had rejected out of hand a Portuguese attempt to bribe him into surrendering Fort van der Dussen, but Johan Nieuhof later established that by then Van Hoogstraten's resolve had already been severely weakened by the attractive offers of rich sugar plantations that the Bahia elite had made. As early as August, it became clear that Van Hoogstraten had double-crossed his superiors and had in fact decided to accept a high post in the Portuguese army he had been offered.[7]

In newspapers and pamphlets of the late 1640s, Van Hoogstraten's name became synonymous with treason. No Amsterdam spin doctor could rectify this story, and time did not heal his reputation. The most reliable account of Van Hoogstraten's treason was written by Mattheus van den Broeck, an educated freeman who had been re-enlisted by the West India Company at the outbreak of the revolt and who, after having been captured by Portuguese troops, heard the story from fellow soldiers who had witnessed the dishonorable surrender. Van den Broeck reported that the major had discussed the bribe with the other senior officers inside the fortress. Of the nine men debating the matter, only three wanted to fight. According to these three, there was no shortage of manpower or victuals, and any attack could have been withstood for quite some time. The other six, however, spurred on by Van Hoogstraten, sacrificed the common good for their personal objectives. Ritmeester Casper van der Ley, thinking of his sugar mill and the lives of his Luso-Brazilian wife and children, considered further resistance "inconvenient." Captain Albert Wedda was prepared to accept the enemy's conditions since he did not want to lose his personal possessions at Cape Santo Agostinho for the sake of the Company. Lieutenant Wenzel Smit was even blunter: he was fed up with the West India Company and just wanted to go home.[8]

Van den Broeck's observations were printed in Amsterdam only in 1651, and the major's duplicity was vilified in even more vigorous fashion in subsequent compendia of the history of Dutch Brazil such as Arnoldus Montanus's *Nieuwe en Onbekende Weereld* (1671) and especially Johan Nieuhof's *Gedenkweerdige Zee en Landreize*, an eyewitness account of Dutch decline in Brazil that was not published until 1682. The deceit was so widely publicized that the name of the entire family suffered from Van Hoogstraten's actions in Brazil. Samuel van Hoogstraten, one of Rembrandt's pupils and author of a famous painting treatise, was also a minor poet in Dordrecht where he met Johann Philipp Mulheiser, the ensign who took his *album amicorum* to Brazil and back in the early 1640s. Mulheiser, in 1642, had encountered Diederick van Hoogstraten who had written a short poem in his album that amounted, ironically enough, to a warning against speaking with a double tongue. Eight years later, when Mulheiser asked Samuel van Hoogstraten to contribute to his album, the embarrassed painter dissociated himself from his distant relative on an adjacent page of the booklet. Just as Judas had been one of the apostles before becoming a traitor, Samuel rhymed in disgust, this conspirator had tarnished the name of his own God-fearing father. By now the memory of treason in Dutch Brazil could lead to personal discomfort even by association.[9]

Authors and printers who were biased in favor of the West India Company allocated blame to Gaspar Dias Ferreira, a planter who had sided with the Dutch in the early 1630s and become a trusted (and roundly despised) adviser to Johan Maurits on matters regarding the *moradores*. Aware of the enmity against him in Brazil, held by Calvinists and Catholics alike, Ferreira returned with the governor-general to The Hague. In October 1645, he was arrested on the recommendation of Sephardic Jews in Amsterdam who, through contacts in Algiers, had obtained information about his persistent collaborating with the court in Madrid.[10] The charges against Ferreira were related to the revolt in Pernambuco. He was accused of deceiving the Dutch by providing both Madrid and Lisbon with politically sensitive information on Brazil and was sentenced to a fine of twelve thousand guilders and an eternal banishment from the United Provinces—a verdict that, unusually, also appeared in print. The authorities appealed to the High Court, but the seven-year prison sentence added to the original verdict was retained and even cut short when Ferreira escaped from his cell and left the country.[11] During the trial, however, documents were found that implicated the authorities in Bahia and Lisbon in organizing the "War of Divine Liberation," unleashing a wave of anti-Portuguese sentiment that had been unthinkable four years earlier when the Portuguese rebellion against Spain had been roundly celebrated in Holland.[12]

The West India Company hired the prominent jurist Dirck Graswinckel to publicly extend the blame from Ferreira and the *moradores* to the plotting Jesuit António Vieira and the colonial regime in Bahia and farther up the chain of command to João IV for not keeping his subjects in check and thereby breaking the stipulations of the Ten Years' Truce concluded in 1641.[13] His treatise was popular enough to warrant a cheaper reprint. In The Hague, wrathful ministers preached so furiously against the disloyalty of the Portuguese that a mob proceeded toward the residence of ambassador Francisco de Sousa Coutinho, where, one observer estimated, "they would certainly have overwhelmed him, dragged him outside, and cut him to pieces, had not the Prince of Orange himself, with his personal guards, intervened and dispersed the crowd." According to Pierre Moreau, who boarded a Recife-bound vessel around this time, the people in 1645 "spoke of nothing else but of avenging such a great treason." Two years later, fears that the life of the Portuguese envoy was again in danger were suppressed by the preemptive arrest of the suspected ringleaders of the plot against him.[14]

Multiple parties and factions that had not actively participated in debates over Dutch Brazil in the 1630s began to raise their voice in the wake of the revolt. The "Jewish nation" of Amsterdam, a small but influential urban group for whom Brazil appeared to be the land on which their future prospects rested, protested most forcefully against the conduct of Ferreira and the Portuguese king.[15] They had petitioned the States General to include a clause in the Ten Years' Truce to the effect that all Dutchman, Jews included, were to receive protection for their persons on Portuguese territory. In the draft of the permanent Luso-Dutch peace treaty of 1648 that would never be signed, the clause was even extended to the entire Portuguese empire.[16] Now their lobbying appeared to have been in vain. Ambassador Sousa Coutinho claimed that what he dreaded most was the frustration of the Sephardim, who had supported the Portuguese cause since the secession from Spain but who now "would condemn me to be stoned." It required intervention from the Amsterdam burgomasters to stop the Sephardic community from publicly insulting Sousa Coutinho and inciting scandal and uproar. The heads of the Amsterdam synagogue warned congregants to stay quiet, on pain of fines. Nonetheless, some continued to spread rumors that discontent and unrest were rife in Lisbon, and even that the king had been arrested by the nobility.[17] As reports trickled through that Portuguese soldiers in Brazil had executed thirteen Jewish captives in cold blood, the Sephardim petitioned the States General to protest to João IV—which they did—demanding the immediate release of Jewish soldiers who had been transferred to the Inquisition. In January 1648, news of the martyrdom of a young Sephardic inhabitant of Dutch Brazil in an auto-da-fé in Lisbon made such an emotional impact in Amsterdam that even Sousa Coutinho could not believe the degree of popular disgust this act aroused.[18]

Yet the ambassador knew how to make use of the discussion culture as well, funding the publication of pamphlets that countered calls for unity or disseminated the Portuguese point of view in such a way that they would create further division.[19] Perhaps the most curious document in this respect was a letter supposedly written by the *moradores* of Pernambuco, printed in Dutch across the border in Antwerp, which completely turned the tables on the West India Company, complaining that it was the planter class who were the victims of the treacherous neglect of the Dutch to live up to the promises they had made. In the early phase of the revolt, the *moradores* claimed to have been caught in the middle of a nasty conflict. Portuguese troops, they asserted, had treated them as if they were Dutch, plundering their houses and sugar mills. The Dutch, however, instead of comforting them and fighting the enemy on their behalf, wrongly blamed the *moradores* for igniting the rebellion. Sigismund von Schoppe, with a party of eighty "wild and furious" Tapuya Indians, had behaved in "tyrannical" fashion—a particularly stinging choice of words since it reminded readers of the supposed Spanish brutalities that had legitimated the Dutch attack on America in the first place. Every time the *moradores* had offered Company soldiers food as a token of their support, the pamphlet continued, Von Schoppe's troops, in turn, had given over their fellow Christians as fodder to their cannibalistic allies. The scheming of the West India Company in the end had left the Pernambucans no other option than to take up arms against the oppressor they had served so loyally for fifteen years.[20]

To Name and Shame

The two battles of Guararapes ended any hope that the revolt would fade away. In July 1648, Broer Jansz reported in his coranto that, in the first clash between Von Schoppe and the Portuguese, many officers and soldiers had died but that "ours have held the field, and the enemy has retreated with great losses."[21] Yet no matter how much Jansz tried to talk down its significance, the news from Guararapes was followed by more pessimism over the future of Dutch Brazil and the West India Company, bitterness over the persistent cacophony of opposing opinions that had led to the neglect of the colony, finger pointing between Amsterdam and the other chambers about who was to blame for the sudden reversal of fortune, and—still—disagreement over what the next move should be. In these already difficult circumstances, news of the second defeat at Guararapes in February 1649 came as a massive blow. In early May, the Amsterdam news merchant Françoys Lieshout reported in his midweek coranto that "rumor has it that our people in Brazil have again suffered a major defeat, with the loss of hundreds of men."[22] That figure proved to be too low. The Company printed a list with the names of the deceased that was made public on the notice board outside the new West India House, a former warehouse near the Amsterdam docks, to communicate to the urban population the fate of their relatives (Figure 34). The sheer length of this particular list, with more than one thousand casualties and "many" injured or in enemy hands, must have further eroded public support for the Brazilian colony, regardless of the meek excuse of a Portuguese ambush printed at the bottom of the sheet (Figure 35).[23]

In terms of the public experience of Dutch Brazil in Amsterdam, the year 1649, in almost every conceivable way, was the mirror image of 1624. Instead of joy, there was now despair; instead of harmony, there was disagreement. "Months and years were wasted through disputes between different chambers and directors," one commentator would later write somewhat hyperbolically, but he had a point.[24] The States General faced a seemingly insurmountable political deadlock: Amsterdam and the States of Holland argued for a complete overhaul of the West India Company, at the very least, while the States of Zeeland pressed for sending yet more troops to save the colony.[25] In relative terms, Zeeland owned the greatest share in the Company, and much of the province's economy depended on its fate. The fall of the share price to as low as 26 percent of its nominal value in February 1649 added a very tangible dimension to the impression in Middelburg that Amsterdam's self-interest had brought Recife to the brink of surrender.[26] The Amsterdam magistrates realized that the widespread

"Amsterdamnified"

FIGURE 34. Jan Veenhuysen, *West Indis Huys*, Amsterdam, 1665, ink on paper, 11.8 × 13.9 cm. Courtesy of Rijksmuseum, Amsterdam, inv. nr. RP-P-OB-15.731.

perception of their abandonment of the Company had led to disgust even among the urban citizens they represented, and it became increasingly clear that the outcome of *their* deliberations, inside city hall, determined the future of Brazil. All eyes were now on Dam Square, to the delight of local pamphleteers. In August, typically for the Dutch discussion culture, the minutes from the meeting of the city council on the fate of the West India Company were out on the street, printed anonymously and signed only with the name of Trajano Boccalini, the famous Italian satirist of the early seventeenth century.[27]

The alleged transcript, announced as a copy of the city council's resolutions, "recorded" the remarks of all thirty-six members of the Amsterdam *vroedschap*. The level of detail in this pamphlet is astounding. Its structure suggests that the author (and his readers) were thoroughly familiar with both the identities and ideas of the various regents and the way meetings of the city council were organized. The suggestion of transparency gently nudged readers in the direction of the author's intended conclusion. The opening statement, by bur-

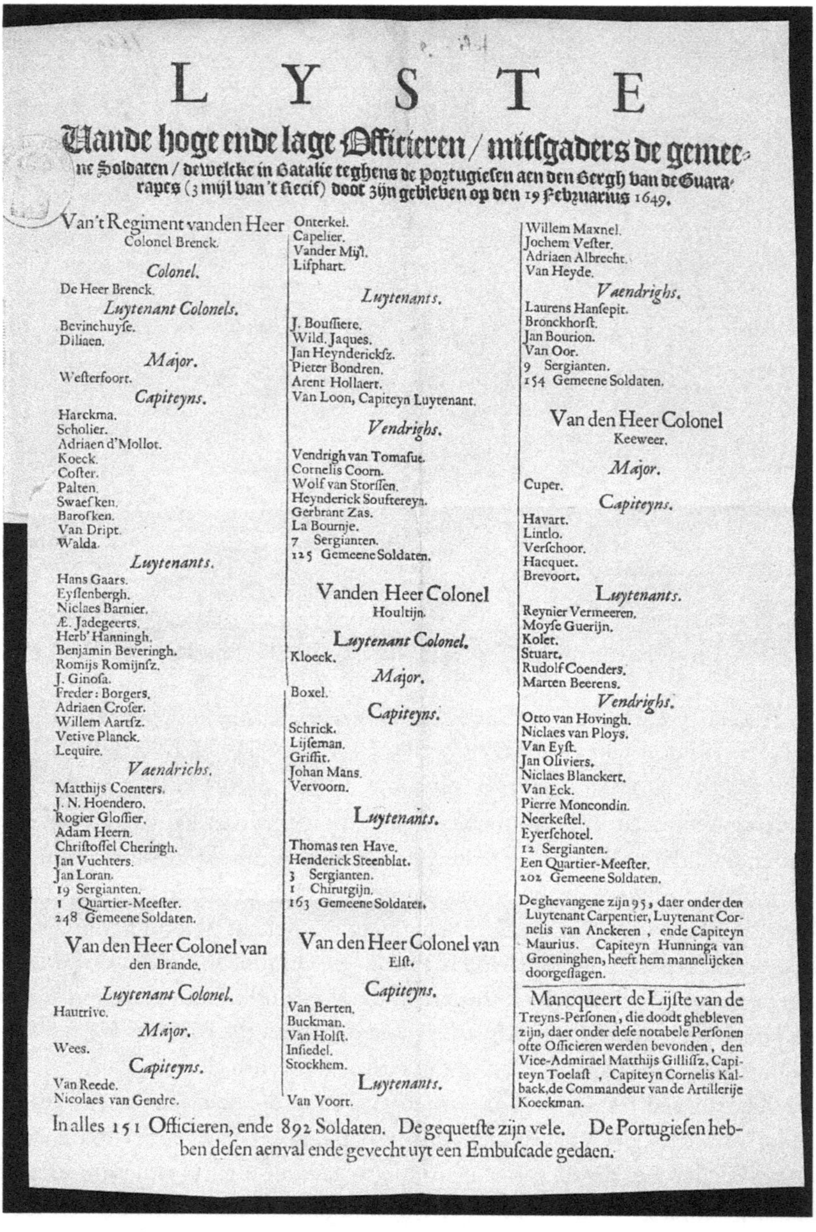

LYSTE

Vande hoge ende lage Officieren / mitsgaders de gemeene Soldaten / dewelcke in Bataljie teghens de Portugiesen aen den Bergh van de Guararapes (3 mijl van 't Recif) door zijn gebleven op den 19 Februarius 1649.

Van 't Regiment vanden Heer Colonel Brenck.

Colonel.
De Heer Brenck.

Luytenant Colonels.
Bevinchuyse.
Dillaen.

Major.
Westerfoort.

Capiteyns.
Harckma.
Scholier.
Adriaen d'Mollot.
Koeck.
Coster.
Palten.
Swaefken.
Barofken.
Van Dript.
Walda.

Luytenants.
Hans Gaars.
Eyssenbergh.
Niclaes Barnier.
Æ. Jadegeerts.
Herb' Hanningh.
Benjamin Beveringh.
Romijs Romijnsz.
J. Ginosa.
Freder: Borgers.
Adriaen Croser.
Willem Aartsz.
Vetive Planck.
Lequire.

Vaendrichs.
Matthijs Coenters.
J. N. Hoendero.
Rogier Glossier.
Adam Heern.
Christoffel Cheringh.
Jan Vuchters.
Jan Loran.
19 Sergianten.
1 Quartier-Meester.
248 Gemeene Soldaten.

Van den Heer Colonel van den Brande.

Luytenant Colonel.
Hautrive.

Major.
Wees.

Capiteyns.
Van Reede.
Nicolaes van Gendre.

Onterkel.
Capelier.
Vander Mijl.
Lisphart.

Luytenants.
J. Boussiere.
Wild. Jaques.
Jan Heynderickfz.
Pieter Bondren.
Arent Hollaert.
Van Loon, Capiteyn Luytenant.

Vendrighs.
Vendrigh van Tomasue.
Cornelis Coorn.
Wolf van Storssen.
Heynderick Souftereyn.
Gerbrant Zas.
La Bournje.
7 Sergianten.
125 Gemeene Soldaten.

Vanden Heer Colonel Houltijn.

Luytenant Colonel.
Kloeck.

Major.
Boxel.

Capiteyns.
Schrick.
Lijseman.
Griffit.
Johan Mans.
Vervoorn.

Luytenants.
Thomas ten Have.
Henderick Steenblat.
3 Sergianten.
1 Chirurgijn.
163 Gemeene Soldaten.

Van den Heer Colonel van Elst.

Capiteyns.
Van Berten.
Buckman.
Van Holst.
Insiedel.
Stockhem.

Luytenants.
Van Voort.

Willem Maxnel.
Jochem Vester.
Adriaen Albrecht.
Van Heyde.

Vaendrighs.
Laurens Hansepit.
Bronckhorst.
Jan Bourion.
Van Oor.
9 Sergianten.
154 Gemeene Soldaten.

Van den Heer Colonel Keeweer.

Major.
Cuper.

Capiteyns.
Havart.
Linclo.
Verschoor.
Hacquet.
Brevoort.

Luytenants.
Reynier Vermeeren.
Moyse Guerijn.
Kolet.
Stuart.
Rudolf Coenders.
Marten Beerens.

Vendrighs.
Otto van Hovingh.
Niclaes van Ploys.
Van Eyst.
Jan Oliviers.
Niclaes Blanckert.
Van Eck.
Pierre Moncondin.
Neerkestel.
Eyerschotel.
12 Sergianten.
Een Quartier-Meester.
202 Gemeene Soldaten.

De ghevangene zijn 95, daer onder den Luytenant Carpenter, Luytenant Cornelis van Anckeren, ende Capiteyn Maurius. Capiteyn Hunninga van Groeninghen, heeft hem mannelijcken doorgeslagen.

Mancqueert de Lijste van de Treyns-Personen, die doodt ghebleven zijn, daer onder dese notabele Personen ofte Officieren werden bevonden, den Vice-Admirael Matthijs Gillissz, Capiteyn Toelast, Capiteyn Cornelis Kalback, de Commandeur van de Artillerije Koeckman.

In alles 151 Officieren, ende 892 Soldaten. De gequetste zijn vele. De Portugiesen hebben desen aenval ende gevecht uyt een Embuscade gedaen.

FIGURE 35. *Lyste van de hoge en lage officieren*, Amsterdam, 1649. Courtesy of Koninklijke Bibliotheek, The Hague, Kn. 6465.

gomaster Antonius Oetgens, insisted that popular pressure to support the Company was high, something he found important:

> If the Company shall not be maintained, however lightly one may think of this, the mob will rise, and attack one or other burgomaster who is not guilty of any crime: because it appears that throughout the country there is talk about the malevolence of this city, so that I understand the gravity of positioning ourselves against the entire government, and of not letting ourselves be moved by the howling of the multitude of miserable and suffering orphans, widows, and other simplefolk who have given their money to the West India Company.[28]

The next burgomaster to speak was Oetgens's nemesis Andries Bicker, who admitted to having abandoned the Company already in the early 1630s when he foresaw that disagreements among the different chambers would be very costly. "Recife I consider to be already lost," he supposedly told his colleagues now, presumably to the horror of many readers.[29] But there were many others who still wanted to save Brazil. One eminent councillor predicted "great joy in the entire city" if the Company would be supported "because many miserable and poor people are tied to it."[30] Doctor Nicolaas Tulp, so famously portrayed by Rembrandt seventeen years earlier, pointed to the historical context of the war against Spain, the way the West India Company had raised spirits in the city, and the extraordinary potential of the settlement in Brazil—alluding to the collective memory of euphoria and appropriation of previous decades. Other councillors supported Brazil after complaining about the bad reputation Amsterdam now enjoyed in rumors and in print.[31] In the end, according to the author, there had been a narrow majority for continuing to support the West India Company. Only the men who expressed their personal loyalty (or kinship) to the rabid Bicker voted to let the Company go bankrupt.[32]

The scathing pamphlet, unusually, named and shamed the magistrates. It was also literally cheap, costing no more than three *stuivers*, and has survived in four different editions—indicating its remarkable popularity.[33] Although the regents probably tried to limit and control public opinion that undermined their authority, they could do little to stop anonymous authors and printers from publishing commercially attractive pamphlets. In 1648 the local booksellers' guild had been ordered to watch out for those "who illegally sell books, courants, tidings etc. on markets, bridges, streets, etc.," but the fact that these measures were regularly repeated suggests they were inadequate. If Amsterdam censorship *was* occasionally successful, authors could bring their inflammatory text to a printer in Haarlem, Leiden, or Utrecht, less than a few hours travel away. "It is generally known," one contemporary observer wrote, "that there are almost no bridges or canals without a table—in some places practically a shop—filled with books, where all can purchase books at a modest price, to their hearts' content."[34] Loyalists, then, had to look for other ways to curtail undesirable media attention.

Predictably, less than a month later, a refutation appeared from the workshop of Abraham de Bruyn, an otherwise untraceable and probably fictional printer who supposedly held shop close to one of Amsterdam's city gates. According to its title, it promised to examine the "false resolution of the burgomasters and city council of Amsterdam."[35] Councillor by councillor, its thirty-six densely printed pages corrected the accusations of the initial pamphlet that had been maliciously intended "to stir up the community and the entire country against the urban magistrates."[36] The author started off by naming seven reasons why burgomaster Oetgens would never form his opinion based on the mockery of "schoolboys." In the process, he displayed a more general concern for the "great injudiciousness and recklessness of those people who throughout the country, on barges and coaches, in alleys and streets, during every wedding and meal, and in all other circles cannot stop talking in this vein," perhaps an indication that part of the establishment felt that public debate had gone too far, even in Amsterdam.[37] Moving on to Andries Bicker's claim that Recife was practically already lost, the author asked his readers: "Is it any wonder that such an old and wise man is pessimistic? Is it really so disgraceful that he deserves to be scaffolded?"[38] Finally, the author dismissed the historical sentiments that were put into the mouth of Nicolaas Tulp by saying that the VOC, individual privateers, and even the monarchs of France, England, and Sweden had assisted the Dutch in countering Spanish force as much as the West India Company had, but, unlike the Company, they had all done so *without* the financial support of the States General.[39]

The Popular View: Chats

The second pamphlet, in reaction to the accusations from Zeeland and political indecision in The Hague, was part of a powerful media campaign emanating from Amsterdam throughout 1649. According to the author of the refutation, it was not just the Bicker clan that strived for the abandonment of Brazil: it was the entire *vroedschap* who practically unisono (and with an avalanche of "good" reasons) resolved that the colony had become a lost cause—at least for a financially unsound and unfairly monopolistic organization like the West India Company. To tip the balance from considering Brazil a difficult plight worth fighting for to a costly conquest that should be abandoned, pamphleteers in the city and across Holland revived an old literary genre to reflect popular discontent and to bend public opinion in their favor. The *praatje* (chat) became the medium of choice in 1649 to influence political discussions on Brazil and the future of the Company.[40]

Praatjes were fictional conversations between characters representing different opinions in Dutch society that reflected real opinions among the middle classes. In 1649, seven of these dialogues were printed in quick succession, each one criticizing Zeeland's staunch loyalty to the West India Company and arguing for the acceptance of the impending loss of Brazil as advocated by Amsterdam. Issued as small pamphlets, they must have had a very high initial impact on the Dutch book market. Three of the seven "Brazilian" *praatjes* describe their function as advice to the States General on how to emerge with credit from the political impasse, and one of them was explicitly endorsed by the author who refuted the fabricated opinions of the Amsterdam *vroedschap*.[41] The first, *Amsterdams Dam-Praetje*, was published in March, during or immediately after the first round of political meetings in The Hague. Before the actual discussion, the pamphlet opened with a short summary of the treatise to explain to readers how they should interpret the dialogue they were about to read. "In the end," the guideline concluded, "it will be proven beyond doubt how detrimental it is for the common good and for all individuals of these provinces that peace is not concluded with Portugal, and also why the West India Company can justifiably be compared to a miscarriage or an untimely born monstrosity" (Figure 36). This rather brusque statement of intent testifies to the strategy of the Amsterdam elite to broaden public discussion by reaching out to those who had not followed every debate on Brazil so far to counter some of the reasonable arguments of their political opponents.[42]

The conversation that takes place at Amsterdam's Dam Square opens innocuously with amicable small talk between three *bewindhebbers* whose names—Isaac van Beeck, Jan Raey, and Eduard Man—correspond to those of real directors of the Amsterdam chamber.[43] Then the leading character, Francisco, whose opinion the author meant to impress on his readership, joins the discussion. Judging from his name, also the first name of Ambassador Sousa

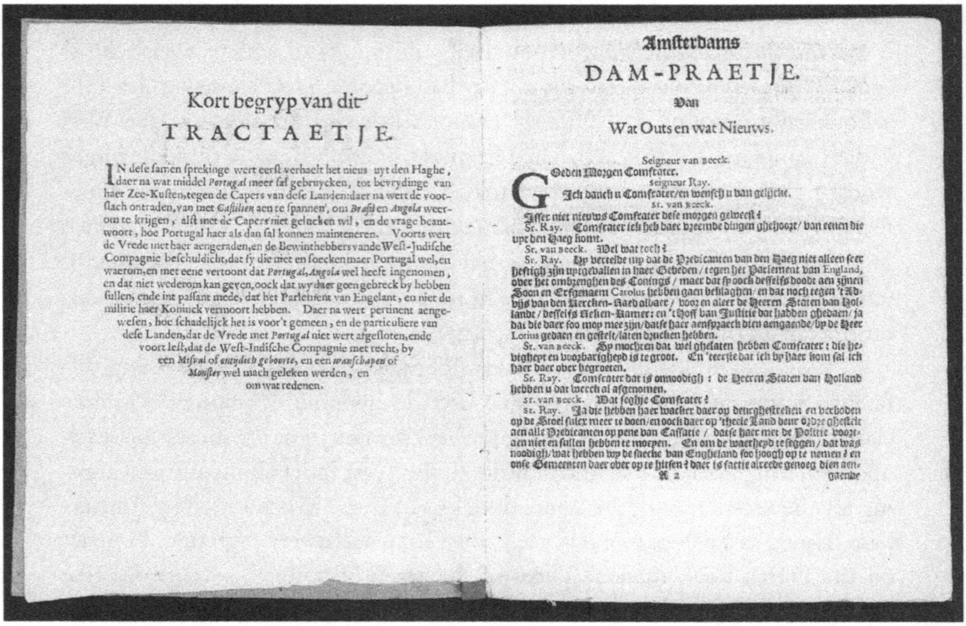

Kort begryp van dit
TRACTAETJE.

IN dese samen sprekinge wert eerst verhaelt het nieus uyt den Haghe, daer na wat middel *Portugal* meer sal gebruycken, tot bevrydinge van haer Zee-Kusten, tegen de Capers van dese Landen: daer na wert de voorslach ontraden, van met *Castilien* aen te spannen, om *Brasil* en *Angola* weerom te krijgen, alst met de Capers niet gelucken wil, en de vrage beantwoort, hoe Portugal haer als dan sal konnen mainteneren. Voorts wert de Vrede met haer aengeraden, en de Bewinthebbers vande West-Indische Compagnie beschuldicht, dat sy die niet en soecken maer Portugal wel, en waerom, en met eene vertoont dat *Portugal*, *Angola* wel heeft ingenomen, en dat niet wederom kan geven, oock dat wy daer geen gebreck by hebben sullen, ende int passant mede, dat het Parlement van Engelant, en niet de militie haer Koninck vermoort hebben. Daer na wert pertinent aengewesen, hoe schadelijck het is voor't gemeen, en de particuliere van dese Landen, dat de Vrede met *Portugal* niet wert afgesloten, ende voort lest, dat de West-Indische Compagnie met recht, by een *Misval* of *ontydich geboorte*, en een *wanschapen* of *Monster* wel mach geleken werden, en om wat redenen.

Amsterdams
DAM-PRAETJE.
Van
Wat Outs en wat Nieuws.

Seigneur van Beeck.
GOeden Morgen Comfrater.
Seigneur Ray.
Ick danck u Comfrater/en wensch u van gelijcke.
Sr. van Beeck.
Isser niet nieuws Comfrater dese morgen geweest?
Sr. Ray. Comfrater ick heb daer vreemde dingen ghehoort/ van eenen die uyt den Haeg komt.
Sr. van Beeck. Wel wat toch?
Sr. Ray. Hy vertelde my dat de Predicanten van den Haeg niet alleen seer hestigh zijn uytgevallen in haer Gebeden/ tegen het Parlement van England, over het ombrenghen des Conings/ maer dat sy oock desselfs doodt aen zijnen Soon en Erfgenaem Carolus hebben gaen beklaghen/ en dat noch tegen 't Advijs van den Kercken-Raed aldaer/ voor en aleer de Heeren Staten van Hollandt/ desselfs Reken-Kamer: en 't Hoff van Justitie dat hadden ghedaen/ ja dat die daer soo moy mee zijn/ datse haer aenspraeck dien aengaende/ by de Heer Lotius gedaen en gestelt/ laten drucken hebben.
Sr. van Beeck. Sy mochten dat wel ghelaten hebben Comfrater: die hevigheyt en voorbarigheyd is te groot. En 't eerste dat ick by haer kom sal ick haer daer over begroeten.
Sr. Ray. Comfrater dat is onnoodigh: de Heeren Staten van Holland hebben u dat werck al afgenomen.
Sr. van Beeck. Wat seghje Comfrater?
Sr. Ray. Ja die hebben haer wacker daer op deurghestreken en verboden op de Stoel sulcx meer te doen/ en oock daer op 't heele Land deur ordre ghestelt aen alle Predicanten op pene van Cassatie/ datse haer met de Politie voortaen niet en sullen hebben te moeyen. En om de waerheyd te seggen/ dat was noodigh/ wat hebben wy de saecke van Engheland soo hoogh op te nemen? en onse Gemeenten daer over op te hitsen? daer is factie alreede genoeg dien aengaende
A 2

FIGURE 36. *Amsterdams Dam-Praetje,* [Amsterdam,] 1649, title page. Courtesy of Koninklijke Bibliotheek, The Hague, Kn. 6477.

Coutinho, he came from Portugal, and, as soon as he enters the conversation, the main issue of the pamphlet is raised. By systematically lining up his arguments and also simply by out-talking the three Company directors in his extensive speaking parts, Francisco undermines the credibility of the *bewindhebbers* and tries to persuade readers that making peace with Lisbon is the only viable option for the authorities in The Hague. He even takes his opponents to a bookshop to quote sizeable sections from an historical work that is meant to convince the others that in spite of the Westphalian Peace agreement the Spanish king still cannot be trusted. The United Provinces, according to Francisco, are better off with an alliance with Portugal, regardless of the recent loss of Angola and São Tomé and the ongoing revolt in Pernambuco.

Here two *bewindhebbers* leave the scene, effectively admitting defeat by no longer countering Francisco's arguments. The message of peace, dictated by the merchant class in Amsterdam yet feared by West India Company loyalists is then reinforced by the *praatje*'s final character, the ungainly drunkard Onkelboer, who in no uncertain terms derides the setup of the Company. "Is it not true," he asks the only remaining director Van Beeck, "that so much has been invested in Brazil, and that the only ones to have benefited are the Company directors?" By putting these words in the mouth of a drunkard, the author uses the rhetorical strategy of showing that even the most simple-minded observer could see what was wrong with the policy of the Heeren XIX.[44] A lot of money would have been saved, Onkelboer continues with remarkable guile, had the Dutch first gained access to the main slave markets in Africa before embarking on Brazil. The current Company, he concludes after listing six different reasons, is nothing but a harmful beast. Faced with this sort of blunt popular opposition the last of the three directors retreats as well. Francisco invites Onkelboer to continue the conversation in his lodgings.

The condemnation of widespread corruption in Brazil was shared by many at home, not just in Amsterdam. Nevertheless, the authors of the seven *praatjes* all published their opinionated views anonymously, as they regarded the contents of the dialogues, and especially the naming of some of the protagonists at city hall or in the boardroom of the Amsterdam chamber, politically too sensitive. The other six *praatjes* that appeared over the next six to nine months had comparable titles and title pages to create a serial effect in the book market. They all followed the agenda laid out in *Amsterdams Dam-Praetje* with slight variations in order to keep the chats attractive for a readership keen on hearing about the ongoing discussions through the perspective of fictional yet believable everyday conversations. The variations give a good impression of the sort of subthemes that were apparently being discussed (or deliberately introduced by the authors in the hope that they would become part of public debate) and put yet more pressure on the States General.

Brasyls Schuyt-Praetjen (Brazilian Chat on the Barge), chronologically the last in the impromptu series of seven, presents a discussion between an officer, a minister, and a merchant "transcribed by an impartial listener." In this chat, several of the issues that had come up over the course of the year featured. The officer who had just returned from Pernambuco complained at length about the way the Company mistreated its soldiers by offering them meager pay and small rations despite the terrible conditions—an evocative line of rhetoric merely a year after the Heeren XIX had sent another five thousand troops to Recife in spite of their sorry financial state. The minister bemoaned the West India Company's refusal to accept Sousa Coutinho's peace offer and proceeded to explain that the Company's current plight struck him as a form of divine retribution, an allusion to the anxiety of the clergy over the Company's lack of Reformed zeal, a problem that had been building for almost two decades. The conclusion to the *praatje*, printed in larger-font verses for additional emphasis and clarity, stated that the Luso-Brazilians were justified in appealing to God to free them from the yoke that had suppressed them for almost twenty-five years: the Dutch, after all, had expressed more reverence for money than for the Lord.[45]

"Amsterdamnification"

Within days of the *Brasyls Schuyt-Praetjen*'s appearance, an equally vicious reaction appeared in print that reminded the audience of the "treacherous" nature of the Portuguese.[46] However, the attempts to mobilize the collective indignation against Bahia and Lisbon no longer resonated after Guararapes. The debate increasingly drifted away from the West India Company's control, as pamphleteers now began to thematize the polarization of the debate itself, an acrimonious form of introspection that further derailed any chance of a constructive discussion on the future of Dutch Brazil. "It is nothing new that folks who consider themselves to be wise on every issue find it necessary to give anonymous and unsolicited advice in matters that concern only the government," one author observed. "But it is worse if they publish their appeal in print, before it has even been seen by those to whom it is addressed. It is bizarre that such writings are then being discussed in meetings of the authorities, without there having been a proper inquest, suggesting that they have been commissioned by those who have no business meddling in these affairs, or who have other agendas than the common good."[47]

This pamphleteer's criticism, it turned out, was drenched in sarcasm as this very pamphlet too thrived on exactly the culture he so righteously criticized. His own text was aimed mainly at another author who, he claimed, "had taken great liberty not only to accuse the directors of the West India Company of small-mindedness, but also to lecture the States General [on the issue of Brazil]. This, more than anything else, indicates that his candor had gone too far."[48] For clarity's sake, he then mentioned the full title of the publication that had aroused his anger. He even stated that the pamphlet he attacked had been printed by the Amsterdam bookseller Johannes van Marel and that it could be purchased in Van Marel's bookshop "In the Globe."[49] Why this practical information was significant is perfectly understandable when we look at the imprint of the text that he wrote in response, which, according to the title page, was also printed in Amsterdam, by Pieter van Marel, who lived in the house called "The Celestial Globe"! If the imprints of both pamphlets are to be believed—and the design of the two title pages and the use of the same font suggest they should—one anonymous commentator here launched his own, inflammatory war of words, exploiting unrest over Dutch Brazil to fuel political particularism and make some easy money. The two pamphlets, moreover, are the only printed works the "Van Marel" family ever produced.[50] This, then, was a perfect example of what English observers meant when they lamented how political debate could be "Amsterdamnified."

The self-confidence of the city reached an all-time high in 1650 when Amsterdam openly rebelled against the new stadtholder William II. The city even had to withstand a military attack by Orangist troops by closing the city gates and arming the militia. Before the conflict could evolve into a full-scale civil war, William II unexpectedly died. The regents in the States of Holland, spurred on by Amsterdam, chose to dismantle the stadtholderate altogether by naming one of their own, the young Dordrecht regent Johan de Witt, as de facto head of state. Dutch Brazil became an integral part of the 1650 prizefight between the city and the stadtholder through the petty and at times painful affair surrounding Admiral Witte de With. De With was already a celebrated naval hero when he was appointed commander of the expedition to rescue Dutch Brazil in 1647. But, once he set sail for the Atlantic, with a fleet assembled with great difficulty and delayed by several months of political wrangling, everything went wrong. From the moment he arrived in Pernambuco in March 1648, he was at loggerheads with the military strategy of the High Council, which focused on the land war and not, as De With desired, on naval battles in Angola and Bahia. Many disagreements and a few unrewarding expeditions later, and weakened by hunger like all of Recife, the admiral, ignoring the demands of the authorities in Dutch Brazil, returned home.[51]

In April 1650, De With arrived in Holland, where two weeks later he was arrested by the guards of William II for insubordination and desertion. That the reckless stadtholder was on a collision course with Amsterdam politicized the case of De With, who held strong anti-Orangist views. The fact that the High Council in Recife intimated that they would be more than happy to send a shipment of brazilwood in case there was not enough material to construct De With's gallows certainly did not help. The issue commanded intense public interest as all the testimonies for and against De With were put into print.[52] The admiral was held in the Gevangenpoort in The Hague for twenty-two weeks, and, as his case dragged on, it became a matter of prestige for the stadtholder, the States of Holland, the Amsterdam Admiralty, and the Amsterdam city council that was not resolved until after William's death in November 1650. Two months later, De With was released with a hefty fine. Amsterdam particularism had triumphed, but the magistrates' relentless criticism of the West India Company and its administrators in Recife—partly intended to mask their own abandonment of the previous two decades—only supported the impression that Brazil was a lost cause. The emerging acceptance that a small coastal settlement, defended by a costly naval presence, was probably the best the West India Company could hope for in the long run opened the door to a harsh and at times infamous public evaluation of the Dutch presence in Brazil for which there had been no audience prior to the early 1650s.

A truly denigrating commentary on the Dutch regime in Brazil was written by Pierre Moreau, a Huguenot from Burgundy who served as secretary to Michiel van Goch, one of the high councillors in Recife. First published in French in 1651, Moreau's report was eagerly translated into Dutch by the professional translator Jan Hendrik Glazemaker and appeared in Amsterdam in 1652 as *Klare en Waarachtige Beschryving der leste beroerten en afval der Portugesen in Brazil* (Clear and Truthful Description of the Recent Troubles and Defection of the Portuguese in Brazil), without, interestingly, the French edition's dedicatory letter that blamed the *moradores* for waging war for causes of "avarice, cruelty, and injustice."[53] In contrast to what the title and (omitted) dedication suggested, Moreau gave an uncompromising account of life in the colony, without holding back any of the unsavory stories that until then had rarely appeared in print. The author also criticized the Portuguese planters, but readers in Amsterdam will have paid special attention to his brutally honest examination of the many Dutch shortcomings and errors of judgment in Brazil.

Moreau's obituary of Dutch Recife, premature but only just, focused on the lack of leadership from High Councillors Hendrick Haecx, Wouter van Schoonenburgh, and the veteran German commander Sigismund von Schoppe. Although he opened his account with a survey of Brazil in the 1630s in which he praised Von Schoppe's qualities as a military strategist, Moreau mainly portrayed him as someone who oversaw the most merciless cruelties in the 1640s when things were no longer going well for the Company. When Dutch troops under Von Schoppe captured Itaparica in the Bay of All Saints in 1646,

> the soldiers spared no-one, and they even killed women and children. Everything was given prey to them, and nothing was forbidden other than initiating fires. Two-thousand inhabitants of the island

died, some by the steel, others by drowning when they fell from the barges which they used to escape into the Bay of All Saints upon the arrival of the Dutch.[54] (Figure 37)

One year earlier a similar scandal had occurred in Cunhaú, Rio Grande, when a group of Tapuyas under the command of Jacob Rabe, a German adventurer in the service of the West India Company, had murdered more than seventy Catholics during Holy Mass. The High Council, who had mobilized the Indians, was blamed for making only a half-hearted attempt to curb indigenous violence against fellow Christians. The dishonorable massacre, Moreau insisted, harmed the Dutch cause in the opening phase of the revolt. The regime in Recife did what they could to deflect the blame, but the illustration included in Moreau's account six years later symbolized Rabe's (and by extension the Company's) quiet approval (Figure 38).[55] For Amsterdammers who were

FIGURE 37. "Sigismund von Schoppe at Itaparica." In Pierre Moreau, *Klare en waarachtige beschryving van de leste beroerten en afval der Portugezen in Brasil.* Amsterdam, 1652, 65. Courtesy of Koninklijke Bibliotheek, The Hague, KW 562 D 20.

Figure 38. "Massacre of Portuguese Colonists by Tapuya Indians." In Pierre Moreau, *Klare en waarachtige beschryving van de leste beroerten en afval der Portugezen in Brasil*. Amsterdam, 1652, 31. Courtesy of Koninklijke Bibliotheek, The Hague, KW 562 D 20.

old enough to remember the lofty Atlantic ambitions from the days of Usselincx and Ruiters, the images in Moreau's pamphlet were the ultimate confirmation of the Company's moral collapse.[56]

Moreau introduced readers to other forms of criticism that provided even more ammunition for the Amsterdam party's reluctance to continue in Brazil. Many New Christians, he claimed, had joined Jews from Amsterdam who worshipped openly as Jews, and together, by making unreasonable demands, they had gradually usurped the possessions of the Christians in Recife. On the plantations, under Dutch rule, the *senhores de engenho* disciplined their slaves in such an inhumane and sadistic way that Moreau shivered to write about it. He had witnessed how slaves who were too tired to work were beaten two or three hundred times until the blood was gushing out from all sides of their bodies. Their wounds were subsequently rubbed with vinegar and salt, a punishment that was sometimes repeated several days in a row. Taken together, these observations amounted to an unprecedented form of public criticism of slavery in Dutch Brazil—long a nontopic in the print media. Of course, Moreau admitted, it is true that these atrocities were not committed exclusively by the Dutch, but they were the consequence of the proverbial miserliness of the West India Company that forced the *moradores* to produce sugar in unrealistically large quantities—an echo of the arguments used by Amsterdammers to make the case for free trade in the late 1630s.

Johan Maurits too was vilified by Moreau for his "scandalous thrift," first because he did not properly protect the sugar planters against roaming bandits and then because he pocketed large amounts of protection money from the most aristocratic ones when he did. During his time in Dutch Brazil, the count, "as they tend to say, skimmed the bowl more than all others before he was pulled out," an accusation that may have struck readers in Amsterdam as believable amid the many stories of corruption. All the sins of the world were on display in Dutch Brazil, Moreau concluded. Nobody went to church, and slaves behaved like beasts because nobody tried to convert them. All ethnic groups intermingled and lived debauched lives, and all Jews and Christians seduced African women before they sold them as cattle are sold in Europe—a very occasional condemnation of the slave trade in a treatise that otherwise accepted the import of forced labor as an inherent part of Dutch Brazil.[57] Moreau's 1652 catalogue of excesses must have made a rapid impression at home. In another *praatje*, published later in the same year, a fictional woman named Grietje listed exactly the same vices in order to explain to two friends the predicament of the West India Company.[58]

Bad Omens

In the late 1630s, Godfried Udemans had criticized the West India Company for not taking seriously its responsibility to convert heathens to Christianity and lay the foundations for a Protestant settlement in the South Atlantic.[59] Even his most devoted readers must have understood that the obstacles for missionary success had increased geometrically since the beginning of the revolt. But for a worldly hierarchy in Recife and The Hague to let things get so far out of hand as to have turned the colony into a veritable Sodom, to use the term of Vicente Soler, divine punishment was a matter of when rather than if. On 3 May 1652, at nine in the morning when the High Council was in session, Dutch Brazil was hit by an earthquake that, in the words of High Councillor Hendrick Haecx, "made the town hall and several other houses in both Recife and Mauritsstad move." Later that same year, the Dutch were gripped by fear again when, in the sky above Recife, there appeared a comet that was clearly visible to the beleaguered population for ten consecutive nights in December. Haecx meticulously described its rise in the southeast on the 15th, its recurring presence and manifestation, the gradual fading of its tail in the days before Christmas, and, ultimately, its disappearance on Boxing Day, which led him to say an anxious prayer, based on 2 Timothy 4:8: "God knows the significance of this apparition, which He shall mercifully make clear unto me, and not to me only but to all others who also love and anticipate His appearing."[60]

Whether news of the earthquake caused a stir in the United Provinces is unknown, but the ominous comet appeared in print (Figure 39). First in the form of a small woodcut, printed in Amsterdam in 1653, with a short textual explanation that ended with the rather faint "God giveth that the result be good for us," and subsequently also in *Hollandse Mercurius*, an annual chronicle of political events modeled on Van Wassenaer's *Historisch Verhael* and produced in Haarlem by Pieter Casteleyn, formerly a reporter for the Amsterdam newspaper of Jan van Hilten.[61] Amsterdammers scrambled for a prognostication of the comet's meaning. A hopeful and even conciliatory explanation of its significance was put forward in another anonymous *praatje* that appeared in 1653, in which two men discussed the future of the West India Company. A man from Holland comforted his friend from Zeeland by saying that it was conceivable that the "early" divine chastisement that came with the comet had been felt by the Dutch, but that the "later" punishment would be directed toward the Portuguese who, with God's assistance, might be subdued.[62] However, a respected scholar like Alexander de Bie, professor of mathematics at the Amsterdam Athenaeum, knew better. In November 1653, in one of the first disputations over which he presided, he wrote that "the rainbow is a sign of God's favor, a comet of His anger." The book of nature, in other words, offered little hope for Dutch Brazil, and, by the time De Bie started to waver on the meaning of comets in the 1660s, conceding they did not necessarily foretell disaster, Recife had long fallen to God's wrath and reverted to Portuguese control.[63]

Brazilian ecology had other arguments in store for Dutch pessimism. In 1649, six years after a small Dutch garrison had been wiped out by the Tapuyas, the West India Company had reoccupied the northern captaincy of Ceará in order to search for silver, thereby hoping to create a new economic lifeline for the colony now that the sugar industry had collapsed.[64] The lore of gold had already been used at the Company's expense by Jan van Hilten back in 1639,

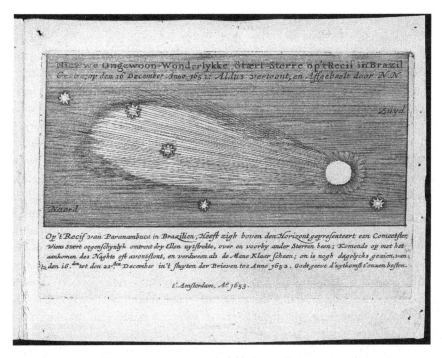

FIGURE 39. *Niewwe ongewoon-wonderlykke Staert-Sterre*, Amsterdam, 1653. Courtesy of Koninklijke Bibliotheek, The Hague, Kn. 7353.

just at the time when the directors had started up a campaign to raise more capital. Van Hilten was well aware that the title of the pamphlet he printed (and wrote?), "The Discovery of Rich Mines in Brazil," would create instant interest. However, the text concluded sarcastically that there were no such mines in the colony, and, in the closing paragraphs, the Amsterdam publisher admitted to this practical "media joke" at the expense of the Company's ardent supporters.[65] But ten years later the hope that precious minerals could be found resurfaced when an expedition under Mathias Beck established Fort Schoonenburg in Ceará to explore the province's rugged interior. A few dozen men, including mountaineers, an engineer, a silversmith, and several African slaves delved into the Serra de Ipiapaba and Serra de Maranguape. It would quickly become clear that Ceará was not the new Potosí, but, in 1649–50, Beck's men found enough silver to convince the High Council to send more workers.[66] Encouraging reports from Ceará briefly lifted spirits in Zeeland, jeered this time by Pieter Casteleyn who wrote in *Hollandse Mercurius* that the Zeeuwen were so eager for pure silver "that they wished the island of Walcheren was surrounded by such mountains, which they would have worked with more pleasure than the dike at Westkappelle" that protected the heart of the province from flooding.[67] In two provinces permanently under threat from the sea, the public spat could not sink much lower than this, and ultimately Beck's search for precious metals in Ceará came to nothing.

Unfortunate campaigns and more generally territorial or economic decay did not merit news maps (or maps in general), but the impulse to visualize events in Brazil was still present in Dutch society.[68] Paintings made in the late 1640s and 1650s symbolized the problems the West India Company faced in holding on to its Atlantic empire. Toward the end of his life, Johan Maurits claimed that he had as many as six painters in his retinue during his time in Recife, of which Albert Eckhout and Frans Post are the best known. One of the other artists may well have been the Antwerp-born marine painter Gillis Peeters. His stay in Brazil is not documented, but some of his surviving work—as well as that of his younger brother Bonaventura—has an unmistakably Brazilian flavor, with touches of exoticism and at times symbolic interpretations of colonial reality.[69] Arguably his most striking painting, signed and dated 1650, depicts a handful of Dutch soldiers, armed with rifles, fighting a large group of Brazilians with bows and arrows (Figure 40). In spite of their superior weaponry, one European has been mortally wounded by an arrow, and the outcome of the battle is not yet clear at the moment Peeters has captured, one year after Guararapes. The rocky landscape, very different from the views produced by Post, looks typically exotic, and the Brazilians are so stereotypical that they could be Tupis as well as Tapuyas. Peeters produced the design at a time when several major incidents, in Ceará and elsewhere in the northeast, had soured the relationship between the West India Company and their indigenous allies.[70] With designs like these, he may have catered primarily for the Antwerp market, where the decline of Dutch Brazil was followed with great interest, but presumably his canvases were also purchased north of the border in Amsterdam.

Two other identifiably "Brazilian" paintings are attributed to Gillis Peeters, and both represent a different, albeit equally problematic, situation for the West India Company. The first, undated, depicts two Dutch ships riding a stormy sea, with as many sloops approaching the coast where an encounter takes place between two Europeans and two Tapuyas. Several palm trees, bending in the wind, highlight the bad conditions the Dutch are facing in Brazil.[71] The second work, signed G.P. and presumably made in the late 1640s

"Amsterdamnified" 151

FIGURE 40. Gillis Peeters, *Battle Between Dutch Soldiers and Indigenous Fighters in Brazil*, c. 1650, oil on canvas, size unknown. Courtesy of RKD Netherlands Institute for Art History, The Hague, no. 366368.

or early 1650s, is a topographic painting of Fort Ceulen at the entrance of the Rio Grande, one of the strongholds the West India Company managed to retain until the very end (Figure 41).[72] The painting once again depicts Dutch vessels fighting the elements. Seascapes dominated by tempests were a popular subgenre of Netherlandish marine painting throughout the seventeenth century, and Bonaventura Peeters was one of its specialists,[73] but it is difficult to detach these representations of impending natural disaster in Brazil from the decline of the colony.[74]

The Brazilian paintings by Gillis and Bonaventura Peeters are not as well known as those by Eckhout and Post, but the brothers almost certainly produced them for a segment of the art market in Amsterdam and beyond with personal experience of Atlantic trade and the deteriorating position of the West India Company in Recife. The seascapes, like the landscapes by Post, were likely made to order. Cornelis Croeger, for example, an Amsterdam ship's captain who had been active in the Brazil trade in the late 1630s and 1640s,

FIGURE 41. Gillis Peeters, *Fort Ceulen*, c. 1652, oil on canvas, 80 × 112 cm. Courtesy of RKD Netherlands Institute for Art History, The Hague, no. 366366.

displayed in his house on the Lauriergracht a painting of his own ship, the *Alckmaer*, before a fortress in Recife, in a black, ebony frame.[75] Such paintings were probably disseminated and absorbed more widely in Dutch society than the materials that remained in the possession of Johan Maurits, at least initially.[76] They also counter the impression that some of Frans Post's images of the late 1640s were trying to disseminate of a prosperous, well-governed colony and instead offer more personalized images of Brazil.[77] Depictions and tales of natural disasters, real or imagined—in the sky, on the ground, in the mountains, or on the water—all contributed to the notion that the fall of Dutch Brazil was inevitable. When news of the surrender arrived, Dutch captives of the Portuguese in Goa, on the other side of the world, may not have believed the news. Supposedly they exclaimed, "Amsterdam perhaps, Recife never!" when they were first told about the fall of Pernambuco.[78] In Amsterdam itself, however, everyone had known what was coming.

Silence

The signing of the Capitulation of Taborda on 26 January 1654 and the triumphal entry of the Portuguese commander-in-chief Francisco Barreto into Recife two days later brought an end to nearly twenty-five years of Dutch rule in northeastern Brazil. The takeover was a courteous affair. Sigismund von Schoppe ceremoniously handed Barreto the keys to the city, while Barreto in turn pledged to treat the defeated inhabitants of Pernambuco well, giving all of them three months to leave, including—to their own surprise—the six hundred Sephardic Jews of Dutch Brazil who had good reason to fear the return of Catholicism. In Recife the Jews had enjoyed more rights than was customary even in Amsterdam, where some of them returned after 1654. Others chose to stay in the Atlantic world, in New Amsterdam where they were barely tolerated or on Curaçao or Barbados where they anxiously anticipated the coming of a second Brazil, which some of them eventually found in Suriname.[79] The Sephardim gradually regained their position as intermediaries in Atlantic trade, connecting Amsterdam to Curaçao and Suriname but did so more quietly than before.[80] Rarely again did the Hebrew nation in Amsterdam make their voices heard as publicly as they had in the late 1640s when Brazil started slipping from the hands of the West India Company.

The Protestant population of Dutch Brazil mostly returned to Europe. Peter Hansen Hajstrup, the officer from Schleswig, documented the chaos that engulfed Recife and Rio Grande in the days after the regime change as hundreds of people including slaves and loyal Brazilians struggled to board one of the ships destined for the United Provinces. After leaving Rio Grande in early February, Hansen did not arrive in Zeeland until the last week of July. After taking a small coach to Middelburg, he spent one of his first nights in an inn called "The Garden of Brazil."[81] No longer was there an incentive for innkeepers of aptly named hostels to recruit conscripts for a tour in the Atlantic world. Instead hundreds of soldiers returning from Recife assembled in The Hague. Here the Heeren XIX expressly forbade the troops, on pain of corporeal punishment, to walk through the streets carrying rifles. But the next day, some four hundred of them announced that they would rather die than hand over their weapons. The grim side of Dutch Brazil had come home. "These men are not paid, nor contented, half wild," news agent Lieuwe van Aitzema explained to the English spymaster John Thurloe. "They are men to frighten people, and chiefly at this time, where there is so much inclination to seditions and tumults."[82] Faced with imminent rebellion and mayhem on the doorstep of the federal government, the authorities gave in and provided the men with two months' pay, ordering them to go to the offices of the Chamber which had employed them. On 23 September 1654, ten years after having been hired by the Company, Hansen finally returned to the West India House in Amsterdam.[83]

One day earlier, taking a barge from The Hague to Amsterdam, Hansen experienced the final heart-breaking moment of his time in the service of the Company. His Tapuya "boy," who had served him for five years, escaped from the barge and ran off into one of the *polders* of Holland. It is unknown what became of him. Perhaps he was captured and displayed at fairs across the countryside, a fate two other Company soldiers had in mind for a "wild" North American Indian they had taken home from New Netherland.[84] In any event, Hansen's "boy" was certainly not the only Brazilian Indian who continued life after Taborda in the United Provinces. Most non-Europeans were probably servants of some sort, but the lives of Luso-Brazilian women who accompanied their husbands, of whom there were many, were occasionally quite privileged. Anna Paes, a prominent lady who had frequented the court of Johan Maurits as the patron of Engenho Nassau near Recife, in May 1645 married Gijsbert de With, a member of the Court of Justice, and converted to Calvinism. Nine years later, in April 1654, she and her husband decided to leave Brazil and move to Dordrecht, and later to The Hague. In one of the pamphlets that deals with the restitution of De With's private property in Pernambuco, including the revenues of his wife's sugar mill, Anna Paes is described as "so beautiful, that it was difficult to look at her without breaking into tears." She lived in Holland for another two decades, her physical presence reminding the local community of a shared past in Brazil.[85]

Some Amerindians turned to the Dutch discussion culture to reignite Dutch interest in regaining part of Brazil's northeast. The most prominent among them was António Paraupaba, leader of the Potiguar Indians in Paraíba, who twice before had made the transatlantic voyage to gather Dutch support. His first remonstrance to the States General in 1654 had very little effect, even though it was supported in the public realm by an anonymous pamphlet from Zeeland and behind the scenes by the Synod of North Holland.[86] The States General merely moved to instruct the Heeren XIX to investigate the status of the Brazilians in Ceará, the remote province where many former allies had sought exile after the return of the Portuguese to Recife. With the exception of a handful of repatriated officers of the West India Company who extended their support to the Indian leader, Paraupaba harvested little sympathy and even fewer results with his pleas, apart from some financial support for his family. Disillusioned about what he perceived to be a lack of loyalty toward the "poor Brazilians," Paraupaba died in 1656 but not before he had petitioned the States General unsuccessfully for a second time, this time asking for "two ships with arms and ammunition." Other Brazilians appealed to the authorities as well, like Domingo Fernandes Carapeba, who had temporarily settled in Amsterdam. His request was not made public, but he too would receive a financial allowance until he decided to move to Tobago, one of the Caribbean provinces of the Dutch Atlantic.[87] When the States General declared war on Portugal in 1657 and sent a fleet to block the Tagus estuary, they did not consider taking the war across the Atlantic, a clear sign that, in spite of indigenous pleas, Brazil was no longer on the political agenda.

The Amerindians who called on the authorities to support their former allies had the misfortune that Brazil no longer generated any headlines to lend public weight to their appeals. The news media were preoccupied throughout 1654 with the peace agreement with Cromwell's England that brought an end to the First Anglo-Dutch War, a more imminent threat to political stability in the United Provinces.[88] The subdued atmosphere in the aftermath of surrender, reminiscent of the fallout of the loss of Bahia in 1625, was interrupted only by a scathing pamphlet that blamed the High Council for its apathetic handling of the situation when the Portuguese fleet had arrived before Recife in December 1653.[89] When hearings on the fall of the colony took place in The Hague ten months later, the triumvirate of Van Schoonenburg, Haecx, and Von Schoppe was accused of a lack of leadership. Von Schoppe had known that there was plenty of food still available in the besieged town but had preferred to negotiate with Portuguese commanders before inevitable dearth would weaken his position. Neither the pamphlet nor the hearings rippled public opinion. Once the immediate political interest had disappeared, Brazil vanished as rapidly from public debate as it had arisen with the arrival of political interest in the early 1620s.

In August 1661, pensionary Johan de Witt and the Count of Miranda do Corvo—the new Portuguese ambassador to the United Provinces—finally concluded their global war with the Treaty of The Hague, which stipulated that the West India Company would no longer demand the restitution of their former possessions in Brazil, Angola, and São Tomé in return for a financial compensation of four million *cruzados*.[90] The Heeren XIX and the States of Zeeland, who until the very end asked for the return of Pernambuco, were once again forced to bow to the political might of Holland. Hence Amsterdam merchants finally regained the opportunity to trade with Portugal and Brazil, something for which they had waged a war of attrition since the early 1630s— initially diplomatically but ultimately in public. In the second half of the 1640s, the print media exploited the polarization to an extent that public discussion on Brazil could be conducted only by anonymous authors and printers whose addresses and names did not exist. At the same time, their rhetoric concretely named and shamed public figures such as the Amsterdam burgomasters and the local directors of the West India Company or used stereotypically ordinary citizens to castigate the corrupted regent class. This so-called Amsterdamnification of political debate on Brazil eroded all remaining support and escalated the downfall of Recife. By then the momentum in the discussion culture had already shifted away from the Atlantic world, on to the more pressing European threats from Restoration England and Louis XIV's France. As its relevance as a political dossier receded, the mythology of Dutch Brazil could begin.

CHAPTER 6

Recollection

As soon as he set foot on European soil after returning from Mauritsstad in the summer of 1644 and building on his many cultural enterprises during his tenure in Recife, Count Johan Maurits of Nassau-Siegen orchestrated a remarkable campaign to construct a stylized memory of his tenure in Dutch Brazil. The inadvertent meltdown of the colony after 1645 helped attach a sense of retrospective authority to the hagiographic reports of his courtiers and (former) allies, meaning that collective nostalgia for Dutch Brazil can be traced back to well before the colony had actually been lost. The notion of *Verzuimd Brazil* (Neglected Brazil), coined by the poet Onno Zwier van Haren in his patriotic hymn *De Geusen* of 1769 (but already in use before then), became intimately connected to the departure of Johan Maurits with whom—in the poet's Romantic phrasing—"the frivolous fortune had disappeared."[1] The idea of Dutch neglect in the post-Johan Maurits years has since the nineteenth century become a catchphrase for a missed opportunity in the Atlantic world. Yet below the surface of this frozen memory there were different recollections of Dutch Brazil too—some of which were more critical of Johan Maurits's time in America.[2]

The most contemptuous murmurings circulated principally in court circles and are collected in the private diary of Willem Frederik of Nassau-Dietz, Johan Maurits's cousin and main rival for prestigious posts in the Dutch army. Louise Henriette, the oldest daughter of the ailing stadtholder Frederik Hendrik, confided to Willem Frederik that the count "has been greedy for eight years in the Indies, and now that he is back here [in October 1644] he immediately wants the best charges." Lieutenant-General Johan Kuin, who had given Johan Maurits a loan of six thousand guilders, related how, during his time in Brazil, he had been deceived by some of the count's "nasty tricks."[3] Scholars in both the Netherlands and Brazil have often failed to recognize that, to contemporaries in the United Provinces, Johan Maurits may have cut a somewhat tragic figure. The way he continued to identify and be identified with his time in Brazil until his death in 1679 is testimony to his nostalgic pride but also to his lack of success in obtaining a position in Europe of similar prestige. In spite of his chronic lack of money that was repeatedly (and maliciously) emphasized by the likes of Willem Frederik, Johan Maurits continued to commission from Albert Eckhout "paintings of all sorts of things from the West Indies from which to make tapestries."[4]

However, just to criticize Johan Maurits's efforts to communicate his personal Dutch Brazilian heritage would be a gross misrepresentation of the artistic and scientific achievements he initiated. Broadly speaking, the count's public relations campaign served two purposes. First, it ensured that he would be remembered as a benevolent, clear-eyed ruler in spite of the accusations of the Heeren XIX that he had too lavishly spent corporate funds on courtly life. Second, it enabled him to use the cultural and intellectual output he had commissioned in Brazil to perform a role in a calculated strategy of gift giving that in due course, he hoped, would lead to a position worthy of his grand ambitions. His three gifts of Brazilian artifacts and paintings to King Frederick III of Denmark (1651), Elector Friedrich Wilhelm of Brandenburg (1652), and King Louis XIV of France (1679) earned him the position of stadtholder of Kleve for the Elector of Brandenburg and several noble distinctions such as membership of the Danish Order of the Elephant, the Order of St. John, and the title Prince of the Holy Roman Empire.[5] But he did not acquire the more prestigious positions he craved in the United Provinces, such as field marshal of the army (despite support from Amsterdam). Nor did he become stadtholder of Holland and Zeeland, a position that came free in 1650 with the premature death of William II, but instead was left vacant for twenty-two years as the regents under Johan de Witt took matters into their own hands. Part of Johan Maurits's public relations campaign must be understood against the background of a stadtholderless period that, from the perspective of the House of Orange-Nassau was the most humbling chapter of the Dutch Golden Age.

Public Relations II

In laying the foundations for a collective memory of Dutch Brazil, Johan Maurits had a ten-year head start, and the self-congratulatory image he constructed was prolonged to the extent that he became colloquially known as

"Maurits the Brazilian."[6] Upon arriving in The Hague after an eight-year absence, the count moved into his newly built urban palace on the Plein—the city's main square and a suitable address for someone aiming to re-enter the political scene in Europe with grandeur. On the outside, his "sugar palace" boasted a frontispiece representing an Indian battle, while inside it was decorated with paintings made "from life" of "all the heathen and barbaric nations, Moors and Mooresses, Negroes, Brazilians, Tapuyas, Hottentots, and other 'wild nations'." Moreover, the palace was scattered with furniture made from brazilwood, cedar, and ivory.[7] During receptions, Johan Maurits exhibited Brazilian treasures to prominent members of the court. In August 1644, only a few days after the count's return from South America, eleven half-naked Indians performed an awkward tableau vivant, probably resembling Albert Eckhout's monumental "Dance of the Tapuyas," before austere Protestant ministers and their wives (Figure 42). A few months later, at a similarly festive occasion, Johan Maurits offered his guests a spicy drink made with Brazilian ingredients, which Leiden professor of medicine Adolph Vorstius described in a letter to Constantijn Huygens as "a gift not worthy of such name."[8] In January 1655, in the count's absence, artifacts from Brazil played a role in an exclusive masquerade in The Hague that is testimony to his impact at court. A

FIGURE 42. Albert Eckhout, *Dance of the Tapuyas*, c. 1640, oil on canvas, 172 × 295 cm. Courtesy of National Museum of Denmark, Copenhagen, inv. nr. N. 38B.

letter written by Elizabeth Stuart to her nephew, future king of England Charles II, attests to the presence of one of Johan Maurits's red-feather capes from Brazil. Writing about Mary Stuart at the masquerade, Elizabeth informed Charles that his sister "was very well dressed like an Amazon."[9]

Away from the court, the count was lauded more categorically for his good government in Brazil. He seamlessly tied these ceremonial appraisals into his program of self-aggrandizement. In November 1644, the Board of Curators of Leiden University organized an official reception when Johan Maurits visited the town for the first time after coming home.[10] From Recife, the count had furnished the university library with a rare multilingual edition of the New Testament in March 1640 when he could not obtain the rarities and artifacts he had originally promised to send. Ultimately, on his return to Holland, he did donate Brazilian and African materials to the curiosity chamber that formed part of the university's botanical garden.[11] In a ceremonial *discursus oratorius* written to congratulate Johan Maurits on returning safely from Brazil, Antonius Thysius, professor of rhetoric, gave a classic example, as one historian has put it, "of how with many words one can say nothing."[12]

Thysius's speech was not initiated by the count himself, but it was flattering enough for Johan Maurits to have it included as a supplement to the first hagiography that appeared in print. The *Mauritias* (1647) of Franciscus Plante was a eulogy in verse of the governor-general's reign in Brazil, printed by Johannes Maire in Leiden at Johan Maurits's expense and sold in Amsterdam by Blaeu. Plante had for eight years been the count's chaplain in Brazil and could write about him from personal experience:

> A commander for whom a vast land, a world within the world opens
> up and whose victory ascends brilliantly in the Brazilian empire. I
> perform my poetic labors for a man of Nassau, and follow once
> more this triumphant leader of royal descent over the waves and the
> vast reaches of the ocean.[13]

Plante, who after returning from Recife became a minister in Breda, modelled his epic on Virgil's *Aeneid*. In twelve books, together comprising well over six thousand verses of bombastic Latin, he praised the Olympian gods for favoring the count of Nassau-Siegen with the task of reigning in Spanish geopolitical ambitions. The 196-page work was published in folio, adorned with copper engravings after designs by Frans Post, and preceded by six laudatory poems, written by stellar names including Constantijn Huygens, Caspar Barlaeus, and

Daniel Heinsius. Yet all Johan Maurits's cultural capital could not prevent that the reception of Plante's *Mauritias* was, at best, mixed. The gifted young classicist Caspar van Kinschot was so critical of the volume that he found it remarkable that Heinsius had written a laudatory poem for it. He called it "a terrible and accursed book," and started composing satires with a friend on bad poets they considered to be a disgrace to Holland, evidently reserving a prominent place for Johan Maurits's former chaplain. When Johann Friedrich Gronovius, a German professor of rhetoric in Deventer, introduced some of his own poetry to friends in 1648, he confessed, "You know what a bad poet I am, I am almost in the same class as the famous gentleman [Franciscus Plante]."[14]

Despite the loud disapproval (and possibly also the envy) of other classicists in Holland, Plante's work—including Thysius's ceremonial address—cannot have made a major impact. The deluxe edition of his eulogy was very expensive, printed as it was in a large font and on high-quality paper, and copies of the presumably fairly small print run were still available twenty years later when slips of paper were pasted on the title pages of the remaining copies to account for Plante's newly acquired honorary doctorate in theology from Oxford.[15] The only contemporary of note to have gone on record in praise of Plante's verses was Caspar Barlaeus. In the final chapter of his *Rerum per Octennium in Brasilia* (1647), alongside Willem Piso's work on Brazilian nature, Barlaeus cited the *Mauritias* as proof "that we were in no way inferior in skills or learning to those whose weapons we conquered with our weapons and whose barbarism we conquered with our mildness."[16]

However, if there was one work on Dutch Brazil that deserved such accolades, it was Barlaeus's own—something of which the author was all too aware. Casper van Baerle was one of the finest humanists of the Dutch Golden Age, an imposing intellectual figure who had been one of the two founding professors of Amsterdam's *Athenaeum Illustre*. The notion of the "Mercator Sapiens," the Wise Merchant, which he launched in his opening lecture in January 1632, must be considered one of the key concepts not only of Northern European humanism in the seventeenth century but also of the collective intellectual identity of Golden Age Amsterdam. Faced with the looming international prestige of the university in Leiden, Amsterdam's *Athenaeum* rapidly developed into the center of applied classical learning in the United Provinces.[17]

Barlaeus had solicited Johan Maurits's attention on two occasions before being commissioned by the count to write his panegyric of Dutch Brazil. In 1639, he had sent a copy of an oration held at the Athenaeum on the victory over the Spanish fleet at Downs to Vrijburg Palace in Recife. Five years later, shortly after Johan Maurits's return to Holland, Barlaeus wrote the long salutation *Mauritius e Brasilia redux*. In the eyes of Johan Maurits, the professor of classical philology and philosophy had both the necessary erudition and the undisputed academic reputation to furnish a fitting tribute that could silence his critics in the Heeren XIX and at court.[18] Moreover, only a man of Barlaeus's standing would be capable of emulating the Amsterdam director Johannes de Laet's *Iaerlijck Verhael* (1644), a history of the West India Company written from inside the boardroom that Johan Maurits so despised.[19] Yet the count was prudent enough to realize that he could not criticize the Company directors too openly if he ever wanted to obtain a leading position in the service of the States General. Barlaeus's convoluted Latin served Johan Maurits's purposes very well for two reasons. First, it was perfectly suited to heap affluent praise on the governor-general by means of typically long-winded comparisons with the best commanders and administrators of ancient Rome. Second, Barlaeus's references to the primary documents from Brazil Johan Maurits had given him, such as handwritten reports by Elias Herckmans and Adriaen van der Dussen, were sufficiently deconstructed or clouded in erudition to remain politically innocuous.[20]

Barlaeus provided a chronological overview of Johan Maurits's tenure in Recife, but more often than not the facts disappear amid the flattery that fills the pages of *Rerum per Octennium* (Figure 43).[21] This becomes especially clear in the sections Barlaeus devotes to the occasions when Johan Maurits's achievements fell short of expectations at home. The best example is provided by the count's unsuccessful campaign to capture Bahia in 1638—a campaign that had aroused widespread optimism in the United Provinces and that Barlaeus himself had followed closely in the Amsterdam newspapers. Whatever his own memories of those heady days may have been, Barlaeus now justified Johan Maurits's attack on Salvador by citing rumors of the Portuguese desire to surrender the city. Once again, the notion of Portuguese complicity had proved to be wishful thinking. In reality, however, Johan Maurits's campaign had been a strategic debacle. Barlaeus, by assigning responsibility for some of Johan Maurits's overly ambitious decision making to Jupiter and Caesar, shrouded his chapter on Bahia in ample layers of literary rhetoric to clear the count of making errors of judgment.

It is abundantly clear that the raison d'être for Barlaeus's book was to make Johan Maurits look good. But Barlaeus was not as uncritical as some scholars have made him out to be, as can be established from his description of the row in Recife between the governor-general and Colonel Christoph Arciszewsky. In April 1639, Arciszewsky had complained about Johan Maurits in

FIGURE 43. Caspar Barlaeus, *Rerum per Octennium in Brasilia*, Amsterdam, 1647, title page. Courtesy of Koninklijke Bibliotheek, The Hague, KW 199 B 1.

a letter intended for the Amsterdam burgomaster Albert Burgh that had led to disrespectful rumors about the count. Barlaeus, in this case, was at pains to point out that "I am not a judge but merely the narrator of this history, and therefore I will not presume either to accuse or excuse Arciszewsky."[22] The reason for being so demonstratively neutral appears to have been Barlaeus's sympathy for the Polish colonel's cause, and, in this chapter, for once, the author refrained from complimenting Johan Maurits on his good government.[23] Barlaeus also rejected some of the count's pleas to gild his time as governor-general in Recife by including information that was factually incorrect. In a letter Johan Maurits wrote to Barlaeus shortly before the latter was to publish his book, he attempted to persuade the author to include an engraving of the castle at the West African outpost of Arguin, "because said castle has been occupied on my orders, during my government [in Brazil]." That was either an unlikely error or a feeble attempt to appropriate even more of the West India Company's Atlantic achievements for himself. Arguin had already been captured in 1633, not five years later as Johan Maurits wanted Barlaeus to believe, and the print ultimately did not make it into the volume. Another of the count's concerns, voiced in the same letter, was that his printed effigy should not be folded when it was included in the book. Here he did get his wish (Figure 44).[24]

How many ordinary readers were privy to the misleading picture presented in *Rerum per Octennium*? Like Plante's *Mauritias*, Barlaeus's three-hundred-page volume of Latin musings was printed in folio, on high quality paper, embellished with four maps and no fewer than fifty-six copper engravings made after designs by Frans Post.[25] It was available in Johan Blaeu's bookshop near the Old Bridge, but financially it must have been out of reach for all but the very happy few in Amsterdam. For the broader public understanding of Dutch Brazil, its impact cannot have been even remotely on a par with that of the pamphlets and *praatjes* appearing with great regularity in the same years. Although Johan Maurits in all likelihood intended *Rerum per Octennium* to be read by his peers, its limited wider impact was a concern to him even before the original edition had been put into print. In the same letter to Barlaeus, the count insisted that "Blaeu should be notified that he ought to give the copies cheaper" and also "that he should promote further the translation in other languages."[26] Johan Maurits's ambition to impose his view of Dutch Brazil on Europe understandably did not stop at the borders of the United Provinces, yet, here too, the outcome did not match his objectives. In the early modern era, Barlaeus's book was translated only into German, published in 1659 in Kleve under Johan Maurits's watchful eye.[27]

FIGURE 44. Theodor Matham, *Portrait of Johan Maurits of Nassau-Siegen*, c. 1644. In Caspar Barlaeus, *Rerum per Octennium in Brasilia*. Amsterdam, 1647, opposite 1. Courtesy of Special Collections, University of Amsterdam, OTM OF 84-7.

Shortly after Barlaeus's panegyric had first appeared in print, the States General sounded out Johan Maurits for another stint as commander in Brazil. The count must have realized that the future of the colony was looking less promising than its past. After 1645, the defenders of Recife for military reasons had largely demolished Mauritsstad, including the count's pleasure house *Boa Vista* and the towers and tropical gardens of his beloved Vrijburg Palace.[28] Johan Maurits, who had warned against the scenario that was now unfolding in Pernambuco, quickly quashed any hope that he was prepared to risk his good name to suppress the revolt. Declining the offer, however, did not enhance his reputation either. According to his cousin Willem Frederik's private diary,

> Count Maurits is held very much in discredit and in low esteem; he has haughtily imagined that he was needed [in Brazil], and has thus set his demands so high, that the Hollanders derided him for it. His friends do not like his attitude, and his enemies are making fun of him—He is completely ruined, in great debt, he is dreaming, full of thoughts and imaginations, and yet he still has all kinds of things made on credit. . . . His Excellency [Stadtholder William II] is less than pleased, as are the States General.[29]

Shortly thereafter, in October 1647, the count accepted the post as stadtholder in Kleve.[30] After the death of William II three years later, Johan Maurits's Schwanenburg Castle became a refuge for the demoted Orange-Nassau family. News from festivals he organized occasionally reached a wider audience in the United Provinces, like the week-long celebrations in 1652 for the wedding of Willem Frederik and Albertina Agnes. Pieter Casteleyn, in the annual *Hollandse Mercurius*, reported in great detail about the mock battles between Romans and Carthaginians in the gardens of Johan Maurits's domicile for which he employed Tapuya Indians to represent African soldiers from classical times.[31] The former governor-general evidently continued to identify (and be identified) with Dutch Brazil. An influential poet like Joost van den Vondel, throughout the 1650s and 1660s, wrote several poems that helped maintain the link between the stadtholder of Kleve and his achievements across the Atlantic, thus contributing to a canonical memory that persisted until long after the colony was lost.[32]

There was more to the count's repatriated court culture than just self-aggrandizement. One striking example of a successful and lasting legacy of Johan Maurits's ambitions in South America was Georg Marcgraf and Willem Piso's *Historia Naturalis Brasiliae*, a scientific study adequately prepared for the press in Holland by Johannes de Laet.[33] For more than a century, the descriptions of tropical flora and fauna in Dutch Brazil, put together mainly by the brilliant Marcgraf, were considered authoritative and reliable by naturalists across Europe. Treasured for its many in situ observations, it was used by generations of botanists and zoologists to contextualize and understand their own findings in all corners of the Americas, from the Antilles to the Andes.[34] But only a decade after *Historia Naturalis Brasiliae* had appeared in 1648, personal ambitions began to obscure the memory of Johan Maurits's scientific achievements too. Since Marcgraf had died on a trip to Angola in 1643, Willem Piso, Johan Maurits's physician, claimed much of the praise for the volume. He even referred to Marcgraf in the preliminaries as "my assistant," surely a convenient misconception of the relationship the two men had forged. Piso had a good reputation, judging from the kind verses Vondel (again) had written on his departure for Brazil in 1636, and he remained a respected physician in Amsterdam after his return.[35] Yet, while Marcgraf's efforts for *Historia Naturalis Brasiliae* harvested great respect as soon as the volume had appeared—one of his manuscripts commanded an extraordinary price at an auction in Haarlem—Piso's contribution was not rated as highly. Perhaps in an attempt to restore his standing as a scholar of medicine, Piso in 1658 decided to publish a volume on the natural history of both Indies, combining his own and Marcgraf's text with the observations of Jacob Bontius in Asia. This second work, *De Indiae Utriusque Re Naturali et Medica*, damaged his credibility beyond repair. According to Georg Marcgraf's older brother, surgeons and apothecaries in Amsterdam sneered that they had helped Piso to "improve" the sections of Marcgraf's work he did not understand.[36]

(Retro)Exoticism

Judging from the continued output in more reflective genres of the Amsterdam book market, the "info lust" for Brazil continued apace despite the all too abrupt ending of the political storyline.[37] Exoticism, which in its popular form focused on the variety and strangeness of the world, began to flourish in the second half of the seventeenth century. This period witnessed, among other developments, the transformation of accurate and detailed knowledge into the more readily consumable and commercially viable framework of the wondrous and marvelous of the "other," non-European world.[38] Part of Johan Maurits's cultural program fell victim to this shifting set of preferences in Dutch society. In the aftermath of Dutch Brazil, there was no-one more apt at riding the wave of popular exoticism than the Haarlem painter Frans Post. Post's gradual transition from making documentary, albeit generally sympathetic, images of Johan Maurits's Brazil between 1637 and 1643 to a style of Brazilian landscape painting that became increasingly decorative as his personal memory of the colony faded has often been noted.[39] Stylistic and political tastes changed too, and Post adapted. In retrospect, the seven surviving paintings that the artist made in Brazil are arguably the most sober ones in his entire oeuvre, which altogether encompasses more than 150 oil paintings and hundreds of illustrations and sketches.

Once again, the question arises: what impact did Post's landscape images of Dutch Brazil have on the mother country? It is clear that there was a market for his Brazilian paintings, which—unlike his colleague Albert Eckhout—Post churned out at a steady rate. In the first fifteen years after his return to Haarlem in 1645, he made at least forty works, some of which are considered to be among the best in his oeuvre.[40] Post, in this phase of his career, never used the same composition twice, suggesting a richly filled sketchbook and, perhaps, a specific demand in the art market from a clientele with a distinctive memory of Brazil. The art historian Daniel Souza de Leao Vieira has argued that the recurring presence of *engenhos* in Post's paintings of the 1650s suggests that it was an affluent urban elite involved in the sugar trade who were the painter's intended market, but, even though that suggestion is very probable, it is difficult to find sufficient evidence to confirm it.[41] Some customers in Holland certainly ordered specific landscapes, such as Peter van der Hagen who lived in the colony at the same time as Post and had a painting made in 1652 as a souvenir of Brazil, or perhaps also because it was fashionable.[42] The composition's vaulted crown—an anomaly in Post's oeuvre—suggests it was made to fit one of the wall arches in Van der Hagen's Amsterdam residence (Figure 45).[43]

Inventories of local households in the later seventeenth century indicate that Post's Brazilian landscapes were purchased and cherished more widely in Golden Age Amsterdam. Maria Zeeman, for example, the widow of Amsterdam marine painter Reinier Nooms, possessed two "Brazilian landscapes by Frans Post" when the inventory of her house near the city's Old Bridge was made in 1682, four years after her death. Johan van Marselis, one of the directors of the Amsterdam Admiralty with a residence on the Keizersgracht and an avid collector of paintings, also owned two landscapes by Post, which still commanded substantial prices at an auction in 1702. Jan Six, a poet, government official, and one of Rembrandt's major supporters in Amsterdam, owned two Posts as well. Presumably, those who had Post's landscapes at home also possessed other Brazilian memorabilia, like the veteran Hendrick Cannegieter whose two Posts complemented his collection of wall maps.[44] For all these

FIGURE 45. Frans Post, *Brazilian Landscape*, 1652, oil on canvas, 282.5 × 210.5 cm. Courtesy of Rijksmuseum, Amsterdam, inv. nr. SK-A-3224.

Amsterdammers, Post's visual reminders of Dutch Brazil, sometimes alongside artifacts, books, or maps, performed a role in their daily lives.

Yet the obvious follow-up question should be *which* image of Brazil the owners acquired from admiring exotic objects or Post's painted landscapes.

Part of the function of Post's works, for the likes of Van der Hagen, Cannegieter, and others who had lived in Pernambuco, was to nurture a form of upmarket nostalgia not dissimilar to soldiers' diaries and other oral accounts of Brazil. In this case, "a" Post could represent as many Dutch Brazils as there were walls to hang his landscapes on. Judging from the way Post's paintings were referred to by notaries making inventories of private possessions in Amsterdam, the notion that they represented a specific Dutch Brazilian past gradually disappeared. Whereas in the 1682 inventory of Maria Zeeman, Post's works are still referred to as "Brazilian," they are increasingly labeled "West Indian" or more generically "Indian." In the Amsterdam inventory of a certain Cornelis Uijtenbogaert from 1710, a notary or clerk even referred to one of Post's compositions as "an East Indian landscape"![45] For commercial reasons no doubt, his paintings occasionally also came to represent other Caribbean sugar colonies, such as Suriname or—in case they came up for auction in Paris—the French island Saint Domingue.[46]

Part of this changing way of understanding Post is explained by the fading public memory of Dutch Brazil, but part of it is also due to the painter's awareness of a shift in demand. In the 1660s, Post produced nearly seventy landscapes that often include a parade of tropical plants and animals and that arguably no longer represented the same colony that had aroused so much public interest in the 1620s, '30s, and '40s.[47] The changing emphasis in Post's compositions reflected the way political concerns for Dutch Brazil (and, with it, the notion of a Dutch Atlantic empire) gradually gave way to a rich iconography that, from the 1670s onward, would be the catalyst of a full-scale global industry of exoticism initiated in the publishing houses of Amsterdam.[48] Post readily incorporated his designs—and, by association, Johan Maurits's patronage of the arts and sciences in Brazil—in this more decontextualized framework. His images reached a wider public through printed books that thrived on the sentiments of exoticism. His engravings—initially intended to accompany the political narratives of Barlaeus and Plante—were in turn copied by others, most notably by Arnoldus Montanus for his retrospective work *De Nieuwe en Onbekende Weereld*, published by Jacob van Meurs in 1671.[49]

Jacob van Meurs was the leading producer of geographical treatises in Amsterdam. He closed the circle of gradual exotification by dedicating Montanus's book on the New World, including a 180-page chapter on (Dutch) Brazil with fifteen engravings after Post, to Johan Maurits. The publisher reminisced about the time "when a Prince of Nassau carried victorious standards in America . . .

and graced [its] rough surface for eight years, to the fear of Portugal, to the progress of Dutch might, and to the awe of the whole world."[50] Johan Maurits, in accepting the honor, tied his name to one of the most sensational and manipulative histories of the colony printed in the seventeenth century. Van Meurs built his career on the production and dissemination of such exotic coffee table books. He started devoting his attention to presenting a round-up of seventy or eighty years of Dutch overseas expansion in the mid-1660s. From his workshop on the Keizersgracht, he assembled a team of authors and translators, like Lambert van den Bosch, Olfert Dapper, Johan Nieuhof, and the German poet Philipp von Zesen, to stockpile information and produce monumental works on the non-European world with great regularity.[51]

Arnoldus Montanus, a Reformed minister from the Holland town of Schoonhoven, served as one of these professional authors, and Van Meurs assigned him to write a volume on America. As part of this work, Montanus opened his chapter on Brazil with a traditional geography, describing the colony's landscape, its climate, its flora and fauna, and the crops and minerals the colony produced. Then he turned his attention to the different captaincies of Portuguese Brazil, beginning in the south and gradually working his way—in space and time—to the captaincies that had made up Dutch Brazil. On his way north along the Brazilian coast, Montanus succinctly told readers about the arrival of the Portuguese, the interlude of "Antarctic France" in Guanabara Bay—without mentioning the religious turmoil that characterized its short-lived existence—the production of sugar in sixteenth-century Portuguese Brazil, and the arrival of French Jesuits in the Maranhão in the 1610s. Wrapping up his survey, Montanus concluded triumphantly that "on this Brazil, finally, the United Netherlands bravely buckled the armor."[52] This was the start of the narrative of rise and decline with which readers in Amsterdam and beyond were so thoroughly familiar through newspapers, pamphlets, and chronicles.

Throughout his chapter, Montanus devoted considerable attention to Brazil's native inhabitants, and it is in these sections that author and illustrator manipulated the existing iconography of (Dutch) Brazil.[53] Other than in discussions about alliances, Brazilian Indians had played a distinctly secondary role in public debate on the colony between 1624 and 1654. During Johan Maurits's rule, the painter Albert Eckhout had been employed to create his famous "ethnographic portraits" of the colony's population. His four couples, Tapuyas, Tupis, Africans, and Mestizos, which represented a hierarchy of civility in Dutch Brazil under Johan Maurits, formed a cycle intended for the decoration of the Great Hall of Vrijburg Palace in Recife.[54] When the count left Brazil, he took the paintings to Europe, but few people in the United Provinces were in the position to admire the larger-than-life portraits before Johan Maurits gave them to Frederick III of Denmark in 1651.[55] Although Eckhout's designs cropped up in notebooks of Brazilian veterans including Zacharias Wagner and Caspar Schmalkalden, and were even copied by John Locke's artist Sylvanus Brownover, these accounts were never published, and their ultimate contribution to the early modern memory of Brazil in the United Provinces is fuzzy. Geographical and ethnological precision is often lacking, and these manuscripts, essentially two-dimensional counterparts of the *Wunderkammern* of late seventeenth-century Europe, merely confirmed existing preconceptions.[56] The painter Jan van Kessel, in Antwerp, included Eckhout's spectacular Tapuyas and many Brazilian artifacts and naturalia in his painted cycle of the four continents, and from the late 1680s tapestries based on Eckhout's cartoons were made in the Gobelins workshops in Paris for customers from as far away as Rome, Malta, and Russia. But all these derivations were exotic rather than ethnographic and blurred the artist's original vision.[57]

The copper engravings of Brazilian Indians in Arnoldus Montanus's *Nieuwe en Onbekende Weereld* purposefully obliterated the ethnographic impulse of Johan Maurits's team of artists. Large sections of Montanus's text—and several newly invented illustrations—were verbatim transcriptions of the first Dutch translation of the Huguenot Jean de Léry's account published shortly before 1600 by Cornelis Claesz. The spectacular and at times very graphic images of cannibalism—and the derogatory message on the level of civility of the Brazilian Indians the chapter contained—reveal a remarkable susceptibility for stereotypes of the pre-Dutch Brazil period that neither the textual and visual accounts by eyewitnesses like Jacob Rabe and Albert Eckhout nor the individual experiences of thousands of colonists and veterans could prevent. Perhaps these old stereotypes had never disappeared completely, but, in the years of the rise and decline of Dutch Brazil, protoanthropological interest had received very little attention in the public realm. Yet now, as the political storyline indefinitely receded, a "media tycoon" like Van Meurs and his gullible author together turned back the clock a good seventy years in a careful program of what we might term "retroexoticism" (Figure 46).

The description of the cannibalistic "Guyamures" (a name for the Aimoré tribe living near Ilheus, derived from a map by Blaeu) as "the most savage people of all America" is a case in point. The Guyamures, Montanus claimed, have "giant-like bodies, white skins, and . . . live without houses as beasts in

FIGURE 46. "Brazilian Cannibalism." In Arnoldus Montanus, *De Nieuwe en Onbekende Weereld*. Amsterdam, 1671, 534. Courtesy of Special Collections, University of Amsterdam, OTM: KF 61-4633.

the open air, devour human flesh like tigers, never fight in companies or armies, but lie in wait to surprise a single man or animal."[58] Like any sixteenth-century Dutch writer on America, Montanus then went on to explain how things had gone from bad to worse by reconciling heathen practices with the influence of Roman Catholicism. The *mamelucos*, for example, the progeny of Portuguese men and Indian women,

> elected a pope, bishops, and priests, introduced the sacrament of penance, read Mass and rosary devotions, called the people to prayer by drumming loudly on hollowed squashes, using books made from bark that contained many superstitious church customs. They regarded as sacred shaking, pointing their tongues, and producing hollow sounds from the chest, for which they chewed a certain herb.[59]

Because of the way Montanus structured his narrative, this information—based on the writings of De Léry and Jan Huygen van Linschoten—appeared to apply to the period *after* the Dutch surrender, thus carrying the implicit judgment that Brazil and the Brazilians had reverted to old ways now that the Portuguese had resumed control.[60]

Few opinion makers in Amsterdam were so categorical in their neglect of the cross-cultural compromises and nuances that had been forged in Dutch Brazil. Yet, at the same time, few could match Van Meurs and his authors for wider impact.[61] The tendency to sacrifice ethnographic accuracy for more stereotypical and visually more attractive representations quickly began to broaden. Romeyn de Hooghe, arguably the leading engraver of his generation, also reverted to the more indiscriminate visual framework that revealed preciously few traces of a distinctive colonial memory. De Hooghe owned a print shop on Dam Square and made book illustrations for many respectable publishers, including Jacob van Meurs. In 1682, he designed two images for the professional author Simon de Vries's four-volume work of *Curious Comments on the Extraordinary Marvels of the East and West Indies*.[62] The first image, "Brasilise suykerwerken" (Brazilian Sugar Mills) depicted three stages of the production process that closely relied on Frans Post's drawings and that readers may have recognized from earlier publications on Dutch Brazil. This illustration was placed alongside a very graphic image of Spanish tyranny in the West Indies that no longer carried any political relevance in the late seventeenth century and was merely intended to evoke the memory of a shared past—a strategy resembling that of Van Meurs and Montanus.

De Hooghe's second Brazilian engraving, entitled "Brasiliaensche kleedingen" (Brazilian Dress), is a textbook example of the amalgamation of ethnographic imagery that suppressed memories of Brazil in the later seventeenth century (Figure 47). It combined several illustrations into one image, beginning on the right with Tapuya Indians consuming what appeared to be an alligator alongside other cannibals cooking a human head and smoke-drying human limbs, hanging in a tree to the extreme left of the composition. Additional "Brazilian man-eaters," according to the legend, are depicted in the background. De Hooghe borrowed many of the ethnographic details, including the feathered headgear of the cannibals in the foreground (as well as probably the alligator) from the first two *America* volumes published by Theodore de Bry in the early 1590s, which were based on European travel accounts of Virginia and Florida.[63] This predilection for outdated iconography was inadvertently confirmed by De Hooghe's addition of English ships and the practice of bathing in

Recollection

FIGURE 47. Romeyn de Hooghe, "Brazilian Dress." In Simon de Vries, *Curieuse Aenmerckingen*. Utrecht, 1682, 3: 99. Courtesy of Koninklijke Bibliotheek, The Hague, KW 534 C 6.

Virginia to the same image, which completed the *capriccio* of Native American cannibalism. At the same time, it crowned the disappearance of a distinctive (and subtler) Dutch vision of Brazilian Indians that West India Company employees had built in Pernambuco, with the convenient side effect of storing and replacing the painful memory of political neglect. Instead, by the 1680s, the Brazilian imagery of the 1580s had once again become en vogue.

Nostalgia

Reliable observations by Willem Piso, Frans Post, and Albert Eckhout thus came under pressure as the memory of Dutch Brazil faded, no longer through modifications made by a partisan press or because of widespread disappointment and anger in Dutch society but mainly because of a drop in attention and a change in taste. Soldiers and colonists who had served the West India Company continued to transmit and even personify the shared Brazilian past in various ways. Undisciplined former conscripts such as the Caribbean pirate "Rock the Brazilian" or the female professional burglar "Brazilian Mary" switched to a career in crime, retrospectively increasing the notion of Brazil as a disorderly colony.[64] Others, like Peter Hansen, returned home (he became a schoolmaster in Flensburg), probably resentful of the West India Company for not paying their salaries as promised.[65] Still others, including Johan Nieuhof and Zacharias Wagner, opted for a future in the East Indies. In December 1670, just as Van Meurs's Amsterdam workshop began the second phase of its dissemination of Montanus's biased coffee-table book by having it translated it into English and German, former Brazilian freeman Mattheus van den Broeck returned from Asia to visit the home of Johann Philipp Mulheiser in Dordrecht, writing in the latter's *album amicorum* the sobering truth that "vigilance is the mother of good adventure."[66] Such a sentiment was not fit (or intended) to make the headlines, but it revealed the quiet lifestyle many Brazilian veterans had reverted to after their return to Europe.

Some veterans, perhaps those with fonder memories of Recife, made an effort to establish a "second" Brazil. In many ways, as Stuart Schwartz has recently argued, the later seventeenth-century Atlantic world was characterized by the desire to find a new Brazil, a great and profitable tropical colony based on coerced labor that facilitated the realization of dreams of wealth and power.[67] In the United Provinces, this was particularly true for ethnic groups that had enjoyed unprecedented liberties and economic expansion, like Sephardic Jews and former Brazilian allies of the West India Company. The latter, under António Paraupaba, had made a premature attempt to put these ideals into print to assemble funding and gather public support, but the States General and the Dutch public were not receptive to these calls so soon after the fall of Recife. The hundreds of Jews who came back to Amsterdam did not wait for the momentum to return and left for English sugar colonies such as Barbados, although a few remained in the Dutch world by setting up communities on Tobago, Curaçao, and along the coast of Guyana.[68] From the later 1650s onward, the enterprising spirit gradually returned. The Dutch were still important players in the transatlantic slave trade, more dominant than they had been during their presence in Pernambuco, and the thought of establishing another plantation colony resurfaced. Both idealists and actual policymakers used the simmering memory of Brazil to shape a more modest Dutch Atlantic future.

The most notable theorist arguing for a return to the tropics was Otto Keye, a student from Gelderland who had left for Brazil in 1639 and progressed through the ranks until he became captain of a company of foot.[69] Once defeat by the Portuguese became inevitable, Keye was one of the Company employees petitioning the States General to take up the cause of loyal Brazilian Indians. His enthusiasm for Brazil did not wane, and, in 1659, he wrote *Het waere onderscheyt tusschen koude en warme landen* (The True Difference Between Cold and Warm Countries), published to entice would-be settlers to the Caribbean rather than to New Netherland, the Dutch colony along the Hudson River that was also looking to attract colonists. According to the Amsterdam poet (and former Company functionary in Recife) Quirijn Spranger, whose verses prefaced Keye's account, the author wrote from experience about a country like Brazil, "where the vines grow grapes four times a year."[70] Keye argued passionately that Guyana had the same conditions of soil and climate as "beautiful, opulent, pleasant, and indeed, invaluable Brazil." More to the point, the author made calculations of the riches to be obtained on the Wild Coast based on lessons learned in Pernambuco, for example, warning against selling slaves to colonists at high prices "because of which the Company itself incurred more damages than profits."[71] The appeal of the Wild Coast was further enhanced by Keye's associate Sir Balthasar Gerbier, who claimed to have knowledge of a "secret" gold mine in the region.[72] Gerbier successfully petitioned the Chamber of Zeeland to finance an expedition, but, when the value of mineral earth turned out to be disappointing, yet again, he publicly criticized the West India Company for failing to support him in occupying a country "just as good as Brazil." In the end, he left for Cayenne, with a charter from the Dutch authorities, where he did not find any gold either.[73]

A genuine opportunity to build another Brazil came in Suriname, the Barbadian-run colony Abraham Crijnssen seized during the Second Anglo-

Dutch War and that was officially transmitted to the Dutch at the Peace of Breda in 1667. The account that reported on the unexpected takeover, written by one of the expedition's participants, immediately set the tone by claiming that, in Suriname, "such beautiful sugar is made as once was produced in Brazil. If [the colony] can be preserved with God's blessing, it is very well suited to be made into another Brazil."[74] For the Sephardim, this turned out to be an accurate prediction. In 1669, they established their own village at Jodensavanne, far enough away from the colony's administrative heart in Paramaribo to freely practice their religion and trade.[75] Many of their liberties were in conformity with the established practice in Dutch Brazil.[76] For the Dutch governors in Fort Zeelandia and the directors in Middelburg, however, the preservation and development of Suriname proved to be an uphill struggle. Very few Europeans were prepared to make the Atlantic crossing to help build another plantation society, daunted perhaps by stories or personal memories of hardship in Pernambuco. In 1675 there were as few as four hundred Europeans left in the colony.[77]

The hopeful notion that Suriname could become a "second Brazil," regardless of the practical difficulties, was particularly strong in the minds of those who had personally experienced the decline and fall of Recife. Johannes Heinsius, the third governor of Suriname, was one of these former colonists. He had been an administrative official at the Council of Justice in Brazil and on return served as a representative of the West India Company in London. When he arrived in Suriname in 1678, the situation in the colony was more desperate than ever before. Various Indian groups who had taken up arms against the Dutch had managed to obtain support from runaway African slaves on the plantations along the Suriname River. European planters had evacuated the countryside and taken shelter in Fort Zeelandia, and Heinsius immediately noticed the parallels between Suriname and Pernambuco on the eve of the Luso-Brazilian revolt, which provided him with an obvious frame of reference. In his first letter to the directors in Zeeland, he noted approvingly that the country was "better than I had imagined, and it can truly be brought to greater perfection than Brazil has ever been for the West India Company, even though in order to win and lose that land we have spent twenty-four years, and millions in good money."[78]

Two days later Heinsius wrote again suggesting possible solutions for the problems he encountered. He proposed to seal off the harbor and construct a new defensive line against intruders from the interior. He also asked for at least two hundred additional troops, more victuals, and more ammunition.

His short-term plan was to create divisions among the Indian groups that were now united against the Dutch and to recruit Indian allies to weather the storm. And, finally, the governor also intended

> to establish a regiment of blacks and to turn them into soldiers, promising them freedom at the end of their four-year tours. In Brazil the Portuguese had a regiment of *Negros* under the command of Henrique Dias, a Negro with one arm, which did more damage to us than any other Portuguese regiment.[79]

Dias had resisted the Dutch occupation since as early as 1633, and his successive feats in the War of Divine Liberation had earned him several royal favors from Lisbon.[80] Heinsius could have seen Dias when the latter led his troops into Recife days after the West India Company had surrendered. The experience of defeat in Brazil had certainly made an impression on Heinsius, and he was adamant not to make the same mistakes twice. In 1679, in a letter to one of the colony's planters, he explained that he needed more soldiers to release others from their military duties, "for it is wrong to hold on to these men for too long, which was an important reason for the loss of Brazil, because they become absolutely reluctant."[81] Heinsius's frame of reference for making policy in Suriname, although at times quite explicit, was not new. Brazil had also provided the blueprint for his predecessors Julius Lichtenberg and Pieter Versterre, as well as for Suriname's inhabitants. A group of prominent colonists submitted a petition to the States of Zeeland in 1671 to finance the building of "public sugar mills" to enable less affluent planters to manufacture their sugar cane there, "as is custom in other countries & also in Brazil."[82]

For the first fifteen years the Dutch were in charge in Suriname, the colony was a Zeeland patroonship, a residue of the political particularism in the final years of Dutch Brazil.[83] The Amsterdam print media expressed some interest in the settlement, but it was by no means comparable to the frenzy that had surrounded Brazil in the second quarter of the seventeenth century. Brief reports of ships departing and arriving were spiced up only occasionally by information on political developments and relations with the region's native inhabitants. The main newspaper reporting on Suriname did not appear in Amsterdam but in Haarlem. Contemporary Amsterdam media like *La Gazette d'Amsterdam* or the *Amsterdamsche Courant* paid hardly any attention to the new Dutch efforts to establish a foothold in the Atlantic world, and no matter how salient information from Suriname became, on Indian uprisings or the progress of the transatlantic slave trade, the colony never stirred up public interest in remotely the same way that Dutch Brazil had done.[84]

The Amsterdam directors, meanwhile, waited patiently for the mood to change. In 1674, the "old" Company went bankrupt, only to be resurrected immediately as the Second West India Company. Despite all the obvious deficiencies, the Amsterdam authorities retained an interest in Suriname. In 1679, as Heinsius was trying to restore order, local merchants began to put pressure on the Chamber of Amsterdam to get involved. A local committee was formed, consisting of prominent magistrates like Johannes Hudde and Nicolaes Witsen, with the brief to talk to merchants in the sugar trade and settlers who had lived in Suriname. Their advice to the burgomasters, based on these interviews, was that the colony could indeed become a "second Brazil" (in more ways than one, in fact, as the Amsterdammers also remained concerned about the Company's monopolistic tendencies). Supported by this hopeful claim, the urban authorities composed a document that mapped out the colony's future, which stipulated freedom of trade for everyone. The involvement of Amsterdam alerted the States of Holland, and ultimately led to the creation of a new administrative body, the Society of Suriname, which took control of the colony in 1682. In political terms, Amsterdam, thus, returned to the Atlantic world. But even then, as Suriname slowly began to fulfill its potential, nostalgic echoes of Recife remained. In 1712, when the veterans of Dutch Brazil had all died and the colony's communicative memory began to disappear, its application as a yardstick for Suriname still retained its value. Officers in Paramaribo claimed that, with better protection against roaming French pirates, Suriname "could be as mighty in terms of population as Brazil, and undeniably richer."[85]

Pride

One group of protagonists whose reputations thrived as eyewitness accounts of Dutch Brazil began to vanish were admirals of the West India Company. Even though their achievements had since been nullified, the feats of Piet Heyn, Hendrick Lonck, and Jan Lichthart were incorporated and embellished in a popular "cult of naval heroes." This cult by association prolonged a distinctive memory of Dutch Brazil that survived alongside the personal cult of Johan Maurits into the eighteenth and nineteenth centuries. The cult of naval heroes was unique because it did not express the triumph of a state, ruler, or religion. Instead, the officer's own actions and character were its principal features, helping admirals to become the most recognizable Dutch folk heroes. In a society where service at sea had both a great nation-building effect and acted as a kind of social cement, admirals were ideally positioned to be heroic icons. Unlike army officers, they were typically born in the United Provinces, usually in Holland or Zeeland, and the navy appealed to the public as a homegrown institution. The admirals' modest backgrounds, as an implicit profession of more egalitarian virtues, became of prime importance in shaping urban and provincial pride and, subsequently, national identity.[86]

The cult emerged in the third quarter of the seventeenth century, when the demand for naval heroes was particularly pressing in the domestic political sphere.[87] In the 1650s, the new regent regime under Johan de Witt needed to legitimize its elimination of the House of Orange from the corridors of power, in the First Stadtholderless Period, which lasted until 1672. The cult of naval heroes was quickly adopted for this purpose. It ticked all the boxes in the search for a recognizable republican identity and was soon also embraced by authors with Orangist sympathies, which helps explain its lasting appeal. Funeral processions, epitaphs, medals, and paintings were designed to honor admirals as "secular saints," but the best way to trace the continued popularity of admirals of Dutch Brazil is by looking at so-called collective biographies, a new genre in the book market.[88] Several of these collective biographies were devoted exclusively to iconic figures of maritime discoveries and expansion, sometimes as part of an international lineup of great navigators but increasingly in a national context. The genre depended for its success on a sizeable number of credible laureates and hence could prosper only by embracing admirals who had been victorious further away from the fatherland, in distant places like Brazil.

Until modern times, the cult of naval heroes remained an established expression of patriotism especially during periods of national crisis. The timing of the cult's surge determined the place it reserved for naval commanders of Dutch Brazil. Antonius Thysius, the Leiden professor of rhetoric who had given a ceremonial speech when Johan Maurits returned from South America, was the first to compile a catalogue of naval triumphs in 1657.[89] Alongside clashes with Dunkirk privateers, battles in the Atlantic formed *Historia Navalis*'s prime subject. The immediate impact of *Historia Navalis*, written in Latin, was limited. Its appearance did not fulfill the author's objective of landing the prestigious job of official historian of the States of Holland. Yet the book would become much more influential when it was translated into the vernacular by Lambert van den Bosch, one of Holland's most popular amateur historians, and published in 1676 as *Leeven en daden der doorlughtige zee-helden* (Lives and Achievements of the Illustrious Naval Heroes). Van den Bosch's first edition followed *Historia Navalis* closely, although he shifted the focus toward individual heroes rather than battles, thus reflecting and shaping the demand for personal tales of glory. The main admirals of Dutch Brazil—Heyn and Lonck—each commanded their own chapter, and Van den Bosch enhanced their status further by placing them alongside "international" celebrities like Christopher Columbus and Amerigo Vespucci.[90]

In *Leeven en daden*'s second edition of 1683, however, Van den Bosch changed the emphasis completely. In an effort to create a pantheon of national heroes, the author dropped the chapters on foreign navigators and extended the list of Dutch naval heroes from a handful to nearly thirty.[91] The illustrious men were now introduced according to a clear, partly provincial hierarchy: the volume opened with admirals from Zeeland, followed by their Holland counterparts. The final section was devoted to lieutenant-admirals, the highest-ranking navy officers. Piet Heyn's biography was moved to this final section and thus received additional emphasis. Lonck, on the other hand, was no longer listed alongside Heyn—or Columbus—but in the company of other, "ordinary" Holland admirals like Jan Lichthart. Rethinking his editorial strategy, Van den Bosch had changed the ranking order of Brazilian naval heroes in the national pantheon.

Whereas *Historia Navalis* did not contain any illustrations, *Leeven en daden* included portraits as well as pictures of Dutch admirals in action—heightening the lasting appeal of Van den Bosch's work. Heyn and Lonck were portrayed in the first edition, but no portrait was included of Jan Lichthart, probably because no image was available.[92] More significant still were the illustrations of admirals in action, and Van den Bosch's description of the conquest of Salvador in 1624 can serve to demonstrate this. Here the newly invented copper engraving shows the key moment of the invasion, the taking of the Forte do Mar first by an unfortunate trumpeter (who was immediately killed) and then by Piet Heyn himself (Figure 48). The image reinforced Heyn's reputation as a naval hero who took his place alongside rather than above the other men, a sure sign of the humble background that formed a key element in the cult of naval heroes. This was recognized by foreigners too, like the English tourist Joseph Taylor, who in 1707 visited Heyn's tomb in Delft and wrote that the glory of his actions in Brazil and other places showed "that heroes were not always born but made."[93]

FIGURE 48. Herman Padtbrugge, "Piet Heyn Enters the Forte do Mar." In Lambert van den Bosch, *Leeven en daden der doorluchtighste zee-helden*. Amsterdam, 1676, 488. Courtesy of Special Collections, University of Amsterdam, OTM: O 63-3891.

The illustration of Heyn leading the charge retained its appeal in the eighteenth century. A second image of the attack on Salvador was published in 1787, at yet another turbulent time in Dutch politics, when the cult of naval heroes picked up new momentum (Figure 49).[94] Even then, writers of national

FIGURE 49. "Piet Hein Conquers the City of St. Salvador." In *Nederlandsche reizen, tot bevordering van den koophandel, na de meest afgelegen gewesten des aardkloots.* Amsterdam and Harlingen, 1787, 14:4. Courtesy of Special Collections, University of Amsterdam, OTM: O 63-5936.

histories still considered the story of Heyn's courageous performance in Bahia relevant to evoke a sense of unity. Amid the echo of historical jubilation, some of the accuracy had been lost, as the memory was now embellished by the survival of the trumpeter. Heyn, as the commanding officer, was depicted in the foreground—understandable from an artistic point of view, but a questionable deviation from the carefully constructed plot—while the admiral's long, curling hair reveals how he has fallen victim to contemporary fashion. The same image was in fact reused in a national history of 1863, more than two centuries after the fall of Recife![95] Although by now Piet Heyn, with a newly grown moustache, looked suspiciously like his even more famous colleague

Figure 50. Jan Frederik Christiaan Reckleben, "Verovering van San Salvador in Brazilië." In J. P. Arend, *Algemeene Geschiedenis des Vaderlands*. Amsterdam, 1863, III-4:40. Courtesy of Special Collections, University of Amsterdam, UBM: 262 B 19.

Michiel de Ruyter, the volume kept alive in popular culture the memory of the capture of Salvador (Figure 50). The victories achieved in Brazil thus remained part of the nation's collective consciousness.

Still, the construction of national sentiment could not gloss over the provincial bickering that had characterized the final stages of Dutch Brazil. The Amsterdam minister Petrus de Lange also wrote a collective biography in the second half of the seventeenth century. In his collection *Batavise Romeyn* of 1661, De Lange too ranked the first Dutch expedition to Brazil among the most important campaigns of the Golden Age, if the length of the chapter is anything to go by. But, in his version, the name of Piet Heyn was not even mentioned once. The attack on the Forte do Mar, moreover, was reduced to a single sentence. Only the Amsterdam admiral Jacob Willekens is referred to by name, and, from the way De Lange constructed the narrative, it is clear that for him Willekens—and not Heyn—was the expedition's true hero.[96] At the time of the conquest, it had been a public secret that the Heeren XIX were disappointed in Willekens for his rather sluggish leadership in Bahia, yet it is unclear whether readers in the early 1660s remembered the fallout of the invasion well enough to be suspicious of De Lange's account.[97] Willekens, the old burgomaster Reynier Pauw's cousin, was almost certainly rehabilitated in the local interest, at the expense of Piet Heyn, who was employed by the Chamber of the Maas and would receive plenty of plaudits anyway. De Lange dedicated his work to the Amsterdam city council with the promise to focus on the heroic feats performed by their fellow citizens. Hence, by publishing a selective version of the conquest of Bahia, De Lange put yet more gloss on the glory of Amsterdam, the city other provinces had criticized, with some justification, for relinquishing Dutch Brazil. His study was reprinted in 1781, ensuring that the idiosyncratic yet powerful view from Amsterdam continued to stand out even at the eve of modernity.

CONCLUSION

Toward a Public Atlantic

After thirty years, the balance sheet of Dutch Brazil contained mostly disappointments. The confident infiltrations of Habsburg America had generated great excitement and remained a source of subdued pride in the Netherlands. Also on the credit side were the lasting achievements of Johan Maurits's team of artists and scientists, which acquired more luster and gained in relative weight as the political memory faded. The main storyline that had captivated the public imagination in the Dutch Golden Age, however, had ended in despair. "The Hollanders have left this Brazilian conquest," Pieter Casteleyn noted in 1655, "having surrendered these wonderful provinces out of pure negligence."[1] That painful conclusion stuck. Under the influence of cultural nationalism, the republican rhetoric of provincial particularism gradually eroded. In accordance, historians extended the blame for surrendering Recife from Casteleyn's "Hollanders" to the West India Company and the nation as a whole. When in the later eighteenth century, in his poem for the fatherland, Onno Zwier van Haren reflected on *Verzuimd Brazil* (Neglected Brazil), it still had enough rueful appeal to become a national catchphrase for what once had been a unique opportunity in the Atlantic world.[2]

Generations of Dutch historians have since echoed Zwier van Haren's lamentation. In 1783, Elie Luzac, the Orangist bookseller and editor of *La Gazette de Leyde*, blamed "the different interests and the protracted quarreling over political decisions for the neglect of these considerable conquests."[3] Hendrik Collot d'Escury, in his *Holland's roem in kunsten en wetenschappen* (1825; Holland's Glory in Arts and Sciences), called the loss of Brazil "perhaps the greatest political mistake we have ever made"—quite a claim from a man who was a member of parliament at the time of writing and would go on to serve as a member of the Council of State.[4] Since the early nineteenth century, as the United Provinces transformed into a constitutional monarchy under the House of Orange-

Nassau, the historiographic appeal of Dutch Brazil lay even more strongly than before in the achievements of Johan Maurits. Pieter Netscher, the first (and last) Dutch historian to have written a synthesis on Dutch Brazil, stressed in the introduction to his *Les Hollandais au Brésil* (1853) "that we congratulate ourselves here to do justice to the memory of this prince."[5] For twentieth-century Dutch historians, Dutch Brazil was practically synonymous with Johan Maurits—as three biographies and a number of collections of essays attest.[6] After the count's departure from Recife, so the canonical story goes, "negligence" arrived, and decline set in. The term *Verzuimd Brazil*, the German historian Hermann Wätjen observed in 1921, still resonated in the nation's collective consciousness.[7]

But the trope of "neglect" is only half the story, as contemporaries had been all too aware, and had little direct relation to the withdrawal of Johan Maurits. The popular participation in political debate over Brazil, and the "Amsterdamnification" of the discussion, had contributed significantly to the rise of negligence in political circles. This process of undermining can be traced all the way back to the days of the invasion of Olinda in 1630. The burgomasters of Amsterdam, after all, had advocated the withdrawal from Pernambuco as part of negotiations to establish a lasting peace with Spain. Although their strategy did not immediately bear fruit, the local regents anticipated the war of attrition they were about to wage on the West India Company's imperial assets by selling their shares when, publicly, Dutch Brazil appeared to be in the ascendancy.[8] If we sidestep nationalist historiography and its emphasis on the "neglect" of the colony and focus instead on contemporary perceptions of Brazil and the role of the Amsterdam print media in fueling these perceptions, the Dutch Atlantic's imperial moment can surpass its romanticized epithet of an isolated "Camelot on the Capiberibe"—to echo the words of Stuart Schwartz— and come to stand for something bigger.[9]

That Dutch Brazil ultimately failed cannot be attributed to any single factor but, as Charles Boxer already noted, the insubordination by the Amsterdam magistrates was a major reason for the colony's demise.[10] The sharpest political minds of the period also pointed to the complicity of local opinion makers. "Listen to what the people of Amsterdam have to say, and transcribe it," Hugo Grotius warned in 1636, "but don't say it out loud, because that can only do harm."[11] This, however, was wishful thinking in the discussion culture of the United Provinces where most, if not all, political information, sooner or later, became public—especially in an information hub like Amsterdam. The storyline that had generated such a media frenzy since the first attack on Salvador in May 1624 simply spun out of control. The chronic poisoning of discussions during and after the free trade controversy eroded popular support for a political operation that had initially united the federation like no other venture. By 1649, a hostile pamphleteer intimated that the city's single most powerful regent, Andries Bicker, had already given up on Brazil. When Zeeland and others wanted to take action, Arnoldus Montanus wryly reflected, "Amsterdam, on the one hand not very inclined towards the Company, on the other hand concerned about her own Portuguese trade, reacted coldly."[12] Without popular or political support at home, the surrender of Recife was inevitable.

In this book I have used the rise and fall of Dutch Brazil to demonstrate the interplay between Atlantic news, information management, and public opinion in the city of Amsterdam. That the Americas had the capacity to dominate public debate in Europe has never been fully appreciated by historians of the early modern Atlantic world, yet the rapid sequence of extreme highs and lows that marked the storyline of Dutch Brazil, and the intense public interest this narrative generated, illustrates the relevance of Atlantic events for Dutch political culture. Generations of scholars in the Netherlands have analyzed how, during the Twelve Years' Truce, heated discussions about the theological direction of the Reformed Church ended in the political execution of Johan van Oldenbarnevelt (1619).[13] Recently, even more scholarship has been devoted to the lynching and mutilation of Johan de Witt by an organized mob in 1672, also as a byproduct of factional divisions within Dutch society.[14] Chronologically anchored between these two nadirs of political desolation lies Dutch Brazil. Despite being five thousand miles away, this was a project that was so unanimously and unreservedly embraced in the 1620s and 1630s, whipped up by skillful patriotic propaganda, that any kind of deflation promised to be of epic proportions. The bitter division of opinions on Dutch Brazil—more than any other topic in the second quarter of the seventeenth century—confirmed that local and provincial particularism in the United Provinces was an endemic aspect of political culture.

The geopolitical significance of Dutch Brazil was much greater than that of the crises and political assassinations of 1618–19 and 1672, which were essentially domestic affairs. Talk about the colony, in Amsterdam and elsewhere, commanded great attention abroad, perhaps more so than any other topic of discussion in the Dutch Golden Age. The Amsterdam print media that channeled public interest in the Atlantic world kept everyone on the same page.

Their concerted coverage of transoceanic events had begun in earnest in anticipation of victory and ended only in anticipation of defeat. Axel Oxenstierna, the Swedish chancellor under Gustavus Adolphus and later Christina, wanted to receive copies of the Amsterdam newspapers every week to keep up with the latest news from Holland.[15] The English ambassador Dudley Carleton, as we have seen, anxiously followed what was being said about Brazil in Amsterdam and then spread the word through letters to London. For Jean-Baptiste Colbert, Louis XIV's minister of finance, the city remained a crucial information exchange, especially for intelligence regarding overseas trade.[16] The West India Company tried to use the public dimension of the Atlantic world to its advantage, and initially its strategy was very effective. The tremendous ignition that was the conquest of Salvador would remain a point of reference for at least two generations. As late as 1680, Nicolaes Jansz Visscher still sold copies of the official news map his grandfather had made in the summer of 1624.[17]

Yet the regents' information management ultimately collided with a more powerful force, the broadly shared belief in Dutch society that ordinary citizens were entitled to some form of participation in politics. The emergence of new media—regular, printed, visual, and cheap—democratized geopolitical knowledge. Atlantic news became a recurring feature of the Amsterdam newspapers, familiarizing a broad audience with the fortunes of the West India Company. While good news could lead to joy, support, or approval, bad news could nurture dissent. Through the lens of Dutch Brazil, we can analyze the impact of political information and establish that the United Provinces were occasionally governed by opinion, for better and for worse. Individual callers at Amsterdam's West India House, regardless of their social background, could nudge Company policy in their favor. Popular unrest could compel the authorities to change course, use force, or give in to specific demands. Amsterdam's Sephardic Jews, regarded as second-class citizens practically everywhere in early modern Europe, effectively petitioned the authorities in The Hague to advance their own commercial agenda. Twice in the 1640s, as the epitome of popular influence, they lobbied the States General to modify the stipulations of diplomatic agreements with the House of Bragança—both times successfully. And, finally, alongside individual agency, popular unrest, and pressure groups, there was always print. Arnoldus Buchelius, a supporter of the West India Company with friends in high places, implied in his diary that the authorities studied pamphlet literature before making important decisions.[18]

It is widely accepted that the extent of openness and political participation in the United Provinces was unique. The embryonic public Atlantic in

Amsterdam emerged in a vibrant urban culture in which a politicized and self-conscious language of public debate and public opinion flourished, an atmosphere that would not come to define European political culture more broadly until much later. In relative terms, its social scope was bigger than elsewhere: burghers, mostly middle-class men with a vested interest in commerce and trade, dominated Dutch discussion culture, but women, ethnic minorities, and the lower classes participated in debates and petitioned the traditional elite as well, challenging the existing patterns of social hierarchy and public life.[19]

The Atlantic world also commanded public interest and invited popular participation elsewhere, in Britain, France, Portugal, and Spain. So how representative is Dutch Brazil? Can its media narrative be used to investigate what a public Atlantic might have looked like in other European societies, where the evidence is sparser? A full comparison between the different guises of a public Atlantic would go beyond the scope of this study.[20] However, a quick survey of how the Western Hemisphere infiltrated political cultures across seventeenth-century Europe might offer arguments for the broader viability of this concept and perhaps an incentive for the reevaluation of how Atlantic information functioned at home. For Dutch Brazil to work as a possible template, the glimpses we have of a public Atlantic elsewhere must resemble it in terms of form and content, if not intensity. Historians now broadly agree that rumors, news, propaganda, public opinion, popular dissent, and collective memory are useful notions to help us understand the political landscape of the past, but they also recognize that some societies offer more tools to investigate these notions than others. For the early modern Atlantic world, the communication circuits of metropolitan societies are still relatively uncharted waters, and it is here that the broader scholarly relevance of discussions on Dutch Brazil in Golden Age Amsterdam might be found.

Rumors and news, which propelled Brazil into the public eye in the United Provinces after a long period of latent interest, circulated everywhere in early modern Europe. The culture of anticipation that characterized Atlantic news in Amsterdam appears to have been just as vibrant in Madrid, for example, where bulletins of the approaching treasure fleets from New Spain and the Tierra Firme generated an annual rhythm of intense interest. After the devastating loss of the Mexican fleet to Piet Heyn in 1628, the prospect of the next batch of silver and gold to cross the ocean created such anxiety in Spain that its safe arrival was celebrated by the publication of a *relacion de sucesos*. This was a form of printed news usually reserved for military victories and royal visits, which emphasized both the immense anticipation surrounding

Atlantic information and its cathartic quality when the news was good.[21] The Spanish cause attracted attention throughout its many territories. In the Southern Netherlands, the frontier province of the composite Habsburg monarchy in the war against the Dutch, news that arrived through Spanish channels of information was printed and, one assumes, avidly followed by loyal readers in Antwerp and Brussels. Although the media landscape differed from the discussion culture north of the border—it celebrated good news yet suppressed information on the loss of Salvador and Olinda to the Dutch until the moment that practically everybody must have been informed about it through word of mouth—here too, as in Amsterdam, the Atlantic world fostered collective anticipation for good news that was about to break.[22]

The monarchy's attempts to manage information from the Americas were not altogether different from the public relations efforts of the West India Company. Annual reports on the treasure fleet in the 1630s commanded ever greater interest in Spain because of the increasingly precarious financial position of the Crown. In September 1638, informed by agents in the Southern Netherlands of a Dutch attack on the Spanish convoy off the coast of Cuba, the Habsburg authorities were relieved to hear that Don Carlos de Ibarra had avoided being captured by spending the winter months in Veracruz. Another Atlantic disaster had been narrowly averted. In Barcelona and Seville, people read newspapers too, but, unlike in Amsterdam, these were mainly intended to defend the centers of power.[23] The rhythm of the transatlantic information flow, however, dictated that news of the treasure fleet would always arrive in the fall, forcing the government to come out and relate the affair to the public. Although it took slightly longer than it would have in Amsterdam, rumors about the encounter in the Caribbean began to circulate in Madrid in November, first in court circles and then on the streets. One of two *relaciones de sucesos*, hastily printed in reaction to public anxiety, triumphantly reported the death of Ibarra's nemesis, the Dutch admiral Cornelis Jol. But as Didier Rault has demonstrated, the *relaciones* were quickly labeled "lies" by readers in Madrid.[24] Not even the Olivares government, then, despite its sway over the printed press in Spain, could smooth away bad news that had crossed the ocean. Soon, as with Dutch Brazil in Amsterdam, Atlantic headlines were overshadowed by conflicts closer to home—in Catalonia and Portugal—that would terrify any public relations strategist.

Portugal was the Atlantic power that arguably resembled the United Provinces most closely. A small country with a distinguished maritime tradition, it had long enjoyed such a privileged position in the Atlantic world in terms of winds, currents, and markets that the Union of the Crowns inevitably led to dissent. News of the capture (and recapture) of Bahia in the mid-1620s launched a wave of anti-Spanish resentment not dissimilar to political particularism in the United Provinces. The fall of Salvador had come as a shock to Lisbon, where the religious orders and parishes organized masses and the clergy preached at least twice a day, asking for the salvation and restoration of Brazil. Here too, although the form of expression was different, Atlantic news resonated until the entire urban space was filled with political information.[25] A procession that saw the harmonious participation of all religious orders graced the streets of Lisbon, beginning at Sé Cathedral in the heart of the city, to demonstrate the shared apprehensions of the Portuguese church and society over the fate of their colony. Only two years earlier the fall of Ormuz to the English, and the feeble reaction to that setback in Madrid, had been a cause of grave concern in Portugal.[26] This time Olivares reacted swiftly and adequately, yet the fact that Madrid had allowed one of its enemies to raid Brazil was reason enough for public outcry.[27]

The pulpit, in particular, was an extremely important platform of protest and political agitation against the Spanish abandonment of the Portuguese Ultramar in the 1620s and 1630s. But the strained relationship spilled over into print as well.[28] The Jesuit Bartolomeu Guerreiro's account of the "Voyage of the Vassals" focused exclusively on the heroic contributions of the Portuguese *fidalgos*, reshaping the collaborative takeover into a legitimation of Lusitanian particularism. In response, the royal chronicler Tomás Tamayo de Vargas issued a Castilian account that served as a reprimand to Guerreiro's patriotism.[29] The public wrangling over the loss and recapture of Bahia continued with Lope de Vega's play *El Brasil restituído*, which hinted at the complicity of the (Portuguese) New Christians in the initial Dutch victory.[30] Yet, in *La Perdida y restauracion de la Bahia de todos los santos*, another partisan play, the Portuguese playwright Juan António Correa did not even mention the New Christians.[31] Clearly, in Iberia, as in the United Provinces, Atlantic events had sufficient power to create different narratives, amplify existing rifts, and affect political culture.

Historian John McCusker singles out Antwerp and later Amsterdam as the places of origin of the Atlantic "information revolution" and contends that the coordinated spread of information "increased the efficiency of an economy by enabling individual businesses to work more productively."[32] In Portugal there was widespread awareness that openness could benefit its prospects in the South Atlantic. Portuguese ambitions may well have included acquiring greater religious liberties in the Iberian world,[33] but their main ambition was to increase the volume of trade. Olivares unequivocally shared this objective, yet his policy to close the Iberian peninsula to hostile traders like the Dutch did not do merchants in Lisbon, Porto, and Viana many favors. The considerable advantage their colleagues in Holland held in the trades and in communication, Portuguese merchants claimed, had generated the explosive wealth of Amsterdam, while, in contrast, the oppression by Spain had closed European markets to Portuguese goods.[34] Free trade, also an important issue in the United Provinces at the same time, would not arrive in Portugal under the Habsburg regime, but the request for more openness reveals that not all foreign observers loathed the relatively unimpeded circulation of information in the Dutch Golden Age.

A perceived lack of information, or (consciously construed) misinformation, especially over a prolonged period of time, could lead to friction, as we have seen. The realities of the Atlantic world—on sensitive topics like religious orthodoxy and slavery—could not match the ambitions formulated at the outset. By the later sixteenth and seventeenth centuries, with the more concerted involvement of the Northern European powers, the Atlantic world had come of age as an arena of geopolitical conflict that was inextricably connected to the balance of power in Europe. At the same time, more and more people went to and returned from the Americas, fragmenting the flow of transoceanic information. Friction on the Iberian peninsula and in the United Provinces over Atlantic issues serves as an important reminder that the political decisions that mattered were still made in Europe. Historians of the Atlantic world, citing the axiom of the movement of people, commodities, cultural practices, and ideas between three continents, have argued for the agency of Amerindian and African societies (and rightly so), but domestic agendas *in* Europe still held great sway over the long-term fortunes of colonies and colonists—certainly in the seventeenth century. Professional opinion makers, with the odd exception, did not cross the ocean. Contemporaries in Amsterdam (and possibly elsewhere in Europe) realized that their own opinions might help consolidate or change the course of Atlantic developments. This not only raised the stakes of public debate in early modern Europe but also raises the significance of a "public Atlantic" for the field of Atlantic history.

The relevance of European politics for the Atlantic world and vice versa also explains why the mainstream media paid so much attention to transoceanic affairs. That Dutch Brazil can provide a model for the role of print culture in a "public Atlantic" is best demonstrated by looking at contemporary developments in Britain. Unlike south of the Pyrenees, the influence of public opinion in early modern England in the 1640s resembled (and rivaled) that of the United Provinces.[35] In 1654, eleven months after Recife had reverted to Portuguese control, Oliver Cromwell dispatched a strong fleet to Hispaniola to end Spanish dominance in the Caribbean and expand the English Atlantic further to the south—a campaign, incidentally, for which Dutch Brazil may have served as an inspiration and whose origin may be traced back to a visit to Parliament in 1641 by Johannes de Laet.[36] The media strategies surrounding Cromwell's "Western Design" were strikingly similar to the way the Amsterdam media had handled the uncertainty around Brazil thirty years before. Rumors abounded of both victory and defeat, news of the campaign's initial failure arrived only after months of delay, and even when it became apparent that the English had taken Jamaica as a consolation prize, its implications were so unclear it took another eight months before Spain formally declared war on the Protectorate.[37]

According to Daniel Bellingradt, "the use of media impulses was seen as an effective way of influencing the political process [in early modern Europe]," occasionally by "mobilizing public opinion for both political and private purposes."[38] The Atlantic world was no exception, as here too the authorities recognized that control over information was of paramount importance. Cromwell in the late 1650s set out on a familiar path by using, and at times teaming up with, the media to frame and withhold information from the general public in order to minimize the damage of the Western Design to his government's (and his personal) reputation. Whereas, initially, the media had imposed different forms of self-censorship in an attempt not to reveal any strategic details to readers abroad, the Protectorate quickly moved to suppress many of the newsbooks when the failure of the planned conquest of Hispaniola came out. Instead, much like the West India Company in Amsterdam, Cromwell turned to a spin doctor: only Marchamont Nedham was allowed to continue his publication of a weekly newsbook, the *Mercurius Politicus*, the content of which was "officially approved." But the authorities' control was not absolute, and, when rumors of disgrace and failure were eventually confirmed, support swelled for domestic opposition to the Protector, most notably for a return of the exiled Stuart prince Charles II.[39]

Just like Dutch Brazil, the Western Design was a matter of international significance. But its immediate political implications were felt most strongly in the mother country, and often the way of reporting Atlantic events was geared toward making a public impact in a specific domestic setting. Just how effective developments in the Western Hemisphere could be in a factional struggle at home had been known throughout Europe since the heyday of

French Brazil, another chapter in Atlantic history with international appeal. Here, again, a variety of political agendas *in* the Old World conditioned the way events were framed and interpreted. The French had discovered that Brazil could be a breeding ground for dissent long before Dutch Brazil came into being. But, intriguingly, the spat between Catholics and Huguenots in Guanabara Bay came into the public eye only when the opportunity was right *in* France, in this case some twenty years after the actual incident, at a time when the Portuguese had long removed the quibbling French from the South Atlantic. The war of words between André Thevet and Jean de Léry became symptomatic for the potential of Atlantic events to dominate and eventually derail European politics. Here too, as in the case of Dutch Brazil, the profile of the Atlantic world had been raised in France earlier, with the forced participation of Tupinamba Indians in Henri II's joyous entry in Rouen—a quintessentially nonrepublican cameo appearance of the Atlantic world in European culture that cannot be found in Amsterdam. Yet the dispute that followed attracted so much coverage that its polemical accounts continued to be printed in France and beyond for many decades and moderated state interest in a French Atlantic world until the emergence of absolutism.

Whereas the Bourbons initially did not participate in the Atlantic race other than in the relatively remote province of New France and a number of islands in the Lesser Antilles, their continued interest in transoceanic developments effectively affirmed the importance of overseas events for the balance of power at home. As an audience for news and opinion, the French were very much engaged in the seventeenth-century Atlantic world, and no one was more apt to exploit the large market in France than Claes Jansz Visscher. His Paraíba news map, published in early 1635, can partly be read as a celebration of the Franco-Dutch alliance that Richelieu and the States General had struck to further thwart Spanish dominance in Europe. For the occasion, Visscher introduced Brazil to the international readership by relating its history since the European discovery, carefully avoiding any denunciation of Roman Catholicism. The first part of the textual description in Dutch and French stressed that the French were "by many" considered to be the colony's true discoverers—an opportunistic (and very unusual) reference to French Brazil as part of the Dutch narrative—and had established a peaceful trade in brazilwood well before their rivals arrived on the scene. The Portuguese, the Jesuits in particular, were responsible for a deterioration in European-indigenous relations. The structure of the text implied that the Dutch had come to restore order in Brazil, a message that was meant to ensure the news map's positive reception in France and serves as further proof of the primacy of European political agendas in constructing a "public Atlantic."[40]

By the time the French entered the Atlantic world in more organized fashion in the aftermath of the War of the Spanish Succession, as Kenneth Banks has shown, political communication—"gathering, analyzing, displaying, storing, and disseminating information and representations of authority"— lay at the heart of the state's task to build an empire from a scattered set of settlements.[41] Banks argues that the vastness of the ocean did not place any major strains on political control for the French, just as Ian Steele before him questioned the scholarly assumption of slowness of communication in the English Atlantic around 1700.[42] Some reservation is in order, however, when it comes to cherishing the directness of communication in the early modern Atlantic world. Even in a sophisticated information society like the United Provinces, the authorities were forced to relinquish some control over political decisions to colonial administrators for reasons of distance, sometimes with major implications. In the case of Dutch Brazil, slow communication (and a lack of metropolitan control) allowed Diederick van Waerdenburgh to demolish Olinda, against the explicit wishes of the Heeren XIX. Johan Maurits was masterful in using distance to his advantage, first in pretending not to know about an impending truce between Portugal and the United Provinces that limited his desire to expand and then in delaying his own departure from Brazil by more than a year.[43]

No matter how much modern terminology we as modern historians use to understand the information flows of the past, there is one difference between then and now that is often overlooked. Distance, as Fernand Braudel observed, remained the "primary enemy" of early modern society, and it was distance that made the "public Atlantic" so idiosyncratic.[44] Distance, in terms of both time and space, generated the unusual culture of anticipation not only in Amsterdam but elsewhere in Europe. Politicians and armchair travelers gradually acquired a level of familiarity with the Atlantic world that belied the everyday delay in communications. Ian Steele, when discussing the role of technological progress in creating a broader metropolitan awareness of life in a distant colony, signals that "increasing familiarity can breed discontent,"[45] something that the case of Dutch Brazil affirms in exemplary fashion. That does not change the fact, however, that every new juncture in Brazil was subjected to the same delay that the initial news stories had suffered.

Amid intense scholarly interest in the Atlantic Ocean as a basin that connected three continents, it is important to remember that, in the most practical terms, it remained a formidable barrier too. If anything, the irregularity and occasional absence of new information created a "public Atlantic" that juxtaposed an episodic news flow with a continuous discussion culture—geared to the colonies' unwavering political relevance at home—that may have even sharpened public debate. This tentative conclusion is reinforced in a seminal article by Will Slauter on transatlantic news in the age of the American Revolution.[46] Although in Britain, by the later eighteenth century, the "culture of anticipation" had become institutionalized to the extent that Slauter terms it a "culture of speculation," the mechanisms—from the viewpoint of the European waterfronts—are identical.[47] From Slauter's investigation of British interest in North America, it appears that the "public Atlantic" observed in this study of Dutch Brazil may have continued at least until the rise of independence movements throughout the Americas.

The public interest in the early modern Atlantic world did not evolve linearly into the global village of today. As the colonial era came to a close in the later eighteenth and early nineteenth centuries, the culture of nationalism dissolved, reframed, and mythologized the Atlantic past, both in the Americas and in Europe.[48] The vehement discussions over Dutch Brazil disappeared almost entirely from the collective memory in the Netherlands, overshadowed by the impressive visual and scholarly legacy of Johan Maurits's circle of artists and scientists. Historians have too long followed suit, neglecting what (from a national point of view) was considered an embarrassing failure, thus overlooking the emphatic impact Dutch Brazil had made on contemporary society, as well as its potential as an important chapter in the history of public opinion and political culture. Because of its premature demise and the subsequent return of the Portuguese, the legacy of Dutch Brazil is difficult to compare with the disengagement in other European cultures that followed the surrender of sovereignty to those whom colonial regimes had always regarded as "natural" subordinates.[49] My choice to focus on Golden Age Amsterdam, with its unrivaled openness, its sophisticated media landscape, and its many pressure groups, presents obvious limitations in addressing the public culture in more centralized societies. At the same time, however, I believe that the transformation of rumors and printed news into public agency, and the scope and social authority of popular reactions to political information from across the ocean observed in the case of Dutch Brazil may provide a useful template for the ways the Atlantic world became a public experience in early modern Europe.

NOTES

✥

INTRODUCTION. AMSTERDAM, DUTCH BRAZIL, AND THE ATLANTIC WORLD

1. Aglionby, *Present State*, 223–24. His travel guide is a translated version of Jean de Parival's *Les Délices de la Hollande* of 1651. See Van Strien, *Touring the Low Countries*, 2.
2. Ray, *Observations*, I, 54.
3. James Howell to his brother, 1 April 1617, as cited in Lesger, *Rise of the Amsterdam Market*, 214.
4. Taylor, *Religion's Enemies*, 6.
5. See most recently Reeves, *Evening News*, 181–86.
6. Price, *Holland and the Dutch Republic*.
7. Harline, *Pamphlets*, 13.
8. Van Nierop, "Popular Participation"; Prak, "Burghers."
9. Temple, *Observations*, 109.
10. Harline, *Pamphlets*, 227. See also, for a broader approach, 't Hart, "Intercity Rivalries." On the Dutch "discussion culture," see Frijhoff and Spies, *Dutch Culture*, 220–25. Good recent studies that take the work of Frijhoff and Spies as their vantage point include Pollmann and Spicer, eds., *Public Opinion*, and Harms, *Pamfletten en publieke opinie*.
11. On the failed attempt to establish a printing press in Brazil, see Schalkwijk, *Reformed Church*, 56.
12. See Pettegree, *The Invention of News*, for a comparative analysis of news in early modern Europe. See Steele, *The English Atlantic*, and Banks, *Chasing Empire*, for explorations of the circulation of political information in the later seventeenth and eighteenth centuries.
13. The sections on early modern Amsterdam that follow here are based on contemporary "city guides" written by Isaac Pontanus, Arnoldus Montanus, and Olfert Dapper; on Abrahamse, *De grote uitleg*, and on an excellent piece by Bakker, "De zichtbare stad." For a good survey in English, see 't Hart, "The Glorious City."
14. Van Selm, *Een menighte treffelijcke boecken*; Schilder, *Monumenta Cartographica Neerlandica VII*. The term "communication circuit" is, of course, Robert Darnton's; see his "What Is the History of Books?"
15. De la Fontaine Verwey, *Uit de wereld van het boek III*; Van Netten, *Koopman in kennis*.
16. The magnificent neoclassical city hall—currently the Royal Palace—was not inaugurated until 1655, one year after the fall of Dutch Brazil.
17. McCusker, "The Demise of Distance."
18. On Van Hilten, Visscher, and their respective reports from the Atlantic world in the 1620s and 1630s, see Van Groesen, "A Brazilian Jesuit," and idem, "A Week to Remember."

19. Siskin and Warner, "This Is Enlightenment," 24. See also Eliassen and Jacobsen, "Where Were the Media."
20. Israel, *The Dutch Republic*, 478–85.
21. Van Groesen, "(No) News."
22. De Vivo, *Information and Communication*, 6. For a more theoretical approach to the notion of the resonating box, see Bellingradt, "The Early Modern City."
23. Boxer, *The Dutch in Brazil*, 236–37, 255–58. Since Boxer, Dutch Brazil has led an historiographically isolated life. The most recent authoritative companion to the field, Canny and Morgan, *The Oxford Handbook*, mentions the colony only in passing. Alison Games emphasizes the "conspicuous absence" of the Dutch in that volume; see her review essay "The *Oxford Handbook*'s Capacious Atlantic," 159. For a discussion of prior scholarship, especially in Brazil, see Rubiés, "Mythologies," 284–96.
24. Much of the scholarship on the Dutch Atlantic has focused on trade. See Postma, *The Dutch in the Atlantic Slave Trade*; Emmer, *The Dutch in the Atlantic Economy*, and idem, *The Dutch Slave Trade*; Klooster, *Illicit Riches*, as well as volumes of essays like Postma and Enthoven, *Riches of Atlantic Commerce*, and Klooster, *Migration, Trade, and Slavery*. A very valuable addition for the seventeenth century promises to be Klooster, *The Dutch Moment*.
25. Emmer and Klooster, "The Dutch Atlantic," 51. See Schmidt, "The Dutch Atlantic," 171–75, who regards Dutch Brazil as the heart of an "exemplary Atlantic." See also Schmidt, *Innocence Abroad* for the role "America" as a political concept played in the early modern Dutch imagination.
26. See the level-headed analysis of Dooley, "News and Doubt."
27. They still troubled the authorities in the later seventeenth and eighteenth centuries; see Steele, *The English Atlantic*; Banks, *Chasing Empire*.
28. *Gerardi Joan. Vossii*, 171: Vossius to Meric Casaubon, 6 May 1630: "Sane, maximus ille Paulus Servita apud Venetos ita semper dictabat, Non esse meliorem viam ac rationem. infringendi vires Hispanorum, quam si Batavi Americam infestent." I owe this reference to Dirk van Miert.
29. Miranda, "Gente de guerra"; Jacobs, "Soldiers of the Company."
30. Mout, "The Youth of Johan Maurits." On Johan Maurits, see first and foremost Van den Boogaart, Hoetink and Whitehead, *Johan Maurits of Nassau-Siegen*. Other volumes include De Werd, *So weit der Erdkreis reicht*; Van den Boogaart and Duparc, *Zo wijd de wereld strekt*; Brunn, *Aufbruch in Neue Welten*. A recent political biography is Cabral de Mello, *Nassau*.
31. Gonsalves de Mello, *Nederlanders in Brazilië*, 12. Large sections of the book's first chapter, devoted to urban life, discuss the rebuilding of Recife according to Dutch custom (46–88).
32. Ibid., 13.

CHAPTER 1. ANTICIPATION

1. Heyns, *Dracht-thoneel*, [H4^v]: *Den Bresiliaen* and [H5^r]: *De Bresiliaensche Vrouwe*. On Heyns, his shop, and his publications, see Meeus, "Zacharias Heyns," 392–94; Moes and Burger, *De Amsterdamsche boekdrukkers*, 4: 174–285.
2. Elias, *De vroedschap*, 1: 191, 205.
3. Amsterdam University Library, 1804 E 11. See Werner, "Le Miroir du Monde"; Meeus, "Zacharias Heyns," 383, 392–93.
4. Meeus, "Zacharias Heyns," 393.

Notes to Pages 18–27

5. Van Groesen, *Representations*, 196–97, 271–75.
6. Jones, "Habits, Holdings, Heterologies," 93.
7. Heyns, *Dracht-thoneel*, [H2^r]: Florida; [H5^v] & [H6^r]: Virginia; [H7^v] & [H8^r]: Strait of Magellan; [H8^v] & [I1^r]: "the South end of the Strait."
8. Meeus, "Inleiding," xiii–xvi; Meeus, "Zacharias Heyns," 393–94.
9. McGrath, "Polemic and History"; Lestringant, "Geneva and America." Davies, "Depictions of Brazilians," discusses representations of Brazilians on French maps from an earlier period.
10. Van Selm, *Een menighte treffelijcke boecken*; Schilder, *Monumenta Cartographica Neerlandica VII*; Sutton, *Early Modern Dutch Prints of Africa*, 21–51.
11. Van Selm, *Een menighte treffelijcke boecken*, 176–79. Amsterdam in 1578 was one of the last cities in Holland to join the Protestant camp; see Van Nierop, "Confessional Cleansing."
12. For the constitutive nature of these three texts in the "invention" of Brazil, see Whitehead, "Historical Writing," 646–50.
13. McGrath, "Polemic and History"; Lestringant, "Geneva and America."
14. Thevet, *Les singularitez*. See Lestringant, *André Thevet*; Lestringant, *Mapping the Renaissance World*.
15. Staden, *Warachtige historie*. On Staden's popularity in the sixteenth-century Low Countries, see Schmidt, *Innocence Abroad*, 33–36.
16. Schmidt, *Innocence Abroad*, 95–99.
17. Silverblatt, "Black Legend," 111–12.
18. Frisch, "In a Sacramental Mode"; Lestringant, "The Philosopher's Breviary."
19. De Léry, *History of a Voyage*, 72–73.
20. Ibid., 164.
21. Spufford, "Literacy, Trade and Religion," 259.
22. Kuijpers, "Lezen en schrijven," 504, 517–18.
23. Meeus, "Inleiding," xii.
24. Van Selm, *Een menighte treffelicke boecken*, 225–53.
25. Enthoven, "Early Dutch Expansion"; Ebert, "Dutch Trade"; Studnicki-Gizbert, *Nation upon the Ocean Sea*.
26. McCusker, "The Demise of Distance," 298.
27. Stols, "Dutch and Flemish Victims"; Wadsworth, "In the Name of the Inquisition," 30–31.
28. *Book Sales Catalogues*, Mf 5347 (see www.bibliopolis.nl).
29. *Book Sales Catalogues*, Mf 2851. This catalog has been facsimilated as *The Auction Catalogue of J. Arminius*.
30. Lechner, "Dutch Humanists' Knowledge," esp. 106; Grafton, *New Worlds*; Elliott, *Old World and the New*.
31. De la Fontaine Verwey, *De Stedelijke Bibliotheek*, 8. The first quote is also from Hooft, who promises "vrij acces," also to those "verre vant verstandt van onze kercken verschelende." All translations from Dutch in this book, unless otherwise noted, are my own.
32. *Catalogus Librorum Bibliothecae*, 35 ("à sacrilego mutilatus")
33. Ibid., 46; Van Groesen, *Representations*.
34. Wintroub, "Civilizing the Savage"; Stols, "Flemish and Dutch Brazil," 168.
35. Van Nierop, "And Ye Shall Hear of Wars," 70–75;
36. Deen, "Handwritten Propaganda."
37. Stolp, *De eerste couranten*, 14–15.

38. McCusker, "The Demise of Distance," 299–300.
39. Stolp, *De eerste couranten*, 49–60.
40. Ibid., 84.
41. Montanus, *Beschryvinge van Amsterdam*, IV, 176: "Dese Brug... ziet men den gantschen dagh, en voornamentlijk tegens den avondt van volck krioelen; daar niet als van Zee en Scheepszaken gehandelt wierdt." For the ordinance on the speedy delivery of letters, proclaimed in 1598, see Lesger, *Rise of the Amsterdam Market*, 240.
42. Brouërius van Nidek and Le Long, *Kabinet van Nederlandsche en Kleefsche Oudheden*, I: 91.
43. *Amsterdams Dam-Praetje*, [C2^v]: "Heb je yets verstaen? Niet met allen ick en heb oock dese morgen aende Brug niet geweest."
44. Harline, *Pamphlets*, 65.
45. Koppenol, *Leids Heelal*, 213. On the performative culture of rhetoricians in the Northern Netherlands, see Van Dixhoorn, "Chambers of Rhetoric."
46. Van Hout, *Loterijspel*, vss. 161–65: S. "Ic wasser zelfs schipper op en ic werde bevracht / Opte Ver en de Boc," B. "Op de Ver ende de Boc? By gans macht, / Wat is dat voor goet?," S. "Mer dat is een haven een stuc deur de lyny in Bresilien. / Men zeylt daer veeltyts van Spaengien, uyt de haven van Sivylgen, / En wert nu by onse Nederlanders mede besocht."
47. Bouwen, the peasant, pronounced "Ver en de Boc" as "Ver ende de Boc," or "the bull and the goat," a clear indication that the scene was intended to amuse the audience.
48. Davids, "Ondernemers in kennis."
49. Ibid., 39; Spufford, "Literacy, Trade and Religion," 255–56.
50. Van Linschoten, *Reys-gheschrift*, 111–14.
51. On the life and work of Van Linschoten, see the various essays in Van Gelder, Parmentier, and Roeper, *Souffrir pour parvenir*.
52. Van Linschoten, *Beschryvinghe*, [††††6^r–††††††2^v], devoted to Brazil; and [†††^{r}], introduction.
53. Waghenaer, *Enchuyser Zee-caert-boeck*, 350. See Schilder and Van Egmond, "Maritime Cartography," 1392–96.
54. "Apendix oft nieu byvoechsel," in Waghenaer, *Thresoor der Zeevaert*.
55. Schilder, *Monumenta Cartographica Neerlandica VII*, 282.
56. Van Gelder, "De wereld binnen handbereik," 15–16.
57. Schmidt, *Innocence Abroad*.
58. Sluiter, "Dutch Maritime Power," 33; Ottsen, *Journael*, 70–71.
59. Goslinga, *The Dutch in the Caribbean*, 53. The claim was made by Emanuel van Meteren. Other contemporary sources do not mention the objective of constructing a fortress.
60. Rijksmuseum, inv.nos. SK-A-2858 & SK-A-1361. See Russell, *Visions of the Sea*, 155.
61. Bruijn, *The Dutch Navy*, 42.
62. IJzerman, "Expeditie naar het Westen," 176.
63. *Niederlendischer Kriegs-Iournal*, fol. 20^r: "der alteste war ein Capitan der Wilder sein hant war picquirt und durchsnitten gleych mann die wammes bey uns thut, und vort gemalet mit allerley farb."
64. Israel, *Dutch Primacy*, 83; Meijer, "Liefhebbers."
65. Ligtenberg, *Willem Usselinx*; Schmidt, *Innocence Abroad*, 176–83.
66. Boxer, *The Dutch in Brazil*, 20–21; Sluiter, "Dutch Maritime Power," 35.
67. De Vries and Van der Woude, *First Modern Economy*, 296–303.
68. Poelwijk, *"In dienste vant suyckerbacken"*, 54–55.

69. Strum, *The Sugar Trade*, 488–541; Ebert, "Early Modern Atlantic Trade."
70. *Resolutiën der Staten-Generaal, nieuwe reeks*, 3: 106.
71. Seed, *Ceremonies of Possession*, 152.
72. *Resolutiën der Staten-Generaal, nieuwe reeks*, 3: 121.
73. "Verzoekschrift van de vrouw van den schipper Dirck de Ruyter."
74. Ruiters, *Toortse der Zee-vaert*, xv.
75. Ibid., Voor-reden.
76. Ibid., 58.
77. Nationaal Archief, The Hague, 4 VEL 710 (Pernambuco); 4 VEL 717 (Bahia); 4 VEL 424 (Rio de Janeiro).
78. Den Heijer, *Geschiedenis van de WIC*, 31–33.
79. Commelin, *Beschryvinge van Amsterdam*, 671.
80. Nationaal Archief, The Hague, 1.11.01.01, inv. no. 256 (Buchelius, "VOC-dagboek," as transcribed by Kees Smit) fol. 99^r. For Buchelius's active involvement in both the VOC and the West India Company, see Pollmann, *Religious Choice*, 147–48.
81. Commelin, *Beschryvinge van Amsterdam*, 1107; Buchelius, "VOC-dagboek," fol. 98^v.
82. Nationaal Archief, The Hague, OWIC, inv. nr. 18B: "Groot Kapitaalboek van de Kamer Amsterdam, 1623–1626."
83. Israel, *Dutch Primacy*, 156–60; Zandvliet, *Mapping for Money*, 248. See De Vivo, *Information and Communication*, 86–87, for the importance of the information gap between professionals and the urban population.
84. Usselincx, *Voortganck*. The eight "West over East" reasons can be found on p. 14. The verses on the title page read, "Westindien kan sijn Nederlands groot gewin / Verkleynt 'svijands macht brengt silver platen in."
85. Elias, *De vroedschap*, 1: lxxviii–lxxix.
86. Buchelius, "VOC-dagboek," fol. 102^r.
87. Ibid., fol. 103^v.
88. *Wonderlicke avontuer*, vss. 1190–1242.
89. *Reys-boeck van het rijcke Brasilien*. The work was composed by "N. G.," identified as Nicolaes van Geelkercken by Voogt, "Reys-boeck."
90. Moerbeeck, *Redenen*, 3–4: "De Portegiese natie die de meeste resistentie of tegenweer sullen doen, synde veel derselve vande Jootsche Religie, voorts merendeels geboren en gesworen vyanden vande Spaensche natie."

CHAPTER 2. JUBILATION

1. Boxer, *Salvador de Sá*, 46–55; Leite, *História da Companhia*, 5: 28–33, 42–47; Edmundson, "The Dutch Power," 238–46. On the stripping of Catholic churches in Brazil, see Schalkwijk, *Reformed Church*, 74–77; Klooster, "Marteling," 325–30.
2. Pettegree, *Invention of News*, 188–90.
3. Raymond, "The Newspaper," 111.
4. Stolp, *De eerste couranten*, 79–88.
5. Van Groesen, "(No) News."
6. *Courante uyt Italien en Duytschlandt*, no. 29 (20 July 1624): "Soo den roep gaet soude de Heer van Dort Toute le Santa in Brisilien ingenomen hebben." See the facsimiles of many early corantos in *Dutch Corantos*, as well as www.delpher.nl/kranten.

7. Borst, "Broer Jansz," 86.

8. *De briefwisseling van Pieter Corneliszoon Hooft*, no. 474: Hooft to Joost Baek, 25 August 1631: "Mijn swaegher Bartelot deed mij gister lezen de loopmaeren van Vezelaer [e.g., the printer of Van Hilten's *Courante*], dien zij zeggen zinlijker te zijn als Broer van UE gemeenlijk komende. Doch gedraeghe mij tot UE oordeel. Altijds vinde in deze ijets dat d' ander niet en melt."

9. As quoted by Reeves, *Evening News*, 139.

10. Beck, *Spiegel*, 157: "Verstont daer oock onder het Volck van de goede Tijdinge uijt West Indien gecommen met eenige rijckgeladene schepen zoo men zeijde."

11. Ibid., 158: "Voormiddags Examineerde S. Ex[cellen]tie in zijn thuijn wel 1½ uijr lang 2 Jesuijten (gevangen op Zee door eene Vlissingschen Vrijbuijter) die van Fernabock uijt Brasilien quamen, willende naer Spagnien om de Cooning t'adviseren, hoe onse vloot de Baije, Stat ende Casteel van Todos-los-Santos ingenomen ende vermeestert hadden." On the role of Maurits of Nassau in Atlantic affairs, see Meuwese, "The States General and the Stadtholder."

12. Beck, *Spiegel*, 159; see Bellingradt, "The Early Modern City," 209.

13. See *Dutch Corantos*, 37–52. Van Hilten generally produced more "exclusives" than Broer Jansz, who instead focused on bringing updates from as many different places as possible: Couvée, "De nieuwsgaring," 26–40, esp. 33. In the first three decades of the newspaper's existence, the publisher would issue an extra edition on only three other occasions. On the messenger who delivered the news from Amsterdam, see *Resolutiën der Staten-Generaal*, 7, no. 397.

14. *Courante Extraordinarij &c.* (27 August 1624): "waer door die . . . vermerckten, ende waren van te vooren oock veradverteert datmen hun aengrypen ende overweldigen wilde." According to Van Hilten, Van Dorth arrived on the thirteenth, "meende dat de Vlote daer noch niet en was, maer met grote blydtschap ende verwonderinghe sagh dat alles soo vergaen was, wenschende dat hy daer by gheweest hadde."

15. Two of the most detailed reports of the Dutch conquest of Bahia in 1624 are Nicolaes van Wassenaer, *Historisch verhael* 8, fol. 3^v–8^r, and fol. 101^r–104^r; and the eyewitness account of the Jesuit Domingo Coelho, whose report is transcribed by Leite, *História da Companhia*, 5: 42–47.

16. *Courante uyt Italien en Duytschlandt*, no. 35 (31 August 1624): "yder Capiteyn beroemt hem in 3. ofte 4. uren 30. ende 40. duysent guldens ghewonnen te hebben, oock eenen Soldaet die maer een been hadde, vont int plonderen eenen Hoetbant vol costelijcke Diamanten, die op eenen grooten schat geexstimeert wort, de Wijn was daer seer abondant yder Soldaet dronck syn volle lust, noch vier ofte vyf persoonen quamen in een Huys ghevallen, vonden daer in een vervallen hoeck een kist staen, sloeghen de selve op creghen daer veel ghelt ende Silver uyt . . . d'eene voor den anderen wilden de buyt hebben, begonnen daerom met malcanderen te vechten."

17. See, for example, Schilder, *Monumenta Cartographica Neerlandica IX*, 478–79.

18. *Dutch Corantos*, 22–26.

19. Harms, "Handel in letteren"; Harline, *Pamphlets*, 87. Salman, *Pedlars*, 176, shows that the number of itinerant booksellers in Amsterdam before 1650 was limited.

20. Van Groesen, "A Week to Remember."

21. Salman, "Het nieuws op straat," 62; Van Groesen, "Reading Newspapers."

22. Lesger, *Rise of the Amsterdam Market*, esp. chap. 6; Lankhorst, "Newspapers in the Netherlands," 152–54; Keblusek, "The Business of News."

23. Beck, *Spiegel*, 143. See also Blaak, *Literacy*, 94.

24. Randall, *Credibility*, 95–120.

25. *De briefwisseling van Pieter Corneliszoon Hooft*, no. 398: Hooft to Joost Baek, 29 September 1630: "De tijdingen van eergisteren maekten mij zoo toghtigh nae 't vervolgh, dat ick, de

veerschujt door onweder met mijne brieven terug gedreven zijnde, eenen bode met dezelve afvejrdighde, om aen naeder bescheidt te geraken."

26. Ibid., no. 1025: Hooft to Joachim van Wikkevoort, 22 June 1640: "Maer, oft goede, oft quaede nieuwmaeren, zij zijn mij altijds welkoom, om dat ze leeren de wereldt kennen"; and no. 378: Hooft to Joost Baek, 18 August 1630: "Zijn geselschap ende 't lezen van zoo veele tijdingen hebben mij te diep inden avont gevoert, om dezen [brief] te verlengen."

27. *Resolutiën der Staten-Generaal*, 8, no. 413.

28. Ibid., no. 426.

29. Van Wassenaer, *Historisch verhael*, 7, fol. 152^v: "op de Frontier Steden, bysonder in 't ghesicht van de Vyandt, als oock binnen Breda, wierdt al het Canon afghelost, op dat sy oock het weten souden, dat Godt de Landen met soo een treffelijcke plaets vereert hadde."

30. "Kronijkje van Cornelis Cornelisz," 124: "Den 29. Augusty victory gehouden door de heele stadt, over de stadt Salvatoor ende Baeye in Westindien." There were also jubilant scenes elsewhere, according to Buchelius, "VOC-dagboek," fol. 103^{rv}: "Den 29 Augusti is int Sticht een danck predicatie ingestelt, an den Almachtigen te loven van sijne vergaende gratie over de Veroveringe in West Indie . . . Sal daer over oock des avonts een publique vieringe geschieden soo hier als tot Amsterdam ende op andere plaetsen van dese provincien."

31. Beck, *Spiegel*, 162: "Men vierde ende triumpheerde hier ende daer dese Vereenigde Nederlanden treffel[ijck] over de West-Indische victorie . . . doen waren de Victorie vieren al meest verbrant, ende het Volck begon zig allenxkens te verliesen." On the political function of religious celebrations in the United Provinces, see Van Rooden, "Dissenters en bededagen."

32. Baudartius, *Memoryen*, 75: "De Portugijsen binnen Amsterdam hebben met een fraye vertooninghe dese Victorie aen-gewesen: ende de Spanjaerden te Lisbona ende in dat gantsche Coninckrijcke, treurden en waren becommert over hare schade" (my italics, MvG). On the Amsterdam Sephardim, see Bodian, *Hebrews of the Portuguese Nation*; Swetschinski, *Reluctant Cosmopolitans*.

33. Haskell, *History and Its Images*, 86–87.

34. Klinkert, *Nassau in het nieuws*, is a good study of Dutch news maps of a slightly earlier period. News maps remained a popular medium throughout the seventeenth century; see Van Nierop, "Profijt en propaganda."

35. On Visscher, see Van Eeghen, "De familie"; Orenstein, "Print Publishers," 189–95; Warren, "Shameful Spectacle."

36. For inventories of topical prints in the Dutch Golden Age, see *Atlas van Stolk*; Muller, *Nederlandsche geschiedenis*. On Gerritsz's role, see Zandvliet, *Mapping for Money*, 164–71; Teensma, "Nederlands-Braziliaans militair inlichtingenwerk," 280–87; Schilder, *Monumenta Cartographica Neerlandica IX*, Ch. 13.

37. Translated from a directive from the Heeren XIX to Admiral Pieter Adriaensz. Ita when leaving for the West Indies in 1628, and quoted in Zandvliet, *Mapping for Money*, 238.

38. Orenstein, "Print Publishers," 191. On advertisements, see *Advertenties voor kaarten*, 3–13; *Tijdingen uyt verscheyde Quartieren* no. 35 (31 August 1624) announces two news maps—the one discussed here, and a second one of the Bay of All Saints; see Schilder, *Monumenta Cartographica Neerlandica IX*, 478–79.

39. *Atlas van Stolk*, no. 1593; Muller, *Nederlandsche geschiedenis*, no. 1508.

40. Boxer, *Salvador de Sá*, 48.

41. See below.

42. *Atlas van Stolk*, no. 1600; Muller, *Nederlandsche geschiedenis*, no. 1509. Visscher testified to drawing the fourteen men *naer't leven* (from life), but could only have seen ten prisoners, as four Jesuits arrived in Rotterdam and were jailed in Dordrecht.

43. Van Groesen, "A Brazilian Jesuit," 447–48.
44. Schurhammer, *Gesammelte Studien IV*, 391–92; Van Groesen, "A Brazilian Jesuit," 448.
45. "Benemen hem het geen daer hy sijn heerschappy / Dus lang me heeft gestut, door groote tyranny / En duysenden vernielt met moorden, hangen, branden / (Gelijck ons Ouders is bekent in dese Landen)."
46. Schmidt, *Innocence Abroad*.
47. Grijp, "Van geuzenlied tot Gedenck-clanck." For a modern edition of the most common "Beggars songs," see *Het geuzenliedboek*. See also Pettegree, *Reformation*, 65–72.
48. Haks, *Vaderland en vrede*, 86–114.
49. Stronks, *Stichten of schitteren*, 39–52.
50. Haselbekius, *Triumph-Dicht* [C1ʳ–D1ʳ]. Exodus 23:27 reads: "I will send my fear before thee, and will destroy all the people to whom thou shalt come, and I will make all thine enemies turn their backs unto thee"; Schalkwijk, *Reformed Church*, 115.
51. Haselbekius, *Triumph-Dicht*, [C2ʳ], vss. 75–84: "Als een Cat starrende met een naersichtigen ooge, / Op de 'vyandlike' Hond, geensins can dueren om hooge: / Schoon sits' al veyligh boven op den boome geklomme," / Noch verlaet-se de plaets, se magh hem niet omme en omme / Huppele' sien: alsoo *starr-oogd'* hyr op dese Geusen, / 't Schrickige *Salvadoor*, oft waeren machtige Reusen. / En dit naere gesicht bracht kranckheyd ooc in syn oogen: / Schoon hadden-s' een veylige plaets, doch konde gedoogen / Dit spel van bove' naar niet langer dus te beschouwen, / Wenscheden haer léven t' *Haes-padje* te meuge' betrouwen."
52. Ibid., [C4ᵛ], vss. 279–82: "Ooc soo is de' Stad-houdre van onse gewaep'nede Knechten / Met noch som'ge getimpd'e Iesuyte' genomen in hechten: / En van daere gescheept nae ons' Hollandische kuste, / Omme te sien, of hun ooc d'hijr-landische Spijse geluste."
53. Pettegree, *Reformation*, 38; Haks, *Vaderland en vrede*, 112–14; Harline, *Pamphlets*, 134–54.
54. Groenhuis, *De predikanten*, 31–38.
55. Revius, *Over-Ysselsche sangen*, 2: 31, vss. 13–16: "Sy claecht dat ghy haer hebt de aerde heten delven, / Met cluyten ende puyn haer schouderen gelae'n, / Sy claecht dat ghy haer hebt het diepste vande zelven; / Doen soeken, om alleen u gelt-sucht te versaen." For the notion of America as the "legitimate wife" of the Spanish king, see Schmidt, *Innocence Abroad*, 227–28. On Revius, see De Bruijn, *Eerst de waarheid*, esp. 55–64, and Stronks, *Stichten of schitteren*, 147–82, who places Revius's work in the context of other ministers' poetry.
56. Baudartius, *Memoryen*, 77–78.
57. Revius, *Over-Ysselsche sangen*, 2: 32: "De Spaensgesinde seyt: (bedeckende sijn toren) / Wy hebben aende Baey soo vele niet verloren. / Maer siet eens, goede vrient, de waerheyt moedernaeckt / Wat God en Maurits u afhandich heeft gemaeckt. / Salvator heet de stat, dat is de Salichmaker, / Voorwaer, die dien ontbeert ontbeert den besten waker. / De Baja draecht den naem der Heyl'gen algelijck, / Die die tesamen mist, sitt die niet suyverlijck? / Daer toe den Heyl'gen Geest int water te verliesen, / En sou Philips het bloet daer over niet bevriesen? / En (boven alle schae) de Hope noch daer by / Eylaes, die niet en hoopt hoe can die wesen bly? / Ja crijcht hy voorts geen gelt vant westen als het tijt is / Ick vrees' dat hy met een oock het Gelove quyt is."
58. Cf. below, Chapter 6.
59. Baudartius, *Memoryen*, 97.
60. Ibid. The opening lines of the poem titled "In laudem Generosi Domini Iohannis a Dort" read, "Lusitanum subigis . . .."
61. Ibid.: "IAN VAN DORT is doot ghebleven in den dienst vant Vaderland, / Synde nu seer hoogh geklommen aen den Indiaenschen cant, / Couverneur van Salvadore, en de Heyl'ge

al te saem, / Waer van hy nu hadd' vercreghen eenen treffelicken naem: / Maer eer hy cond' hoogher klimmen heeft de DOOT hem neer-gelecht. / Daer leyt nu desen held moedich, s'Vaderlands getrouwe knecht; / Lieve Leser, wilt ghedencken wat s'wereldts eer en goet sy, / Eer dat ghy het sult vermoeden, sult ghy hier oock liggen by."

62. Teellinck, *Davids danckbaerheyt*. Psalm 116:12–14 reads, "What shall I render unto the Lord for all his benefits toward me / I will take the cup of salvation, and call upon the name of the Lord / I will pay my vows unto the Lord now in the presence of all his people." Teellinck also stated that, with the Dutch victory, the door to missionary work had opened. See Westerink, *Met het oog van de ziel*, 1–36.

63. For a detailed account of the conflict between Remonstrants and Counter-Remonstrants, see Kaplan, *Calvinists and Libertines*.

64. Van Wassenaer, *Historisch verhael*. See Kannegieter, "Dr. Nicolaes Jansz. van Wassenaer."

65. Weekhout, *Boekencensuur*, 88; *Resolutiën der Staten-Generaal*, 8, nos. 219, 1900, as well as several resolutions for the year 1626.

66. Van Groesen, "A Brazilian Jesuit," 455–65.

67. Van Wassenaer, *Historisch verhael*, 8, fol. 4^v: "Dominicus Kohello, Pater Provincialis van Brasil, heeft hem, terwijl hy alhier in hechting in S. Clarae klooster was, altoos getoont een Man van een sacht gemoed, minnelick in "t spreken, goed van oordeel, en promptelijck de Latijnsche Tale gebruyckende, van de Griecksche of Hebreeusche gantsch geen kennisse hebbende. . . . Sijn Mede broeders, en bysonder sijn Socius, hielt hem in groote reputatie, om dat hy van sijn jonckheyd as voor yet raers ghehouden wierd onder de synen . . . Sy meenden dat het yet wat Goddelijckx in hem was, en dies als een bysonder Man van hen ge-eert wiert."

68. Nelson, "The Jesuit Legend," 95.

69. Van Wassenaer, *Historisch verhael*, 8, fol. 4^v: "Hier op scheen het hem mede te refereren, . . . om dat hy meer was dan de Gouverneur selfs, ja meer dan Koningh, die sulckx niet wel nemen soude, dat men soo een Heyligh Man in soo een verachte plaetse steldede: daer op hem gheantwoort wierdt, dat de vrye luyden onder 't Commendo van de Koningh niet en staen, veel min sijn gramschap in dien deele konden aen-nemen, maer dat hy wel so gheleyt en getracteert soude werden, als yemant van onse landen in Spangien gevanghen."

70. Ibid., fol. 6^r: "Soo veel als het stuck aenging . . . dat hy zijn devoir in zijn Ampt niet gedaen hadde, dat s'Coninckx ordre in 't houden van de Soldaten op die plaets niet gevolgt was, verklaerde de Pater heel contrarie te zijn, also hem bekent was, en voor de Coning sulckx mede wilde sustineren, dat hy alles na de last van sijn Majesteyt uytgevoert hadde: te weten, dat die Batarije aen het water uyt 's Conincx inkomen, en schattinge der Ingesetenen, nae zijn vermoghen gevordert was."

71. Ibid., fol. 5^r: "Onder andere discoursen viel dit mede voor, dat de Pater bekende, dat haer Portugysen sulckx over quam, van wegen de Coningh van Spaengien, die een yeder op syn hals kreegh, en soo veel Rijcken hadde, die hy qualijck alle conde regeren: Datter mede vele synder Oversten waren, die het so grof maeckteden, dat sy de Ondersaten tot disperatie brochten, uyt het welck Oorlogen ontstonden: Dat sy door sulcken geconcipieerden haet nu soo een goedt deel van Oost-Indien verloren hadden, en men bestont also West-Indien mede aen te tasten, 't beginsel van de Bahia nemende."

72. The Jesuits did support the Crown, for example, on the important issue of prohibition of Indian slavery. For these and other controversies in Bahia, see Schwartz, *Sovereignty and Society*, 117–21, 136, 169, 209.

73. Van Wassenaer, *Historisch verhael*, 8, fols. 5^{rv}: "Op het welck hy ophet alderdiepste syns gemoets suchtende, exclameerde: O lieve Coning Sebastiaen, onse lieve Vader en Heer, wy beklag-

hen met droefheyt u dood, en 't sedert u aflyven zijn wy in verdriet gekomen, o ongeluckighe uyre die u van ons scheyde, O heyloose veltslagh die u van ons weg nam: doen ghy over ons regeerde waren wy vrienden van de gantsche werelt, door onse Coopmanschappen der Specerijen, 't zedert u aflyven zijn wy in den haet van een yeder gheraeckt, om onser sonden wille, die wy bedreven hebben . . . Sy meenen soo sy onder 't rijck van Spaengien niet en stonden, dat sy van de gantsche wereldt gheadoreert, versocht, en op haer havenen sonder eenigh perijckel ghehandelt soude werden, als in voortijden geschiede, datter niemant eenigh quaet in haer Landen overquam, die haer na de gheleghentheydt van de plaets voegdede."

74. Van Groesen, "A Brazilian Jesuit," 448–49.

75. Van Wassenaer, *Historisch verhael*, 8, fol. 5^v: "In 't mentie maken van haer Ordre, gaf hy wel te kennen, dat die buyten andere gehaet wiert, als oock de redenen, beschuldigt synde, dat sy die zijn, die Coningen, Vorsten, Princen teghens malkanderen ophitsen, ende oorsake van groote oorloghen zijn, ja niet en schromen Coningen of om te brengen in 't gesicht van alle menschen, of door heymelijcke lagen van Bospoeder, ende andersints, als in onse eeuwe al te veel gebleken is." Van Wassenaer presumably referred to the English gunpowder plot of November 1605.

76. On anti-Jesuit rhetoric in early modern Europe, see: Nelson, "The Jesuit Legend."

77. Van Wassenaer, *Historisch verhael*, 8, fol. 5^v: "'t welck hy excuseerde teghens haer Ordre te zijn, dat sy haer niet met den vleeschelijcken arm (soo sy de Koninghen en Regenten noemen) moeyen moeten: . . . Dat zy altemet op plaetsen daer de Gouverneurs weynigh raets hebben, sijn zy wel in de Raet geroepen, om met hen van stucken de Regeringhe aengaende te consuleren, maer tot den Oorlogh eenige consultatie te geven, dat is hen op haer salighheyd verboden. Dese Pater selfs protesteerde voor Godt en zijn Heylighe Engelen, met devotie zijn ooghen nae den Hemel slaende, dat hy de waerheyt sprack, dat hy in zijn tijt tot dit hooge Ampt gheroepen zynde, in de Bahia, van de Gouverneur in een Ghenerale vergaderingh, . . . gevordert synde, om te consuleren, of hy de Binnelantsche Indianen, die zijn volck doot geslagen, geplondert, ja wegh gevoert hadden, en Rebellen waren, niet mocht beoorlogen, dat hy daer op gheantwoordt heeft, op sulckx te consulteren, hen van haer Generael die binnen Romen sidt, verboden was sub paene excommunicationis, en dies uyt de vergaderingh met sulcken antwoort vertrock: Statuerende daer by, dat alle die sulcx deden, dat sy geen oprechte Jesuyten waren, haer Ordre niet voldoende."

78. Alden, *Making of an Enterprise*, 479–87.

79. Van Wassenaer, *Historisch verhael*, 8, fols. 5^v–6^r: "maer dattet hen geoorlooft was de Coningen te Raden tot onderhout van haer religie, tot voortplantinge van dien: Hoe sulckx dan geschiet, laten wy hier in medio: geen plaets synde om hier daer van te spreken. Soo veel als my aengaet ick mach gaerne sulcke velitationes hooren, en "t myne daer op infereren, het oordeel staet dan aen den derde, die als Auditor daer by sidt: Het geloof of het accepteren wil niet gedwonghen zijn: het staet een yeder vry yemants segghen aen te nemen of te verwerpen."

80. Weekhout, *Boekencensuur*, 88.

81. *Atlas van Stolk*, nos. 1594–1597; Muller, *Nederlandsche geschiedenis*, nos. 1508 A-G; Paas, *German Political Broadsheet*, 4, nos. P 1038–1043.

82. Paas, *German Political Broadsheet*, 4, no. P 1038; *Atlas van Stolk*, no. 1594.

83. For a study of so-called "transmediation" in an early modern Dutch context, see Schmidt, *Inventing Exoticism*, 294–95.

84. Andries van Eertvelt (1590–1652) was one of the first Southern Netherlandish marine painters, with a considerable reputation in his native Antwerp. There is hardly any literature on Van Eertvelt, but see Preston, *Seventeenth-Century Marine Painters*, 19.

85. *Inventarissen van de inboedels*, 1: 202: "Derthien groote stucken schilderie met slechte swarte lijsten, te weten de stadt Nova Batavia, Mexico, St. Maerten, Porta de St. Vera Crux, St. Salvador, Malacca, 't fort Nassau, Tarnati ende andere onbekende plaetsen door Knipbergen ende andere gedaen."

86. Meisner, *Thesauri philo-politici*, 6, [B3^v]: "Haec Maxima Dona Vigescunt," with the *subscriptio* "Corporis, Ingenii donis, sortisque coruscat / Si quis; haec tria sunt maxima dona Dei"; "Wer Gsundt, Klug und von gutem Glück / Der hat von Gots drey schöner Stück: / Welcher sie nun von Ihm kan habn, / Der hat fürwar die grösten Gabn." The Latin and German texts were written by Johann Ludwig Gottfried.

87. Schwartz, "Voyage of the Vassals," 752–55.

88. De Boer, "De val van Bahia"; Edmundson, "The Dutch Power," 247–54.

89. Sir Dudley Carleton to William Trumbull, 4 August 1625, British Library, Add. Ms. 72274, fol. 167^r. I am grateful to David Coast for providing me with these transcriptions.

90. Goldgar, *Tulipmania*, 220–21.

91. *Resolutiën der Staten-Generaal*, 7, no. 2889; *Courante uyt Italien en Duytschlandt* 33 (16 August 1625): "soo wortet nog van veelen in twijffel ghetrocken."

92. Carleton to Trumbull, 1 September 1625, British Library, Add. Ms. 72274, fol. 175^v.

93. For *El Brasil Restituído*, see Shannon, *Visions of the New World*, 163–89. For Maíno, see Brown and Elliott, *A Palace for a King*, 193–202.

94. Leiden University, Coll. BN 054-16-001, *La Rivee* [sic!] *de l'arme navalle de Spaigne devant la Baye au Bresil* (s.l., 1625). See Storms, "Cartografie in camouflage."

95. See Van Groesen, "(No) News," for the interaction between the media in the Northern and Southern Netherlands. A recent analysis of the media landscape in the Southern Netherlands is Arblaster, *From Ghent to Aix*, esp. chaps. 3–5 about Antwerp news publisher Abraham Verhoeven.

96. Paas, *German Political Broadsheet*, 4, no. P 1058.

CHAPTER 3. APPROPRIATION

1. De Laet, *Iaerlijck verhael*, 1: 84–85: "Dit hebben soo meest vernomen uyt t'ghene de Spaensche selfs daer van hebben uytgegeven, want uyt de onse gheen recht bescheyt hebben konnen bekommen, hoewel naer dat "tvolck t'huys gekommen was, daer nauw ondersoeck by de Hoog. Mog. Heeren Staten woerde ghedaen; de bekentenissen soo verscheyden, ende de beschuldingen d'een van d'ander soo vele, ende teghen den anderen strijdende zijde, datter qualijck yets sekers van te segghen is."

2. *Resolutiën der Staten-Generaal*, 7, nos. 1266, 1280, 1327, 2165, 2325, 2889. The resolutions of the States General for 1626 and later years can be found at www.historici.nl/resources.

3. Van Groesen, "A Brazilian Jesuit," 467–68.

4. Van Groesen, "Lessons Learned."

5. Aldenburgk, *Reise nach Brasilien*.

6. [Teellinck], *De tweede wachter*, [G1^v]: "Want aldus spreect de Heere: Siet inde stadt die nae mijnen naem genaemt is, beginne ick te plagen, ende soudt ghy onghestraft blijven? Ghy en sult niet onghestraft blijven." Arnoldus Buchelius was equally critical; see Pollmann, *Religious Choice*, 148.

7. Dutra, "Matias de Albuquerque," 117–66.

8. Valerius, *Neder-landtsche Gedenck-clanck*, 256–60; Grijp, "Van geuzenlied tot Gedenck-clanck," 128.

9. Van Wassenaer, in his *Historisch Verhael*, was particularly conscientious in covering these expeditions. The best modern discussion of Dutch actions in the Atlantic between 1624 and 1630 is Goslinga, *The Dutch in the Caribbean*, 210ff.

10. On this campaign, see *Westafrikaanse reis*.

11. Goslinga, *The Dutch in the Caribbean*, 168–69; Zandvliet, *Mapping for Money*, 165–66.

12. *Atlas van Stolk*, nos. 1646–1647.

13. Ibid., no. 1646: "De Capiteyn Padilha, die voor desen den Colonel Dort by embuscade om-ghebracht hadt, verweerde sich dapper, maer wierd eyndtlijck door sijn Schilt inde slincker borst ter neder geschoten, 't welck sijn volck seer descourageerde."

14. Israel, *The Dutch Republic*, 497–99, 506–7.

15. *Correspondance de Rubens*, 4: 426: Rubens to Pierre Dupuy, 1 June 1628: "Pare che gli Ollandesi faccino qualche apparato, per tentar un' impresa non penetrata da noi sin adesso . . . Quei Stati fanno la guerra più nociva al re di Spagna, a spese de' particolari e particolarmente per la compagnia occidentale, che ha mandato fuor una flotta gagliardissima, si non m'inganno, verso la baya de todos los Santos, per impadronirsi di novo della città di S.-Salvador, persa da loro contro il suo costume assai vilmente."

16. Zandvliet, *Mapping for Money*, 191; Teensma, "Nederlands-Braziliaans militair inlichtingenwerk," 282–83.

17. Boxer, *The Dutch in Brazil*, 40.

18. *Particuliere notulen*, 4, no. 1432.

19. National Maritime Museum, Greenwich, inv. no. MEC 0029, where the reverse side of the medal made by A. van der Wilge depicts Pernambuco and the silver fleet alongside Frederik Hendrik's triumphs in Grol and Wesel. The obverse side was dedicated to the siege of Den Bosch. See Bizot, *Histoire Metallique*, 167: "Ce fut pour la conquête de ces trois Villes & pour les heureux progrés de la Compagnie des Indes Occidentales, que les Estats firent fraper cetter Medaille en 1631 à l'honneur du Prince d'Orange."

20. Van Wassenaer, *Historisch Verhael*, 19, fol. 17^v, who provided so much detail in 1624, only devoted a single sentence to the celebrations and public prayers in Holland. Examples of single-sheet popular songs are *Schimp-Ghedicht van Fernabuco* and *Batavier gaet hem verblye*.

21. Van Groesen, "(No) News."

22. Baers, *Olinda*, 33: "Teghen Paesschen hebben de Heeren Raden de Hooft-parochie kercke van Olinda doen openen, schoon maecken ende prepareren, inde welcke dat ick op Paesdach de eerste Predicatie hebbe ghedaen ende oock de volghende daghen ghepredickt, hebbe oock den Doop aldaer aen een seecker Soldaet bedient. . . . Daer sijn oock vele swarten ende swartinnen inde Kercke ghecomen, die welcke naer hare maniere toeghemaeckt stil ende devootich saten ende neerstich toehoorden." Baers's work was published by Hendrick Laurensz, one of the heirs to the estate of Cornelis Claesz.

23. Ibid., 8: "Want hebbende mijn camer recht onder sijn camer, soo hebbe ick gehoort ende can betuygen, dat hy alle avont ende morghen, knielende aen sijn bedde, inde presentie van alle sijn knechts, het avont ende morgen gebet seer aendachtich heeft ghebeden ende ghedaen, ende niet alleene dat, maer oock snachts wacker wordende, is dicwils uyt syn bedde opghestaen ende heeft teghen een stoel gekniele, ende aldaer sijn gebedt, dat ick 't wacker sijnde hooren conde, uytghestort, ende voorts altemet meenich uyre in sijn bedde legghende, met suchten ende bidden tot Godt doorghebracht."

24. Boxer, *The Dutch in Brazil*, 37, 49.

25. Richshoffer, *Brasilianisch und West Indianische Reiße Beschreibung*, 55. Richshoffer's account was not published until 1677.

26. Van Wassenaer, *Historisch Verhael*, 19, fol. 23^v: "Eyndelijck dat de Generael Loncq met 40. Musquettiers buyten de Stadt Olinda gaende, van by-na 300 Swarten, die in een Embuscade laghen, was overvallen gheweest, ende waren de sijne op vijf na alle doodtgheslaghen, ende ten ware den Generael te paerde geweest ende sich door de snellickheydt ghesalveert hadde, soude sonder twijfel oock in de handen der Swarten vervallen ende doodtgheslagen zijn gheweest."

27. Schwartz, "Voyage of the Vassals," 745–46; Boxer, *The Dutch in Brazil*, 42–45.

28. Van Nederveen Meerkerk, *Recife*, 46–53; Hefting, "High Versus Low," esp. 201–05.

29. *Gedenkschriften*, 1: 609: "Andere scepen laeter van Fernambuco uytgevaeren, ende dese maend mede aengekomen, verhaelen, dat het met de Stadt nu wel staet, synde deselve wel *natura loci* niet geheel sterk; maer de forten van *Antony Vast*, ende 't Recif sulx, dat die onwinbaer worden gehouden, ende met 500. man bewaert kunnen worden . . . waer mede de Plaetse nu versekert synde, heeft de Gouverneur syne handen dies te vryer, om landinwaerts in te kunnen marcheren."

30. Richshoffer, *Brasilianisch und West Indianische Reiße Beschreibung*, 72: "Den 7. [Febr. 1631] zu Nachts umb 9. Uhren, brandten und schossen wir so wohlen allhie als auch in der Stadt Victoriam, weilen nunmehr Jahr und Tag verflossen, daß wir mit der Hülff Gottes nicht allein diese Plätze eingenommen, sondern auch erhalten haben."

31. Gonsalves de Mello, *Nederlanders in Brazilië*, 40, 45–46.

32. Den Heijer and Brommer, *Grote Atlas*, 1: 157; Sutton, *Capitalism*, 83–86.

33. Massing, "From Dutch Brazil to the West Indies," esp. 184–86. See also Schwartz, "A Commonwealth Within Itself," 163.

34. Zandvliet, *Mapping for Money*, 169. For a French translation of Gerritsz's notes, see Bondam, "Journaux et nouvelles."

35. Respectively, Leiden University, BN 051-09-007; Muller, *Nederlandse geschiedenis*, no. 1656; *Atlas van Stolk*, no. 1711; *Veroveringh van de stadt Olinda*.

36. For Merian's reproductions, see the unfolding maps in Gottfried, *Historia Antipodum*, 32–33. For Hollar, see *Éloge de la navigation hollandaise*, 104–5.

37. Schmidt, "Mapping an Empire," 550–52; Harley, "Maps, Knowledge, and Power," 71–73; see also Seed, *Ceremonies of Possession*, chap. 6.

38. Zandvliet, *Mapping for Money*, 169.

39. For some of the terminology used here, see Harley, "Silences and Secrecy."

40. See also the many manuscript maps that remained unavailable to the general public in Den Heijer and Brommer, *Grote Atlas*.

41. Buchelius, "VOC-dagboek," fol. 38^v: "Meenende daerdoor den viant plaets te openen, ende occasie te geven om haer te overrompelen, maer behoorden veeleer te bedencken, dat dese plaetsen al over de LXXX jaeren voor haer bij den Portugesen genoch bekent sijn geweest, ende dat het weynich profiteert, dat sij haere saecken aldaer so secreet meenen te houden. Dat se veeleer achterdencken met sulcx causeren, dat haeren saecken niet al te recht en gaen, ende die meenen te verdonckeren voor de gemeene participanten, waerover grote doleantiën gemaect ende onder andere faulten in verscheyde boecxkens gedivulgeert worden." Buchelius's comment from 1620 actually concerned the VOC, the Dutch East India Company, but it can easily be projected onto Brazil.

42. *Courante uyt Italien en Duytschlandt*, no. 21 (25 May 1630); no. 29 (20 July 1630); no. 30 (27 July 1630); no. 41 (12 October 1630); Van Groesen, "(No) News."

43. Van Wassenaer, *Historisch Verhael*, 18, fol. 88^v; *Copie vande Missive*, [A4^r]: "zijnde . . . een plaetse die ghesecondeert ende versien wordende onwinnelick is."

44. *Van varen en van vechten*, 1: 238–42: "Geoctroyeerde Heeren vry / Der West Indische Compagny / Gheluck komt u toe wenden, / U Helden maeckt nu herten bly / Secours wiltse haest senden."

45. Herckmans, *Der Zee-vaert Lof*, 203: "Dus werd de stad verheert; sta vast nu buyten schanssen, / Borstweeren van 't Recif en opghetranste transsen. / De schup geraeckt in de aerd, me plant het grof gheschut, / In 't kort daer is gheen hoop die hier den Spangiaerd stut."

46. On Herckmans's poetry, see Dams, "Elias Herckmans." On the Chile expedition, see Schmidt, "Exotic Allies," 460–68.

47. Bredan, *Desengaño a los pueblos del Brasil*.

48. *De briefwisseling van Pieter Corneliszoon Hooft*, no. 402: Hooft to Albert Burgh, 5 October 1630: "Krijghen wij dat vaer-water, alleen, ick zie ons Salomons tijden koomen, en 't zilver voor slijk t' Amsterdam op straet leggen."

49. *Cort ende warachtich Verhael* is the only surviving Dutch pamphlet on the clash between Pater and Oquendo. The Habsburgs, ironically, had a medal struck to commemorate the *victory* of Oquendo over Pater: National Maritime Museum, Greenwich, inv. no. MEC 0085.

50. Gonsalves de Mello, *Nederlanders in Brazilië*, 40–42.

51. See the extremely detailed account by Johannes de Laet, *Iaerlijck verhael*, 4: 71–92. The news map is *Atlas van Stolk*, no. 1762. The text was translated from Dutch into French by Daniel Bredan, who four years earlier had published a Spanish version of the pamphlet to arouse support for the West India Company.

52. Schmidt, "Exotic Allies." The Dutch efforts to court the natives in the northeastern captaincies had begun as early as 1625: Meuwese, "Subjects or Allies," 116–17.

53. Boxer, *The Dutch in Brazil*, 59.

54. Both news maps, the one depicted here and the "official" one issued by Blaeu, included a version of what was termed an "authentic story" (*Auctentijck Verhael*) of the campaign.

55. Zandvliet, *Mapping for Money*, 177.

56. Ibid., 175–76.

57. Den Heijer and Brommer, *Grote Atlas*, 1: 171.

58. De la Fontaine Verwey, *Uit de wereld van het boek III*, 169; Zandvliet, *Mapping for Money*, 204–06; Den Heijer and Brommer, *Grote Atlas*, 1: 171.

59. Storms, "De kaart van Nederlands Brazilië."

60. The list of names that were "Dutchified" is, of course, much longer and includes, for example, the main streets in Recife. See Van Nederveen Meerkerk, *Recife*, 96; Gonsalves de Mello, *Nederlanders in Brazilië*, 60–61, 64. For the perceived political importance of the language of geography, see Schmidt, "Mapping an Empire."

61. On Duck's development as a painter of guardroom scenes, see Rosen, *Soldiers at Leisure*, 82–100. There is surprisingly little literature on cartographic material in Dutch genre painting, but see Welu, "Vermeer."

62. All examples here are from the online version of the Getty Provenance Index (Hendrix, N-2287; Nason, N-2281; Alewijn, N-2349; Van Ceulen, N-2204). See also Van Groesen, "Officers," 54.

63. De Vries and Van der Woude, *First Modern Economy*, 326–29; Poelwijk, *"In dienste vant suyckerbacken"*, 86.

64. Hochstrasser, *Still Life*, 187–204; Den Heijer, *Geschiedenis van de WIC*, 54.

65. All of these cases and quotes are from Hondius, "Black Africans." See also Schorsch, *Jews and Blacks*, 93–101.

66. Cf. above, p. 78.

Notes to Pages 92–95   213

67. Meuwese, "Indigenous Leaders," 214.
68. *Suiker, verfhout & tabak*, 69; Meuwese, *Brothers in Arms*, 137.
69. "Bernard O'Brien's Account," 421–22. See also Vaughan, *Transatlantic Encounters*, 102. On Manuel de Moraes, see Boxer, *The Dutch in Brazil*, 267–69; Dams, "Manoel de Moraes."
70. Moreau, *Klare en waarachtige beschryving*, 86–87; Gonsalves de Mello, *Nederlanders in Brazilië*, 52.
71. Hansen Hajstrup, *Memorial und Jurenal*, 65: "mit ein Madame die so schön auff geputzt wahr, daß menniger solte gemeint [haben], eß wehre ein Adelß Jumfer geweßen."
72. Miranda, "Zielkopers"; Van Alphen, "The Female Side."
73. Richshoffer, *Brasilianisch und West Indianische Reiße Beschreibung*, 6. The New-York Historical Society owns a booklet with forty-nine watercolor flags of the West India Company. Sierksma, "Een 17de eeuws vaandelboek" dates the manuscript to the early to mid-1630s.
74. On life on board, see Klooster, "Bootsgezellen," 48–53.
75. Baers, *Olinda*, 36: "sijnde oock aldaer vergadert vele lief-hebbers, die hem [i.e., Lonck] oock inhaelden, ende met hare Jachten (in sulcken getale datmen die selvighe niet tellen en conde, wesende het water schier bedeckt van schepen) betoonende alderley teeckenen van vreucht ende blijtschap. . . . Te Amsteldamme aengecomen sijnde, sijn wij . . . midden door het gedrang vant volck, vermits 'twelcke datmen schier de straten niet conde ghebruycken, geleyt gheworden op 't West-Indische Huys."
76. Richshoffer, *Brasilianisch und West Indianische Reiße Beschreibung*, 133–34: "Den 5. umb Mittag arrivirten wir glücklich daselbsten an, da sich dann bey dem außsteigen viel Volcks und sonderlich von Weibsbildern befunden, welche theyls nach ihren Männern, Söhnen order Brüdern gefragt, deren dann etliche durch der ihrigen Widerkunfft erfreuet, viel aber wegen derselben verlust zum höchsten betrübet worden, dessen ungeachtet, brachten sie Brandten- und Frantzen-wein, auch Essenspeisen zum freundlichen Willkom, darnach seind wir auff das West-Indianische Hauß geführet worden, und daselbsten unsere Gewehr abgeleget, in dem hinmarschiren aber das übrige Pulver dergestalten verschossen, daß sich fast niemand an den Fenstern hat dörffen blicken lassen, welches dann lauter Freüden-schütz gewesen."
77. For a wonderful view of Amsterdam's "intimate Atlantic," see Romney, *New Netherland Connections*, esp. chaps. 1 and 2.
78. On the directors of the West India Company, see Noorlander, "'For the Maintenance of the True Religion.'" On Burgh's visits to Domingo Coelho in 1625 and 1626, see Sterck, "Een historische rozenkrans," 83–85 and, more succinctly, Van Groesen, "A Brazilian Jesuit," 468. On Man's role in the English church in Amsterdam, see Sprunger, *Dutch Puritanism*, 108.
79. Nationaal Archief, The Hague, OWIC, inv. no. 14: Minutes of the Directors of the Amsterdam Chamber, 1 January 1635–31 December 1636.
80. Van Nierop, "Popular Participation."
81. Van der Heijden and Van den Heuvel, "Sailors' Families."
82. Romney, *New Netherland Connections*, 28–30.
83. Nationaal Archief, The Hague, OWIC 14, fols. 12^{rv}. The news from Paraíba was mentioned by Jan van Hilten two days later, on 24 February, but the directors had probably been informed already on the eighteenth through the official letters of the Political Council in Recife to the Heeren XIX. The States of Holland discussed the news and the appropriate measure of celebration on that same Thursday; see *Particuliere notulen*, 7: 253.
84. Gelderblom, *Zuid-Nederlandse kooplieden*, 229–32.
85. Nationaal Archief, The Hague, OWIC 14, fol. 15^{r}. The original reference to the salary slip reads *haer gedruckte ceeltgen*.

86. Nationaal Archief, The Hague, OWIC 14, fol. 29ʳ.
87. See Davids, "White Collar Workers."
88. Both examples from Nationaal Archief, The Hague, OWIC 14, fol. 34ʳᵛ (directors' meeting of 24 May 1635).
89. Nationaal Archief, The Hague, OWIC 14, fol. 12ʳᵛ. *De Windhond* also had five Portuguese captives on board, perhaps another reason Croon was told to take care of its cargo; see Nationaal Archief, The Hague, OWIC 14, fol. 13ʳ.
90. *Particuliere notulen*, 7: 248–49.
91. *Extract uyt den Brief.*
92. The position of the Company is made abundantly clear in *Consideratien en redenen*.
93. Israel, *The Dutch Republic and the Hispanic World*, 223–49. See *Particuliere notulen*, vols. 6 and 7, passim, for the requests for more money from the Heeren XIX.
94. Usselincx, *Waerschouwinge*, [A3ᵛ]. The pamphlet is dated 16 January 1630.
95. See, for example, *Pertinent Bericht* and *Extract uyt den Brief,* as well as the news maps discussed above. On Hooft reading newspapers, see Van Groesen, "(No) News," 752–57.
96. *Briefwisseling van Hugo Grotius*, 4, no. 1578; Grotius to Nicolaas van Reigersberch, 30 January 1631: "Farnembuck, soo de onse nae de tresves luysteren, is apparent dispute te sullen veroorsaecken." Many of these letters are discussed in Nellen, *Hugo de Groot*.
97. *Briefwisseling van Hugo Grotius*, 5, no. 1851: Willem van Oldenbarnevelt to Grotius, 21 June 1633: "Dit sal noch grooter hapermarckt in den trefves maecken."
98. Ibid., 5, no. 1858: Willem van Oldenbarnevelt to Grotius, 5 July 1633: "Waerdenburch wt Farnabucq gekommen sijnde sal de waerheyt van de importantie van de Westindiën wel weten te decifreren."
99. Ibid., 5, no. 1859: Willem van Oldenbarnevelt to Grotius, 12 July 1633: "Het schijnt weynich apparentie tot handeling is, tensij de Westindissche compagnie contentement gedaen wert, daer ick weynich apparentie toe sien."
100. *Reden van dat die West-Indische Compagnie*, 5–6: "Daer zijn persoonen, mede van aensien ende qualiteyt in dese onse Landen, die met kleynachtinghe van dese West-Indische Compagnie spreken, die selve seer luttel estimerende . . . wat sullen [Die Historien-Schrijvers] . . . van ons seggen ofte gedencken . . . als die gene, so om eenen bedrieghlijcken ende onsekeren Pays ofte Trefues, sulcken Conqueste, die mee te estimeren is, quiteren?"
101. Ibid., 9: "Behooren wij niet met alle onse verstandt ende krachten daer naer te arbeyden . . . om sulck een vasticheydt . . . te conserveeren, verbeteren ende exorneren, op dat wy andere Nacien het oorsake geven haar Negotien meer ende meer in onse quartieren te soecken."
102. Weststeijn, "Dutch Brazil," 188–93.
103. Boxer, *The Dutch in Brazil*, 67–70. The count's Atlantic crossing to Brazil has been documented in sketches by Frans Post in an album currently in the collection of Het Scheepvaartmuseum, Amsterdam, inv. no. A.3457. See Corrêa do Lago and Corrêa do Lago, *Frans Post*, 372–77.

CHAPTER 4. FRICTION

1. *De briefwisseling van Pieter Corneliszoon Hooft*, 3, no. 928: Barlaeus to Hooft, 23 Aug 1638: "In Brasilia spes non levis nostros erigit, futurum ut urbe St. Salvatoris propediem potiantur. Sed haec aliaque ex fastis hebdomadalibus intellexisti, chartulis tam ficti pravique tenacibus, quam veri nunciis."

2. *Briefwisseling van Hugo Grotius*, 9, no. 3681: Van Reigersberch to Grotius, 19 July 1638: "De Westindische Compagnie sorgt om off, soo de Baia is conquesteert, die van behoorlijck garnisoen te voorsien, ofte soo de onse schade hebben geleden, wederom die te verstercken." The rumors had already reached Van Reigersberch in April: ibid., no. 3547.

3. Boxer, *The Dutch in Brazil*, 84–108; Schmidt, "The Dutch Atlantic," 174.

4. See *Fontes para a história do Brasil Holandês*, 2: 188, for the encounter between Adriaen van Bullestrate and Johann Philipp Mulheiser when the latter was commanding a small unit just outside Recife in January 1642.

5. Koninklijke Bibliotheek, The Hague, KW 129 F 6.

6. Ibid., fol. 7^r (Johan Maurits); fol. 16^r (Van Bullestrate); fol. 17^r (Lichthart); fol. 18^r (Soler); fol. 26^r (Herckmans); fol. 193^r (Mortamer); fol. 238^r (Piso).

7. Ibid., fol. 18^v (Bachiler); fol. 69^r (Vogellius); fol. 156^v (Scot): "Mutate nomine de te loquitur Poeta mi charissime Mulheisere . . . apud Barbaros."

8. Ibid., fol. 200^r (Eduardus); fol. 201^r (Van Dooreslaer)—both were Reformed ministers. See Schalkwijk, *Reformed Church*, 168–85, for the uphill task these preachers faced in converting Brazilians to the Reformed faith. Eduardus, according to Schalkwijk (178), was of English descent. He must have known Mulheiser from his time in Leiden, where both studied theology at the same time. The list of ministers Mulheiser met in Holland is too long to include here, but reads like a comprehensive who's who of the Dutch Reformed Church in the mid-1640s.

9. Ibid., fol. 128^r (Gerardus Vossius); fol. 175^v (Isaac Vossius); fol. 138^r (Golius); fol. 129^r (Barlaeus). Barlaeus's inscription for Mulheiser reads, "Philosophandum, sed paucis" (Discourse philosophically, but not to many). Barlaeus, *History of Brazil*. In her introduction (xiii–xiv), Ebeling-Koning points out that it was precisely in the fall of 1644 that Johan Maurits and Barlaeus discussed their publishing plans.

10. Koninklijke Bibliotheek, The Hague, KW 129 F 6, fol. 56^r (Thysius). On Thysius's problems during the writing of *Historia Navalis*, which remained unpublished until 1657, see Van Groesen, "Heroic Memories," 215.

11. Ibid., fol. 15^r (Cats); fol. 3^r (Elizabeth Stuart); fol. 10^r (Appelboom); fol. 13^v (Boswell).

12. Ibid., fol. 160^r (Revius); fol. 81^v (Spranckhuysen).

13. Ibid., fol. 265^v (visitors from Bad Bergzabern); fol. 273^v (Georg David Mülheuser); fol. 274^r (Johann Martin Mülhauser).

14. Ibid., fol. 244^v (Golijath).

15. Hansen Hajstrup, *Memorial und Jurenal*. See also Kraack, "Flensburg."

16. On the revolt and its repercussions in the Amsterdam print media, see Chapter 5 below.

17. Hansen Hajstrup, *Memorial und Jurenal*, 69–70, 72–74, 78, 82.

18. Ibid., 68, 91–92. See Boxer, *The Dutch in Brazil*, 124–25, for Portuguese views of Dutch drinking habits in Brazil. There were strong disagreements and personal clashes much higher up in the army's hierarchy as well: Johan Maurits and Christoph Arciszewsky, in the words of minister Soler, were "conflicting powers," occasionally to the detriment of the army's campaigns in Brazil; see *Vincent Joachim Soler's Seventeen Letters*, 57: Soler to André Rivet, 2 April 1639.

19. Hansen Hajstrup, *Memorial und Jurenal*, 83, 100.

20. Ibid., 77, 79.

21. Van Dillen, *Bronnen tot de geschiedenis*, 3, nos. 262, 399, 500, 652, 672.

22. The census of 1645–46, to which I have made minor adjustments to reflect the situation before the Portuguese revolt, can be found in Nationaal Archief, The Hague, OWIC 61, doc. 51. It is included as Appendix 1 in Wiznitzer, "The Number of Jews."

216 Notes to Pages 108–112

23. Hansen, *Memorial und Jurenal*, 89–90. Like the Portuguese before (and after) them, the Dutch struggled with the problem of runaway slaves in the northeast: see Anderson, "The Quilombo of Palmares," esp. 548–52.

24. Van den Boogaart and Emmer, "The Dutch Participation"; Postma, *The Dutch in the Atlantic Slave Trade*, 18–22.

25. See the graphic illustration in Wagner, "*Thierbuch*," fol. 106^r.

26. Bredero, *Moortje*, vss. 233–36: "Onmenschelyck ghebruyck! Godlóóse schelmery! / Dat-men de menschen vent, tot paartsche slaverny! / Hier zynder oock in stadt, die sulcken handel dryven, / In Farnabock: maar 't sal Godt niet verhoolen blyven."

27. Oey-de Vita and Geesink, *Academie en schouwburg*, 104, 107, 109–10, 114, 184. The first performance in the fencing school took place less than three weeks after the Dutch had completed the conquest of Elmina.

28. Postma, *The Dutch in the Atlantic Slave Trade*, 11; Priester, "Nederlandse houding," 39–41.

29. Evenhuis, *Ook dat was Amsterdam*, 2: 163–64.

30. This book is discussed in detail by Van Eijnatten, "War, Piracy and Religion," esp. 197, with further references. See also Schmidt, *Innocence Abroad*, 244–45, 262–64; Groenhuis, *De predikanten*, 36–37.

31. Udemans, *'t Geestelyck roer*, 360–66. For the quotes and passages I emphasize, see ibid., 360: "dit is een swaer stuck"; 361 for his references to John 8:34, quoted here, and Romans 6:16, and to the curse of Ham, and for his conclusion that "hy was waerdigh te vervallen in de vuylste, ende swaerste slavernie, overmidts hy het soete jock van synen schepper niet en wilde onderworpen zijn"; 363 for the example of Angola.

32. Ibid., 363: "Aengaende de Heydenen of Turcken, die moghen van de Christenen tot slaven ghebruyckt worden, midts datse in eene rechtvaardighe Oorloghe gevangen: of van hare Ouders, of andere deughdelicke Meesters, voor eenen rechten prijs gekocht zijn, gelijck verhaelt wordt, dat ordinaris gheschiedt in Angola. Want dit accordeert met de Goddelicke Wet, Levit. 25.vers. 44.45.46." On the same page, Udemans argued for the conversion of slaves as part of his legitimation. See ibid., 364: "ende derhalve en mogen sy de selve niet verkoopen aen Spaengjaerden, Portugijsen of andere wreede menschen"; and 364–65: "Trouwe slaven, insonderheydt die vrome Christenen worden, moeten eerlijck beloont, ende naer sekeren tijdt van jaren vry ghelaten worden."

33. Haefeli, "Breaking the Christian Atlantic," 136–40. The term "ethical compass" is Van Eijnatten's, "War, Piracy and Religion," 194.

34. Van Quelen, *Kort verhael*, [B4^r]: "Den handel der Swarten van Angola, Guinae &c., is als het zaet, 't welck de Compagnie moet in d'aerde smijten, om uyt Fernanbuc een ongeloooffelijcke inkomste te trecken . . . daer en is niet aen te twijffelen hoe datter aldaer meer sullen wesen, hoe het lande beter sal gebout worden, en de Compagnie soo veel te grooter winste trecken."

35. *Trou-hertighe onderrichtinge*, [B2^r]: "Sullen oock de particuliere wel sorge dragen dat de slaven, tot een beter conditie verkocht werden alse van natuere sijn, om in de Gerformeerde religie onder-wesen te werden? of niet meer letten waer sij 't meeste gelt voor hare lichamen connen crijghen, het mach met hare zielen gaen soo het wil, daer de Compagnie het aen haer hebbende, volghens de ordre die op hare vercoopinghe ghestelt is, daer voor sorghe sal draghen, om te meer seghen over desen handel te ghenieten, en dese vercoopinghe onder de Christenen te institueren, die voor particuliere persoonen niet en betaemt."

36. Joosten, *Kleyne wonderlijcke wereldt*, 70: "Het andere zijn swarte menschen die van Angola gebracht worden, by heele scheepen vol, ende werden verkocht op 't Recif; die daer nae op Olinde gekocht werden, die slaven moeten voor al haer leven eeuwigh dienen, en de kost

moeten zy selve besorghen; op de maniere ghelijck den Turck met de Christenen handelt: maer den Turck handelt ghemeen noch beter met de Christenen." For Usselincx's complaint, see Priester, "Nederlandse houding," 48.

37. *Reglement by de West-Indische Compagnie.* Later, too, slavery appears to have been a nonissue. In 1665, in a disputation at Amsterdam's *Athenaeum Illustre*, one student echoed Udemans's work in claiming that Christianity does not forbid slavery—but this was not part of a wider debate, judging from its isolated inclusion in a work of mixed theses: Van Miert, *Humanism in an Age of Science*, 281.

38. See Haefeli, *New Netherland*, with considerable attention to Dutch Brazil, esp. in chap. 3.

39. *Korte Onderrichtinghe*, [B3^v]: "dat wy middel sullen hebben om het heylighe Evangelium onder de Heydenen en wilde menschen te propageren."

40. Noorlander, "'For the Maintenance of the True Religion'," 78–84. Schalkwijk, *Reformed Church*, 95–96, claims that a committee for Indian affairs was already in place in Amsterdam in 1621.

41. For the frequent clashes between Company officials and the clergy in North America at the same time, see Rink, "Private Interest."

42. Udemans, *'t Geestelyck roer*, 317: "Om nu het huys des Heeren in beyde de Indien wel te bouwen . . . daer moet oock goede orde en discipline zijn."

43. Ibid., 318–19: "Soo heeft oock elcke Compagnie . . . die Authoriteyt, om alle die gene, die in haren dienst zijn, eerst met vriendelijcke vermaningen, en goede exempelen: ende wanneer die niet en helpen, met eenige boeten of andere penen, te drijven tot waerneminge van den openbaren Godsdienst"; ibid., 321: "Soo datse . . . als onwillighe kinderen, door vreese van Politijcke macht, tot de Kercke moeten ghetrocken worden: verwachtende dat middeler tijdt, God de Heere hare herten sal gewilligh maken, ende trecken door het gehoor van sijn H. Woort . . . of anders sal den bouw van de Kercke Christi aldaer, ten deele door de blindtheydt van de Heydenen, ten deele, ende insonderheydt door de ongeregeltheyt en goddeloosheyt van de genaemde Christenen, traghelijck voortgaen."

44. Ibid., 357: "Aengaende de . . . vrage, of men de Portugijsen, die onder onse Jurisdictie, in Oost- ende West-Indien wonen, om eenighe Politijcke redenen, niet en soude moghen toelaten de openbare oeffeninge van de Paepsche Religie? Daer op antwoorden wy rondt uyt, neen."

45. Israel, "Religious Toleration," 21. See also "Classicale acta."

46. Feitler, "Jews and New Christians"; Klooster, "Communities of Port Jews," 134–37. On Kahal zur Israel and a second synagogue in Dutch Brazil, established on Antonio Vaz in 1637, see Gonsalves de Mello, *Gente da Nação*, 230ff.

47. "Classicale acta," 348: "Wenschen de broeders gesamentlijck dat d'oude gravamina, aengaan de grote vrijheyt der Joden en Papisten, ongeregeltheyt onder de Negros, ontheylinge des Sabbaths, vloecken en sweren etc. eenmaal mochten afgedaan worden." Seventeen copies of Udemans's book were available for readers in Recife on the eve of the Portuguese revolt; see Nationaal Archief, The Hague, OWIC 60, doc. 80: *Memorie vande volgende boeken althans berustende opt magazijn der stuckgoederen [te Recife], 9 juni 1645*. See also Teensma, "Resentment in Recife."

48. "Classicale acta," 410–11: "Nopende het 1^e gravamen, handelende van de ontheylinge des Sabbaths . . . dat de Deput. op alle abusen, oock bij de Negros gepleeght, wel zullen letten. . . . Wat aengaet het 2^e gravamen, 'twelck spreeckt van Godlasteraeren, vloecken ende lichtveerdich sweeren, als oock de vrijheyt der Joden . . . dat de placcaten, daer tegen gestatueert, vernieuwt ende geexecuteert worden. . . . Het 3^e gravamen, sprekende van de stouticheyt der Papisten in 't gemeen . . . als oock in 't bijsonder datse nieuwe capellen timmeren, cruycen

oprechten, processien doen, onder het dexel van begravingh, affgoderije voortplanten, onder het dexel van comoedien."

49. Wiznitzer, *Jews in Colonial Brazil*, 81, 86, 129; Swetschinski, *Reluctant Cosmopolitans*, 115, 232–33. On the clandestine printing of Hebrew books in Amsterdam, see Fuks-Mansfeld, "The Hebrew Book Trade."

50. On Soler, see Teensma, "Brazilian Letters"; Gonsalves de Mello, "Vincent Joachim Soler"; Joosse, "Soler als predikant"; and throughout Schalkwijk, *Reformed Church*.

51. Boxer, *The Dutch in Brazil*, 128, called this description "one of the most curious accounts of the colony." Boudewijn du Preys invested six hundred guilders in the Company in the mid-1620s, according to his entry in the Amsterdam Groot-Kapitaalboek.

52. Throughout, I follow the English translations in *Vincent Joachim Soler's Seventeen Letters*, 41–44.

53. *Vincent Joachim Soler's Seventeen Letters*, 11–12: Soler to the directors of the Chamber of Zeeland, 8 June 1636.

54. Evenhuis, *Ook dat was Amsterdam*, 2: 358–59.

55. *Vincent Joachim Soler's Seventeen Letters*, 59: Soler to Rivet, 2 April 1639.

56. Ibid., 74: Soler to Rivet, 6 May 1640.

57. Schalkwijk, *Reformed Church*, 218–23. See Nationaal Archief, The Hague, OWIC 60, doc. 80.

58. Moreau, *Klare en waarachtige beschryving*, 45.

59. Reesse, *De suikerhandel van Amsterdam*, 194.

60. On the tension between republicanism and empire in Dutch Brazil and the way it was used by champions of free trade, see Weststeijn, "Republican Empire."

61. *Vertoogh by een Lief-hebber*, [A2r]: "hoe dat de onghefondeerde sustenue der Zeeuwen ende andere buyten-Cameren op 't sluyten vanden vryen handel, de Compagnie als participanten niet alleen schadelijck is: Maer dat sulcx volgende de gheheele ruyne vande Compagnie int cort ghebooren sal worden"; ibid.: "sullen haer Soldaten met 15. stuyvers ter weecke de magazijnen leedich coopen, ende daer mede de groote geimagineerde proffijten . . . haer selven toebrengen, voorwaer een slecht Fondament. Nu ist haer om de eere te doen, datse besitters zijn van groote landen, dat is die Princen . . . eenen eeretitel. Maer de Administrateurs van Weduwen en Wesen middelen een Goddeloose hovaerdye"; ibid., [A3r]: "Segghen als recht is den Tiran Duc d'Alva omt invoeren vanden thienden penninck, heeft den Coninck van Spangnien de Nederlanden doen verliesen, ende wanneer wy van alles rekening souden geven wel 50. ten hondert, ende en connen daer met noch niet volstaen."

62. *Examen over 't Vertoogh*, 3: "dat het by een goet ghehersent mensche in gheen consideratie sal mogen vallen; soo ist dan noch dat daer mede d'Autheur by eenighe eenvoudighe oft aen zijne zijde doch wat hellende persoonen desen roem sich niet en mach aentrecken, als oft hy sonder contradictie ghewonnen sake hadde"; ibid.: ". . . in 't selve werck niet en vindet . . . dan passien sonder stijl, sonder ordre, sonder fondament, sonder grondich verstandt, vol van exclamatien, vol ydele vertoninghen, vol woorden van extremiteyten ende dreyghementen."

63. Ibid., 7: "onversadelijcken begeerlijckheyt."

64. Ibid., 12: "waer in hy dan betoont aen d'eene zijde dat hy in die nederlantsche saecken een Portugijs vreemdelingh is; ende aen d'ander zijde een onbedacht periculeus fomenteerder der Portugijschen vyandtlijcke ghemoederen." The lasting power of the trope of "tyranny" at the hands of the Duke of Alva in the United Provinces is discussed by Sawyer, "Tyranny of Alva."

65. *Examen over 't Vertoogh*, 15: "'Twelck also alles in een goede harmonie weder ghebrocht zijnde."

66. *Briefwisseling van Hugo Grotius*, 7, no. 2895: Grotius to Nicolaas van Reigersberch, 18 December 1636: "Wat resolutie in uE. quartieren sal werden genomen op het onderhouden van de Compaignie, sal ick mede garen verstaen. Wilt bij Numerianus' [i.e., Amsterdam's, Grotius occasionally used coded language in his letters] volck luisteren ende overschrijven, maer niet seggen, insonderheit in dese tijden, dat sulcx niet dan quaedt can doen."

67. Ibid., 8, no. 2996: Grotius to Nicolaas van Reigersberch, 18 March 1637: "In de saecke van Brasyl sie ick dat Heufd gelijck oock in andere saecken seer is gepassioneert tegen Hollant. Ick sal garen de insichte van beide zijden verstaen om daervan met oordeel te connen spreecken." For Grotius's ideas on free trade, see Van Ittersum, "Long Goodbye," esp. 402.

68. Ibid., 8, no. 3079: Nicolaas van Reigersberch to Grotius, 18 May 1637: "ter beyder sijden met wat te veel animositeyt"; ibid., 8, no. 3118, 16 June 1637: "Het different, dat tusschen de camers was op het drijven van den handel in Brasil, is vereffent ende blijft de negotie bij de Compagnie. De bewinthebbers crijgen goede opinie van dat werck ende sijn niet buyten hope van haest te hooren, dat de Bahy de Todos los Santos in hare handen soude wesen."

69. Buchelius, "VOC-dagboek," fol. 127^r: "Sijn oeck daertoe dienende verscheide boecxkens van dese materie, waerbij soo d'eene als d'andere opinie voorgestaen wert, soo bij gescrifte als den drucke gemeen gemaeckt. Waerover de bewinthebberen mette Staten seer besich sijn ome het beste te verkiesen." The phrase "governed by opinion" forms the title of Dagmar Freist's book of 1997.

70. *Briefwisseling van Hugo Grotius*, 9, no. 3458: Nicolaas van Reigersberch to Grotius, 15 February 1638: "ende doet dat verschil de compagnie seer groote schade."

71. Ibid., 9, no. 3475: Grotius to Nicolaas van Reigersberch, 27 February 1638: "Dat den vrijen handel niet van alle, maer van eenige goederen goed soude doen . . . is het advys altijd geweest van Matelief ende eenige anderen. In Westindië gelove ick, dat noch meerder redenen daertoe dienen, ende soude een proeve daervan connen werden genomen soo lang de compagnie sulcx soude behaegen."

72. Ibid., 9, no. 3533: Nicolaas van Reigersberch to Grotius, 19 April 1638: "Dat de Westindische Compagnie haer different onder den andere, sonder intercessie ende autoriteyt van yemant, heeft gevonden, geeft niet alleen groot contentemente aen de regeerynge, maer aen de participanten int particulier." For the outcomes of the prolonged discussions, see Boxer, *The Dutch in Brazil*, 81–82.

73. Ibid., 9, no. 3892: Nicolaas van Reigersberch to Grotius, 18 December 1637: "De Engelschen meenen, dat het in Brasyl wel quaelijck soude mooge afloopen, ende anderen seggen mij oock, dat het beleit van de Westindische Compaignie door oneenicheit wat los gaet."

74. Deen, "Handwritten Propaganda," 211.

75. Eisenstein, *Divine Art*, 52–53.

76. On the politics of particularism, see Price, *Holland and the Dutch Republic*.

77. Taylor, *Religion's Enemies*, 6.

78. See, for example Buchelius, "VOC-dagboek," fol. 119^r; *Briefwisseling van Hugo Grotius*, 13, no. 5628: Nicolaas van Reigersberch to Grotius, 1 March 1642. On the proposed merger with the VOC, see Den Heijer, "Plannen voor samenvoeging."

79. *Briefwisseling van Hugo Grotius*, 9, no. 4659: Nicolaas van Reigersberch to Grotius, 21 May 1640.

80. Israel, *Dutch Primacy*, 163; Van Dillen, "Effectenkoersen," 9–10; Den Heijer, *De geoctrooieerde compagnie*, 101. On the tulip craze of the late 1630s and its effects, see Goldgar, *Tulipmania*, esp. chap. 5.

81. Den Heijer, *De geoctrooieerde compagnie*, 98. See Joseph de la Vega, *Confusion de confusiones* (Amsterdam, 1688), as cited by Petram, *De bakermat van de beurs*, 7.

82. Elias, *De vroedschap*, 1: xc; Den Heijer, *De geoctrooieerde compagnie*, 142; Ligtenberg, *Usselinx*, 192–93.

83. Goldgar, *Tulipmania*, 247–51.

84. Dudok van Heel, "Wie mogen wij," 51n6.

85. Van Winter, *Westindische Compagnie*, 6–11.

86. See, for example, Willemsen, "Beleggers."

87. Van Winter, *Westindische Compagnie*, 27–28, 36–38; see *Verhooginghe vande Capitalen*.

88. Noorlander, "'For the Maintenance of the True Religion'," 85–86, and more extensively in the same author's "Serving God and the Mammon," 86–91.

89. For this decision and the remainder of the paragraph, see Boxer, *The Dutch in Brazil*, 146, 155–57.

90. Cabral de Mello, *Olinda Restaurada*, 301, shows how share prices continued to fall in the months after Johan Maurits's departure from Recife, from 95 percent in July 1643 to 37 percent in August 1644.

CHAPTER 5. "AMSTERDAMNIFIED"

1. Cabral de Mello, *Olinda Restaurada*. The qualification of Amsterdam's position as blind obstruction is from Alexander van der Capellen, the Gelderland representative in the States General: *Gedenkschriften*, 2: 190. For the two battles of Guararapes, both narrowly lost by the Dutch, see Boxer, *The Dutch in Brazil*, 196–98, 213–16.

2. *Amsterdams Tafel-Praetje*, [B3^{rv}].

3. *Dutch Corantos*, 70–82.

4. A particularly fierce pamphlet accusing the West India Company of corruption, *Brasilsche Geltsack*, appeared in 1647.

5. *Tijdingen uyt verscheyde Quartieren*, no. 35 (2 Sept 1645); *Courante uyt Italien en Duytschlandt*, no. 35 (2 Sept 1645).

6. Bick, "Governing the Free Sea," esp. chap. 2, is a microhistory of Dutch politics and information management in the wake of the Portuguese revolt.

7. Nieuhof, *Gedenkweerdige Brasiliaense zee- en lantreize*, esp. 96–98.

8. Van den Broeck, *Journael*, 17. See also Van Groesen, "Officers," 45–47.

9. Koninklijke Bibliotheek, The Hague, KW 129 F 6, fols. 239^v and 240^r, for the inscriptions of Samuel and Diederick van Hoogstraten, respectively.

10. Boxer, *The Dutch in Brazil*, 165–71; De Bruin, *Geheimhouding en verraad*, 524–26.

11. The only surviving copy in print of the verdict against Ferreira is *Brieven, confessie*, 70–73. See also De Bruin, *Geheimhouding en verraad*, 524–26.

12. Cabral de Mello, *Braziliaanse affaire*, 48, 51–54.

13. [Graswinckel], *Aen-spraeck*. See Van de Haar, *Diplomatieke betrekkingen*, 113.

14. Moreau, *Klare en waarachtige beschryving*, [*2^v], 45. See also Montanus, *Nieuwe en Onbekende Weereld*, 513, 523.

15. Israel, "Dutch Sephardi Jewry," 383.

16. Klooster, "Essequibo Liberties," 79.

17. Swetschinski, *Reluctant Cosmopolitans*, 231; Israel, *Dutch Primacy*, 170.

18. Israel, "Dutch Sephardi Jewry," 368–78. For more background, see Wiznitzer, "Jewish Soldiers." For Sousa Coutinho, see his *Correspondência diplomatica*.

19. Van de Haar, *Diplomatieke betrekkingen*, 115. Nonetheless, I agree with Boxer in rejecting claims that Sousa Coutinho was primarily responsible for the Dutch failure to rescue Brazil; see *The Dutch in Brazil*, 257.

20. *Manifest door d'Inwoonders*, 3–4. See also Schmidt, *Innocence Abroad*, 281–88, who, by placing it alongside Kieft's War in New Netherland, draws attention to the wider context of Dutch "tyranny" in the 1640s.

21. *Tijdingen uyt verscheyde quartieren*, no. 27 (4 July 1648): "doch by de Onse het Veldt behouden en den Vyandt met groot verlies geretireert."

22. *Ordinarisse Middel-Weeckse Courante*, no. 19 (4 May 1649): "Alhier [in The Hague] is den roep dat ons volck in Brasilien weder een groote schade gheleden hebben ende eenige hondert mannen verlooren."

23. *Lyste vande hooge en de lage officieren*.

24. *Hollantse Mercurius . . . 1654*, 29.

25. Van de Haar, *Diplomatieke betrekkingen*, 116–21.

26. The notion that Amsterdam was responsible for the impending loss of Brazil is demonstrated very forcefully by Boxer, *The Dutch in Brazil*. For the Company share price in 1649, see Goslinga, *The Dutch in the Caribbean*, 509.

27. *Copye vande Resolutie*.

28. Ibid., [A1^v]: "indien de Compag. niet gemainteneert en wordt, ende 'tis oock te vreesen, hoe licht men het oock wil op-nemen, dat het Grau eens mocht op de been komen, ende haer aen d' een of d' ander Burgemeester dieder geen schult in heeft vergrypen: want het schynt ende men roept het heele Landt deur op de quawille van dese Stadt, soo dat icker groote swarigheyt in sie, met ons soo te kanten tegen de heele regeringen, endat dat wy ons niet laten bewegen, door 't gekarm van so veel bedructe ende onnosele Wesen, Weduwen, ende andere eenvoudige menschen, die haer gelt aen de West-Ind. Comp. hebben gegeven."

29. Ibid., [A2^r]: "Het Recif hou ic al verloren."

30. Ibid., [A3^v]: "datter een generale blydschap sou komen over de heele Stadt . . . om datter so veel bedructe ende arme menschen aen vast zijn."

31. Ibid., [B4^r]: "om also doende, te toonen dat by dese stadt noch kleynmoedigheyt, veel min die gepresumeerde quade wille is, die op eenige Heeren Regenten van dese stadt, so men hoort ende in verscheiden blauwe boexkens gedruct siet, gepresumeert," supposedly the contribution of the powerful burgomaster Cornelis de Graeff.

32. Tulp's contribution is the most extensive one, *Copye vande Resolutie*, [A3^v]–[B2^r]

33. Account of books purchased by Lieuwe van Aitzema, in Keblusek, *Boeken in de Hofstad*, 336. The different editions are also listed in the Knuttel catalogue, with the same title, as Nos. 6470, 6471, and 6472.

34. Harline, *Pamphlets*, 88.

35. *Examen van de Valsche Resolutie*.

36. Ibid., 3: "en waert mogelijck der selven goede Gemeente, mitsgaders oock 't heele Landt tegen haer op te hitsen."

37. Ibid., 4–5: "ende d'een of d'ander van die Ed. Regeeringe op te dringen, vresende van de school-Jongens . . . selfs bespot te worden" / ". . . het groot onverstant, en de stoutigheyt van dese luyden, die het heele landt deur op schuyten en wagens, in stegen en straten op alle bruyloften en maeltijden en by na in alle geselschappen de mondt daer van vol hebben."

38. Ibid., 9: "Wel is dan wonder dat een out wijs man swaer hoofdich is?"

39. Ibid., 16–17: "maer also heeft oock gedaen d'Oost-Indische Comp. en de particuliere Capers van dese Landen, ghelijck oock mede sijn Majest. van Vranckrijck, Engelandt, Sweden en andere die met Spaengien directelijck of indirectelijck ghekrakeelt en gheoorlocht hebben."

40. At the same time, there was tension too in the Company's other American colony, New Netherland. See Jacobs, *New Netherland*, 145–49.

41. *Examen van de Valsche Resolutie*, 4–5. For a survey of these seven *praatjes*, see Dingemanse and Meijer Drees, "'Praatjes' over de WIC," esp. 115–17. See also Emmer and Klooster, "The Dutch Atlantic," 50, who focus on another 1649 *praatje* that emphasizes the lack of Dutch migrants to sustain an Atlantic challenge.

42. *Amsterdams Dam-Praetje*, [A1ᵛ]: "Kort begryp van dit tractaetje": "Daer na wert pertinent aengewesen, hoe schadelijck het is voor 't gemeen, en de particuliere van dese Landen, dat de Vrede met Portugal niet wert afgesloten, ende voort lest, dat de West-Indische Compagnie met recht, by een misval van ontijdich geboorte, en een wanschapen of Monster wel mach geleeken worden, en om wat redenen."

43. Boxer, "Salvador Correia de Sá," 511; Dingemanse and Meijer Drees, "'Praatjes' over de WIC," 117–22.

44. For similar strategies on the stage in Amsterdam, see Meeus, "Peasant as a Mouthpiece."

45. *Brasyls Schuyt-Praetjen*, with the concluding verses on [C4ʳ]: "Met recht mogen de Brasilische Portogysen seggen, Godt sal ons verlossen van 't Hollandtsche Jock soo swaer / 't Welck ons heeft onder-druckt seer naer vijf-en-twintigh Jaer . . . Om dat d'Hollanders rijckdom voor haer God hebben ge-eert, / soo heeft Godt al haer werck tot niet ghekeert."

46. *De Portogysen goeden buyrman*.

47. *Korte observatien*, [A2ʳ]: "Ten is niet nieus, dat Lieden die hare wijsheydt ende vernuft alles toe-schrijven, sich aen-nemen Raedt te geven, in saken die de Regeringe aengaen, daer niet toe versocht zijnde; dan dat sonder naem sich derven aen de Hooghste Regeringe, 'tselve gaet wat verder, insonderheydt, als haer aen-spraken in Druck uyt-geven, eer dat de selve gesien zijn by de gene, aen de welcke sy die adresseren: ende is vry vreemt, dat sulcke Schriften werden aen-gesien, ende in de Vergaderingen vande Regeerders gebracht, sonder datter onder-soeck op wert gedaen; wesende te vermoeden dat sulcke zijn aen-gestelt ende gestijft werden, by de gene die het niet en betaemt, en die daer yets anders meer voor hebben, als wel behoorde." See also Harline, *Pamphlets*, 160–61.

48. *Korte observatien*, [A2ʳ]: "neemt hy so groote vryheydt, om niet alleen de Bewindthebberen vande Geoctroyeerde West-Indische Compagnie haer kleyn verstant te verwijten; maer oock de Ho. Regeringe te scholieren, so dat sijne vrymoedicheyt al vry verre sich uyt streckt."

49. Ibid. The initial pamphlet is entitled *Vertooch aen de Hoogh en Mogende heeren Staten Generael*.

50. This claim is based on the Short Title Catalogue Netherlands (STCN; www.stcn.nl). Neither of the Van Marels is mentioned in the exhaustive archival overview of the Amsterdam book trade by Kleerkooper and Van Stockum, Jr., *De boekhandel te Amsterdam*, suggesting that Van Marel was not their real name.

51. Van Hoboken, *Witte de With*; Doedens, *Witte de With*, 69–88.

52. [Cramer], *Voor-looper*.

53. Gonsalves de Mello, *Nederlanders in Brazilië*, 14, calls Moreau "one of the classic sources for this period," but Boxer, for example, repeatedly questions his authority. Apart from Benjamin Schmidt (*Innocence Abroad*, 291ff), few scholars have since written on Moreau. Moreau dedicated his book to César, Duke of Vendôme, an illegitimate son of King Henri IV.

54. Moreau, *Klare en waarachtige beschryving*, 64–65.

55. Ibid., 30–31. On Jacob Rabe, see Meuwese, *Brothers in Arms*, 172–73; Van den Boogaart, "Infernal Allies," 528–29.

56. There were similar excesses in New Netherland around the same time; see Merwick, *Shame and the Sorrow*, 133–79.

57. Moreau, *Klare en waarachtige beschryving*, 7, 9–11, 17–18.

58. *Het Hollants wijve-praetjen*, [B2ʳ].

59. Haefeli, "Breaking the Christian Atlantic," 136.

60. "Dagboek van Hendrik Haecxs," 291, 293–94. See also Schalkwijk, *Reformed Church*, 62. The comet was also visible "for 19 days" in Fort Ceulen in Rio Grande: Hansen Hajstrup, *Memorial und Jurenal*, 100.

61. *Nieuwe ongewoon-wonderlykke Staert-Sterre*; *Hollandtse Mercurius . . . 1652*, 117.

62. *West-Indisch Discours*, 16. For the relationship between news and prognostications, see Reeves, *Evening News*, 2–6.

63. Vermij, *Calvinist Copernicans*, 182–83; Van Miert, *Humanism in an Age of Science*, 73–74; Jorink, *Reading the Book of Nature*, 145, who emphasizes that De Bie here relies on Genesis 9:13.

64. *Information from Ceará*, 33–36.

65. *Ontdeckinghe van Rijcke Mijnen in Brasil*.

66. Krommen, *Mathias Beck*, 58–70. The second group of men sent to Ceará included Peter Hansen; see Hansen Hajstrup, *Memorial und Jurenal*, 86–89.

67. *Hollandse Mercurius . . . 1652*, 106.

68. Alpers, *The Art of Describing*, 162–65.

69. Larsen, "Some Seventeenth-Century Paintings," 127, assumes that Gillis Peeters crossed the Atlantic. Zandvliet, *Mapping for Money*, 244, is inclined to believe that he did not and that his paintings are based on the maps and views of others. Some of Peeters's early work appears to have been influenced by Andries van Eertvelt, who painted the exoticized cityscape of Bahia after Claes Jansz Visscher; see Figure 17.

70. Meuwese, *Brothers in Arms*, 176–80.

71. Zandvliet, *Mapping for Money*, 244, suggests the painting may represent Dutch-Potiguar encounters in Baía da Traição around 1625 and may have been in the possession of the stadtholder before 1632. Larsen, "Neu entdeckte Brasilien-Bilder," 2: 937, dates the panel c. 1640 on stylistic grounds. If my reading of the painting on historical grounds makes sense, it must be dated later still, in the second half of the 1640s when the Dutch were losing their grasp on Brazil.

72. Zandvliet, *Mapping for Money*, 296n90.

73. Larsen, "Some Seventeenth-Century Paintings," 125.

74. This much is confirmed in a printed catalogue of meaningful disasters by the Amsterdam author Van Zanten, *Spiegel*, 190–91, which reserved a prominent place for the famine that struck Recife in 1646, forcing the colonists "to feed themselves on the herbs, roots, and leaves that grew in the graveyards" and almost drove them to surrender to the Portuguese at that time.

75. Belonje, "Capiteyn Croeger," reports the captain's 1659 inventory that includes "1 stuckje vant schip *Alckmaer* ende lantcasteel vant Recife met een aerdich geteeckent met een swarte ebbe lijst."

76. For a similar suggestion, see Alpers, *The Art of Describing*, 163; Honour, *New Golden Land*, 82–83.

77. Larsen, "Neu entdeckte Brasilien-Bilder," 2: 937. On Post's designs for engravings from the late 1640s, see Van den Boogaart, "A Well-Governed Colony."

78. Schwartz, "Looking for a New Brazil," 41.

79. Klooster, "Networks of Colonial Entrepreneurs"; Goodfriend, "Practicing Toleration," 105–12; Schwartz, "Looking for a New Brazil," 48, 51–52.
80. Israel, "Jews in Dutch America," 342–47.
81. Hansen Hajstrup, *Memorial und Jurenal*, 102–19. The inn was called "Hoff von Brasilien."
82. *A Collection of the State Papers of John Thurloe*, 2: 521.
83. Hansen Hajstrup, *Memorial und Jurenal*, 120–21.
84. Jacobs, *New Netherland*, 397–98.
85. Hulsman, "Gisberth de With en Anna Paes"; *Kort, Bondigh ende Waerachtigh Verhael*, no. 68.
86. Schalkwijk, *Reformed Church*, 98.
87. Meuwese, *Brothers in Arms*, 182–85, where he also mentions the petitions of several free blacks. See also the same author's "From Dutch Allies to Portuguese Vassals." For a transcript of António Paraupaba's requests, see Hulsman, "Brazilian Indians."
88. De Bruin, "Political Pamphleteering," 79–81.
89. See also Boxer, *The Dutch in Brazil*, 243–44.
90. *Articulen van Vrede ende Confederatie*. See Cabral de Mello, *Braziliaanse affaire*, 139–59; Van de Haar, *Diplomatieke betrekkingen*, 162–79.

CHAPTER 6. RECOLLECTION

1. Zwier van Haren, *De Geusen*, 69: "Verzuimd Brasil; ô ryke gronden, / Wier aard' is Diamant en goud; / Ik hoor uw overgaaf verkonden, / Nu Bankert u niet meer behoud! / Vergeefs heeft Post Olinda's kerken / Verwoest, voor onse nieuwe Werken. / Met Nassau wykt het wuft geluk; / De Plaats, de naamen, zyn verlooren, / Die d'Overwinnaar had verkooren / In 't heedendaagse Fernaambuk." See Van der Vliet, *Onno Zwier van Haren*, 319–40, for an extensive discussion of *De Geusen*. For this poem and for the section on naval heroes in this chapter, see Van Groesen, "Heroic Memories."
2. On the concept of "frozen memory," see Assmann, "Memory, Individual and Collective," 216–17.
3. *Gloria Parendi*, 81, 302. On Willem Frederik's strained relationship with Johan Maurits, see Kooijmans, *Liefde in opdracht*, 57–60, 67–68.
4. *Gloria Parendi*, 436; Egmond and Mason, "Albert E(e)ckhout," 123–24.
5. The scholarship on Johan Maurits's three gifts is abundant. See Joppien, "The Dutch Vision," esp. 321–28; Françozo, "Global Connections," 120–22. On Johan Maurits as Stadtholder of Kleve, see Opgenoorth, "Johan Maurits as Stadholder of Cleves."
6. Cabral de Mello, *Nassau*; Bouman, *Johan Maurits van Nassau*; Van Balen, *Johan Maurits in Brazilië*.
7. This description is based on Hennin, *Zinrijke gedachten*, 111–17, and the journal of William Lord Fitzwilliam of June 1663, in Van Strien, *Touring the Low Countries*, 188. For images of Johan Maurits's furniture, see *O Brasil e os Holandeses*, 63.
8. Françozo, "Global Connections," 115; Bots, "Johann Moritz," 104. The full story of Johan Maurits's impressive court spectacles is told more extensively in Françozo, *De Olinda a Holanda*, 169–202
9. Françozo, "Global Connections," 118, with further references, and Françozo, "Dressed like an Amazon," which discusses two paintings by Adriaen Hanneman. The first painting, *Por-*

trait of Mary Stuart (c. 1655), belongs to the English Royal Collection and is housed at St. James's Palace in England; the second, *Posthumous Portrait of Mary I Stuart with a Servant* (c. 1664), is property of the Mauritshuis in The Hague.

10. *Bronnen tot de geschiedenis der Leidsche universiteit*, 2: 283.

11. Ibid., 4: 311, a resolution of the university curators from 1711 that bemoans the sorry state of some of Johan Maurits's artifacts. On the New Testament in twelve languages, see Duparc, "Zeldzaam geschenk."

12. Van den Besselaar, "Franciscus Plante," 52.

13. Plante, *Mauritiados*. Both the translations and much of the information in the following paragraph are based on Eekhout, "The Mauritias"; and Van den Besselaar, "Franciscus Plante."

14. Eekhout, "The Mauritias," 379–81, 390–91; Van den Besselaar, "Franciscus Plante," 47–48, who adds slanderous accusations of fighting, stealing, drinking, and whoring to Plante's supposed list of vices in Brazil. On this circle of Latinists around Nicolaas Heinsius, see also Rademaker, "Oorlog en vrede."

15. Eekhout, "The Mauritias," 380n11.

16. Barlaeus, *History of Brazil*, 314.

17. On Barlaeus's role in the establishment of the Amsterdam *Athenaeum Illustre*, see Van Miert, *Humanism in an Age of Science*, 45–55.

18. Van Berckel-Ebeling Koning, "Preface," x–xi, xiii.

19. On De Laet, see Bremmer, "Correspondence of Johannes de Laet," one of a number of contributions in a special issue of *Lias* devoted to Johannes de Laet. On the animosity between De Laet and Barlaeus, which dated back to the Arminian controversy of the late 1610s when Barlaeus had been denied the chair in logic at Leiden because of his liberal beliefs, see Rubies, "Mythologies," 310.

20. Van Berckel-Ebeling Koning, "Preface," xvii–xviii.

21. Ibid., xviii–xix.

22. Barlaeus, *History of Brazil*, 106. See also Warnsinck, "Christoffel Artichewsky," 4: lxxi.

23. Van Berckel-Ebeling Koning, "Preface," xviii–xix.

24. Van der Veldt, "An Autograph Letter." For the cooperation between Blaeu and Barlaeus, see Sutton, *Capitalism*, 88–93.

25. Van den Boogaart, "A Well-Governed Colony."

26. Van der Veldt, "An Autograph Letter," 312.

27. Barlaeus, *Geschichte in Brasilien*. It was reprinted in Latin in 1660, also in Kleve; see Dams, "Production, Communication, and Comprehension," 225. The first printed translation in Dutch did not appear until 1923 (*Nederlandsch Brazilië onder het bewind van Johan Maurits Grave van Nassau*); the first Portuguese translation dates from 1940 (*História dos feitos recentemente praticádos durante oito años no Brasil*); the first English edition was published as late as 2011 courtesy of Blanche T. van Berckel-Ebeling Koning (Barlaeus, *History of Brazil*).

28. Moreau, *Klare en waarachtige beschryving*, 32–33; Nieuhof, *Gedenkweerdige Brasiliaense Zee- en lantreize*, 139. On Boa Vista, see van Nederveen Meerkerk, *Recife*, 149–50, who reports that the villa was still standing in 1654; and Terwen, "Buildings," 98. On the gardens of Vrijburg, see Da Silva and Mota Alcides, "Collecting and Framing the Wilderness."

29. *Gloria Parendi*, 432 (25 September 1647): "Graf Mauritz iss heel in discredijt en door dit werck in kleinachting gekomen; hij heeft sich te veul geimagineert, dat hij al te nootwendich wass en daerom sulcke hooghen eisch gedaen, daer de Hollanders mit spotten; het staet sijn vrunden niet aen, en sijn vianden die maeckten sich lustich daermede.—Hij iss heel ten achteren en gerouineert, vol schulden, iss half of hij droomde, vol gedachten en reveriën, en laet

noch alle dingen op credijt maecken. . . . S. H. iss niet wel op Graf Mauritz tevreden, de Staten-General oock."
30. Opgenoorth, "Johan Maurits as Stadholder of Cleves."
31. *Hollandtse Mercurius . . .1652*, 28–31.
32. Schenkeveld-Van der Dussen, "Vondel und Johann Moritz."
33. Marcgraf and Piso, *Historiae Naturalis Brasiliae*. On Marcgraf, see the exhaustive analysis in Whitehead and Boeseman, *Portrait of Dutch 17th-Century Brazil*, as well as several exemplary articles by Peter Whitehead, including "The Biography of Georg Marcgraf," and "Georg Markgraf and Brazilian Zoology." See also North, "Georg Markgraf." More recent is *Information from Ceará*.
34. Safier, "Beyond Brazilian Nature"; Freedberg, "Science, Commerce, and Art," 389–97.
35. Pies, *Willem Piso*, 42–48, provides many details in an otherwise rather apologetic biography of his ancestor. See also Elias, *De vroedschap*, 2: 761.
36. Piso, *De Indiae utriusque*. See Cook, *Matters of Exchange*, 213–24; Whitehead and Boeseman, *Portrait of Dutch 17th-Century Brazil*, 30.
37. The term "info lust" was coined by Blair and Stallybrass, "Mediating Information," 139.
38. Schmidt, *Inventing Exoticism*, as well as Mason, *Infelicities*, 3.
39. Correa do Lago and Correa do Lago, *Frans Post*, who divide Post's artistic career into four phases of increasing exoticism (and diminishing quality).
40. Ibid., 115–89.
41. Souza Leão Vieira, "Topografias Imaginárias"; on Post's sugar mills, see also Massing, "From Dutch Brazil to the West Indies," 186–87.
42. Uitenhage de Mist-Verspyck, "'Gezicht in Brazilie'," 55.
43. Correa do Lago and Correa do Lago, *Frans Post*, 138–41, with references to Sousa-Leão, *Frans Post*, 26, 68ff.
44. Getty Provenance Index, Archival Inventories and Sales Catalogs N-42 (Zeeman), N-A24 (Marselis), and N-3868 (Cannegieter). Cannegieter had been an administrator in Rio Grande in the 1650s; see Hansen Hajstrup, *Memorial und Jurenal*, 93. The paintings owned by Jan Six are currently in the collection of Het Scheepvaartmuseum in Amsterdam; see Corrêa do Lago and Corrêa do Lago, *Frans Post*, 154–57. See also Parker Brienen, "Who Owns Frans Post?" 230–37.
45. Getty Provenance Index, Archival Inventory N-434: "Een Oost-Indisch landtschapje van Post."
46. Parker Brienen, "Who Owns Frans Post?" 237–38. Souza Leão Vieira, "Topografias Imaginárias," Inventários Notariais, Table 4, even includes a later reference to Post's landscapes as Chinese.
47. Corrêa do Lago and Corrêa do Lago, *Frans Post*, 191–295.
48. Schmidt, *Inventing Exoticism*, 25–81.
49. Montanus, *Nieuwe en Onbekende Weereld*.
50. Van Meurs, "Opdragt," in Montanus, *Nieuwe en Onbekende Weereld* [*3ᵛ]: "die over America zeeghaftige standaerden voerde . . . hoe een Nassouwsche Vorst haer woeste boodem acht jaer betreeden heeft, tot schrik van Portugal, voort-zetting der Nederlandsche moogendheid, en verwondering des gantschen aerdboodems."
51. Schmidt, *Inventing Exoticism*, 27–28, 42–43; Blair and Stallybrass, "Mediating Information," 139–40.
52. Montanus, *Nieuwe en Onbekende Weereld*, 399: "Om dit Brasil eindelijk gespte 't Vereenigde Nederland stoutmoedig 't harnas aen."
53. The following section is based on Van Groesen, "Arnoldus Montanus."

54. Parker Brienen, *Visions of Savage Paradise*, 171–99. See also Buvelot, *Albert Eckhout*, and Berlowicz, *Albert Eckhout volta ao Brasil*.

55. Joppien, "The Dutch Vision," 321–28.

56. Both handwritten accounts have been edited and published in the later twentieth century: Wagner, *"Thierbuch"*; *Wundersamen Reisen des Caspar Schmalkalden*. On Wagner, see Spohr, *Zacharias Wagner*; on Schmalkalden, Collet, *Welt in der Stube*, 94–131.

57. Anderson, "Material Mediators"; Teixeira, *The "Allegory of the Continents"*; Bremer-David, *"Le Cheval Rayé"*; Whitehead and Boeseman, *Portrait of Dutch 17th-Century Brazil*, 90–94 (on Van Kessel), 107–40 (on tapestries).

58. Montanus, *Nieuwe en Onbekende Weereld*, 383.

59. Ibid., 532: "Zy verkooren een Mameluksche paus, bisschoppen en priesters: onderhielden de biecht: lasen missen en roosenhoedjens: riepen 't volk tot 't gebed door 't geklop op geholde kalabassen: gebruikten boeken, van boom-schorsen gemaekt: de boeken begreepen in kris-krassen veel bygeloovige kerkzeden: stelden groote heiligheid in 't beeven, uit-steeken der tonge en een hol geluid, voortgebragt uit de borst, tot welke verrichting een zeker kruid knaeuwden."

60. A similar sentiment can be found in a poem dedicated to Johan Maurits by Joost van den Vondel, *Jaghtzang*, vss. 85–92: "Men zagh dien braven helt de Braziljaensche Reuzen / Verschricken met zijn knods, den Lissebonschen Taegh / De horens en het hooft, in d'andre weereldt kneuzen, de menscheneeters stout verstooren in hun laegh. / De wilde woestheit, langs de kust, uit schrick geweecken / Geschoolen in haer bosch en ruighten uit ontzagh / Begon op zijn vertreck haer hooft weêr op te steecken, / te groeien, daer Olinde in puin begraven lagh."

61. Schmidt, *Inventing Exoticism*, 27–28.

62. De Vries, *Curieuse Aenmerckingen*.

63. De Bry, *America*, 2, ills. 14 and 26. See Van Groesen, *Representations*.

64. On Rock the Brazilian, see Exquemelin, *De Americaensche Zeerovers*; Lunsford, *Piracy and Privateering*, 62–63. On Brazilian Mary, a member of the Band of Hees that infested the countryside of Holland, Utrecht, and Gelderland in the late 1650s, see Egmond, *Underworlds*, 55.

65. Hansen traveled to Amsterdam in March/April 1656 to get paid, but to no effect.

66. Koninklijke Bibliotheek, The Hague, KW 129 F 6, fol. 352^r: "La vigilancia es la madre de bona vintura."

67. Schwartz, "Looking for a New Brazil."

68. Klooster, "Networks of Colonial Entrepreneurs."

69. Leiden University Library, ms. BPL 2610: *Album Amicorum Otto Keye* (1637–1640).

70. Keye, *Het waere onderscheyt*, [(^)4^v]. Spranger went on to become director of Dutch Cayenne in the 1660s.

71. Ibid., 159. See Schwartz, "Looking for a New Brazil," 52–57.

72. Sellin, *Treasure, Treason and the Tower*, 21–23.

73. Gerbier, *Waarachtige verklaringe*; Octroy, [A1^v]: "immers so goet als dat van Brasil." Gerbier also translated Keye's treatise into English: *A sommary description manifesting that greater profits are to bee done in the hott than in the could parts off the coast off America* (Rotterdam, 1660).

74. Van Westhuysen, *Waerachtich Verhael*, [A3^r]: "waer soo schoone Suyckeren werden ghemaeckt, als oyt Brasijl gegeven heeft; ende soo het onder Godts zeghen kan behouden werden, is seer bequaem om een ander Brasijl van te maecken."

75. Frankel, "Antecedents and Remnants."

76. Klooster, "Essequibo Liberties."

77. Games, "Cohabitation," 217, 232; Zijlstra, "Competing for European Settlers," 159.

78. Archief Staten van Zeeland, no. 2035, 310–12: Johannes Heinsius to the Chamber of Zeeland, 28 December 1678: "vinde het lant vrij beter als ick selve hadde ge-imageneert, en is waerlijck in corte jaren tot grooter perfectie te brengen als Brasil oijt voor de West-Indische Compie. is geweest, hoewel dat deselve soo om dat landt te winnen als te verliesen vier en twintigh jaren heeft doorgebraght beneffens veele milioenen aen geldt." I am grateful to Suze Zijlstra for pointing me in the direction of this and other documents from Suriname.

79. Buve, "Gouverneur Johannes Heinsius," 17–18: "Ben van intentie een compie. negros op te reghten en tot soldaten te maken, belovende haer ten eijnde van vier jaeren dienst vrijdom; In Brasil hadden de portugesen een regiment negros onders den collonel *Henriques Dias*, een neger met één arm, t'welck ons meer afbreuck gedaen heeft als eenige ander regiment van de portugesen."

80. Mattos, "'Black Troops'."

81. Archief Staten van Zeeland, no. 2035, 322–23: Johannes Heinsius to an unknown planter, 10 April 1679: "Ick ben seer verlangende na soldaten om d'oude te mogen licentieeren, sijnde een seer quade sake dat men de luijden over haer tijt hout, t'welck een groote oorsake vant verlies van Brasil is geweest, want de luijden dan t'eenemael onwillich worden."

82. Archief Staten van Zeeland, no. 2035, 225: Petition of planters from Suriname, 11 March 1671: "dat vanwegen Ued: Mog: op bequame plaetsen publijcqe molens zouden worden gebouwt, . . . om de daeromme leggende plantagien het riet uijt te maelen, gelijck die herom leggende planters oock zouden gehouden zijn hun riedt aen zoodaenighe meulen ter maling te brengen & dat op zoodanige conditien, gelijck in de Landen & oock in Brasijl, gebruickelijck zijn."

83. Enthoven, "Suriname and Zeeland"; Zijlstra, "Competing for European Settlers."

84. *Voyages of Adriaen van Berkel*, 22–34.

85. Van der Meiden, *Betwist bestuur*, 36–39, 81. The term "communicative memory," defined as the orally transmitted memory that lasted for three generations, was coined by Assmann, "Communicative and Cultural Memory."

86. The seminal article on naval heroes is Lawrence, "Hendrick de Keyser's Heemskerk Monument." See also Esser, "Der Staten Rechterhant"; Harreld, "'How Great the Enterprise'."

87. Lawrence, "Hendrick de Keyser's Heemskerk Monument"; Scholten, *Sumptuous Memories*.

88. See Bell, *Cult of the Nation*, 108–19, for an elaborate discussion of the merits of this genre.

89. Cf. above; Thysius, *Historia Navalis*.

90. Van den Bosch, *Leeven en daden der doorlughtige zee-helden*.

91. Both the "nationalization" and the increasing number of illustrious men are typical of the genre's development; see Bell, *Cult of the Nation*, 130, for a similar development in eighteenth-century France.

92. Van den Bosch, *Leeven en daaden der doorluchtigste zeehelden*, 283.

93. Lawrence, "Hendrick de Keyser's Heemskerk Monument," 272; Van Strien, *Touring the Low Countries*, 127–28.

94. *Nederlandsche reizen*, 14: 4: "Ondanks het geweldig vuuren, zo van de Batterye als van het Strand, volvoerde hy zo dapper en kloekmoedig deezen last, dat eerst zyn Trompetter, vervolgens hy zelve en voorts het overige Bootsvolk die Sterkte beklommen. Dit was een zeer stout bedryf." See Van Sas, *Metamorfose van Nederland*, 71.

95. Arend, *Algemeene Geschiedenis des Vaderlands*, III-4: 40.

96. De Lange, *Bataviase Romeyn*, 155–59.

97. L'Honoré Naber, *Piet Heyn*, lxiv. According to Arnoldus Buchelius, the Heeren XIX reprimanded Willekens for having been too passive in battle.

CONCLUSION. TOWARD A PUBLIC ATLANTIC

1. *Hollandtse Mercurius . . . 1654*, 30: "Alsoo hebben de Hollanders na een besittinge van 24. Jaren dese Brasiliaense Conquesten weder verlaten, ende uyt een puyre negligentie die treffelijcke Ghewesten versuymt."
2. Zwier van Haren, *De Geusen*, 69. See my "Heroic Memories," 207.
3. Luzac, *Hollands Rijkdom*, 4: 143: "Maar het is niet minder buiten twijfel, dat een verschil van belangen en geduurige twisten, zoo over de besluiten welken men diende te neemen, alsover de middelen hoe dezelven uit te voeren, niet minder toebragten tot het verwaarlozen van de behoudenis van dit aanzienelijk gedeelte der veroveringen, wlken wy, geduurende den oorlog tegen Spanje gemaakt hadden" See also 1: 335: "Bij dit alles kwam nog de nationaale jalouzij, die nimmer ophoudt van zaad van tweespalt te strooijen."
4. Collot d'Escury, *Holland's roem*, 2: 113, 291–305, with the quote "De grootste fout, welke wij veelligt immer in het staatkundige begaan hebben" on 291.
5. Netscher, *Les Hollandais*, viii. See Van den Boogaart, "As perspectivas da Holanda," 50–52.
6. Fabius, *Johan Maurits*; Van Balen, *Johan Maurits in Brazilië*; Bouman, *Johan Maurits van Nassau*. The best volume of essays is Van den Boogaart, Hoetink and Whitehead, *Johan Maurits van Nassau-Siegen, 1604–1679*.
7. Wätjen, *Das Holländische Kolonialreich*, 8.
8. Israel, *The Dutch Republic and the Hispanic World*, 223–49; Den Heijer, *De geoctrooieerde compagnie*, 142. Cf. above.
9. Schwartz, "Looking for a New Brazil," 41.
10. Boxer, *The Dutch in Brazil*, 255–58.
11. *Briefwisseling van Hugo Grotius*, 7, no. 2895: Grotius to Nicolaas van Reigersberch, 18 December 1636: "Wat resolutie in uE. quartieren sal werden genomen op het onderhouden van de Compaignie, sal ick mede garen verstaen. Wilt bij Numerianus' volck luisteren ende overschrijven, maer niet seggen, insonderheit in dese tijden, dat sulcx niet dan quaedt can doen."
12. Montanus, *Nieuwe en Onbekende Weereld*, 525: "Amsterdam, eensdeels niet zeer genegen tot de West-Indische maetschappy, andersdeels bekommert voor 't verlies van haer Portugeesche handel, hield zich koel."
13. See, among many others, Kaplan, *Calvinists and Libertines*; Van Deursen, *Bavianen en slijkgeuzen*.
14. Haks, *Vaderland en vrede*; Reinders, *Printed Pandemonium*; Panhuysen, *Rampjaar 1672*.
15. Keblusek, "The Business of News," 211–12.
16. Soll, *The Information Master*, 24–25.
17. Van der Waals, *Prints in the Golden Age*, appendix 5.
18. Buchelius, "VOC-dagboek," fol. 127^r: "Sijn oeck daertoe dienende verscheide boecxkens van dese materie, waerbij soo d'eene als d'andere opinie voorgestaen wert, soo bij gescrifte als den drucke gemeen gemaeckt. Waerover de bewinthebberen mette Staten seer besich sijn ome het beste te verkiesen."
19. Boyte, "The Pragmatic Ends," 341–42.
20. As Trevor Burnard points out in his article "The Idea of Atlantic History," www.oxfordbibliographies.com/, Atlantic history in general "is better at tracing connections than comparisons" (last visited 27 August 2015).
21. The news pamphlet is titled *Relacion verdadera y cierta de la desseada y felize venida de la Flota de Nueva España, y galeones de Tierra Firme, y de la Armada Real del Mar Occeano,*

Granada, 1630. On printed news in Golden Age Spain, see Ettinghausen, "The News in Spain." The story of this fleet has been captured in great detail in Rahn Phillips, *Six Galleons*.

22. Van Groesen, "(No) News."
23. Ettinghausen, "'Tabloids' y 'Broadsheets'."
24. Rault, "La información y su manipulación." Jol died only in 1641 at São Tomé.
25. Cf. De Vivo, *Information and Communication*, 6.
26. *Memorial de Pero Roiz Soares*, 465–67.
27. Schwartz, "Voyage of the Vassals"; Boxer, *Salvador de Sá*, 40–68.
28. Camenietzki and Pastore, "1625, Fire and Ink," 5.
29. Ibid., 7–9.
30. Shannon, *Visions of the New World*, 163–89.
31. Camenietzki and Pastore, "1625, Fire and Ink," 12–13.
32. McCusker, "The Demise of Distance," 298–305.
33. Schwartz, *All Can Be Saved*.
34. Studnicki-Gizbert, *A Nation upon the Ocean Sea*, 128.
35. See mainly the essays in Raymond, *News, Newspapers, and Society*, and Raymond, *News Networks*.
36. Bremmer, "Correspondence of Johannes de Laet," 158.
37. Greenspan, "News and the Politics of Information."
38. Bellingradt, "The Early Modern City," 205.
39. Greenspan, "News and the Politics of Information," 12–14.
40. Van Groesen, "Text, Image, News."
41. Banks, *Chasing Empire*, quote on 5.
42. Steele, *The English Atlantic*, 5–6; see Banks, *Chasing Empire*, 5.
43. Gonsalves de Mello, *Nederlanders in Brazilië*, 40, 45–46; Boxer, *The Dutch in Brazil*, 108, 156.
44. Braudel, *The Mediterranean*, II-1: 358–69.
45. Steele, *The English Atlantic*, ix.
46. Slauter, "Forward-Looking Statements."
47. Ibid., 761.
48. For the powerful Brazilian mythology of Dutch Brazil, see Cabral de Mello, *Rubro veio*.
49. See the collected essays in Van Groesen, *The Legacy of Dutch Brazil*.

BIBLIOGRAPHY

PRINTED PRIMARY SOURCES

Advertenties voor kaarten, atlassen, globes e.d. in Amsterdamse kranten, 1621–1811. Ed. P. C. J. van der Krogt. Utrecht: Hes, 1985.

Aglionby, William. *The Present State of the United Provinces of the Low Countries.* 2nd rev. ed. London, 1671.

Aldenburgk, Johann Gregor. *Reise nach Brasilien, 1623–1626.* Ed. S. P. L'Honoré Naber. The Hague: Nijhoff, 1930.

Amsterdams Dam-Praetje, van wat outs en wat nieuws, en wat vreemts. Amsterdam, 1649. [Kn. 6477]

Amsterdams Tafel-Praetje van wat goets en wat quaets en wat noodichs. Gouda, 1649. [Kn. 6479]

Arend, J. P. *Algemeene Geschiedenis des Vaderlands, van de vroegste tijden tot op heden.* 5 vols. Amsterdam: Schleijer, 1863.

Articulen van Vrede ende Confederatie tusschen den Koning van Portugael ende de Staten Generael. s.l., 1661. [Kn. 8518]

Auctentijck Verhael van de Belegheringhe ende veroveringhe van Porto Calvo. Amsterdam, 1637.

The Auction Catalogue of J. Arminius. Ed. Carl Bangs. Utrecht: Hes, 1985.

Baers, Johannes. *Olinda, ghelegen int Landt van Brasil.* Amsterdam, 1630.

Barlaeus, Caspar. *Geschichte in Brasilien unter der Regierung dess Durchleuchtigen Hoch-gebohrne Fürsten und Herrn Iohannis Mauriti.* Kleve, 1659.

———. *The History of Brazil Under the Governorship of Count Johan Maurits of Nassau, 1636–1644.* Ed. and trans. Blanche T. van Berckel Ebeling-Koning. Gainesville: University Press of Florida, 2011.

———. *Rerum per Octennium in Brasilia.* Amsterdam, 1647.

Batavier gaet hem verblye, Singioor krijcht de Popeleye. Utrecht, 1630.

Baudartius, Willem. *Memoryen ofte Cort Verhael der gedenck-weerdichste so kercklicke als werltlicke gheschiedenissen.* Arnhem, 1624.

Beck, David. *Spiegel van mijn leven: een Haags dagboek uit 1624.* Ed. Sven E. Veldhuijzen. Hilversum: Verloren, 1993.

"Bernard O'Brien's Account of His Adventures." In *English and Irish Settlement on the River Amazon, 1550–1646*, ed. Joyce Lorimer, 72–74, 80, 113–14, 414–31. London: Hakluyt Society, 1989.

Bizot, Pierre. *Histoire metallique de la Republique de Hollande.* Paris, 1687.

Bondam, E. J., ed. "Journaux et nouvelles tirées de la bouche de marins hollandais et portugais de la navigation aux Antilles et sur les cotes du Bresil." *Annaes da Bibliotheca Nacional do Rio de Janeiro* 29 (1907): 99–179.

Book Sales Catalogues of the Dutch Republic, 1599–1800. Ed. H. W. de Kooker and Bert van Selm. [microfiche collection]
Bosch, Lambert van den. *Leeven en daden der doorlughtige zee-helden*. Amsterdam, 1676.
———. *Leeven en daaden der doorluchtigste zeehelden*. Amsterdam, 1683.
Brasilsche Gelt-sack, waer in dat klaerlijck vertoont wort, waer dat de participanten van de West-Indische Compagnie haer geldt ghebleven is. "Recife." 1647. [Kn. 5547]
Brasyls Schuyt-Praetjen, Ghehouden tusschen een Officier, een Domine, en een Coopman, noopende den Staet van Brasyl. s.l., 1649. [Kn. 6482]
Bredan, Daniel. *Desengaño a los pueblos del Brasil, y demas partes en las Indias Occidentales*. Amsterdam, 1630.
Bredero, Gerbrand Adriaensz. *Moortje*. Amsterdam, 1617.
Briefwisseling van Hugo Grotius. Ed. P. C. Molhuysen et al. 17 vols. The Hague: Nijhoff, 1928–2001.
De briefwisseling van Pieter Corneliszoon Hooft. Ed. Hendrik W. van Tricht. 3 vols. Culemborg: Tjeenk Willink, 1976–79.
Brieven, confessie ... The Hague, 1662. [Kn. 8645]
Broeck, Mattheus van den. *Journael, ofte Historiaelse Beschrijvinge van Matheus vanden Broeck*. Amsterdam, 1651.
Bronnen tot de geschiedenis der Leidsche universiteit. Ed. P. C. Molhuysen. 7 vols. The Hague: Nijhoff, 1913–24.
Brouërius van Nidek, Mattheus, and Isaac Le Long. *Kabinet van Nederlandsche en Kleefsche Oudheden*. 3rd ed. 8 vols. Amsterdam, 1792–1803.
Bry, Theodore de. *America*. 13 vols. Frankfurt and Oppenheim, 1590–1634.
Buchelius, Arnoldus, "VOC-dagboek, 1619–1639." Unpublished transcription by Kees Smit, 2011.
Catalogus Librorum Bibliothecae Civitatis Amstelodamensis. Amsterdam, 1622.
"Classicale acta van Brazilië." *Kroniek van het Historisch Genootschap* 29 (1873): 298–317, 322–71, 375–419.
A Collection of the State Papers of John Thurloe. Ed. Thomas Birch. 7 vols. London, 1742.
Collot d'Escury, Hendrik. *Holland's roem in kunsten en wetenschappen*. 7 vols. The Hague and Amsterdam, 1824–44.
Commelin, Caspar. *Beschryvinge van Amsterdam*. Amsterdam, 1693.
Consideratien en redenen der E. Heeren bewindhebberen vande geoctroijeerde West-Indische Compagnie. Haarlem, 1629. [Kn. 3912]
Copie vande Missive, gheschreven byden Generael Weerdenburch, aende Ho. Mo. Heeren Staten Generael. The Hague, 1630. [Kn. 3995]
Copye vande Resolutie van de Heeren Burgemeesters ende Rade tot Amsterdam Op 't stuck vande West-Indische Compagnie. s.l., 1649. [Kn. 6469]
Correspondance de Rubens et documents épistolaires concernant sa vie et ses oeuvres. Ed. M. Rooses and Ch. L. Ruelens. 6 vols. Antwerp, 1887–1909.
Correspondência diplomatica de Francisco de Sousa Coutinho durante a sua embaixada em Holanda. Ed. Edgar Prestage and Pedro de Azevedo. 3 vols. Coimbra: Imprensa da Universidade, 1920–55.
Een cort ende warachtich Verhael vande vermaerde Seestrijdt. Middelburg, 1631. [Kn. 4153]
Courante uyt Italien en Duytschlandt &c. Amsterdam, 1618–69.
[Cramer, Barent]. *Voor-looper van D. Hr. Witte Cornelissz de With, Admirael van de West-Indische Compagnie, noopende den Brasijlschen handel*. s.l., 1650. [Kn. 6628]
"Het dagboek van Hendrik Haecxs, lid van den Hoogen Raad van Brazilië (1645–1654)." Ed. S. P. L'Honoré Naber. *Bijdragen en Mededeelingen van het Historisch Genootschap* 46 (1925): 126–311.

Dutch Corantos 1618–1650: A Bibliography Illustrated with 334 Facsimile Reproductions of Corantos Printed 1618–1625. Ed. Folke Dahl. The Hague, 1946.
Examen over 't Vertoogh. s.l., 1637. [Kn. 4515]
Examen van de Valsche Resolutie vande Heere Burgemeesters ende Raden tot Amsterdam Op 't stuck vande West-Indische Compagnie. Amsterdam, 1649. [Kn. 6473]
Exquemelin, Alexander O. *De Americaensche Zeerovers*. Amsterdam, 1678.
Extract uyt den Brief vande Politijcque Raeden in Brasil. The Hague, 1635. [Kn. 4384]
Fontes para a história do Brasil Holandês. Ed. Jose Antônio Gonsalves de Mello. 2 vols. Recife: Fundação nacional pró-memória, 1981.
Gedenkschriften van Jonkheer Alexander van der Capellen. Ed. R. J. van der Capellen. 2 vols. Utrecht, 1777–78.
Gerardi Joan. Vossii et clarorum virorum ad eum Epistolae. Augsburg, 1691.
Gerbier, Balthasar. *Waarachtige verklaringe vanden Ridder Balthasar Gerbier*. The Hague, 1656.
Het geuzenliedboek. Ed. E. T. Kuiper and P. Leendertz, Jr. 2 vols. Zutphen: Thieme, 1924–25.
Gloria Parendi: Dagboeken van Willem Frederik, stadhouder van Friesland, Groningen en Drenthe, 1643–1649, 1651–1654. Ed. Jacob Visser and Gees van der Plaat. The Hague: Nederlands Historisch Genootschap, 1995.
Gottfried, Johann Ludwig. *Historia Antipodum oder Newe Welt*. Frankfurt, 1631.
[Graswinckel, Dirck]. *Aen-spraeck aan den getrouwen Hollander*. The Hague, 1645. [Kn. 5227 and 5228]
Hansen Hajstrup, Peter. *Das Memorial und Jurenal des Peter Hansen Hajstrup (1624–1672)*. Ed. Frank Ibold, Jens Jäger, and Detlev Kraack. Neumünster: Wachholtz, 1995.
Haselbekius, Johannes. *Triumph-Dicht, over de Gheluckighe Ver-overinghe van de Spaensche Silver-Vlote, Geschiet den 8. Septemb. Anno 1628. Item, over de rasse Ver-overinghe van de Bahia de Todos os Sanctos. Den 10. Maij, Anno 1624*. Leeuwarden, 1629.
Hennin, J. *De zinrijke gedachten toegepast op de vijf sinnen, van 's menschen verstand*. Amsterdam, 1681.
Herckmans, Elias. *Der Zee-vaert Lof*. Amsterdam, 1634.
Heyns, Zacharias. *Dracht-thoneel waer op het fatsoen van meest alle de kleedren . . . met corte woorden in rijm beschreven wordt*. Amsterdam, 1601.
———. *Le miroir du monde, ou, epitome du Theatre d'Abraham Ortelius*. Amsterdam, 1598.
Hollandtse Mercurius: Behelzende het ghedenckweerdighste in christenryk voor-ghevallen. 41 vols. Haarlem, 1651–91.
Het Hollants wijve-praetjen, tusschen drie gebueren Trijntje, Grietje en Neeltje. Haarlem, 1652. [Kn. 7233]
Hout, Jan van. *Loterijspel*. Leiden, 1596.
Information from Ceará from Georg Marcgraf (June-August 1639). Ed. Ernst van den Boogaart and Rebecca Parker Brienen (= *Brasil Holandês—Dutch Brazil*, vol. 5). Petrópolis: Index, 2002.
Inventarissen van de inboedels in de verblijven van de Oranjes en daarmede gelijk te stellen stukken 1567–1795. Ed. S. W. A. Drossaers and Th. H. Lunsingh Scheurleer. 3 vols. The Hague: Nijhoff, 1974.
Joosten, Jacques. *De kleyne wonderlijcke werelt*. Amsterdam, 1649.
Keye, Otto. *Het waere onderscheyt tusschen koude en warme landen*. The Hague, 1659.
Kort, Bondigh ende Waerachtigh Verhael van 't schandelijk overgeven ende verlaten vande voornaemste Conquesten van Brasil. Middelburg, 1655. [Kn. 7655]
Korte observatien op het vertoogh, door een ongenaemden uyt-gegeven . . . nopende de voor-gaende ende tegenwoordige Proceduren van Brasil. Amsterdam, 1647. [Kn. 5559]
Korte Onderrichtinghe ende vermaeninge aen alle lifhebbers des Vaderlandts, om liberalijcken te teeckenen inde West-Indische Compagnie. Rotterdam, 1622. [Kn. 3363]

"Kronijkje van Cornelis Cornelisz." *Archief voor Kerkelijke en Wereldsche Geschiedenissen, inzonderheid van Utrecht* 6 (1849): 9–222.

Laet, Johannes de. *Iaerlijck verhael van de verrichtinghen der Geoctroyeerde West-Indische Compagnie.* Ed. S. P. L'Honoré Naber. 4 vols. The Hague: Nijhoff, 1931–37.

Lange, Petrus de. *Batavise Romeyn; ofte alle de voornaemste Heldendaden.* Amsterdam, 1661.

Léry, Jean de. *History of a Voyage to the Land of Brazil, Otherwise Called America.* Ed. and trans. Janet Whatley. Berkeley: University of California Press, 1990.

Linschoten, Jan Huygen van. *Beschryvinghe van de gantsche Custe van Guinea, Manicongo, Angola, Monomatapa.* Amsterdam, 1596.

———. *Reys-gheschrift vande Navigatien der Portugaloysers in Orienten.* Amsterdam, 1595.

Luzac, Elie. *Hollands Rijkdom.* 4 vols. Leiden, 1780–83.

Lyste vande hooge en de lage officieren, mitsgaders de gemeene soldaten, dewelcke in Batalie teghens de Portugiesen aen den Bergh van de Guararapes . . . doot zijn gebleven. s.l. [1649]. [Kn. 6465]

Manifest door d'Inwoonders van Parnambuco uytghegeven. Antwerp, 1646. [Kn. 5354] / s.l., s.a. [Kn. 5355]

Marcgraf, Georg, and Willem Piso. *Historiae Naturalis Brasiliae.* Amsterdam, 1648.

Meisner, Daniel. *Thesauri philo-politici.* 6 vols. Frankfurt, 1625.

Memorial de Pero Roiz Soares. Ed. M. Lopes de Almeida. Acta Universitatis Conimbrigensis. Coimbra: [Par ordem da Universidade], 1953.

Moerbeeck, Jan Andries. *Redenen, waeromme de West-Indische Compagnie dient te trachten het Landt van Brasilia den Coninck van Spangien te ontmachtigen.* Amsterdam, 1624. [Kn. 3541]

Montanus, Arnoldus. *Beschryvinge van Amsterdam.* Amsterdam, 1665.

———. *De Nieuwe en Onbekende Weereld: of beschryving van America en 't Zuid-land.* Amsterdam, 1671.

Moreau, Pierre. *Klare en waarachtige beschryving van de leste beroerten en afval der Portugezen in Brasil.* Amsterdam, 1652.

Nederlandsche reizen, tot bevordering van den koophandel, na de meest afgelegen gewesten des aardkloots. 14 vols. Amsterdam and Harlingen, 1787.

Niederlendischer Kriegs-Iournal, oder täglich Register. [Amsterdam, 1605?].

Nieuhof, Johan. *Gedenkweerdige Brasiliaense zee- en lantreize.* Amsterdam, 1682.

Niewwe ongewoon-wonderlykke Staert-Sterre op 't Recif in Brazil. Amsterdam, 1653. [Kn. 7353]

Octroy van de Hoog: Moog: Heeren Staten Generael, aengaende de Colonie op de Wilde Kust van America. s.l., 1659. [Kn. 8175a]

Ontdeckinghe van Rijcke Mijnen in Brasil. Amsterdam, 1639. [Kn. 4634]

Ordinarisse Middel-Weeckse Courante. Amsterdam, 1638–69.

Ottsen, Hendrik. *Journael van de reis naar Zuid-Amerika (1598–1601).* Ed. J. W. IJzerman. The Hague: Nijhoff, 1918.

Particuliere notulen van de vergaderingen der Staten van Holland, 1620–1640. Ed. E. C. M. Huysman and V. L. Vree. 7 vols. The Hague: Instituut voor Nederlandse Geschiedenis, 1992–2005.

Pertinent Bericht van alle de particulariteiten soo sich hebben toegedragen in West-Indien. The Hague, 1634. [Kn. 4347]

Piso, Willem. *De Indiae utriusque re naturali et medica libri quatuordecim.* Amsterdam, 1658.

Plante, Franciscus. *Mauritiados Libri XII.* Amsterdam, 1647.

De Portogysen goeden buyrman. Ghetrocken uyt de registers van sijn goet gebuerschap . . . Dienende tot antwoort op het ongefondeerde Brasyls-schuyt-praetjen. "Lisbon," 1649. [Kn. 6483]

Quelen, Augustus van. *Kort verhael vanden Staet van Fernanbuc.* Amsterdam, 1640. [Kn. 4689]

Ray, John. *Observations Topographical, Moral & Physiological; Made in a Journey Through Part of the Low-Countries, Germany, Italy, and France.* London, 1673.

Reden van dat die West-Indische Compagnie oft Handelinge, niet alleen profijtelijck, maer oock noodtsaeckelijck is, tot behoudenisse van onsen Staet. s.l., 1636. [Kn. 4425]

Reglement by de West-Indische Compagnie... over het open-stellen vanden handel op S.Paulo de Loando. The Hague, 1648. [Kn. 5790a]

Resolutiën der Staten-Generaal, nieuwe reeks. Ed. A. Th. van Deursen, J. G. Smit, and J. Roelevink. 7 vols. The Hague: Rijks Geschiedkundige Publicatiën, 1971–94.

Revius, Jacobus. *Over-Ysselsche sangen en dichten.* Ed. W. A. P. Smit. 2 vols. Amsterdam: Uitgeversmaatschappij Holland, 1930–35.

Reys-boeck van het rijcke Brasilien, Rio de la Plata ende Magellanes. Dordrecht, 1624. [Kn. 3540]

Richshoffer, Abraham. *Brasilianisch und West Indianische Reiße Beschreibung.* Ed. S. P. L'Honoré Naber. The Hague: Nijhoff, 1930.

Ruiters, Dierick. *Toortse der Zee-vaert.* Vlissingen, 1623.

Schimp-Ghedicht van Fernabuco. s.l., 1630

Staden, Hans. *Warachtige historie ende beschrivinge eens lants in America ghelegen.* Antwerp, 1558.

Suiker, verfhout & tabak: het Braziliaanse handboek van Johannes de Laet, 1637. Ed. Benjamin Teensma. Zutphen: Walburg Pers, 2009.

Taylor, John. *Religion's Enemies.* London, 1641.

[Teellinck, Ewout]. *De tweede wachter, brenghende tijdinghe vande nacht, dat is, van het overgaen vande Bahia.* The Hague, 1625. [Kn. 3607]

Teellinck, Willem. *Davids danckbaerheyt voor Gods weldadicheyt.* Middelburg, 1624. [Kn. 3561]

Temple, William. *Observations upon the United Provinces of the Netherlands.* London, 1673.

Thevet, André. *Les singularitez de la France antarctique, autrement nommée Amérique.* Antwerp, 1558.

Thysius, Antonius. *Historia Navalis.* Leiden, 1657.

Tijdingen uyt verscheyde Quartieren. Amsterdam, 1619–71.

Trou-hertighe onderrichtinge, aen alle hooft-participanten, en lief-hebbers vande Ge-octroyeerde West-Indische Compagnie. s.l., 1643. [Kn. 5021]

Udemans, Godfried. *'t Geestelyck roer van 't coopmans schip.* 2nd rev. ed. Dordrecht, 1640.

Usselincx, Willem. *Voortganck vande West-Indische Compaignie.* Amsterdam, 1623. [Kn. 3426]

———. *Waerschouwinge over den Treves.* Vlissingen, 1630. [Kn. 4017]

Valerius, Adriaen. *Neder-landtsche Gedenck-clanck.* Haarlem, 1626.

Van varen en van vechten. Verzen van tijdgenooten op onze zeehelden en zeeslagen, lof- en schimpdichten, matrozenliederen. Ed. Daniël F. Scheurleer. 3 vols. The Hague: Nijhoff, 1914–16.

Verhooginghe vande Capitalen inde West-Indische Compagnie. The Hague, 1639. [Kn. 4633]

Veroveringh van de stadt Olinda. Amsterdam, [1630]. [Kn. 3996]

Vertooch aen de Hoogh en Mogende heeren Staten Generael. Amsterdam, 1647. [Kn. 5558]

Vertoogh by een Lief-hebber des Vaderlants vertoont. s.l., 1637. [Kn. 4514]

"Verzoekschrift van de vrouw van den schipper Dirck de Ruyter . . . 1618." *Bijdragen en Mededeelingen van het Historisch Genootschap* 2 (1879): 112–13.

Vincent Joachim Soler's Seventeen Letters 1636–1643. Ed. Benjamin Teensma. Rio de Janeiro: Editora Index, 1999.

Vondel, Joost van den. *Jaghtzang aen den doorluchtighsten vorst en heer J. Mauritius.* Amsterdam, 1656.

The Voyages of Adriaen van Berkel to Guiana. Ed. Martijn van den Bel, Lodewijk C. Hulsman, and Lodewijk Wagenaar. Leiden: Sidestone Press, 2014.

Vries, Simon de. *Curieuse aenmerckingen der bysonderste Oost en West Indische verwonderenswaerdige dingen.* 4 vols. Utrecht, 1682.

Waghenaer, Lucas J. *Enchuyser Zee-caert-boeck.* Amsterdam, 1598.

———. *Thresoor der Zeevaert.* 4th ed. Amsterdam, 1602.

Wagner, Zacharias. *The "Thierbuch" and "Autobiography" of Zacharias Wagener.* Ed. Cristina Ferrão and José Paulo Monteiro Soares. Rio de Janeiro: Editora Index, 1997.

Wassenaer, Nicolaes van. *Historisch verhael alder ghedenck-weerdichste geschiedenisse.* 21 vols. Amsterdam, 1622–35.

De Westafrikaanse reis van Piet Heyn, 1624–1625. Ed. Klaas Ratelband. 2nd ed. Zutphen: Walburg Pers, 2006.

West-Indisch Discours, verhandelende de West-Indische Saecken. s.l., 1653. [Kn. 7454]

Westhuysen, Abraham van. *Waerachtich Verhael van de Heerlijk overwinning van Pirmeriba ende de reviere Serename.* The Hague, 1667.

Wonderlicke avontuer van twee goelieven. Ed. Eddy Grootes. Muiderberg: Coutinho, 1984.

Die wundersamen Reisen des Caspar Schmalkalden nach West- und Ost-Indien 1642–1652. Ed. Wilhelm Joost. Leipzig: Brockhaus Verlag, 1983.

Zanten, Laurens van. *Spiegel der gedenckweerdighste wonderen.* Amsterdam, 1661.

Zwier van Haren, Onno. *De Geusen: Proeve van een vaderlands gedicht.* Zwolle, 1776.

SECONDARY LITERATURE

Abrahamse, Jaap Evert. *De grote uitleg van Amsterdam: Stadsontwikkeling in de zeventiende eeuw.* Bussum: Thoth, 2010.

Alden, Dauril. *The Making of an Enterprise: The Society of Jesus in Portugal, Its Empire, and Beyond, 1540–1750.* Stanford, Calif.: Stanford University Press, 1996.

Alpers, Svetlana. *The Art of Describing: Dutch Art in the Seventeenth Century.* Chicago: University of Chicago Press, 1983.

Alphen, Marc van. "The Female Side of Dutch Shipping: Financial Bonds of Seamen Ashore in the 17th and 18th Century." In *Anglo-Dutch Mercantile Marine Relations, 1700–1850,* ed. Jaap R. Bruijn and Willem F. J. Mörzer Bruyns, 125–32. Amsterdam: Nederlands Scheepvaartmuseum, 1991.

Anderson, Carrie. "Material Mediators: Johan Maurits, Textiles, and the Art of Diplomatic Exchange." *Journal of Early Modern History* 20, 1 (2016): 63–85.

Anderson, Robert Nelson. "The *Quilombo* of Palmares: A New Overview of a Maroon State in Seventeenth-Century Brazil." *Journal of Latin American Studies* 28, 3 (1996): 545–66.

Arblaster, Paul. *From Ghent to Aix: How They Brought the News in the Habsburg Netherlands, 1550–1700.* Leiden: Brill, 2014.

Assmann, Aleida. "Memory, Individual and Collective." In *The Oxford Handbook of Contextual Political Analysis,* ed. Robert E. Goodin and Charles Tilly, 210–24. Oxford: Oxford University Press, 2006.

Assmann, Jan. "Communicative and Cultural Memory." In *Cultural Memory Studies: An International and Interdisciplinary Handbook,* ed. Astrid Erll, Ansgar Nünning, and Sara Young, 109–18. Berlin: De Gruyter, 2008.

Atlas van Stolk: Katalogus der historie-, spot- en zinnebeelden betrekkelijk de geschiedenis van Nederland. 10 vols. Amsterdam, 1893–1935.

Bakker, Boudewijn. "De zichtbare stad, 1578–1713." In *Geschiedenis van Amsterdam, II-1: Centrum van de wereld: 1578–1650*, ed. Willem Frijhoff and Maarten Prak, 17–101. Amsterdam: SUN, 2004.
Balen, Willem van. *Johan Maurits in Brazilië*. The Hague: Leopold, 1941.
Banks, Kenneth J. *Chasing Empire Across the Sea: Communication and the State in the French Atlantic, 1713–1763*. Montreal: McGill-Queen's University Press, 2003.
Bell, David A. *The Cult of the Nation in France: Inventing Nationalism, 1680–1800*. Cambridge, Mass.: Harvard University Press, 2001.
Bellingradt, Daniel. "The Early Modern City as a Resonating Box: Media, Public Opinion, and the Urban Space of the Holy Roman Empire, Cologne, and Hamburg, ca. 1700." *Journal of Early Modern History* 16, 3 (2012): 201–40.
Belonje, Johan. "Capiteyn Croeger." *Maandblad Amstelodamum* 65 (Jan/Feb. 1978): 1–3.
Berckel-Ebeling Koning, Blanche T. "Preface." In Caspar Barlaeus, *The History of Brazil Under the Governorship of Count Johan Maurits of Nassau, 1636–1644*, ed. and trans. Berckel-Ebeling Koning, ix–xxiii. Gainesville: University Press of Florida, 2011.
Berlowicz, Barbara, ed. *Albert Eckhout volta ao Brasil/Returns to Brazil (1644–2002)*. Copenhagen: Nationalmuseet, 2002.
Besselaar, José van den. "Franciscus Plante und seine 'Mauritias'." In *Soweit der Erdkreis Reicht: Johann Moritz von Nassau-Siegen, 1604–1679*, ed. Guido de Werd, 47–56. Kleve: Stadt Kleve, 1979.
Bick, Alexander. "Governing the Free Sea: The Dutch West India Company and Commercial Politics, 1618–1645." Ph.D. dissertation, Princeton University, 2012.
Blaak, Jeroen. *Literacy in Everyday Life: Reading and Writing in Early Modern Dutch Diaries*. Leiden: Brill, 2009.
Blair, Ann, and Peter Stallybrass, "Mediating Information, 1450–1800." In *This Is Enlightenment*, ed. Clifford Siskin and William Warner, 139–63. Chicago: University of Chicago Press, 2010.
Bodian, Miriam. *Hebrews of the Portuguese Nation: Conversos and Community in Early Modern Amsterdam*. Bloomington: Indiana University Press, 1997.
Boer, Michel G. de. "De val van Bahia." *Tijdschrift voor Geschiedenis* 58 (1943): 38–49.
Boogaart, Ernst van den. "As perspectivas da Holanda e do Brasil do 'Tempo dos Flamengos'." In *Brasil Holandês: História, memória e patrimônio compartilhado*, ed. Hugo Coelho Vieira, Nara Neves Pires Galvão, and Leonardo Dantas Silva, 47–63. São Paulo: Alameda, 2012.
―――. "Infernal Allies: The Dutch West India Company and the Tarairiu." In *Johan Maurits van Nassau-Siegen, 1604–1679: A Humanist Prince in Europe and Brazil*, ed. Van den Boogaart et al., 519–38. The Hague: Johan Maurits van Nassau Stichting, 1979.
―――. "A Well-Governed Colony: Frans Post's Illustrations in Caspar Barlaeus's History of Dutch Brazil." *Rijksmuseum Bulletin* 59, 3 (2011): 236–71.
Boogaart, Ernst van den, and Frederik J. Duparc, eds. *Zo wijd de wereld strekt*. The Hague: Johan Maurits van Nassau Stichting, 1979.
Boogaart, Ernst van den, and Piet Emmer. "The Dutch Participation in the Atlantic Slave Trade, 1596–1650." In *The Uncommon Market: Essays in the Economic History of the Atlantic Slave Trade*, ed. Henry A. Gemery and Jan S. Hogendorn, 353–75. New York: Academic Press, 1979.
Boogaart, Ernst van den, Hendrik Richard Hoetink, and Peter J. P. Whitehead, eds. *Johan Maurits van Nassau-Siegen, 1604–1679: A Humanist Prince in Europe and Brazil*. The Hague: Johan Maurits van Nassau Stichting, 1979.

Borst, Henk. "Broer Jansz in Antwerpse ogen: De Amsterdamse courantier na de slag bij Kallo in 1638 neergezet als propagandist." *De zeventiende eeuw* 25, 1 (2009): 73–89.

Bots, Hans. "Johann Moritz und seine Beziehungen zu Constantijn Huygens." In *Soweit der Erdkreis Reicht: Johann Moritz von Nassau-Siegen, 1604–1679*, ed. Guido de Werd, 101–06. Kleve: Stadt Kleve, 1979.

Bouman, Paul. *Johan Maurits van Nassau: De Braziliaan*. Utrecht: Oosthoek, 1947.

Boxer, Charles R. *The Dutch in Brazil, 1624–1654*. Oxford: Clarendon, 1957

———. "Salvador Correia de Sá e Benevides and the Reconquest of Angola in 1648." *Hispanic American Historical Review* 28, 4 (1948): 483–513.

———. *Salvador de Sá and the Struggle for Brazil and Angola, 1602–1682*. London: Athlone, 1952.

Boyte, Harry C. "The Pragmatic Ends of Popular Politics." In *Habermas and the Public Sphere*, ed. Craig Calhoun, 340–55. Cambridge, Mass.: MIT Press, 1992.

O Brasil e os Holandeses, 1630–1654. Ed. Paulo Herkenhoff and Evaldo Cabral de Mello. Rio de Janeiro: Sextante Artes, 1999.

Braudel, Fernand, *The Mediterranean and the Mediterranean World in the Age of Philip II*. 2 vols. New York: HarperCollins, 1972.

Bremer-David, Charissa. "*Le Cheval Rayé*: A French Tapestry Portraying Dutch Brazil." *J. Paul Getty Museum Journal* 22 (1994): 21–29.

Bremmer, Rolf H., Jr. "The Correspondence of Johannes de Laet (1581–1649) as a Mirror of His Life." *Lias: Sources and Documents Relating to the Early Modern History of Ideas* 25, 2 (1998): 139–64.

Brown, Jonathan, and John H. Elliott. *A Palace for a King: The Buen Retiro and the Court of Philip IV*. 2nd rev. ed. New Haven, Conn.: Yale University Press, 2003.

Bruijn, Enny de. *Eerst de waarheid, dan de vrede: Jacob Revius, 1586–1658*. Zoetermeer: Boekencentrum, 2012.

Bruijn, Jaap R. *The Dutch Navy of the Seventeenth and Eighteenth Centuries*. Columbia: University of South Carolina Press, 1993.

Bruin, Guido de. *Geheimhouding en verraad: De geheimhouding van staatszaken ten tijde van de Republiek (1600–1750)*. The Hague: SDU, 1991.

———. "Political Pamphleteering and Public Opinion in the Age of De Witt (1653–1672)." In *Pamphlets and Politics in the Dutch Republic*, ed. Femke Deen, David Onnekink, and Michel Reinders, 63–96. Leiden: Brill, 2011.

Brunn, Gerhard, ed. *Aufbruch in Neue Welten: Johann Moritz von Nassau-Siegen (1604–1679): der Brasilianer*. Siegen: Johann Moritz, 2004.

Burnard, Trevor. "The Idea of Atlantic History," www.oxfordbibliographies.com/ (last visited 27 August 2015)

Buve, Raymond. "Gouverneur Johannes Heinsius: De rol van Van Aerssen's voorganger in de Surinaamse Indianenoorlog, 1678–1680." *New West Indian Guide/Nieuwe West-Indische Gids* 45, 1 (1966): 14–26.

Buvelot, Quentin, ed. *Albert Eckhout: A Dutch Artist in Brazil*. Zwolle: Waanders, 2004.

Cabral de Mello, Evaldo. *De Braziliaanse affaire: Portugal, de Republiek der Verenigde Nederlanden en Noord-Oost Brazilie, 1641–1669*. Trans. and rev. ed. of *O negócio do Brasil*. Zutphen: Walburg Pers, 2005.

———. *Nassau: Governador do Brasil Holandês*. São Paulo: Companhia das Letras, 2006.

———. *Olinda Restaurada: Guerra e Açúcar no Nordeste, 1630–1654*. São Paulo: Editora da Universidade de São Paulo, 1975.

———. *Rubro veio: O imaginário da restauração pernambucana*. Rio de Janeiro: Editora Nova Fronteira, 1986.

Camenietzki, Carlos Ziller, and Gianriccardo Grassia Pastore. "1625, Fire and Ink: The Battle of Salvador in Accounts of the War." *Topoi: Revista de História* 2 (2006): 1–28.

Canny, Nicholas, and Philip D. Morgan, eds. *The Oxford Handbook of the Atlantic World, 1450–1850*. Oxford: Oxford University Press, 2011.

Collet, Dominique. *Die Welt in der Stube: Begegnungen mit Aussereuropa in Kunstkammern der Frühen Neuzeit*. Göttingen: Vandenhoeck & Ruprecht, 1997.

Cook, Harold J. *Matters of Exchange: Commerce, Medicine, and Science in the Dutch Golden Age*. New Haven, Conn: Yale University Press, 2007.

Corrêa do Lago, Pedro, and Bia Corrêa do Lago, eds. *Frans Post (1612–1680): Catalogue Raisonné*. Milan: 5 Continents Editions, 2007.

Couvée, Dirk H. "De nieuwsgaring van de eerste courantiers." In *Pers, propaganda en openbare mening*, ed. J. Barents, 26–40. Leiden: Stenfert Kroese, 1956.

Dams, Britt. "Elias Herckmans: A Poet on the Borders of Dutch Brazil." In *The Dutch Trading Companies as Knowledge Networks*, ed. Siegfried Huigen, Jan L. de Jong, and Elmer Kolfin, 19–37. Leiden: Brill, 2010.

———. "Manoel de Moraes: Spelen met de grenzen van de eigen identiteit in Nederlands Brazilië." *Tijdschrift voor Geschiedenis* 124, 1 (2011): 4–15.

———. "Production, Communication, and Comprehension of Knowledge of the New World: Ethnographic Descriptions in Caspar Barlaeus' *Rerum per Octennium*." *Journal of Early American History* 2, 3 (2012): 223–46.

Darnton, Robert. "What Is the History of Books?" *Daedalus* 111, 3 (1982): 65–83.

Davids, Karel. "Ondernemers in kennis: Het zeevaartkundig onderwijs in de Republiek gedurende de zeventiende eeuw." *De zeventiende eeuw* 7, 1 (1991): 37–48.

———. "White Collar Workers of the VOC in Amsterdam, 1602–1795." In *Working on Labor: Essays in Honor of Jan Lucassen*, ed. Marcel van der Linden and Leo Lucassen, 191–212. Leiden: Brill, 2012.

Davies, Surekha. "Depictions of Brazilians on French Maps, 1542–1555." *Historical Journal* 55, 2 (2012): 317–48.

Deen, Femke. "Handwritten Propaganda: Letters and Pamphlets in Amsterdam During the Dutch Revolt, 1572–1578." In *Pamphlets and Politics in the Dutch Republic*, ed. Deen, David Onnekink, and Michel Reinders, 205–26. Leiden: Brill, 2011.

Deursen, Arie Th. van. *Bavianen en slijkgeuzen: Kerk en kerkvolk in de tijd van Maurits en Oldenbarnevelt*. 4th rev. ed. Franeker: Van Wijnen, 2010.

van Dillen, J. G., ed. *Bronnen tot de geschiedenis van het bedrijfsleven en het gildewezen in Amsterdam*. 3 vols. The Hague: Nijhoff, 1929–1974.

———. "Effectenkoersen aan de Amsterdamsche Beurs, 1723–1794." *Economisch-Historisch Jaarboek* 17 (1931): 1–46.

Dingemanse, Clazina, and Marijke Meijer Drees. "'Praatjes' over de WIC en Brazilië: Literaire aspecten van gesprekspamfletten uit 1649." *De zeventiende eeuw* 21, 1 (2005): 112–27.

Dixhoorn, Arjan van. "Chambers of Rhetoric: Performative Culture and Literary Sociability in the Early Modern Northern Netherlands." In *The Reach of the Republic of Letters: Literary and Learned Societies in Late Medieval and Early Modern Europe*, ed. Dixhoorn and Susie Speakman Sutch, 1: 119–57. 2 vols. Leiden: Brill, 2008.

Doedens, Anne. *Witte de With 1599–1658: Wereldwijde strijd op zee in de Gouden Eeuw*. Hilversum: Verloren, 2008.

Dooley, Brendan, "News and Doubt in Early Modern Culture: Or, Are We Having a Public Sphere Yet?" In *The Politics of Information in Early Modern Europe*, ed. Dooley and Sabrina Baron, 275–90. London: Routledge, 2001.

Dudok van Heel, S. A. C. "Wie mogen wij als de stichter van de katholieke huiskerk 'De Drie Bonte Kraayen' in de Oude Teertuinen beschouwen?" *Maandblad Amstelodamum* 75 (May/June 1988): 49–54.

Duparc, Frederik J. "Een zeldzaam geschenk van Johan Maurits aan de Leidse Universiteit." In *Een vorstelijk archivaris: Opstellen voor Bernard Woelderink*, ed. Johan ter Molen et al., 105–10. Zwolle: Waanders, 2003.

Dutra, Francis A. "Matias de Albuquerque and the Defense of Northeastern Brazil, 1620–1626." *Studia: Revista Semestral* 36 (1973): 117–66.

Ebert, Chris. "Dutch Trade with Brazil Before the Dutch West India Company, 1587–1621." In *Riches from Atlantic Commerce: Dutch Transatlantic Trade and Shipping, 1585–1817*, ed. Johannes Postma and Victor Enthoven, 49–75. Leiden: Brill, 2003.

———. "Early Modern Atlantic Trade and the Development of Maritime Insurance to 1630." *Past and Present* 213 (2011): 87–114.

Edmundson, George. "The Dutch Power in Brazil (1624–1654): Part I: The Struggle for Bahia (1624–1627)," *English Historical Review* 11 (1896): 231–59; *English Historical Review* 14 (1899): 676–99.

Eeghen, Isabella H. van. "De familie van de plaatsnijder Claes Jansz Visscher." *Maandblad Amstelodamum* 77 (1990): 73–81.

Eekhout, R. A. "The Mauritias: A Neo-Latin Epic by Franciscus Plante." In *Johan Maurits van Nassau-Siegen, 1604–1679: A Humanist Prince in Europe and Brazil*, ed. Ernst van den Boogaart et al., 377–93. The Hague: Johan Maurits van Nassau Stichting, 1979.

Egmond, Florike. *Underworlds: Organized Crime in the Netherlands, 1650–1800*. London: Polity, 1993.

Egmond, Florike, and Peter Mason. "Albert E(e)ckhout, Court Painter." In *Albert Eckhout: A Dutch Artist in Brazil*, ed. Quentin Buvelot, 108–27. Zwolle: Waanders, 2004.

Eijnatten, Joris van. "War, Piracy and Religion: Godfried Udemans' *Spiritual Helm* (1638)." In *Property, Piracy and Punishment: Hugo Grotius on War and Booty in De Iure Praedae—Concepts and Contexts*, ed. Hans W. Blom, 192–214. Leiden: Brill, 2009.

Eisenstein, Elizabeth L. *Divine Art, Infernal Machine: The Reception of Printing in the West from First Impressions to the Sense of an Ending*. Philadelphia: University of Pennsylvania Press, 2011.

Elias, Johan. *De vroedschap van Amsterdam, 1578–1795*. 2 vols. Haarlem: Loosjes, 1903–05.

Eliassen, Knut Ove, and Yngve Sandhei Jacobsen. "Where Were the Media Before the Media? Mediating the World at the Time of Condillac and Linnaeus." In *This Is Enlightenment*, ed. Clifford Siskin and William Warner, 64–86. Chicago: University of Chicago Press, 2010.

Elliott, John H. "Afterword: Atlantic History: A Circumnavigation." In *The British Atlantic World, 1500–1800*, ed. David Armitage and Michael J. Braddick, 233–49. Basingstoke: Palgrave Macmillan, 2002.

———. *The Old World and the New, 1492–1650*. Cambridge: Cambridge University Press, 1970.

Éloge de la navigation hollandaise au XVIIe siècle: Tableaux, dessins et gravures de la mer et de ses rivages dans la collection Frits Lugt. Ed. Maria van Berge-Gerbaud. Paris: Fondation Custodia, 1989.

Emmer, Pieter C. *The Dutch in the Atlantic Economy, 1580–1880: Trade, Slavery, and Emancipation*. Aldershot: Ashgate/Variorum, 1998.

———. *The Dutch Slave Trade, 1500–1850*. New York: Berghahn, 2006.
Emmer, Pieter C., and Wim Klooster. "The Dutch Atlantic, 1600–1800: Expansion Without Empire." *Itinerario* 23, 2 (1999): 48–69.
Enthoven, Victor. "Early Dutch Expansion in the Atlantic Region, 1585–1621." In *Riches from Atlantic Commerce: Dutch Transatlantic Trade and Shipping, 1585–1817*, ed. Enthoven and Johannes Postma, 17–47. Leiden: Brill, 2003.
———. "Suriname and Zeeland: Fifteen Years of Dutch Misery on the Wild Coast, 1667–1682." In *Proceedings of the International Conference on Shipping, Factories, and Colonization*, ed. John Everaert and Jan Parmentier, 249–60. Brussels: Koninklijke Academie voor Overzeese Wetenschappen, 1996.
Esser, Raingard. "Der Staten Rechterhant: Niederländische Seehelden in der Literatur des 17. Jahrhunderts." In *"Mars und die Musen": Das Wechselspiel von Militär, Krieg und Kunst in der Frühen Neuzeit*, ed. Jutta Nowosadtko and Matthias Rogg, 59–74. Berlin: Lit Verlag, 2008.
Ettinghausen, Henry. "The News in Spain: *Relaciones de Sucesos* in the Reigns of Philip III and IV." *European History Quarterly* 14, 1 (1984): 1–20.
———. "'Tabloids' y 'Broadsheets': La prensa española y sus lectores en el primer tercio del siglo XVII." In *Las relaciones de sucesos: Relatos facticos, oficiales y extraordinarios*, ed. Patrick Begrand, 17–33. Besançon: Presses Universitaires Franche-Comté, 2006.
Evenhuis, R. B. *Ook dat was Amsterdam: De kerk der hervorming in de Gouden Eeuw*. 5 vols. Amsterdam: Ten Have, 1965–78.
Fabius, A. N. J. *Johan Maurits, de Braziliaan (1604–1679)*. Utrecht: Bruna, 1914.
Feitler, Bruno. "Jews and New Christians in Dutch Brazil, 1630–1654." In *Atlantic Diasporas: Jews, Conversos, and Crypto-Jews in the Age of Mercantilism, 1500–1800*, ed. Richard L. Kagan and Philip D. Morgan, 123–51. Baltimore: Johns Hopkins University Press, 2009.
Fontaine Verwey, Herman de la. *De Stedelijke Bibliotheek van Amsterdam in de Nieuwe Kerk, 1578–1632*. Meppel: Krips, 1980.
———. *Uit de wereld van het boek III: In en om de "Vergulde Sonnewyser."* Amsterdam: Nico Israel, 1979.
Françozo, Mariana. "Dressed like an Amazon: The Transatlantic Trajectory of a Red Feather Coat." In *Museums and Biographies*, ed. Kate Hill, 187–99. London: Boydell and Brewer, 2012.
———. "Global Connections: Johan Maurits of Nassau-Siegen's Collection of Curiosities." In *The Legacy of Dutch Brazil*, ed. Michiel van Groesen, 105–23. New York: Cambridge University Press, 2014.
———. *De Olinda a Holanda: O gabinete de curiosidades de Nassau*. Campinas: Unicamp, 2014.
Frankel, Rachel. "Antecedents and Remnants of Jodensavanne: The Synagogues and Cemeteries of the First Permanent Plantation Settlement of New World Jews." In *The Jews and the Expansion of Europe to the West, 1450–1800*, ed. Paolo Bernardini and Norman Fiering, 394–436. New York: Berghahn, 2001.
Freedberg, David. "Science, Commerce, and Art: Neglected Topics at the Junction of History and Art History." In *Art in History, History in Art: Studies in Seventeenth-Century Dutch Culture*, ed. Freedberg and Jan de Vries, 377–428. Los Angeles: Getty Center, 1992.
Freist, Dagmar. *Governed by Opinion: Politics, Religion and the Dynamics of Communication in Stuart London, 1637–1645*. London: Tauris, 1997.
Frijhoff, Willem, and Marijke Spies. *Dutch Culture in a European Perspective*, vol. 1, *1650: Hard-Won Unity*. Assen: Van Gorcum, 2004.

Frisch, Andrea. "In a Sacramental Mode: Jean de Léry's Calvinist Ethnography." *Representations* 77, 1 (2002): 82–106.
Fuks-Mansfeld, R. "The Hebrew Book Trade in Amsterdam in the Seventeenth Century." In *Le Magasin de l'Univers: The Dutch Republic as the Centre of the European Book Trade*, ed. C. Berkvens-Stevelinck et al., 155–68. Leiden: Brill, 1992.
Games, Alison. "Cohabitation, Suriname-Style: English Inhabitants in Dutch Suriname After 1667." *William and Mary Quarterly* 72, 2 (2015): 195–242.
———. "The *Oxford Handbook*'s Capacious Atlantic." *Slavery and Abolition* 34, 1 (2013): 158–65.
Gelder, Roelof van. "De wereld binnen handbereik: Nederlandse kunst- en rariteitenverzamelingen, 1585–1735." In *De wereld binnen handbereik: Nederlandse kunst- en rariteitenverzamelingen, 1585–1735*, ed. Ellinoor Bergvelt and Renee Kistemaker, 15–38. Zwolle: Waanders, 1992.
Gelder, Roelof van, Jan Parmentier, and Vibeke Roeper, eds. *Souffrir pour parvenir: De wereld van Jan Huygen van Linschoten*. Haarlem: Arcadia, 1998.
Gelderblom, Oscar. *Zuid-Nederlandse kooplieden en de opkomst van de Amsterdamse stapelmarkt (1578–1630)*. Hilversum: Verloren, 2000.
Goldgar, Anne. *Tulipmania: Money, Honor, and Knowledge in the Dutch Golden Age*. Chicago: University of Chicago Press, 2007.
Gonsalves de Mello, Jose Antônio. *Gente da Naçao: Cristaôs-novos e judeus em Pernambuco, 1543–1654*. Recife: Fundacâo Joaquim Nabuco, 1996.
———. *Nederlanders in Brazilië (1624–1654): De invloed van de Hollandse bezetting op het leven en de cultuur in Noord-Brazilië*, trans. and rev. ed. of *Tempo dos Flamengos*. Zutphen: Walburg Pers, 2001.
———. "Vincent Joachim Soler in Dutch Brazil." In *Johan Maurits van Nassau-Siegen, 1604–1679: A Humanist Prince in Europe and Brazil*, ed. Ernst van den Boogaart et al., 247–55. The Hague: Johan Maurits van Nassau Stichting, 1979.
Goodfriend, Joyce. "Practicing Toleration in Dutch New Netherland." In *The First Prejudice: Religious Tolerance and Intolerance in Early America*, ed. Chris Beneke and Christopher S. Grenda, 98–122. Philadelphia: University of Pennsylvania Press, 2011.
Goslinga, Cornelis. *The Dutch in the Caribbean and on the Wild Coast, 1580–1680*. Gainesville: University Press of Florida, 1971.
Grafton, Anthony. *New Worlds, Ancient Texts: The Power of Tradition and the Shock of Discovery*. Cambridge, Mass.: Belknap Press of Harvard University Press, 1992.
Greenspan, Nicole. "News and the Politics of Information in the Mid-Seventeenth Century: The Western Design and the Conquest of Jamaica." *History Workshop Journal* 69, 1 (2010): 1–26.
Grijp, Louis-Peter. "Van geuzenlied tot Gedenck-clanck." *De zeventiende eeuw* 10, 1 (1994): 118–32; *De zeventiende eeuw* 10, 2 (1994): 266–76.
Groenhuis, Gerrit. *De predikanten: De sociale positie van de gereformeerde predikanten in de Republiek der Verenigde Nederlanden voor ±1700*. Groningen: Wolters-Noordhoff, 1977.
Groesen, Michiel van. "Arnoldus Montanus, Dutch Brazil, and the Re-Emergence of Cannibalism." In *Transformations of Knowledge in Dutch Expansion*, ed. Susanne Friedrich, Arndt Brendecke, and Stefan Ehrenpreis, 93–120. Berlin: De Gruyter, 2015.
———. "A Brazilian Jesuit in Amsterdam: Anti-Spanish and Anti-Catholic Rhetoric in the Dutch Golden Age, 1624–1626." *Archivum Historicum Societatis Iesu* 160 (2011): 445–70.
———. "Heroic Memories: Admirals of Dutch Brazil in the Rise of Dutch National Consciousness." In *The Legacy of Dutch Brazil*, ed. Van Groesen, 207–28. New York: Cambridge University Press, 2014.
———, ed. *The Legacy of Dutch Brazil*. New York: Cambridge University Press, 2014.

———. "Lessons Learned: The Second Dutch Conquest of Brazil and the Memory of the First." *Colonial Latin American Review* 20, 2 (2011): 167–93.

———. "(No) News from the Western Front: The Weekly Press of the Low Countries and the Making of Atlantic News." *Sixteenth Century Journal* 44, 3 (2013): 739–60.

———. "Officers of the West India Company, Their Networks, and Their Personal Memories of Dutch Brazil." In *The Dutch Trading Companies as Knowledge Networks*, ed. Siegfried Huigen, Jan L. de Jong, and Elmer Kolfin, 39–58. Leiden: Brill, 2010.

———. "Reading Newspapers in the Dutch Golden Age." *Media History*, forthcoming.

———. *The Representations of the Overseas World in the De Bry Collection of Voyages (1590–1634)*. Leiden: Brill, 2008.

———. "Text, Image, News: The Amsterdam Spin-Doctor Claes Jansz Visscher and the Dutch West India Company." In *Visualizing the Text from Manuscript Culture to the Age of Caricature*, ed. Christina Ionescu and Lauren Beck. Newark: University of Delaware Press, forthcoming.

———. "A Week to Remember: Dutch Publishers and the Competition for News from Brazil, 26 August–2 September 1624." *Quaerendo* 40, 1 (2010): 26–49.

Haar, Cornelis van de. *De diplomatieke betrekkingen tussen de Republiek en Portugal 1640–1661*. Groningen: Wolters, 1961.

Haefeli, Evan. "Breaking the Christian Atlantic: The Legacy of Dutch Tolerance in Brazil." In *The Legacy of Dutch Brazil*, ed. Michiel van Groesen, 124–45. New York: Cambridge University Press, 2014.

———. *New Netherland and the Dutch Origins of American Religious Liberty*. Philadelphia: University of Pennsylvania Press, 2012.

Haks, Donald. *Vaderland en vrede, 1672–1713: Publiciteit over de Nederlandse Republiek in oorlog*. Hilversum: Verloren, 2013.

Harley, J. B. "Maps, Knowledge, and Power." In *The New Nature of Maps: Essays in the History of Cartography*, ed. Harley, 51–81. Baltimore: Johns Hopkins University Press, 2001.

———. "Silences and Secrecy: The Hidden Agenda of Cartography in Early Modern Europe." In *The New Nature of Maps: Essays in the History of Cartography*, ed. Harley, 84–107. Baltimore: Johns Hopkins University Press, 2001.

Harline, Craig. *Pamphlets, Printing, and Political Culture in the Early Dutch Republic*. Dordrecht: Nijhoff, 1987.

Harms, Roeland. "Handel in letteren: De ambulante boekhandel in actueel drukwerk in zeventiende-eeuws Amsterdam." *De zeventiende eeuw* 23, 2 (2007): 216–29.

———. *Pamfletten en publieke opinie: Massamedia in de zeventiende eeuw*. Amsterdam: Amsterdam University Press, 2011.

Harreld, Donald J. "'How Great the Enterprise, How Glorious the Deed': Seventeenth-Century Dutch Circumnavigations as Useful Myth." In *Myth in History, History in Myth: Proceedings of the Third International Conference of the Society for Netherlandic History*, ed. Laura Cruz and Willem Frijhoff, 17–31. Leiden: Brill, 2009.

't Hart, Marjolein. "The Glorious City: Monumentalism and Public Space in Seventeenth-Century Amsterdam." In *Urban Achievement in Early Modern Europe: Golden Ages in Antwerp, Amsterdam and London*, ed. Patrick O'Brien et al., 128–50. Cambridge: Cambridge University Press, 2001.

———. "Intercity Rivalries and the Making of the Dutch State." In *Cities and the Rise of States in Europe, A.D. 1000 to 1800*, ed. Charles Tilly and Wim P. Blockmans, 196–217. Boulder, Colo.: Westview, 1994.

Haskell, Francis. *History and Its Images: Art and the Interpretation of the Past.* New Haven, Conn.: Yale University Press, 1993.

Hefting, Oscar F. "High Versus Low: Portuguese and Dutch Fortification Traditions Meet in Colonial Brazil (1500–1654)." In *First Forts: Essays on the Archaeology of Proto-Colonial Fortifications*, ed. Eric Klingelhofer, 189–208. Leiden: Brill, 2010.

Heijden, Manon van der, and Daniëlle van den Heuvel. "Sailors' Families and the Urban Institutional Framework in Early Modern Holland." *History of the Family* 12, 4 (2007): 296–309.

Heijer, Henk den. *De geoctrooieerde compagnie: De VOC en WIC als voorlopers van de naamloze vennootschap.* Amsterdam: Kluwer, 2005.

———. *De geschiedenis van de WIC.* Zutphen: Walburg Pers, 1994.

———. "Plannen voor samenvoeging van VOC en WIC." *Tijdschrift voor Zeegeschiedenis* 13, 2 (1994): 115–30.

Heijer, Henk den, and Bea Brommer, eds. *Grote Atlas van de West-Indische Compagnie/Comprehensive Atlas of the Dutch West India Company*, vol. 1, *De Oude WIC 1621–1674/The Old WIC, 1621–1674.* Voorburg: Asia Maior, 2011.

Hoboken, Willem J. van. *Witte de With in Brazilië, 1648–1649.* Amsterdam: Noord-Hollandsche Uitgevers Maatschappij, 1955.

Hochstrasser, Julie Berger. *Still Life and Trade in the Dutch Golden Age.* New Haven, Conn.: Yale University Press, 2007.

Hondius, Dienke. "Black Africans in Seventeenth-Century Amsterdam." *Renaissance and Reformation* 31, 2 (2008): 87–105.

L'Honoré Naber, S. P. *Piet Heyn en de Zilvervloot.* Utrecht: Kemink, 1928.

Honour, Hugh. *The New Golden Land: European Images from the Discoveries to the Present Time.* New York: Pantheon, 1975.

Hulsman, Lodewijk. "Brazilian Indians in the Dutch Republic: The Remonstrances of Antonio Paraupaba to the States General in 1654 and 1656." *Itinerario* 29, 1 (2005): 51–78.

———. "Gisberth de With en Anna Paes: De geschiedenis van het huwelijk van een Dordtenaar en een Braziliaanse in de 17e eeuw." *Oud Dordrecht* 23, 2 (2005): 52–62; 23, 3 (2005): 36–45; 24, 1 (2006): 61–70.

IJzerman, J. W., "De expeditie naar het Westen onder Paulus van Caerden." In *Journael van de reis naar Zuid-Amerika (1598–1601)*, ed. IJzerman, 167–215. The Hague: Nijhoff, 1918.

Israel, Jonathan I. *Dutch Primacy in World Trade, 1585–1740.* Oxford: Oxford University Press, 1989.

———. *The Dutch Republic and the Hispanic World, 1606–1661.* Oxford: Oxford University Press, 1982.

———. *The Dutch Republic: Its Rise, Greatness, and Fall, 1477–1806.* Oxford: Oxford University Press, 1995.

———. "Dutch Sephardi Jewry, Millenarian Politics, and the Struggle for Brazil (1645–1654)." In *Diasporas Within a Diaspora*, ed. Jonathan I. Israel, 355–84. Leiden: Brill, 2002.

———. "The Jews in Dutch America." In *The Jews and the Expansion of Europe to the West, 1450–1800*, ed. Paolo Bernardini and Norman Fiering, 335–49. New York: Berghahn, 2001.

———. "Religious Toleration in Dutch Brazil (1624–1654)." In Israel and Stuart B. Schwartz, *The Expansion of Tolerance: Religion in Dutch Brazil, 1624–1654*, 13–32. Amsterdam: Amsterdam University Press, 2007.

Ittersum, Martine J. van. "The Long Goodbye: Hugo Grotius' Justification of Dutch Expansion Overseas, 1615–1645." *History of European Ideas* 36, 4 (2010): 386–411.

Jacobs, Jaap. *New Netherland: A Dutch Colony in Seventeenth-Century America*. Leiden: Brill, 2005.

———. "Soldiers of the Company: The Military Personnel of the West India Company in Nieu Nederlandt." In *Jacob Leisler's Atlantic World in the Later Seventeenth Century*, ed. Hermann Wellenreuther, 11–31. Berlin: Lit Verlag, 2009.

Jones, Ann Rosalind. "Habits, Holdings, Heterologies: Populations in Print in a 1562 Costume Book." *Yale French Studies* 110 (2006): 92–121.

Joosse, L. J. "Soler als predikant in Delft, 1645–1665." *Documentatieblad voor de geschiedenis der Nederlandse Zending en Overzeese Kerken* 4 (1997): 24–42.

Joppien, Rüdger, "The Dutch Vision of Brazil: Johan Maurits and His Artists." In *Johan Maurits van Nassau-Siegen, 1604–1679: A Humanist Prince in Europe and Brazil*, ed. Ernst van den Boogaart et al., 297–376. The Hague: Johan Maurits van Nassau Stichting, 1979.

Jorink, Eric. *Reading the Book of Nature in the Dutch Golden Age, 1575–1715*. Leiden: Brill, 2010.

Kannegieter, J. Z. "Dr. Nicolaes Jansz. van Wassenaer (1571/1572–1629)." *Jaarboek Amstelodamum* 56 (1964): 71–99.

Kaplan, Benjamin J. *Calvinists and Libertines: Confession and Community in Utrecht, 1578–1620*. Oxford: Oxford University Press, 1995.

Keblusek, Marika. *Boeken in de Hofstad: Haagse boekcultuur in de Gouden Eeuw*. Hilversum: Verloren, 1997.

———. "The Business of News: Michel Le Blon and the Transmission of Political Information to Sweden in the 1630s." *Scandinavian Journal of History* 28, 3/4 (2003): 205–13.

Kleerkooper, M. M., and W. P. van Stockum, Jr. *De boekhandel te Amsterdam voornamelijk in de 17e eeuw*. 2 vols. The Hague: Nijhoff, 1914–16.

Klinkert, Christi. *Nassau in het nieuws: Nieuwsprenten van Maurits van Nassaus militaire ondernemingen uit de periode 1590–1600*. Zutphen: Walburg Pers, 2005.

Klooster, Wim. "De bootsgezellen van Brazilië." *Tijdschrift voor Zeegeschiedenis* 33, 2 (2014): 41–56.

———. "Communities of Port Jews and Their Contacts in the Dutch Atlantic World." *Jewish History* 20, 2 (2006): 129–45.

———. *The Dutch Moment in Atlantic History: War, Trade, and Settlement in the Transformation of the Americas*. Ithaca, N.Y.: Cornell University Press, forthcoming.

———. "The Essequibo Liberties: The Link Between Jewish Brazil and Jewish Suriname." *Studia Rosenthaliana* 42–43 (2010–11): 77–82.

———. *Illicit Riches: Dutch Trade in the Caribbean, 1648–1795*. Leiden: KITLV Press, 1998.

———. "Marteling, muiterij en beeldenstorm: Militair geweld in de Nederlandse Atlantische wereld, 1624–1654." In *Geweld in de West: Een militaire geschiedenis van de Nederlandse Atlantische wereld, 1600–1800*, ed. Victor Enthoven, Henk den Heijer, and Han Jordaan, 313–43. Leiden: Brill, 2013.

———. ed. *Migration, Trade, and Slavery in an Expanding World*. Leiden: Brill, 2009.

———. "Networks of Colonial Entrepreneurs: The Founders of the Jewish Settlements in Dutch America, 1650s and 1660s." In *Atlantic Diasporas: Jews, Conversos, and Crypto-Jews in the Age of Mercantilism, 1500–1800*, ed. Richard L. Kagan and Philip D. Morgan, 33–49. Baltimore: Johns Hopkins University Press, 2009.

Knuttel, Willem P. C. *Catalogus van de pamfletten-verzameling berustende in de Koninklijke Bibliotheek*. 9 vols. The Hague: Algemeene Landsdrukkerij, 1889–1920.

Kooijmans, Luuc. *Liefde in opdracht: Het hofleven van Willem Frederik van Nassau*. Amsterdam: Bert Bakker, 2000.

Koppenol, Johan. *Leids heelal: Het Loterijspel (1596) van Jan van Hout*. Hilversum: Verloren, 1998.
Kraack, Detlev. "Flensburg, an Early Modern Centre of Trade: The Autobiographical Writings of Peter Hansen Hajstrup (1624–1672)." In *The North Sea and Culture (1550–1800)*, ed. Juliette Roding and Lex Heerma van Voss, 235–46. Hilversum: Verloren, 1996.
Krommen, Rita. *Mathias Beck und die Westindische Kompagnie: Zur Herrschaft der Niederländer im Kolonialen Ceará*. Cologne: Köln University, 2001.
Kuijpers, Erika. "Lezen en schrijven: Onderzoek naar het alfabetiseringsniveau in zeventiende-eeuws Amsterdam." *Tijdschrift voor Sociale Geschiedenis* 23, 4 (1997): 490–522.
Lake, Peter, and Steven Pincus. "Rethinking the Public Sphere in Early Modern England." *Journal of British Studies* 45, 2 (2006): 270–92.
Lankhorst, Otto. "Newspapers in the Netherlands in the Seventeenth Century." In *The Politics of Information in Early Modern Europe*, ed. Brendan Dooley and Sabrina Baron, 151–59. London: Routledge, 2001.
Larsen, Erik. "Neu entdeckte Brasilien-Bilder von Frans Post, Abraham Willaerts und Gillis Peeters I." *Weltkunst* 72, 2/6 (2002): Teil 1: 162–64, Teil 2: 936–37.
———. "Some Seventeenth-Century Paintings of Brazil." *Connoisseur* 175, 704 (Oct 1970): 123–31.
Lawrence, Cynthia. "Hendrick de Keyser's Heemskerk Monument: The Origins of the Cult and Iconography of Dutch Naval Heroes." *Simiolus: Netherlands Quarterly for the History of Art* 21, 4 (1992): 265–95.
Lechner, Jan, "Dutch Humanists' Knowledge of America." *Itinerario* 16, 2 (1992): 101–13.
Leite, Serafim. *História da Companhia de Jesus no Brasil*. 10 vols. Lisbon: Livraria Portugália, 1938–50.
Lesger, Clé. *The Rise of the Amsterdam Market and Information Exchange: Merchants, Commercial Expansion, and Change in the Spatial Economy of the Low Countries, c. 1550–1630*. Aldershot: Ashgate, 2006.
Lestringant, Frank. *André Thevet: Cosmographe des derniers Valois*. Geneva: Droz, 1991.
———. "Geneva and America in the Renaissance: The Dream of the Huguenot Refuge, 1555–1600." *Sixteenth Century Journal* 26, 2 (1995): 285–95.
———. *Mapping the Renaissance World: The Geographical Imagination in the Age of Discovery*. Berkeley: University of California Press, 1994.
———. "The Philosopher's Breviary: Jean de Léry in the Enlightenment." *Representations* 33 (1991): 200–11.
Ligtenberg, Catharina. *Willem Usselinx*. Utrecht: Oosthoek, 1914.
Lunsford, Virginia W. *Piracy and Privateering in the Golden Age Netherlands*. New York: Palgrave Macmillan, 2005.
Mason, Peter. *Infelicities: Representations of the Exotic*. Baltimore: Johns Hopkins University Press, 1998.
Massing, Jean Michel. "From Dutch Brazil to the West Indies: The Paper Image of the Ideal Sugar Plantation." In *Studies in Imagery II: The World Discovered*, ed. Jean Michel Massing, 172–95. London: Pindar, 2007.
Mattos, Hebe, "'Black Troops' and Hierarchies of Color in the Portuguese Atlantic World: The Case of Henrique Dias and His Black Regiment." *Luso-Brazilian Review* 45, 1 (2008): 6–29.
McCusker, John J. "The Demise of Distance: The Business Press and the Origins of the Information Revolution in the Early Modern Atlantic World." *American Historical Review* 110, 2 (2005): 295–321.
McGrath, John. "Polemic and History in French Brazil 1555–1560." *Sixteenth Century Journal* 27, 2 (1996): 385–97.

Meeus, Hubert. "Inleiding." In *Zacharias Heyns: Dracht-thoneel*, facsimile edition, ix–xx. Amsterdam: Buijten & Schipperheijn, 1989.

———. "The Peasant as a Mouthpiece of Public Opinion in Sixteenth- and Seventeenth-Century Dutch Theatre." In *Drama, Performance and Debate: Theatre and Public Opinion in the Early Modern Period*, ed. Jan Bloemendal, Peter Eversmann, and Elsa Strietman, 193–211. Leiden: Brill, 2013.

———. "Zacharias Heyns, Sometime Apprentice to Moretus, Becomes the First Merchant/Publisher in Amsterdam." *Quaerendo* 38, 4 (2008): 381–97.

Meiden, Gerard van der. *Betwist bestuur: Een eeuw strijd om de macht in Suriname 1651–1753*. Amsterdam: De Bataafsche Leeuw, 1986.

Meijer, Albert. "'Liefhebbers des Vaderlandts ende beminders van de commercie': De plannen tot oprichting van een generale Westindische Compagnie gedurende de jaren 1606–1609." *Archief: Mededelingen van het Koninklijk Zeeuwsch Genootschap der Wetenschappen* (1986): 21–70.

Merwick, Donna. *The Shame and the Sorrow: Dutch-Amerindian Encounters in New Netherland*. Philadelphia: University of Pennsylvania Press, 2006.

Meuwese, Mark. *Brothers in Arms, Partners in Trade: Dutch-Indigenous Alliances in the Atlantic World, 1595–1674*. Leiden: Brill, 2012.

———. "From Dutch Allies to Portuguese Vassals: Indigenous Peoples in the Aftermath of Dutch Brazil." In *The Legacy of Dutch Brazil*, ed. Michiel van Groesen, 59–76. New York: Cambridge University Press, 2014.

———. "Indigenous Leaders and the Atlantic World: The Parallel Lives of Dom Antônio Filipe Camarão and Pieter Poty, 1600–1650." In *Atlantic Biographies: Individuals and Peoples in the Atlantic World*, ed. Meuwese and Jeffrey A. Fortin, 213–33. Leiden: Brill, 2013.

———. "The States General and the Stadtholder: Dutch Diplomatic Practices in the Atlantic World Before the West India Company." *Journal of Early American History* 3, 1 (2013): 43–58.

———. "Subjects or Allies: The Contentious State of the Tupi Indians in Dutch Brazil, 1625–1654." In *Bridging the Early Modern Atlantic World*, ed. Caroline A. Williams, 113–30. Farnham: Ashgate, 2009.

Miert, Dirk van. *Humanism in an Age of Science: The Amsterdam Athenaeum in the Golden Age, 1632–1704*. Leiden: Brill, 2009.

Miranda, Bruno R. F. "Gente de guerra: Origem, cotidiano e resistência dos soldados do exército da Companhia das Índias Ocidentais no Brasil (1630–1654)." Ph.D. dissertation, Leiden University, 2011.

———. "Zielkopers, Zielverkopers and Other Dealers: The Recruitment of Soldiers for the West India Company." Unpublished paper, 2011.

Moes, Ernst Wilhelm, and C. P. Burger, Jr. *De Amsterdamsche boekdrukkers en uitgevers in de zestiende eeuw*. 4 vols. Amsterdam: Van Langenhuysen, 1900–1915.

Morgan, Philip D., and Jack P. Greene. "Introduction: The Present State of Atlantic History." In *Atlantic History: A Critical Appraisal*, ed. Greene and Morgan, 3–33. Oxford: Oxford University Press, 2009.

Mout, Nicolette. "The Youth of Johan Maurits and Aristocratic Culture of the Early Seventeenth Century." In *Johan Maurits van Nassau-Siegen, 1604–1679: A Humanist Prince in Europe and Brazil*, ed. Ernst van den Boogaart et al., 13–38. The Hague: Johan Maurits van Nassau Stichting, 1979.

Muller, Frederik. *De Nederlandsche geschiedenis in platen: Beredeneerde beschrijving van Nederlandsche historieplaten, zinneprenten en historische kaarten*. 3 vols. Amsterdam, 1863–70.

Nederveen Meerkerk, Hannadea C. van. *Recife: The Rise of a 17th-Century Trade City from a Cultural-Historical Perspective*. Assen: Van Gorcum, 1989.

Nellen, Henk. *Hugo de Groot: Een leven in strijd om de vrede, 1583–1645*. Amsterdam: Balans, 2007.

Nelson, Eric. "The Jesuit Legend: Superstition and Myth-Making." In *Religion and Superstition in Reformation Europe*, ed. Helen Parish and William G. Naphy, 94–115. Manchester: Manchester University Press, 2002.

Netscher, Pieter Marinus. *Les Hollandais au Brésil: Notice historique sur les Pays-Bas et le Brésil au XVII siècle*. The Hague: Belinfante, 1853.

Netten, Djoeke van. *Koopman in kennis: De uitgever Willem Jansz Blaeu in de geleerde wereld van zijn tijd (1571–1638)*. Zutphen: Walburg Pers, 2013.

Nierop, Henk van. "'And Ye Shall Hear of Wars and Rumours of Wars': Rumour and the Revolt of the Netherlands." In *Public Opinion and Changing Identities in the Early Modern Netherlands*, ed. Judith Pollmann and Andrew Spicer, 69–86. Leiden: Brill, 2007.

———. "Confessional Cleansing: Why Amsterdam Did Not Join the Revolt (1572–1578)." In *Power and the Cities in the Netherlandic World*, ed. Wim Klooster and Wayne Te Brake, 85–102. Leiden: Brill, 2006.

———. "Popular Participation in Politics in the Dutch Republic." In *Resistance, Representation, and Community: The Origins of the Modern State in Europe, 13th to 18th Centuries*, ed. Peter Blickle, 272–90. Oxford: Clarendon, 1997.

———. "Profijt en propaganda: Nieuwsprenten en de verbeelding van het nieuws." In *Romeyn de Hooghe: De verbeelding van de late Gouden Eeuw*, ed. Henk van Nierop et al., 66–85. Zwolle: Waanders, 2008.

Noorlander, Danny L. "'For the Maintenance of the True Religion': Calvinism and the Directors of the Dutch West India Company." *Sixteenth Century Journal* 44, 1 (2013): 73–95.

———. "Serving God and the Mammon: The Reformed Church and the Dutch West India Company in the Atlantic World." Ph.D. dissertation, Georgetown University, 2011.

North, J. D. "Georg Markgraf: An Astronomer in the New World." In *Johan Maurits van Nassau-Siegen, 1604–1679: A Humanist Prince in Europe and Brazil*, ed. Ernst van den Boogaart et al., 394–423. The Hague: Johan Maurits van Nassau Stichting, 1979.

Oey-de Vita, E., and M. Geesink. *Academie en schouwburg: Amsterdams toneelrepertoire, 1617–1665*. Amsterdam: Huis aan de Drie Grachten, 1983.

Opgenoorth, Ernst. "Johan Maurits as Stadholder of Cleves." In *Johan Maurits van Nassau-Siegen, 1604–1679: A Humanist Prince in Europe and Brazil*, ed. Ernst van den Boogaart et al., 39–53. The Hague: Johan Maurits van Nassau Stichting, 1979.

Orenstein, Nadine et al. "Print Publishers in the Netherlands, 1580–1620." In *Dawn of the Golden Age: Northern Netherlandish Art, 1580–1620*, ed. Ger Luijten et al., 167–200. Amsterdam and Zwolle: Waanders, 1993.

Paas, John Roger. *The German Political Broadsheet, 1600–1700*. 12 vols. Wiesbaden: Harrassowitz, 1985–2012.

Panhuysen, Luc. *Rampjaar 1672: Hoe de Republiek aan de ondergang ontsnapte*. Amsterdam: Atlas, 2011.

Parker Brienen, Rebecca. *Visions of Savage Paradise: Albert Eckhout, Court Painter in Colonial Dutch Brazil*. Amsterdam: Amsterdam University Press, 2006.

———. "Who Owns Frans Post? Collecting Frans Post's Brazilian Landscapes." In *The Legacy of Dutch Brazil*, ed. Michiel van Groesen, 229–47. New York: Cambridge University Press, 2014.

Petram, Lodewijk. *De bakermat van de beurs: Hoe in zeventiende-eeuws Amsterdam de moderne aandelenhandel ontstond*. Amsterdam: Balans, 2011.

Pettegree, Andrew. *The Invention of News: How the World Came to Know About Itself.* New Haven, Conn.: Yale University Press, 2014.

———. *Reformation and the Culture of Persuasion*. Cambridge: Cambridge University Press, 2005.

Pies, Eike. *Willem Piso (1611–1678): Begründer der kolonialen Medizin und Leibarzt des Grafen Johann Moritz von Nassau-Siegen in Brasilien*. Düsseldorf: Interma-Orb, 1981.

Poelwijk, Arjan. *"In dienste vant suyckerbacken": De Amsterdamse suikernijverheid en haar ondernemers, 1580–1630*. Hilversum: Verloren, 2003.

Pollmann, Judith. *Religious Choice in the Dutch Republic: The Reformation of Arnoldus Buchelius (1565–1641)*. Manchester: Manchester University Press, 1999.

Pollmann, Judith, and Andrew Spicer, eds. *Public Opinion and Changing Identities in the Early Modern Netherlands*. Leiden: Brill, 2007.

Postma, Johannes. *The Dutch in the Atlantic Slave Trade, 1600–1815*. Cambridge: Cambridge University Press, 1990.

Postma, Johannes, and Victor Enthoven, eds. *Riches of Atlantic Commerce: Dutch Transatlantic Trade and Shipping, 1585–1817*. Leiden: Brill, 2003.

Prak, Maarten. "Burghers, Citizens, and Popular Politics in the Dutch Republic." *Eighteenth-Century Studies* 30, 4 (1997): 443–52.

Preston, Rupert. *The Seventeenth Century Marine Painters of the Netherlands*. Leigh-on-Sea: F. Lewis, 1974.

Price, Leslie. *Holland and the Dutch Republic in the Seventeenth Century: The Politics of Particularism*. Oxford: Clarendon, 1994.

Priester, L. R. "De Nederlandse houding ten aanzien van de slavenhandel en slavernij, 1596–1863." MA thesis, Erasmus University Rotterdam, 1986.

Rademaker, Cor S. M. "Oorlog en vrede in de neolatijnse literatuur in de Noordelijke Nederlanden rond 1648: Dichters, redenaars en geleerden." *De zeventiende eeuw* 13, 1 (1997): 245–52.

Rahn Phillips, Carla. *Six Galleons for the King of Spain: Imperial Defense in the Early Seventeenth Century*. Baltimore: Johns Hopkins University Press, 1986.

Randall, David. *Credibility in Elizabethan and Early Stuart Military News*. London: Pickering & Chatto, 2010.

Rault, Didier. "La información y su manipulación en las relaciones de sucesos: Encuesta sobre dos relatos de batallas navales entre españoles y holandeses (1638)." *Criticón* 86 (2002): 97–116.

Raymond, Joad, ed. *News, Newspapers, and Society in Early Modern Europe*. London: Frank Cass, 1999.

———, ed. *News Networks in Seventeenth-Century Britain and Europe*. London: Routledge, 2006.

———. "The Newspaper, Public Opinion, and the Public Sphere in the Seventeenth Century." In *News, Newspapers, and Society in Early Modern Europe*, ed. Raymond, 109–40. London: Frank Cass, 1999.

Reesse, Jan Jacob. *De suikerhandel van Amsterdam van het begin der 17de eeuw tot 1813*. Haarlem: Kleynenberg, 1908.

Reeves, Eileen. *Evening News: Optics, Astronomy, and Journalism in Early Modern Europe*. Philadelphia: University of Pennsylvania Press, 2014.

Reinders, Michel. *Printed Pandemonium: Popular Print and Politics in the Netherlands, 1650–72.* Leiden: Brill, 2013.

Rink, Oliver. "Private Interest and Godly Gain: The West India Company and the Dutch Reformed Church in New Netherland, 1624–1664." *New York History* 75, 3 (1994): 245–64.

Romney, Susanah Shaw. *New Netherland Connections: Intimate Networks and Atlantic Ties in Seventeenth-Century America.* Chapel Hill: University of North Carolina Press, 2014.

Rooden, Peter van. "Dissenters en bededagen: Civil religion ten tijde van de Republiek." *Bijdragen en Mededelingen Betreffende de Geschiedenis der Nederlanden* 107, 4 (1992): 703–12.

Rosen, Jochai. *Soldiers at Leisure: The Guardroom Scene in Dutch Genre Paintings of the Golden Age.* Amsterdam: Amsterdam University Press, 2010.

Rubiés, Joan Pau. "Mythologies of Dutch Brazil." In *The Legacy of Dutch Brazil*, ed. Michiel van Groesen, 284–317. New York: Cambridge University Press, 2014.

Russell, Margarita. *Visions of the Sea: Hendrick C. Vroom and the Origins of Dutch Marine Painting.* Leiden: Brill, 1983.

Safier, Neil. "Beyond Brazilian Nature: The Editorial Itineraries of Marcgraf and Piso's *Historia Naturalis Brasiliae*." In *The Legacy of Dutch Brazil*, ed. Michiel van Groesen, 168–86. New York: Cambridge University Press, 2014.

Salman, Jeroen. "Het nieuws op straat: Actueel drukwerk in het vroegmoderne distributienetwerk." In *Het lange leven van het pamflet: Boekhistorische, iconografische, literaire en politieke aspecten van pamfletten, 1600–1900*, ed. Salman, José de Kruif, and Marijke Meijer Drees, 56–67. Hilversum: Verloren, 2006.

———. *Pedlars and the Popular Press: Itinerant Distribution Networks in England and the Netherlands, 1600–1850.* Leiden: Brill, 2013.

Sas, Niek van. *De metamorfose van Nederland: Van oude orde naar moderniteit, 1750–1900.* Amsterdam: Amsterdam University Press, 2004.

Sawyer, Andrew. "The Tyranny of Alva: The Creation and Development of a Dutch Patriotic Image." *De zeventiende eeuw* 19, 2 (2003): 181–211.

Schalkwijk, Frans L. *The Reformed Church in Dutch Brazil (1630–1654).* Zoetermeer: Boekencentrum, 1998.

Schenkeveld-Van der Dussen, M. A. "Vondel und Johann Moritz." In *So weit der Erdkreis Reicht: Johann Moritz von Nassau-Siegen, 1604–1679*, ed. Guido de Werd, 117–26. Kleve: Stadt Kleve, 1979.

Schilder, Günter. *Monumenta Cartographica Neerlandica VII. Cornelis Claesz (c. 1551–1609): Stimulator and Driving Force of Dutch Cartography.* Alphen aan den Rijn: Canaletto, 2003.

———. *Monumenta Cartographica Neerlandica IX. Hessel Gerritsz (1580/81–1632): Master Engraver and Map Maker, Who "Ruled" the Seas.* Houten: Hes & De Graaf, 2013.

Schilder, Günter, and Marco van Egmond. "Maritime Cartography in the Low Countries During the Renaissance." In *The History of Cartography Volume 3* (Part II): *Cartography in the European Renaissance*, ed. David Woodward, 1384–1432. Chicago: University of Chicago Press, 2007.

Schmidt, Benjamin. "The Dutch Atlantic: From Provincialism to Globalism." In *Atlantic History: A Critical Appraisal*, ed. Jack P. Greene and Philip D. Morgan, 163–87. Oxford: Oxford University Press, 2009.

———. "Exotic Allies: The Dutch-Chilean Encounter and the (Failed) Conquest of America." *Renaissance Quarterly* 52, 2 (1999): 441–73.

———. *Innocence Abroad: The Dutch Imagination and the New World, 1570–1670.* Cambridge: Cambridge University Press, 2001.

———. *Inventing Exoticism: Geography, Globalism, and Europe's Early Modern World*. Philadelphia: University of Pennsylvania Press, 2015.

———. "Mapping an Empire: Cartographic and Colonial Rivalry in Seventeenth-Century Dutch and English North America." *William and Mary Quarterly* 54, 3 (1997): 549–78.

Scholten, Frits. *Sumptuous Memories: Studies in Dutch Seventeenth-Century Tomb Culture*. Zwolle: Waanders, 2003.

Schorsch, Jonathan. *Jews and Blacks in the Early Modern World*. Cambridge: Cambridge University Press, 2004.

Schurhammer, Georg. *Gesammelte Studien IV: Varia*. Rome: Institutum Historicum S.I., 1965.

Schwartz, Stuart B. *All Can Be Saved: Religious Tolerance and Salvation in the Iberian Atlantic World*. New Haven, Conn.: Yale University Press, 2008.

———. "A Commonwealth Within Itself: The Early Brazilian Sugar Industry, 1550–1670." In *Tropical Babylons: Sugar and the Making of the Atlantic World, 1450–1680*, ed. Stuart B. Schwartz, 158–200. Chapel Hill: University of North Carolina Press, 2004.

———. "Looking for a New Brazil: Crisis and Rebirth in the Atlantic World After the Fall of Pernambuco." In *The Legacy of Dutch Brazil*, ed. Michiel van Groesen, 41–58. New York: Cambridge University Press, 2014.

———. *Sovereignty and Society in Colonial Brazil: The High Court of Bahia and Its Judges, 1609–1751*. Berkeley: University of California Press, 1973.

———. "The Voyage of the Vassals: Royal Power, Noble Obligations, and Merchant Capital Before the Portuguese Restoration of Independence, 1624–1640." *American Historical Review* 96, 3 (1991): 735–62.

Seed, Patricia. *Ceremonies of Possession in Europe's Conquest of the New World, 1492–1640*. Cambridge: Cambridge University Press, 1995.

Sellin, Paul R. *Treasure, Treason and the Tower: El Dorado and the Murder of Sir Walter Raleigh*. Farnham: Ashgate, 2011.

Selm, Bert van. *Een menighte treffelijcke boecken: Nederlandse boekhandelscatalogi in het begin van de zeventiende eeuw*. Utrecht: Hes, 1987.

Shannon, Robert M. *Visions of the New World in the Drama of Lope de Vega*. New York: Peter Lang, 1989.

Sierksma, Klaas. "Een 17de eeuws vaandelboek van de West-Indische Compagnie." *Mars et Historia* 20, 5 (1986): 31–44.

Silva, Maria Angelica da, and Melissa Mota Alcides. "Collecting and Framing the Wilderness: The Garden of Johan Maurits (1604–79) in North-East Brazil." *Garden History* 30, 2 (2002): 153–76.

Silverblatt, Irene. "The Black Legend and Global Conspiracies: Spain, the Inquisition, and the Emerging Modern World." In *Rereading the Black Legend*, ed. Margaret R. Greer, Walter Mignolo, and Maureen Quilligan, 99–116. Chicago: University of Chicago Press, 2007.

Siskin, Clifford, and William Warner. "This Is Enlightenment: An Invitation in the Form of an Argument." In *This Is Enlightenment*, ed. Siskin and Warner, 1–33. Chicago: University of Chicago Press, 2010.

Slauter, Will. "Forward-Looking Statements: News and Speculation in the Age of the American Revolution." *Journal of Modern History* 81, 4 (2009): 759–92.

Sluiter, Engel. "Dutch Maritime Power and the Colonial Status Quo, 1585–1641." *Pacific Historical Review* 11, 1 (1942): 29–41.

Soll, Jacob. *The Information Master: Jean-Baptiste Colbert's Secret State Intelligence System*. Ann Arbor: University of Michigan Press, 2009.

Sousa-Leão, Joaquim de. *Frans Post, 1612–1680*. Amsterdam: Van Gendt, 1973.
Souza Leão Vieira, Daniel de. "Topografias Imaginárias: A paisagem política do Brasil Holandês em Frans Post, 1637–1669." Ph.D. dissertation, Leiden University, 2010.
Spohr, Otto H. *Zacharias Wagner: Second Commander of the Cape*. Cape Town: Balkema, 1967.
Sprunger, Keith L. *Dutch Puritanism: A History of English and Scottish Churches of the Netherlands in the Sixteenth and Seventeenth Centuries*. Leiden: Brill, 1982.
Spufford, Margaret. "Literacy, Trade and Religion in the Commercial Centres of Europe." In *A Miracle Mirrored: The Dutch Republic in European Perspective*, ed. Karel Davids and Jan Lucassen, 229–83. Cambridge: Cambridge University Press, 1995.
Steele, Ian K. *The English Atlantic, 1675–1740: An Exploration of Communication and Community*. Oxford: Oxford University Press, 1986.
Sterck, J. F. M. "Een historische rozenkrans." In *Oud en nieuw over Joost van den Vondel*, ed. Sterck, 82–86. Amsterdam: De Spieghel, 1932.
Stolp, Annie. *De eerste couranten in Holland*. Haarlem: Enschede, 1938.
Stols, Eddy. "Dutch and Flemish Victims of the Inquisition in Brazil." In *Essays on Cultural Identity in Colonial Latin America: Problems and Repercussions*, ed. Jan Lechner, 43–62. Leiden: TCLA, 1988.
———. "Flemish and Dutch Brazil: The Story of a Missed Opportunity." *Low Countries* 3 (1995–96): 163–71.
Storms, Martijn. "Cartografie in camouflage: Sluis (1604) wordt Salvador de Bahia (1625)." *De Boekenwereld* 29, 5 (2013): 24–27.
———. "De kaart van Nederlands Brazilië door Georg Marcgraf." *Caert-Thresoor* 30, 2 (2011): 37–46.
Strien, Kees van. *Touring the Low Countries: Accounts of British Travellers, 1660–1720*. Amsterdam: Amsterdam University Press, 1998.
Stronks, Els. *Stichten of schitteren: De poëzie van zeventiende-eeuwse gereformeerde predikanten*. Houten: Den Hertog, 1996.
Strum, Daniel. *The Sugar Trade: Brazil, Portugal and the Netherlands (1595–1630)*. Stanford, Calif.: Stanford University Press, 2013.
Studnicki-Gizbert, Daviken. *A Nation upon the Ocean Sea: Portugal's Atlantic Diaspora and the Crisis of the Spanish Empire, 1492–1640*. Oxford: Oxford University Press, 2007.
Sutton, Elizabeth. *Capitalism and Cartography in the Dutch Golden Age*. Chicago: University of Chicago Press, 2015.
———. *Early Modern Dutch Prints of Africa*. Farnham: Ashgate, 2012.
Swetschinski, Daniel M. *Reluctant Cosmopolitans: The Portuguese Jews of Seventeenth-Century Amsterdam*. London: Littman Library of Jewish Civilisation, 2000.
Teensma, Benjamin. "The Brazilian Letters of Vicent Joachim Soler." In *Documents in the Leiden University Library* [= *Dutch Brazil-Brasil Holandes*, vol. 1], 51–70. Rio de Janeiro: Editora Index, 1997.
———. "Nederlands-Braziliaans militair inlichtingenwerk van de West-Indische Compagnie, 1629–1654." In *Geweld in de West: Een militaire geschiedenis van de Nederlandse Atlantische wereld, 1600–1800*, ed. Victor Enthoven, Henk den Heijer, and Han Jordaan, 277–311. Leiden: Brill, 2013.
———. "Resentment in Recife: Jews and Public Opinion in 17th-Century Dutch Brazil." In *Essays on Cultural Identity in Colonial Latin America*, ed. Jan Lechner, 63–78. Leiden: TCLA, 1988.

Teixeira, Dante Martins. *The "Allegory of the Continents" by Jan van Kessel "The Elder" (1626–1679): A Seventeenth-Century View of the Fauna in the Four Corners of the Earth*. Petrópolis: Editora Index, 2002.
Terwen, J. J. "The Buildings of Johan Maurits van Nassau." In *Johan Maurits van Nassau-Siegen, 1604–1679: A Humanist Prince in Europe and Brazil*, ed. Ernst van den Boogaart et al., 54–141. The Hague: Johan Maurits van Nassau Stichting, 1979.
Uitenhage de Mist-Verspyck, I. A. "'Gezicht in Brazilie' door Frans Post: een onderzoek naar de oorspronkelijke bestemming van het schilderij." *Bulletin van het Rijksmuseum* 12, 2 (1964): 50–56.
Vaughan, Alden T. *Transatlantic Encounters: American Indians in Britain, 1500–1776*. Cambridge: Cambridge University Press, 2006.
Veldt, James van der. "An Autograph Letter of John Maurice of Nassau, Governor of the Dutch Colony in Brazil (1636–1644)." *The Americas* 3, 3 (1947): 311–18.
Vermij, Rienk. *The Calvinist Copernicans: The Reception of the New Astronomy in the Dutch Republic, 1575–1750*. Amsterdam: Koninklijke Nederlandse Akademie van Wetenschappen, 2002.
Vivo, Filippo De. *Information and Communication in Venice: Rethinking Early Modern Politics*. Oxford: Oxford University Press, 2007.
Vliet, Pieter van der. *Onno Zwier van Haren (1713–1779): Staatsman en dichter*. Hilversum: Verloren, 1996.
Voogt, J. W. F. "Het 'Reys-boeck van het rijcke Brasilien': Amerika op kaarten in pamfletten omstreeks 1600." *Kartografisch Tijdschrift* 18, 3 (1992): 7–14.
Vries, Jan de, and Ad van der Woude. *The First Modern Economy: Success, Failure, and Perseverance of the Dutch Economy, 1500–1815*. Cambridge: Cambridge University Press, 1997.
Waals, Jan van der, ed. *Prints in the Golden Age: From Art to Shelf Paper*. Rotterdam: Exhibition catalogue, Museum Boymans-Van Beuningen, 2006.
Wadsworth, James E. "In the Name of the Inquisition: The Portuguese Inquisition and Delegated Authority in Colonial Pernambuco, Brazil." *The Americas* 61, 1 (2004): 19–52.
Warnsinck, J. C. M. "Christoffel Artichewsky." In Johannes de Laet, *Iaerlijck verhael van de verrichtinghen der Geoctroyeerde West-Indische Compagnie*, ed. S. P. L'Honoré Naber, 4, xxv–lxxiii. 4 vols. The Hague: Nijhoff, 1931–37.
Warren, Maureen. "A Shameful Spectacle: Claes Jansz. Visscher's 1623 News Prints of Executed Dutch 'Arminians'." In *Death, Torture and the Broken Body in European Art, 1300–1650*, ed. John R. Decker and Mitzi Kirkland-Ives, 207–30. Farnham: Ashgate, 2015.
Wätjen, Hermann. *Das Holländische Kolonialreich in Brasilien: Ein Kapitel aus der Kolonialgeschichte des 17. Jahrhunderts*. The Hague: Nijhoff, 1921.
Weekhout, Ingrid. *Boekencensuur in de Noordelijke Nederlanden: De vrijheid van drukpers in de zeventiende eeuw*. The Hague: SDU, 1998.
Welu, James A. "Vermeer: His Cartographic Sources." *Art Bulletin* 57, 4 (1975): 529–47.
Werd, Guido de, ed. *So weit der Erdkreis reicht: Johann Moritz von Nassau-Siegen, 1604–1679*. Kleve: Stadt Kleve, 1979.
Werner, Jan W. H. "Le Miroir du Monde, uitgegeven te Amsterdam door Zacharias Heyns in 1598, een korte toelichting." In *Le Miroir du Monde*—facsimile edition, 3 pp. Weesp: Robas, 1994.
Westerink, H. *Met het oog van de ziel: Een godsdienstpsychologische en mentaliteitshistorische studie naar mensvisie, zelfonderzoek en geloofsbeleving in het werk van Willem Teellinck (1579–1629)*. Zoetermeer: Boekencentrum, 2002.

Weststeijn, Arthur. "Dutch Brazil and the Making of Free Trade Ideology." In *The Legacy of Dutch Brazil*, ed. Michiel van Groesen, 187–204. New York: Cambridge University Press, 2014.

———. "Republican Empire: Colonialism, Commerce and Corruption in the Dutch Golden Age." *Renaissance Studies* 26, 4 (2012): 491–509.

Whitehead, Neil L. "Historical Writing About Brazil, 1500–1800." In *The Oxford History of Historical Writing*, vol. 3, *1400–1800*, 640–60. Oxford: Oxford University Press, 2012.

Whitehead, Peter J. P. "The Biography of Georg Marcgraf (1610–1643/4) by His Brother Christian, Translated by James Petiver." *Journal of the Society for the Bibliography of Natural History* 9, 3 (1979): 301–14.

———. "Georg Markgraf and Brazilian Zoology." In *Johan Maurits van Nassau-Siegen, 1604–1679: A Humanist Prince in Europe and Brazil*, ed. Ernst van den Boogaart et al., 424–71. The Hague: Johan Maurits van Nassau Stichting, 1979.

Whitehead, Peter J. P., and Marinus Boeseman. *A Portrait of Dutch 17th-Century Brazil: Animals, Plants and People by the Artists of Johan Maurits of Nassau*. Amsterdam: North-Holland, 1989.

Willemsen, René T. H. "Beleggers in een nieuwe compagnie: Het aandeelhoudersregister van de Kamer Enkhuizen der VOC." In *Souffrir pour parvenir: De wereld van Jan Huygen van Linschoten*, ed. Roelof van Gelder, Jan Parmentier, and Vibeke Roeper, 65–79, 173–81. Haarlem: Arcadia, 1998.

Winter, P. J. van. *De Westindische Compagnie ter Kamer Stad en Lande*. The Hague: Nijhoff, 1978.

Wintroub, Michael. "Civilizing the Savage and Making a King: The Royal Entry Festival of Henri II (Rouen, 1550)." *Sixteenth Century Journal* 29, 2 (1998): 465–94.

Wiznitzer, Arnold, "Jewish Soldiers in Dutch Brazil (1630–1654)." *Publications of the American Jewish Historical Society* 46, 1 (1956): 40–50.

———. *Jews in Colonial Brazil*. New York: Columbia University Press, 1960.

———. "The Number of Jews in Dutch Brazil (1630–1654)." *Jewish Social Studies* 16, 2 (1954): 107–14.

Zandvliet, Kees. *Mapping for Money: Maps, Plans and Topographic Paintings and Their Role in Dutch Overseas Expansion During the 16th and 17th Centuries*. Amsterdam: Batavion Lion, 2002.

Zijlstra, Suze. "Competing for European Settlers: Local Loyalties of Colonial Governments in Suriname and Jamaica, 1660–1680." *Journal of Early American History* 4, 2 (2014): 149–66.

INDEX

Acosta, José de, 25, 43
Aglionby, William, 1
Aitzema, Lieuwe van, 153
alba amicorum, 103–6, 176
Albertina Agnes of Nassau, 166
Albuquerque, Matias de, 80, 123
Aldenburgk, Johann Gregor, 73
Alewijn, Frederik van, 90
Algiers, 132
Allart, Huych, 88
Alva, Duke of, 118, 120–21
Amsterdam, passim; Admiralty, 32–33, 34, 62, 143, 168; Athenaeum Illustre, 28, 148, 161, 217n37; Bank of Exchange, 6–7, 124; Corn Exchange, 5–6; Dam Square ("the Dam"), 5–7, 19, 25, 52, 127–28, 135, 139, 174; demographics, 23–24; harbor district, 26, 92, 124; Latin School, 59; Old Bridge, 5–6, 15, 88, 164, 168; Old Church, 6, 25; New Bridge, 27–29; New Church, 6–7, 25, 52; Op 't Water (On the Waterfront), 5–6, 19, 43; Paalhuys, 27, 29; private libraries, 24–26; public library, 25–26; Schouwburg, 109; Beurs (Stock Exchange), 6–7, 123–24; town hall, 6–7, 52, 135–38, 199n16; Rapenburg, 34; Rasphuis, 54; Vlooienburg, 51; Weeskamer (Orphan Chamber), 23; West India House, 39, 47, 52, 54, 80, 93–97, 100, 125, 190; West India House (New), 134–35, 154; Zuiderkerk, 65
Angola, 12, 68, 108, 111–12, 127, 140, 143, 155, 167. *See also* Luanda
Antarctic France (France Antarctique). *See* French Brazil

Antonio Vaz, 80, 89, 106, 217n46. *See also* Mauritsstad
Antwerp, 6, 15, 26, 63, 65, 68, 133, 150, 172, 192, 193
Appelboom, Harald, 105
Arciszewsky, Christoph, 85, 162, 164, 215n18
Arguin, 164
Arminian controversy, 8, 52, 60, 189, 225n19
Arminius, Jacobus, 25
atlases, 16. *See also* maps
Azores, the, 34

Bachiler, Samuel, 104
Baek, Joost, 98
Baers, Johannes, 78, 93
Bahia, 24, 29, 31, 37, 44, 52, 62–63, 75, 121, 130, 143, 155, 162, 193. *See also* Salvador de Bahia
Barbados, 153, 177
Barlaeus, Caspar, 102, 105, 160, 161–65, 170, 225n19
Barreto, Francisco, 153
Baudartius, Willem, 51, 59–61, 63
Bay of All Saints, 31, 36–37, 41, 44, 46, 52, 58, 66, 68, 144–45. *See also* Forte do Mar; Itaparica; Salvador de Bahia
Beck, David, 46, 50–51
Beck, Mathias, 149–50
Beeck, Isaac van, 139–41
Beer, Leonart de, 35
Behaim, Stephen Carl, 92
Benguela, 103
Berckenrode, Balthasar Florisz van, 5–6
Bernard of Saxe-Weimar, 103

betting, 68
Bicker, Andries, 99, 124, 137–39, 189
Bicker, Cornelis, 124, 139
Bicker, Laurens, 31
Bie, Alexander de, 148
"Black Legend," 20–21, 31, 56, 118, 120, 133, 174
Blaeu, Johan, 5, 7, 85, 88, 90, 160, 164, 172
Blaeuwenhaen, Pieter, 95, 97
Blommaert, Samuel, 88
Bontemantel, Hans, 88
Bontius, Jacob, 167
Bosch, Lambert van den, 171, 182–83
Boswell, William, 105
Brazilian Indians: indiscriminate mentions of, 47, 64, 85, 113, 115–17, 126, 150, 153–54, 159, 171, 176–77; stereotypical representations of, 14–15, 18, 20–21, 30, 33–34, 37, 151, 159, 172–75
brazilwood, 54, 122, 159, 196
Breda, Siege of (1625), 51, 73
Bredan, Daniel, 84, 212n51
Bredero, Gerbrand Adriaensz, 108–9
Breton, Richard, 19–20
Broeck, Mattheus van den, 130–31, 176
Brownover, Sylvanus, 172
Bry, Theodore de, 18, 21, 26, 174
Buchelius, Arnoldus, 39, 41, 121–22, 190, 209n6, 228n97
Bullestrate, Adriaen van, 104
Burgh, Albert Coenraedtsz, 51, 84, 88, 94, 164
Bussen, Susanna, 95–96

Caerden, Paulus van, 31–33, 43
Calabar, Domingos Fernandes, 84, 130
Canary Islands, 30, 31
Cannegieter, Hendrick, 168, 170
cannibalism, 20–21, 133, 172–74
Cape Santo Agostinho, 98, 130–31
Cape Verde, 29
Capellen, Alexander van der, 220n1
Carleton, Sir Dudley, 68, 190
Carapeba, Domingo Fernandes, 155
Carpentier, Servatius, 97
cartography. *See* maps
Casteleyn, Pieter, 148, 150, 166, 187

Cats, Jacob, 105
Ceará, 3, 102, 148–50, 154
celebrity culture, 60, 75, 180–86
censorship, 19, 83, 122, 138, 195
Ceulen, Matthias van, 78, 89–90, 94, 97
charity, 124–25
Charles II, king of England (r. 1660–85), 160, 195
chats, 128, 138–42, 147, 148, 164
chronicles, 61–65, 148, 171
Claesz, Cornelis, 5, 7, 19–24, 26, 29–30, 33, 43, 172
Coelho, Domingo, 54–55, 62–64, 72
Colbert, Jean-Baptiste, 190
collective biographies, 181–85
Collot d'Escury, Hendrik, 187
corantos, handwritten, 16, 27
corantos, printed. *See* newspapers
Correa, Juan António, 193
costume books, 14, 16, 18
Courante uyt Italien en Duytschlandt. *See* Hilten, Jan van
Crijnssen, Abraham, 177
Croeger, Cornelis, 151–52
Cromwell, Oliver, 155, 195
Cunhaú, 145
Curaçao, 153, 177

Dapper, Olfert, 171
Dias, Henrique, 179
Dooreslaer, David van, 117, 215n8
Dorth, Johan van, 46–47, 50, 53, 60, 75, 78
Duck, Jacob, 90–91
Dussen, Adriaen van der, 162
Dutch Brazil, passim; demographics, 107–8; as Garden of Eden/paradise, 41–42, 116, 177; invasion of (1624), 44–71, 187, 190; invasion of (1630), 72, 77–82, 187, 188; memory of, 73, 78, 131, 137, 156, 157–69, 176–78, 180–86, 187; resistance against, 47, 84, 118, 125; revolt against Dutch regime (1645–54); Roman Catholics in, 112, 114–15, 117, 126, 131, 145. *See also* "War of Divine Liberation"
Dutch Revolt, 8, 19, 26, 56–57, 137

East India Company, Dutch. *See* VOC
Eckhout, Albert, 150–51, 157, 159, 168, 171–72, 176
Eduardus, Johannes, 215n8
education, 23, 28, 92
Eertvelt, Andries van, 65–66, 223n69
Elizabeth Stuart, 105, 160
Elmina, São Jorge de, 10, 102
embedded journalism, 45, 52, 58, 93, 103. *See also* news maps
emblem books, 67–68
exoticism, 150, 167–76
eyewitnesses, 73, 78, 100, 103, 172, 194

feast days. *See* public celebrations
Fernando de Noronha, 3, 29
Ferreira, Gaspar Dias, 131–32
Fort Ceulen (*Reis Magos*), 3, 84, 89, 104, 151–52
Fort Ernestus, 104
Fort Schoonenburgh (Fortaleza), 3, 149
Fort van der Dussen, 130–31
Forte do Mar (Bahia), 44, 52, 62, 68, 75, 182–86
Francis Xavier, 63
Frederick III, king of Denmark, 158, 172
Frederik Hendrik, stadtholder of Orange-Nassau (r. 1625–47), 67, 77, 97, 101, 132, 157
Frederikstad, 89
free black people (in Amsterdam), 90–91, 224n87
free trade controversy, 9, 100, 103, 117–23, 139, 147, 189
French Brazil, 19–21, 43, 171, 196
Friedrich Wilhelm, elector of Brandenburg, 158

Gakelius, Petrus, 60
Geelkercken, Nicolaas van, 41–42
Gerbier, Balthasar, 177
Gerritsz, Hessel, 52, 65, 75–76, 80–82, 88
Gijsselingh, Johan, 78
Glazemaker, Jan Hendrik, 144
Goch, Michiel van, 144
Golijath, Cornelius, 106

Golius, Jacob, 105
Graswinckel, Dirck, 132
Gronovius, Johann Friedrich, 161
Grotius, Hugo, 99, 109, 121–22, 188
Grynaeus, Simon, 25
Guanabara Bay. *See* Rio de Janeiro
Guararapes, Battle(s) of, 106, 127, 134, 142, 150
Guerreiro, Bartolomeu, 193
Guinea, 30, 108, 111–12. *See also* Elmina
Guyana, 177

Haecx, Hendrick, 144, 147–48, 155
Hagen, Pieter van den, 168–70
Hakluyt, Richard, 34
Halsberch, Johannes, 25
Hanneman, Adriaen, 224n9
Hansen Hajstrup, Peter, 92, 106–8, 130, 153–54, 176
Haselbeeck, Johannes, 58–59
Hasselaer, Pieter, 15
Heemskerck, Cornelis van, 31
Heinsius, Daniel, 161
Heinsius, Johannes, 178–79
Heinsius, Nicolaas, 225n14
Henri II, king of France (r. 1547–59), 19, 26, 196
Herckmans, Elias, 83, 104, 162
Heyn, Piet, 44, 60, 63, 68, 75–76, 125, 180, 182–86, 191
Heyns, Peeter, 16–17
Heyns, Zacharias, 14–20, 22–24, 26, 92
Hilten, Jan van, 7, 45–47, 68, 83–85, 87, 128–29, 148–49, 204n13, 213n83
Hispaniola, 195
Hoing, Jacob Gerritsz, 39
Holland, States of, 2, 33, 97–98, 134, 143, 156, 180, 181, 213n83
Hollar, Wenceslaus, 82
Hooft, Cornelis Pieterszoon, 25–26, 201n31
Hooft, Pieter Corneliszoon, 50, 84, 98, 102
Hooghe, Romeyn de, 174–75
Hoogstraten, Diederick van, 130–31
Hout, Jan van, 28, 31
Howell, James, 1
Hudde, Johannes, 180

Hüttich, Johan, 25
Huygens, Constantijn, 159, 160

Ibarra, Don Carlos de, 192
Ignatius of Loyola, 63
Inga, Athanasius, 42
Inquisition, 24, 35, 133
Isabella, archduchess of the Southern Netherlands (r. 1598–1633), 72, 98
Itamaracá, 3, 83, 84, 108, 127
Itaparica, 3, 52

Jacobsz, Rombout, 51
Jamaica, 195
Jans, Jannetje, 95–96
Jansz, Barent, 17
Jansz, Broer, 20, 42–43, 45–46, 49, 84, 128–29, 134, 204n13
Jesuits, 18, 39, 46, 54–56, 62–64, 85, 114, 171, 196
Jews, Sephardic: in Amsterdam, 23, 34, 51, 80, 91, 100, 102, 109, 114–15, 117, 131–33, 153, 176–78, 190; in Pernambuco, 108, 112, 114–17, 133, 146–47, 153, 177. See also New Christians
João IV, king of Portugal (r. 1640–56), 12, 132–33
Johan Maurits of Nassau-Siegen, governor-general of Dutch Brazil (r. 1637–44), 12, 89, 101–5, 108, 114–17, 122–23, 125–26, 129, 131, 147, 150, 152, 154, 157–68, 170–72, 180, 181, 187, 188, 197, 198, 215n18
Jol, Cornelis, 103, 111, 192, 230n24
Jonghe, Clement de, 88–89
Joosten, Jacques, 112

Kessel, Jan van, 172
Keye, Otto, 177
Kieser, Eberhard, 67
Kinschot, Caspar van, 161
Knibbergen, François van, 67
Kuin, Johan, 157

Laet, Johannes de, 72, 162, 166, 195, 225n19
Lampe, Barent, 83
Lampsins, Cornelis, 123
Lange, Petrus de, 185–86

Langren, Jacob Florisz van, 30–31
Las Casas, Bartolomé de, 20–21, 56
Leiden, 28, 38, 103, 105, 116, 160, 161, 225n19
Léry, Jean de, 20–22, 25, 30, 31, 34, 42, 43, 172, 174, 196
Ley, Casper van der, 131
Lichtenberg, Julius, 179
Lichthart, Jan, 103, 104, 180, 182
Liebergen, Daniel van, 94
Lieshout, Françoys, 134
Linschoten, Jan Huygen van, 29–30, 36, 174
Lisbon, 24, 51, 133, 193–94
literacy, 23, 26
Locke, John, 172
Lonck, Hendrick, 77–78, 81, 84, 92, 93, 180, 182
Lope de Vega, Felix, 68, 193
Louis XIV, king of France (r. 1648–1715), 158
Louise Henriette of Orange-Nassau, 157
Luanda, São Paulo de, 75, 103, 112. See also Angola
Luzac, Elie, 187

Madrid, 68, 192
Magellan, Strait of, 18
Maíno, Juan Bautista, 68
Maire, Johannes, 160
Man, Eduard, 94, 139–40
maps, 17, 24, 82–83, 85, 88–90, 150, 168–69
Maranhão, 3, 102, 104, 126, 171
Marcgraf, Georg, 88, 166–67
Marel, Johannes van, 142–43
Marel, Pieter van, 142–43
Marselis, Johan van, 168
Matanzas, 75
Matham, Theodor, 165
Maurits, stadtholder of Orange-Nassau (r. 1587–1625), 8, 46, 59, 73
Mauritsstad, 89, 104, 108, 125, 148, 157, 166
Meisner, Daniel, 67–68
Menasseh ben Israel, 115
Mendonça de Furtado, Diogo, 44, 54–55, 62, 72
Merian, Matthias, 82
Meteren, Emanuel van, 202n59
Meurs, Jacob van, 170–72, 174, 176

Index

Middelburg, 10, 35, 134, 153, 178. *See also* Zeeland
Mine, Jacques de la, 97
Miranda do Corvo, Count of, 155
Moerbeeck, Jan Andries, 42
Montaigne, Michel de, 22, 25
Montanus, Arnoldus, 131, 170–74, 176, 189
moradores, 84, 108, 111, 114, 126, 128–31, 133, 144
Moraes, Manuel de, 92
Moreau, Pierre, 132, 144–47
Mortamer, Pieter, 104
Mulheiser, Johann Phillip, 103–6, 131, 176
Münster, Sebastian, 25–26
mutiny, 32, 68

Nedham, Marchamont, 195
New Amsterdam. *See* New Netherland
New Christians, 24, 34, 42, 100, 146, 193
New France, 196
New Netherland, 10, 153, 154, 177, 221n20, 222n40, 223n56
news maps, 52–58, 75, 80–82, 85, 89–90, 150, 190, 196, 205n34
newspapers, 27, 44–50, 73, 77–78, 84, 98, 100, 102, 128–30, 134, 162, 171, 179, 190, 192, 195, 203n6
Nieuhof, Johan, 130–31, 171, 176
Nooms, Reinier, 168

O'Brien, Bernard, 92
Oetgens, Antonius, 137–38
Oldenbarnevelt, Johan van, 8, 34, 52, 189
Oldenbarnevelt, Willem van, 99
Olinda, 3, 72, 77–78, 82, 84, 109, 123, 192; demolition of, 80, 89, 197
Olivares, Duke of, 78, 98, 192, 193–94
Oquendo, Don Antonio de, 212n49
Ortelius, Abraham, 16–17, 26
Ottsen, Hendrik, 31
Oxenstierna, Axel, 190

Padilha, Francisco, 75
Padtbrugge, Herman, 183
Paes, Anna, 154
paintings, 32, 90–91, 150–51, 167–69, 171–72

pamphlets, 34, 58, 85, 103, 115, 117–21, 128, 130, 135, 138–47, 164, 171, 190
Paraíba, 3, 83, 85–86, 89, 92, 95–98, 100, 108, 127, 154, 196
Paraupaba, Antonio, 154–55, 176
Pater, Adriaen, 84, 212n49
Pathuys, Nicolaes, 124
patriotism, 32, 46, 56, 60, 72, 83, 103, 120, 182–86
Pauw, Adriaen, 65
Pauw, Reynier, 15, 41, 186
Peace of Münster (1648), 12. *See also* Peace of Westphalia
Peace of The Hague (1661), 155
Peace of The Hague (1667), 178
Peace of Westphalia (1648), 140
Peeters, Bonaventura, 150–51
Peeters, Gillis I, 150–52
Pernambuco, 2, 3, 24, 30–31, 37, 77, 80, 83, 108, 112, 133, 143, 153–55, 166, 170, 178, 188
Philip II, king of Spain (r. 1558–98), 20, 89, 118
Philip IV, king of Spain (r. 1621–65), 12, 46, 59, 72, 98
piracy, 176, 180
Piso, Willem, 104, 161, 166–67, 176
Plancius, Petrus, 34
Plante, Franciscus, 160–61, 164, 170
Plantin, Christopher, 15
Plasse, Cornelis van de, 42
poetry, 57–60, 62, 83
Porto Calvo, 85, 87–88, 102
Portuguese Restoration (1640), 12, 102, 123, 133, 192
Post, Frans, 150–52, 160, 164, 167–70, 174, 176, 214n103
Potiguar Indians, 92, 154–55, 223n71. *See also* Brazilian Indians
praatjes. *See* chats
Preys, Boudewijn du, 115, 218n51
privateering, 128, 181
prostitution, 92
public celebrations, 51, 71, 77

Rabe, Jacob, 145, 172
Raey, Jan, 94–95, 97, 139–40

Ray, John, 1
Reael, Laurens, 88
Recife, 3, 12, 13, 72, 77–78, 82, 92, 97, 101, 103, 106, 108, 123, 127, 130, 134, 137–38, 141, 147–48, 154, 157, 160, 161, 200n31; as stumbling block for peace with Spain, 98–99; defensive structures around, 79, 83, 89, 129; hunger in, 84, 97, 103, 106, 116, 143, 223n74; surrender of, 107, 128, 152–53, 155–56, 176–79, 195
recruiting, 92–93
Reepmaecker, Jacob, 94
Reigersberch, Nicolaas van, 121–23
Rembrandt (van Rijn), 131, 137, 168
Revius, Jacobus, 58–59, 106
Richshoffer, Ambrosius, 78, 93–94
Rio de Janeiro, 3, 19–20, 35, 37, 43, 171, 196
Rio de la Plata, 31
Rio Grande (province), 3, 80, 83, 108, 127, 145, 153, 226n44
Rio Grande (river), 3, 89, 104, 151
Rivet, André, 116
"Rock the Brazilian," 176
Rubens, Peter Paul, 77
Ruiter, Godefroy, 95
Ruiters, Dierick, 35–37, 52, 83, 108, 146
Ruyter, Michiel de, 184–85
rumors, 45–46, 102, 137, 195, 215n2

Saint Domingue, 170
Salvador de Bahia, 3, 18, 31, 35, 37, 44–71, 72–73, 75–78, 80, 102, 162, 182–85, 189, 192, 193
São Tomé, 12, 103, 127, 140, 155, 230n41
São Vicente, 29
Sarpi, Paolo, 12
Schenkenschans, Siege of (1636), 101
Schmalkalden, Caspar, 172
Schoonenburgh, Wouter van, 144, 155
Schoppe, Sigismund von, 84, 133–34, 144–45, 153, 155
Sebastianism, 63
Sergipe, 3, 35, 102
sermons, 57–58, 193
Setterich, Nicolaes van, 94

silver, 84, 148–50
Six, Jan, 168
slave trade, 104, 107–12, 122–23, 130, 141, 147, 177, 180
slavery, 107–13, 146–47, 194, 217n37
slaves: in Brazil, 78, 92, 108, 113, 117, 147, 149, 153, 171, 179, 216n23; in Europe, 26, 91; in Suriname, 178
Smit, Wenzel, 131
Smout, Adriaen, 58
Society of Jesus. *See* Jesuits
Soler, Vicente Joachim, 104, 115–17, 125, 147, 215n18
songs, 57, 74, 77, 83
Sousa, Fernando de, 31
Sousa, Luis de, 35
Sousa Coutinho, Francisco de, 132–33, 139–41
Spínola, Ambrogio, 51, 73
Spranckhuysen, Dionysius, 106
Spranger, Quirijn, 177
Staden, Hans, 20–21, 36
States General, 2, 31–33, 37, 42, 51, 62, 65, 98, 100, 112, 117, 121, 125, 129, 132–33, 134, 138–39, 141–42, 147, 162, 166, 176, 177, 190, 196
Stoop, Willem, 69
sugar: consumption, 90; planters. *See moradores*; production, 85, 89, 108, 118, 123, 129, 146, 168, 174, 178–79; refining (in Amsterdam), 34, 90
Suriname, 10, 153, 170, 177–80
Swartenhondt, Jochem, 31–33
Synod of Dordrecht (1618–1619), 8, 52, 60

Tamayo de Vargas, Tomás, 193
tapestries, 172
Tapuya Indians, 20, 133, 145–46, 148, 150, 154, 166, 171, 174. *See also* Brazilian Indians
Tavernier, Melchior, 65
Taylor, John, 1
Taylor, Joseph, 182
Teellinck, Ewout, 73
Teellinck, Willem, 60, 113
Teixeira, Marcos, 44
Temple, Sir William, 4

Ten Years' Truce (1641), 12, 102, 132, 197
Texel, 41, 47, 93
theater, 28, 108–9, 222n44
The Hague, 11, 38, 46, 97, 105, 121, 125, 129, 131, 132, 143, 153–55, 159. *See also* States General
Thevet, André, 19–21, 26, 196
Thirty Years' War (1618–48), 12, 65, 103
Thurloe, John, 153
Thysius, Antonius, the Younger, 105, 160, 181–82
Tobago, 155, 177
Toledo, Don Fadrique de, 68–69
tolerance, 112–17, 125–26
Torre, Count of, 102–3, 123
translation, 65, 70, 80, 84, 117
travel accounts, 16–22, 33, 107
treason, 106, 130–31, 133
treasure fleet, 74, 79, 125, 191–92
tulipmania, 123
Tulp, Nicolaes, 137–38
Tupinamba (Tupi) Indians, 21–22, 26, 117, 171, 196. *See also* Brazilian Indians
Twelve Years' Truce (1609–21), 2, 8, 9, 33–35, 43, 189

Udemans, Godfried, 109–11, 113–14, 117, 147
Uijtenbogaert, Cornelis, 170
Union of the Crowns (1580–1640), 11–12, 21, 59, 63, 74, 193
Usselincx, Willem, 34, 40, 98, 108, 112, 146

Valerius, Adriaen, 74
Veenhuysen, Jan, 135
Verdonck, Adriaen, 84
Versterre, Pieter, 179
Verzuimd Brazil, 157, 187–88
Vieira, Antonio, 132
Villegagnon, Nicolas Durand de, 19, 21–22
Vingboons, Johannes, 88
Vingboons, Philips, 88
Visscher, Claes Jansz, 7, 39, 51–58, 60, 62, 65, 68, 70, 75, 80–83, 85–86, 88, 100, 190, 196
Visscher, Nicolaes Jansz, 190

VOC, 25, 27, 31–34, 40, 58, 59, 95, 113, 122, 138, 176, 211n41
Vogelaer, Marcus de, 95
Vogellius, Nicolaus, 104
Vondel, Joost van den, 166
Vorstius, Adolph, 159
Vossius, Gerardus, 104–5
Vossius, Isaac, 105
Vries, Simon de, 174–75
Vroom, Hendrik Cornelisz, 32, 40, 65

Waerdenburgh, Diederick van, 77–78, 80, 83, 99, 197
Waghenaer, Lucas Jansz, 30
Wagner, Zacharias, 172, 176
"War of Divine Liberation," 12, 106, 117, 127–33, 140, 142, 157, 166, 178–79
Wassenaer, Nicolaes van, 61–65, 83, 148
Wedda, Albert, 131
West India Company, passim; administrative setup, 37–38; Amsterdam Chamber, 40–41, 72, 84, 92, 94–97, 113, 124–25, 156, 180; bankruptcy, 180; foundation, 33–34, 37–40, 43, 113, 123; foreign soldiers in service of, 12, 65, 92–93, 103–7; "Grand Design," 40, 42; Heeren XIX, 2, 37–38, 54, 68, 75, 78, 95, 98, 100, 108, 111, 113–14, 122–23, 125–26, 129, 141, 153, 154, 155, 157, 162, 186, 197, 213n83; as information managers, 50–57, 65–67, 71, 73, 78, 80–82, 100, 190; maintenance of monopoly, 40, 100, 103, 117–23; mismanagement, 122, 128, 140–41, 144, 147; share prices, 123–24, 134, 220n90; shareholders, 40, 100, 107, 123–26
Western Design, 195
Wijckersloot, Cornelis van, 97
Wild Coast. *See* Guyana
Willekens, Jacob, 41, 46, 60, 65, 68, 186
Willem Frederik of Nassau-Dietz, stadtholder of Groningen and Friesland (r. 1640–64), 157–58, 166
Willems, Catharina, 35
William II, stadtholder of Orange-Nassau (r. 1647–50), 143–44, 158, 166

With, Gijsbert de, 154
With, Witte de, 143–44
Witsen, Nicolaes, 180
Witt, Johan de, pensionary of Holland (r. 1651–72), 143, 155, 158, 181, 189
Wotton, Henry, 46

Zeeland, province, 10, 33, 37, 98, 116–17, 122, 125, 128, 134, 138–39, 149–50, 155, 177, 179, 189
Zeeman, Maria, 168, 170
Zesen, Philipp van, 171
Zimmermann, Wilhelm Peter, 70–71
Zwier van Haren, Onno, 157, 187

ACKNOWLEDGMENTS

The idea for this book first came to me in 2005, as I was preparing to teach a BA seminar in "Nederlandse Geschiedenis" at the University of Amsterdam that introduced me to the wealth and variety of publications on the rise and fall of Dutch Brazil. How was it possible that nobody had written a full-length study about this exceptional historical venture for fifty years?! Fortunately, at the time, I did not realize it would take me another ten to do so. I am happy to have the chance here to express my gratitude to all those people who followed (part of) my journey from idea to index. My interest in Dutch Brazil was given an early boost during a period as Dr. Ernst Crone Fellow at Het Scheepvaartmuseum in Amsterdam, where Joost Schokkenbroek's tireless encouragement helped me on my way. Without pressure to produce something polished immediately, the fellowship enabled me to study what had happened in Salvador (and in Amsterdam printing shops) in the years 1624 and 1625. The incongruity between collective euphoria and collective memory taught me a lot about the persistence of patriotic perspectives on history, and the narrative potential of national defeat.

Soon thereafter the project received the blessing of the Netherlands Organisation for Scientific Research (NWO). I am grateful for their generosity and their flexibility. Finding the right framework for the story I wanted to tell lasted longer than I had somewhat naively imagined. The participants in the 2011 conference "The Legacy of Dutch Brazil" challenged me to sharpen my thinking on what made the colony unique and representative of something broader at the same time, and I am indebted to all of them for accepting my invitation to take a fresh look at the "Time of the Flemings." The reactions I received after giving a paper on early modern newspapers at the "Global Dimensions" conference, organized by Surekha Davies that same year, made me realize that perhaps the perspective of the Amsterdam print media offered the best escape route from the relatively isolated historiography of the West India Company.

Since then, the general idea of this work has been presented to critical audiences at the Low Countries Seminar of the Institute of Historical Research in London, the European History Seminar at Columbia University, and the Renaissance and Early Modern Studies Seminar at Brown University. I am grateful to the respective organizers, and to everyone who came to listen and nudged my impressionistic ambitions in the right direction by asking me questions I could not answer. The book has also benefited greatly from two extended periods I spent away from home, first as a research fellow at Birkbeck in London, and then in 2013 as Queen Wilhelmina Visiting Professor at Columbia University in New York, where the manuscript began to take its final shape. I am very grateful to Evan Haefeli for inviting us to come to New York City. There, amid the everyday linguistic and topographic reminders of New Amsterdam, I finally figured out a way to write about "my" Amsterdam—and about Recife.

Over the years, many different people have helped me in a variety of ways, often simply by reassuring me that the combination of Dutch Brazil and public debate was a topic worth pursuing. They include Carlos Alberto Asfora, Alex Bick, Remmelt Daalder, Kate Delaney, Chris Ebert, Mariana Françozo, Roelof van Gelder, Martha Howell, Jaap Jacobs, Wim Klooster, Kris Lane, David Onnekink, Judith Pollmann, Joan-Pau Rubiés, Benjamin Schmidt, Stuart Schwartz, and Diederick Wildeman. At the University of Amsterdam, Henk van Nierop once again provided all the support I needed, and every now and then nurtured the belief that I was on the right track. Marten Jan Bok, Guy Geltner, Helmer Helmers, Geert Janssen, Clé Lesger, Djoeke van Netten, and Suze Zijlstra helped me with practical advice, literature references, and encouragement. I am thankful to James Kennedy and all my now former colleagues at the History Department for having made the last five years in particular so inexplicably enjoyable. PW Zuidhof regularly checked to see if I was still interested in things other than Dutch Brazil, and hopefully will continue to do so. Paul Knevel, finally, deserves a special mention for having been an exemplary neighbor for the entire duration of the project, and for always having been prepared to discuss, among many other things, the intricacies of history writing, the rise of academic newspeak, the virtues of upsinging, and even occasionally—and invariably very helpfully—Dutch Brazil. I shall miss his companionship now that I have set sail for Leiden.

Across the Atlantic, Peter Mancall's immediate enthusiasm inspired me to start thinking about finishing the book, and Robert Lockhart's expert guidance at Penn Press then helped it over the line. Two reviewers for the Press endorsed and criticized the manuscript, challenging me to rethink and reconfigure some of the elements I had already accepted could not be improved. I am grateful for the energy and time they invested in this book. In the final stages, the Stichting Amsterdamse Historische Reeks generously provided funding for the inclusion of fifty images. But my greatest debt lies at the homefront—and lately at the Amsterdam waterfront, where Dutch Brazil was so eagerly debated more than three hundred and fifty years before. Maartje, Felix, and David have together provided me with a present that is infinitely more engaging than the past, offering me enough diversion not to let my hobby become my work. As any opinionated Amsterdammer from the Golden Age would acknowledge, a four-way discussion is perhaps more cacophonous than a simple conversation, and it often takes a bit longer too, but it is certainly more than twice as much fun.

Lightning Source UK Ltd.
Milton Keynes UK
UKHW040935070419
340603UK00006B/222/P